Jacqueline
Bouvier Kennedy Onassis

A Life

The Hidden Jesus: A New Life

Diana—The Last Year

Notorious: The Life of Ingrid Bergman

Rebel: The Life and Legend of James Dean

The Decline and Fall of the House of Windsor

A Passion for Life: The Biography of Elizabeth Taylor

Marilyn Monroe: The Biography

Blue Angel: The Life of Marlene Dietrich

Laurence Olivier: A Life

Madcap: The Life of Preston Sturges

Lenya: A Life

Falling in Love Again: Marlene Dietrich (photo-essay)

The Kindness of Strangers: The Life of Tennessee Williams

The Dark Side of Genius: The Life of Alfred Hitchcock

Stanley Kramer, Film Maker

Camerado: Hollywood and the American Man

The Art of Alfred Hitchcock

Jacqueline
Bouvier Kennedy Onassis

A Life

DONALD SPOTO

ST. MARTIN'S PRESS ❧ NEW YORK

Library of Congress Cataloging-in-Publication Data

Spoto, Donald.
    Jacqueline Bouvier Kennedy Onassis : a life / Daniel Spoto.—1st ed.
        p. cm.
    Includes bibliographical references and index.
    ISBN 0-312-24650-1
    1. Onassis, Jacqueline Kennedy, 1929–94. 2. Celebrities—
United States—Biography.   3. Presidents' spouses—United States—
Biography.   I. Title.

CT275.O552 S68 2000
973.922'092—dc21
[B]

                                                        99-056263

First Edition: March 2000

10 9 8 7 6 5 4 3 2 1

FOR LEWIS FALB AND GERALD PINCISS,

WITH ADMIRATION AND AFFECTION,

AND WITH GRATITUDE FOR TWENTY YEARS OF FRIENDSHIP

True happiness
Consists not in the multitude of friends,
But in the worth and choice.

BEN JONSON, *Cynthia's Revels* (1600)

Contents

Acknowledgments

*M*y litany of saints includes the names of generous people who provided important assistance.

At the East Hampton Library, Long Island, Dorothy King brought to light important articles in local newspapers and archives about young Miss Jacqueline Bouvier and her family in the 1920s and 1930s.

Sandra Chewnick, head of the Chapin School, and Eleanor Southworth, Chapin's archivist, opened up critical documents relative to my subject's early education.

At the Holton-Arms School, Trish Meyers, director of public relations, efficiently delivered data about Jacqueline's time there.

At Miss Porter's School, archivist Shirley Langhauser was equally helpful in locating crucial material she cheerfully made available to me.

In the archives of the George Washington University, Dagne Yemam pointed the way to pertinent papers and documents.

THE JOHN F. KENNEDY Library at Columbia Point in Boston is, of course, the major repository for materials relative to that President's term of office. There is also an astonishingly large volume of data on Jacqueline Bouvier Kennedy, First Lady from 1961 to 1963. A clear path through the massive files and helpful direction during my visits there were made possible by June Payne, Rosie Atherton and Maura Porter.

The staffs of the Library of Congress, the New York Public Library, the Beverly Hills Public Library, and the libraries of the cities of Los Angeles and Santa Monica are, as any researcher or visitor knows, unfailingly gracious and helpful, and I record my thanks to them all herewith.

AS FIRST LADY, Jacqueline Kennedy personally directed a two-year restoration program of the executive mansion. It was, then, necessary for me to visit the White House; thanks to Jeremy Bernard, I was able to do so. When I arrived, my host, Sean Maloney, staff secretary and assistant to the President of the United States, welcomed me and provided a private tour.

Gregory Dietrich again provided expert help as my New York–

based research assistant: as before, his scholarship, persistence and timeliness were invaluable over the course of several years.

Kyra Larkin, senior editor at *Quest* magazine, kindly provided a copy of an important essay from a past issue of that periodical.

For various special kinds of assistance, I am also grateful to John Darretta, Angela Lutomski, Peter McQuillan, Irene Mahoney, Ruth Prigozy and Kirtley Thiesmeyer.

I also owe a particular debt to William C. Eller II, who completely redesigned and reconstructed my home and office while I was working on this book. I'm grateful for Bill's application of his unique gifts as artisan and craftsman, just as I am for the inestimable gift of his loyal friendship.

THIS BOOK COULD not have been completed without the kindness and generosity of those who agreed to be interviewed, for their recollections provide some of the richest material in this book. I am glad and grateful to record my thanks to the following people for their time and effort on my behalf:

Letitia Baldrige, Betty Beale Graeber, DeVallon Bolles, Ben Bradlee, John H. Davis, Grant Dilman, Muriel Dobbin, James Fitzgerald, John Kenneth Galbraith, Gwen Gibson, Edwin Guthman, Eugene C. Kennedy, William La Riche, Scott Moyers, Edna O'Brien, Stephen Rubin, Pierre Salinger, Arthur M. Schlesinger Jr., Paul Sidey, Alvin Spivak, Helen Thomas, Bruce Tracy, Marianne Velmans, Gunilla von Post, Tillie Weitzner, Arthur Wilde and Harris Wofford.

FOR OVER TWENTY years, I have been represented by Elaine Markson, my wise and perceptive agent—and, I rejoice to say, a precious friend. Whatever I can say to express my thanks for her devotion and guidance is much less than she deserves.

In the offices of Elaine Markson Literary Agency, I am in every way supported and assisted by a vigilant congress of gifted people who look after my interests: Geri Thoma, Sally Wofford Girand, Elizabeth Sheinkman, Elizabeth Clementson, Sara De Nobrega and Gary Johnson.

The manuscript of this book was expertly edited by Ruth Coughlin, to whom I offer my admiring gratitude. In the offices of St. Martin's

Press, editorial assistant Patricia Fernandez dispatched a wide variety of responsibilities with unfailing grace and patience.

ON THE DEDICATION page appear the names of two friends with whose affectionate camaraderie and constancy I have been blessed for twenty years. Lewis Falb and Gerald Pinciss are the rarest and truest kind of people: successful as professors, writers and academic administrators, they are also (more to the point) men of depth and insight, keen of wit and sharp in discernment. Gerry and Lewis have been with me through both bright and cloudy times, and their devotion to me and my work has never faltered. They embody every graceful, empathetic quality Jackie most valued. I know she would have shared my loving estimation of them.

D. S.
Los Angeles
August 1999

I had three chairs in my house:
one for solitude, two for friendship, three for society.

—HENRY DAVID THOREAU, *Walden*

Part One

❧

Miss Bouvier
1929-1952

CHAPTER ONE

1929

To escape New York City's annual waves of summer heat and humidity, the privileged few find suburban or rural retreats. The breezy New Jersey shore or the cool hills of Pennsylvania, the rocky coast of Maine, the dunes of Cape Cod, an island off the Connecticut banks: these are among the most popular and desirable sanctuaries for a week, a month or longer. But the proximity of Long Island has always made it especially attractive to New Yorkers. About a hundred miles east of the city is a collection of sleepy hamlets, rustic and quiet—except from late May to early September.

Native Americans once dwelt there, and some villages of eastern Long Island still bear names from that bygone culture: Quogue, Cutchogue, Shinnecock, Sagaponack, Amagansett, Montauk. With the arrival of the British in the seventeenth century, sturdy English names were added: the county itself was named for Suffolk, and soon there were Calverton, Jamesport, Water Mill, North Haven and a medley of towns stretching over thirty miles and known collectively as the Hamptons—Westhampton, Westhampton Beach, Hampton Bays, Bridgehampton, Southampton and with proud, orthographic insistence on the separation of two words, East Hampton.

By the end of the nineteenth century, East Hampton was well established as a haven for a few wealthy citizens. The village, according to a journalist of the time, "excluded the vulgar parvenus that so often make life wretched at the conventional summer resort"—perhaps because the distance of six miles to the nearest railroad stop, at Bridgehampton, "keeps off the rabble." The "summerites," as the seasonal visitors were known, at first rented from year-round residents: only in the next decades did they build their own vast estates. "None seeks it except such as wish for comfortable quietude," wrote a reporter for a New York City newspaper about East Hampton in 1894. "It is distinctively a village of cottages. No hotel, no band, no merry-go-round, no Vanity Fair... The natives of East Hampton live in their back lots in summer. Their homes are, almost without exception, leased to wealthy city people, who will pay extravagant prices to occupy during the summer months these queer old homesteads, many of them more than one hundred, some more than two hundred years old."

According to a well-bred woman writing at the same time, the village was "almost completely unknown" to those who did not brave the railroad from New York. "How we suffered to get there!" she confided to her diary. "Four hours of torture from suffocating clouds of smoke and dust, prostrating heat from parboiled cars and endless jerky stops at every crossroad. Not until the always revivifying first whiff of sea air did we cease to bemoan our folly on this hideous journey." Once there, however, she apparently forgot these hardships, for she went often.

DURING THE SUMMER of 1929, America was dancing on an economic volcano, but East Hampton's summer denizens were blissfully high-stepping the Charleston and the Black Bottom at merry weekend parties. On the oppressively hot and humid Sunday, July 28, Janet Lee Bouvier was driven fifteen miles to the nearest hospital, in Southampton. An hour later, her husband, John Vernou (Jack) Bouvier III, dictated telegrams announcing the birth of a girl they at once named Jacqueline Lee, the two names neatly honoring him and his father as well as the infant's maternal grandfather. The baby, according to doctors' calculations, was a month overdue but arrived easily, serene and healthy. Weighing eight pounds, Jacqueline Lee Bouvier had a dramatic tuft of brunette hair, silken ivory skin and, it was soon determined, velvet-brown eyes.

Twenty-one-year-old Janet Bouvier was an earnest, bright, ambitious socialite. Her great-grandfather had come to New York from Ireland during the nineteenth-century famine; his son became a teacher and city school administrator and married a pretty nurse named Mary Norton, also from hardy Irish stock. Their son, James Thomas Lee, Janet's father, was born in New York on October 2, 1877. He attended City College of New York, where he took a diploma in engineering in 1896; three years later he earned his law degree from Columbia University.

James T. Lee was the clan's first real success story in the New World. A short, stocky man with a prominent nose, an expressive mouth and intense dark eyes, he munched cigars, did not suffer fools gladly and interrupted his business day at three o'clock for a half hour of boxing lessons. He married the gentle Irishwoman Margaret Merritt in 1903, and she bore him three daughters—Marion, Janet (born December 3, 1907) and Winifred. From Margaret, the girls learned the craft of housewifery; from James, a sense of determination and the fine art of ingratiating oneself into polite society.

In the sparring ring as in business, James Lee fought to win and usually did. After quitting his six-dollar-a-week job as a law clerk, he opened his own office, whence he gazed down to see the first work on what was to become the Seventh Avenue subway. Almost at once, he purchased properties along the proposed route, which soon quadrupled in value as Manhattan business became more firmly entrenched above Fourteenth Street.

By 1910, Lee was involved mostly in real estate and banking, and to hell with the practice of general law. He built several of the city's grandest residences, among them the luxury building at 998 Fifth Avenue, which offered elite apartments with as many as twenty-three rooms. For the units he built at 740 Park Avenue, he advertised leases on twelve- and fourteen-room apartments for the outrageous sum of $2,000 per month. Friends and colleagues told him that he was mad, but Lee was resolute. "Better a bad decision today than a good one three weeks late," he replied gruffly. This odd wisdom was justified within six months, when he announced that all the units at 740 Park had been leased. Other successful investments soon followed, and eventually Lee complemented his property speculation with positions as vice president of the Chase National Bank and, later, president and chairman of the New York Central Savings Bank. By 1922, his real estate holdings amounted to $35 million.

A conservative Republican, James Lee had little social grace. His lack of polish and his Irish Catholic heritage were distinct liabilities in both town and country, but would not stop Lee from improving his family's social fortunes. Eager for their daughters to be accepted in the right circles and to marry into so-called good families, the Lees began, as early as 1920, to pass the summers near the established "old money" families of East Hampton. Here he installed his family in a splendid house called Avery Place, on Lily Pond Lane, where the Lees and their three daughters repaired, accompanied by Margaret's mother, a plain woman who cooked, sewed and laundered for them all. Old Mrs. Merritt's only compensation, however, was the summer's lodging; otherwise, the family treated Grandma like a servant and never included her in events involving outsiders, because they considered her thick Irish brogue a threat to their grand social aspirations.

JANET ATTENDED A private girls' academy, then Sweet Briar and Barnard Colleges; at eighteen, she was presented to society by her parents at a tea dance. Slim, neat, bright and energetic, she had a practiced patrician manner and a lively interest in anything social; this made her an agreeable presence at any fashionable event. At her father's insistence, she mastered all the requisite graces quickly. In her teens, she learned to play a ferocious game of bridge, to speak good French, and to excel in just about every sport, particularly riding, for which she had a great passion. Her slight build, small bosom and athletic legs were no liabilities either at the hunt club or on the dance floor: if she took no prizes at the latter, she more than compensated as an expert horsewoman who accumulated one blue ribbon after another at shows in the city and the country.

Quietly confident and calmly aggressive, Janet was an independent thinker; she was also, it seems, not particularly warm or emotional, but sentiment rarely softens one fiercely dedicated to establishing a secure place in society. Nevertheless, she knew how to flatter the male ego, and although dozens of young ladies were prettier and many just as wealthy, Janet had no trouble attracting beaux in Manhattan or East

Hampton. Among her many talents, none was more refined than know-ing the proper word to impress at the right moment.

Her social skills were, however, exercised with such apparent ease that she never offended—even when she claimed that her family was related to "the Lees of Maryland." She may have meant "of Virginia," for there are no Maryland Lees. But few people, it seems, caught the gaffe. Ever her father's daughter, Janet had her cap set for a brilliant marriage to the wealthy heir of a properly old family. She would not grow up to be like her grandmother, whom (also like her father) she virtually ignored. Mrs. Merritt ceased to exist outside Avery Place, and the Lees of Maryland rode on triumphantly. In this complex game, with its subtle class snobberies, Janet Lee was scarcely the only player. It was, after all, an era brilliantly captured in F. Scott Fitzgerald's unctuously ingratiating character, the popular arriviste Jay Gatsby, born James Gatz.

SIXTEEN YEARS OLDER than Janet, John Vernou Bouvier III (born in 1891) came from precisely the class of people the Lees most admired. His great-great-grandfather Michel Bouvier—the surname means "cowherd" or "cattle driver"—emigrated from the south of France and settled in Philadelphia, where he prospered as a carpenter, cabinet-maker and designer of first-rate furniture. As he traveled around the eastern United States, Bouvier's talents as an artisan quickly expanded to speculation: his success enabled him to acquire 153,000 acres of coal-rich land in West Virginia and choice Main Line real estate.

After the death of his first wife, Michel Bouvier married Louise Vernou, daughter of a tobacconist; of his nine children, only two sons survived. He saw his children married into Philadelphia's venerable families—the Drexels, Ewings and Pattersons, for example. To cap his career, he bought two seats on the New York Stock Exchange and built a thirty-room Renaissance palazzo on North Broad Street—a sump-tuous residence boasting two reception rooms and large formal dining room, a conservatory, library, gaming room, chapel, formal gardens and lavish fountains, for which he had reserved some of his finest imported marble. Michel Bouvier died at eighty-two in 1874.

His surviving sons, Michel and the first John Vernou Bouvier, in-vested wisely and poured more millions into the family fortune: by

1914, the Bouviers had amassed a sum equivalent to $40 million in later valuation. The Bouvier wealth increased still further during the 1920s, thanks to real estate holdings in the Middle Atlantic states and enormous investments in a number of successful companies; by 1929, the aggregate, it was confidently asserted, would guarantee the Bouviers' opulent lifestyle for generations to come.

Most important of all to the Bouviers, their wealth and intermarriage with prestigious American families put their names in the New York *Social Register* in 1899—no easy feat for Catholics at that time— and there they remained for sixty years, until the death of Jacqueline's father. The Bouvier name, as donor, is also etched on an altar at St. Patrick's Cathedral. John Vernou Bouvier wed Caroline Ewing, one of the great beauties of New York society, of whom it was said that she was a great hostess who made their home on East Twenty-sixth Street a glittering salon during the city's belle epoque.

Until Bouvier's death, his son, also named John Vernou, kept "Jr." appended to his name. Born in 1864, he graduated with honors from Columbia University Law School, became a trial lawyer, and was so successful that he opened his own firm. John Vernou Bouvier Jr., Jacqueline's grandfather, was so highly regarded by no less an influential lawmaker than Supreme Court Justice Benjamin Cardozo that he was appointed major judge advocate for the army during the Great War. Forever after, he delighted in being addressed as Major Bouvier. The bulk of his wealth, however, came from his association with his uncle, M. C. Bouvier, a Wall Street tycoon for whom he put aside his law practice and worked, to their mutual financial advantage.

As consequential as wealth and military title were for him, neither satisfied the Major's constant ambition to improve his social status. To that end, he successfully sought membership in Manhattan's Union and Racquet Clubs and, on Long Island, the Maidstone and Piping Rock Clubs. His name was also on the roster of fashionable associations in Washington, D.C., Florida and Cuba. In 1890, he married Maude Sargeant, the handsome, English-born daughter of a rich pulp merchant and paper manufacturer. They had five children—dark-haired John Vernou Bouvier III, born in 1891; the fairer William Sergeant Bouvier, born in 1893 and always known as Bud; honey-blond Edith, called Edie

(1894); and the redheaded twins, Maude and Michelle (1905), who bobbed their hair but not their names.

The children were born on an estate called Woodcroft in Nutley, New Jersey. Subsequently, the family relocated to a series of ever grander Fifth Avenue addresses, and eventually they settled permanently into a sumptuous, twenty-four-room apartment at 765 Park Avenue, a home lavishly decorated with, among other accessories, Italian marble and French wood. The Bouviers' first summer residence in East Hampton was a clapboard-and-shingle house called Wildmoor, on Appaquogue Road, which the Major bought about 1910; in 1925, he purchased an additional estate on Further Lane called Lasata ("place of peace" in an American Indian dialect). With the twitter of summer's first cuckoo, the family betook themselves to Long Island, and there the Bouviers remained in stately splendor until the pumpkin harvest.

The Major typified a sort of Victorian gentility. His hair was trimmed twice weekly, and long after they were fashionable, he continued to wear spats and English tweeds; high, starched collars; a mustache tortured several times daily into neatness with wax; and, even in summer, a tie with an Edwardian suit jacket.

BUT THERE WAS an even more remarkable eccentricity.

Apparently unsatisfied with the family genealogy, John Vernou Bouvier Jr.—a man who was otherwise a stickler for accuracy— eventually published a little book called *Our Forebears* in which, with shameless gravity, he invented the most outrageous accounts of a noble ancestry. These stories he had told for years with rhapsodic fervor.

The line of Bouviers, Jack's father insisted without a shred of evidence, had sprung from the patrician house of Fontaine and included illustrious French patriots and titled aristocrats from the royal courts. With that stroke of his imaginative pen, a modest Provençal clan was at once transformed into a family of barons and marquises. Every Bouvier child and grandchild was thenceforth subjected to excerpts from Grandfather's solemn family saga, which was understood to be true.

John Davis, Jackie's first cousin and later the scrupulously accurate historian of the Bouvier clan, felt that Jack's father was not a deliberately deceptive charlatan. "I think," Davis reflected, "[that] it was simply inconceivable to him that the residents of the palatial mansions of his grandfather, uncle and aunts could have stemmed from anything but noble stock." The proudly American, flag-waving Republican John Vernou Bouvier Jr. never appreciated the irony of his arrant pretense to blue blood.

No wonder, then, that his children and grandchildren assimilated an unfortunate kind of *folie de grandeur,* a sense that their progenitors were so eminent, their privileged place so much their due, that the Bouviers were a tribe apart. For lesser mortals even to meet them ought to be benediction enough in this life.

But families are nothing if not complex. The Bouvier haughtiness was tempered by the reminder that *noblesse* ought to *oblige:* Grandpa loved to insert French phrases, however hackneyed, into any available chink in the conversation. Because they had impeccable manners and a concomitant respect for the comfort of anyone they met, the Bouvier offspring projected politeness and even genuine warmth of the kind that had never characterized the Lees. Remarkable for these qualities was Maude Sargeant Bouvier, Jackie's paternal grandmother—a highly refined woman whose love of nature bore fruit in numerous horticultural prizes. At Lasata, Grandma Bouvier often took Jackie around the gardens, pointing out this flower and that plant and spicing her instruction with legends and folklore about each species.

Regarding religious affiliation, the Bouviers were like the Lees— nominally Roman Catholic, but scarcely devout. Fervent defenders of their faith only if someone attacked it, they worshiped mostly at the altars of money, position and influence.

JOHN VERNOU (JACK) Bouvier III, who was Janet's husband and Jacqueline's father, graduated without distinction from Yale in 1914 and then served in the Signal Corps during the war. His father's influence secured Jack a position with the Wall Street brokerage firm of Henry Henty & Co. and bought him a place on the New York Stock Exchange. Hence Jack was, for the record, a stockbroker.

But his real career was that of playboy and roué. Charming and poised, he cultivated a life of pleasure, was indifferent to the worlds of art and culture and had no interest in matters of the mind or spirit. But Jacqueline would later say that to the world he cut "a most devastating figure," with his movie-star good looks, expressive mouth, high forehead, intense, sensuous eyes, pencil-thin mustache and dark hair invariably slicked with brilliantine. All this was highlighted by a perpetual dusky tan, combining to produce an effective sorcery with women that earned him the sobriquet "Black Jack" while still in school. Expelled from one preparatory school and barely tolerated at the second, he graduated, a year late, from Yale. His respectable position as a stockbroker notwithstanding, Jack Bouvier excelled most of all at gambling, womanizing and prodigiously consuming liquor. Unlike his brother, Bud, who never did much of anything, Jack was for a time what would later be called a functioning alcoholic.

More than once before he married, Jack had proposed to one junior miss or another while they were both gulping contraband whiskey during a weekend spree—Prohibition be damned. On April 7, 1920, for example, *The New York Times* reported Jack's engagement to Miss Eleanor Carter, "a first cousin of Lady Acheson of England." The wedding never occurred, thanks to the timely intervention of Miss Carter's parents, who dragged her back home and arranged a marriage to a Baltimore tycoon.

The newspaper reference to Lady Acheson had been included at the insistence of Jack's father and with the willing collaboration of the *Times*. Thus did one of America's leading newspapers avidly advance the cause of the Yankee caste system, which mimicked many characteristics of English country life. In this spirit, there was horseback riding in rigidly prescribed costume; tea or a cocktail hour; a fresh wardrobe several times daily; the christening of estates like the Lees' Avery Place and the Bouviers' Woodcroft and Lasata; and the retention of servants for every possible task. There was, as well, a timetable for genteel pastimes: letter writing in the morning room; luncheon at poolside; games at the club; cards and billiards after supper. The twin forks that formed the land of Long Island's eastern extremity seemed like fingers, pointing directly to Mother England, where, it was presumed, civility, manners and values were virtues that America ought gratefully to replicate.

Rich but reckless, Jack realized a handsome income during the 1920s. But he led an irresponsibly high life, spending prodigally on clothes, gambling, whiskey, cars and women; by the end of each year he had usually saved little. Some family members claimed he made and lost more than $7 million during that decade, and often his father or his uncle, who was even richer, had to rescue him from creditors—until in 1929 the worsening economy forced the Major to survey his own assets with more than ordinary caution.

BY 1927, TWENTY-YEAR-OLD Janet Lee had met and sufficiently charmed the young Bouvier twins, Maude and Michelle, so thoroughly that she was often invited to summer parties at Lasata. Inevitably, she met Jack, for whom she was initially just another diversion. For her part, Janet was at once struck by the dashing, courtly and apparently wealthy John Vernou Bouvier, the third of that name.

During the following winter in Manhattan, Janet and Jack met frequently, danced and attended parties at the Waldorf and jazz fests in speakeasies. By spring 1928, her persistence, occasionally artfully disguised as indifference, had sustained Jack's interest. The notorious, somewhat louche playboy would at last be tamed by a gentlewoman—and one, it could not be ignored, who was sixteen years younger. Their engagement was announced at Easter.

As time would reveal, the couple shared one paramount concern: the acquisition of money and the indulgence of its rewards. Jack's parents had to admit that they seemed a good match, for Janet was a serious girl without any apparent social liability or ill repute; the Lees, of course, were delighted with a further link to wealth, which mattered more to them than ancestry. "Long Island society mostly bases its claims on money rather than lineage," wrote that formidable, clear-eyed doyenne Mrs. John King Van Rensselaer in *The Social Ladder* in 1924. "Wealth and worth are interchangeable terms."

In addition, Jack was undoubtedly warmhearted and generous, whereas Janet was, as even her parents admitted, a bit statuesque, too reserved, her manner a trifle arch. Jack's drinking, frequently to excess in public, was dismissed by Janet's family as devil-may-care high spirits—a reaction typical of that era. As for poor, alcoholic Bud, he was shuttled off to various clinics and retreats in Connecticut, New Jersey and as far away as California; he was not much seen by anyone, and died of drink at the age of thirty-six, two months after Jacqueline's birth.

The wedding was held on Saturday, July 7, 1928, at St. Philomena's Church, East Hampton. The little frame church on Buell Lane, decorated with a profusion of white ribbons and flowers, was filled to overflowing with five hundred guests, and the Lees hosted a reception afterward at Avery Place, where an orchestra played popular tunes, rags and tangos. Next morning, the newlyweds sailed for Europe aboard the *Aquitania*. When they returned and settled into Jack's bachelor apartment at the end of August, it was just in time for another family wedding, that of his sister Maude.

But as the year drew to a close and the Manhattan party season shifted into high gear, Janet and many of those in their circle found it difficult to ignore either her husband's excessive drinking or his insouciant visits to mistresses both familiar and newfound. In this regard, his conduct became more and more irksome and embarrassing—Janet's cool, evidently complaisant attitude notwithstanding. She rode her horses, she shopped, she hosted teas and suppers, and she appeared to all to be a proper society wife. Her husband went to his office, dashed around city and country in his black convertible, disappeared for an evening or overnight, bewitched women and impressed men. But after Jack came perilously close to falling into an alcoholic coma at the traditional New Year's Eve revelry, the Lees had doubts about their daughter's future.

FEARING A POSSIBLE early dissolution of the marriage, the Bouviers consulted their attorneys and financial advisers. Not to worry, they said: all would be well, whatever the outcome between Jack and Janet. But then came the announcement that forestalled any talk of divorce: Janet was pregnant.

In their optimism, the lawyers and accountants were taking their cue from no less than the country's leader. "Ours is a land filled with millions of happy homes blessed with comfort and opportunity," declared President Herbert Clark Hoover in his inaugural address to the American people on March 4, 1929. "I have no fears for the future. It is bright with hope!"

But on that sunny, cold day in Washington, the gleam was mostly in the skies and on the faces of victorious Republicans taking office with the new chief executive, who had solidly defeated his opponent,

the Democratic governor of New York, Alfred E. Smith. On the dubious premise that Jazz Age prosperity would continue forever, Hoover
had successfully mobilized the support of tycoons and moguls.

The facts of life for ordinary people belied any national euphoria,
however. Throughout the 1920s, a greater and greater share of income
went to an ever smaller number of extremely wealthy citizens, the
Bouviers and Lees among them. But while businesses prospered as
never before, workers received salaries less and less proportionate to
what they produced for the rich. From 1923 to 1929, for example,
productivity per person-hour grew by 32 percent while workers' pay
increased by only 8 percent. To make matters worse, the Revenue Act
of 1926 decreased by almost 70 percent the taxes of those making a
million dollars or more. Corporate profits rose 65 percent in the same
period, with the result that the rich became opulently so, and the poor
came perilously close to penury: each of the top .1 percent of American
families took in salaries equal to that of the entire bottom 42 percent.

The causes of the incongruity are, in retrospect, easy to identify.
After the treaties ending the war in 1919, a kind of myopic, jingoistic
individualism gripped the country during the Roaring Twenties. International and social concerns were not much emphasized by politicians
or pundits, while new wealth, new fun, new fashions and a new im-
pudence seemed to many the most desirable goals. Modern manufac-
turing techniques produced enormous quantities of goods, and an
unprecedented array of new radios, automobiles and household appli-
ances appeared in stores everywhere.

But demand had to keep pace with supply, and fresh, powerful and
sometimes intimidating strategies for marketing and promotion were
devised by the newly authoritative advertising industry. "The key to
economic prosperity is the organized creation of dissatisfaction." Such
was the shameless assertion of a General Motors executive in 1929 as
he summed up the spirit of the decade. With alarming rapidity, ordinary people had been persuaded that they actually needed more and
more possessions, greater and greater luxuries. That the exhortations
were effective was because of another contrivance: credit, which is only
a euphemism for debt. "Buy now, pay later" was the last push against
the backs of those who had already been convinced by advertising that
(a) all their needs could be met; (b) all their needs could be met by

material goods; and (c) all their needs could be met by material goods *immediately*. "Why wait? Be the first one in your neighborhood to own . . ."

But even as the General Motors officer sniffed and perhaps lit a dollar cigar, his employees were accumulating so much debt that they could no longer continue to buy every attractive new item that appeared in the shop windows and in the mail-order catalogs; much less could they contemplate a new automobile.

By late winter 1929, the average gross pay for a white-collar worker in New York City was $33.50 for a fifty-hour week (not much more than it had been a decade earlier), but withholding taxes took more than half that amount. Credit was stretched to the limit, and comparatively few people had notable savings. A day of disaster was imminent for the nation—beginning with the fat, sleek corporations that counted on the purchases of ordinary men and women. While Hoover concluded his inaugural speech to wild applause that March, company stocks everywhere were gradually but continually declining.

The situation worsened that July, but the richest residents of New York City, which was home to the greatest number of the nation's wealthy, believed for the most part that any crisis would be appropriately managed by Washington wizards. Surely, nothing could prevent any successful businessman from being one of the first to avail himself of exciting, luxurious new opportunities. On July 7, for example, Jack pointed out to Janet a news item: Transcontinental Air Transport began the first cross-country service by plane. At a one-way cost of $351.94, passengers could depart New York's Pennsylvania Station on Monday and, traveling in trains by night and on planes by day, would arrive at Glendale Airport, near downtown Los Angeles, late Wednesday. Jack said this would be a good idea for a change of pace that summer. The impending birth of Jacqueline quashed that idea.

AFTER THE CHILD'S birth, the family returned to Grandfather Bouvier's Lasata, where the clan was in residence that summer and where relatives and a platoon of servants scurried about, trying to outdo one another in providing luxuries for mother and child. Janet liked to pronounce her baby's name "Jack-leen," but her husband applied no such affectation: his daughter was "Jackie," and so she was addressed by family and friends throughout her life. Soon a nursemaid named Bertha Newey was employed, and in proper British fashion she was charged with the care of the little girl, and eventually of a second daughter as well.

Set back from Further Lane and approached by a long, curving drive, Lasata was in fact a manor composed of fourteen acres planted thick with maple, linden, willow and fruit trees. The property included a cornfield and apple orchard, stables, a paddock with a horse-jumping ring, a tennis court, formal sunken gardens maintained with Renaissance precision by the gardener and his staff, marble statuary, a fish pool, fountains and, everywhere, a brilliance of flowers.

But if the secondary elements of the estate were dazzlingly luxuriant, the house itself, a mixture of English country and eastern Long Island colonial, was downright opulent. Ivy clung to its stucco walls, reaching almost to the shingled roof; surrounded by lush green lawns and shaded by ancient elms, Lasata seemed to emerge from its surroundings like a medieval castle. Here, if anywhere, it was possible to forget Manhattan's frenetic pace and to believe Grandpa's fantastic fables of ancestral grandeur.

The fifteen-room house, built in 1916, had seven bedrooms, each decorated in exquisite taste: English chintz in one chamber, chinoiserie in another, beach pastels in a third. Downstairs, at the head of a Jacobean refectory table set with gold utensils and Limoges plates, the Major presided over polite dinner conversation among the family and their guests, the men invariably dressed in white shirt, coat and tie, the women in long-sleeved dresses, stockings and high-heeled shoes. At mealtimes as elsewhere, every gentleman's hair seemed to glisten with brilliantine, while the ladies took up hot curling irons so they might appear with fashionable marcel waves. Speech was measured, manners were impeccable; there were neither raised voices nor interruptions. Nothing was awry; everything was accomplished *comme il faut,* planned according to the complex rituals of a meticulous courtliness. But this was no social hypocrisy: manners, it was believed, expressed an essential esteem for human dignity.

The expansive living room, a mix of French, English, Victorian and Early American styles, contained many items from two centuries of Bouvier residences: red damask walls and silk furniture coverings,

Louis XV gilt-framed mirrors, velour draperies, card and chess tables, marble busts, a grand piano, a wall of books, an Empire clock and Chippendale chairs crafted, it was claimed, by Jackie's great-great-grandfather soon after his immigration from France.

Things were simpler, more quaint but no less pleasant elsewhere in East Hampton, with its saltbox cottages, old windmills and serene village green, its ponds and nearby potato fields, its paths and lanes bordered by wooden fences draped in wild roses and honeysuckle. Only a handful of other places could be compared with Lasata, but the prevalent tone of life reflected an adherence to a virtual religion of comfort and refinement among the wealthy and to a cult of elegant simplicity elsewhere. East Hampton, as Mrs. Van Rensselaer noted in 1924, "clings to the conservative fashions and manners of bygone days." While some locals still traveled by horse-drawn carriage and lived in shanties near the two-lane highway, they shared with their wealthier neighbors the formalities of common courtesy and an abhorrence of noise and incivility.

In such splendor, set in a graceful and cultivated hamlet, Janet, Jack and their daughter remained until late autumn 1929—and to it they returned during the next decade, not only every summer but also frequently off-season. Lasata and its ambience provided, along with the refinements of Park Avenue, the atmosphere in which Jackie lived until adolescence, when even greater luxuries would surround her.

CHAPTER TWO

1930-1936

*T*he summers of Jackie's childhood, which extended from May to October, may fairly be described in one word: white. Everywhere could be seen people in white suits and polo whites, tennis whites and sailing whites, white shoes and hats. Women wore white pearls, men white boutonnieres. Clothes were changed often, for freshness was impossible in those summers before air-conditioning, and servants were kept busy washing, pressing and spot cleaning.

These tasks could also be dispatched by the staff at the Maidstone Club, where—although it strictly observed Prohibition—Jack stashed a bottle or three, entertained friends and business colleagues and blatantly lunched with his mistress of the moment. Still, the Maidstone Club was to all appearances a temple of respectability, the achievement of which, the members were certain, had much to do with the frank exclusion of Jews, blacks and (unless they belonged to or married into a member family) actors. With these restrictions in place, the club thrived for decades. As long as nothing *seemed* out of place or ill mannered, a roué like Jack could take calculated risks. In summertime he and his mistresses looked fresh, crisp and handsome in their seasonal whites. Such appearances were of primary concern to the administrators of the Maidstone. Besides, often enough Jack and friend were joined for tea by Janet, whose equestrian skills quickly earned her a position of some esteem: more than one year she was voted Junior Master of the Suffolk Hounds.

But not all of life was so tidy.

Paternity moderated neither Jack's drinking nor his philandering. It was not unusual for the police to be summoned when, inebriated, Jack drove his car off the road or into the shallow pond in the town center of East Hampton. As for sexual indiscretions, a photograph of the Bouviers at a riding event documents Janet gazing rapturously off— presumably at the horse and rider—while between her and Jack is a lovely woman, her fingers slyly, romantically intertwined with his. Usually, he and his mistresses were more circumspect.

But such emblems of affection were not much in evidence between husband and wife, at home or in public—hence Jackie grew up seeing few signs of love between those supposedly joined by it. Nor was her mother a demonstrative woman; an embrace and a kiss were far more often forthcoming from Jack or from grandparents.

By an odd set of circumstances, the aristocratic life of the Bouviers was not much altered by the Great Depression, which began with the collapse of the stock market in October 1929, when Jackie was three months old. When the losses were assessed that winter, her grandfather, on whom her father greatly depended, still had $4 million, although just weeks earlier his portfolio had been twice that size. Still rich in municipal and corporate bonds, the Major found himself in the awkward position of taking instructions from his uncle (M. C. Bouvier) as his employer. It was this formidable tycoon who decided that all the family reins must thenceforth be held in tight check.

This meant no more bailouts for Jack, who had no savings and was immediately affected by a sharp decline in his commissions as stockbroker because of the hugely reduced trading volume. His only resource for loans and luxuries, therefore, was Janet's father, but now that Jack was both impecunious as well as intemperate and unfaithful, James Lee began to regard him as something of an annoyance. Only the comfort of his daughter and the well-being of his granddaughter prompted Lee to come to the aid of his son-in-law, which he did not with cash but with real estate. Instead of the hefty loan Jack requested, Lee instead offered him an eleven-room apartment at 740 Park Avenue, where Jack, Janet and Jackie could live rent-free, in sybaritic splendor.

As a sign of his willingness to dedicate himself to hard work and to amend his insouciant life, Jack was required to resign from all his clubs except the Maidstone, and Lee made it clear that thenceforth, Big Father-in-Law would be watching. This did not, however, produce the desired effect; on the contrary, the Bouvier marriage, now laced with suspicion and contempt, deteriorated further.

On December 22, 1929, five-month-old Jacqueline Lee Bouvier was baptized at the Church of St. Ignatius Loyola, on Park Avenue, where she would later be confirmed.

EARLY IN THE new year, Janet was compelled to put a good face on the disintegration of another marriage—that of her own parents. James and Margaret Lee had led separate lives for years, and although they never legally divorced, after 1930 they had little contact.

By the time Jackie marked her second birthday in East Hampton the following summer, there was more marital bad fortune. Her father's sister Edith was abandoned by her husband, Phelan Beale. An animated soul with a keen wit, Edie had preferred seductive tangos to staid cotillions. She had also charted the career of a singer, dancer and actress, but her parents had more traditional plans and, alas, forced her into a respectable, loveless marriage. With her husband's departure and with three children, thirty-five-year-old Edie Beale had to rely on her family for support. Eventually, they installed her in a house near the beach. Somehow, Aunt Edie kept her good spirits, and at family gatherings and at Jackie's birthday parties, Edie needed no encouragement to break into song. A chorus or two from the works of Sigmund Romberg, Irving Berlin or George Gershwin, sung by Edie, could always be counted on to enliven the festivities.

Surrounded by a family with so many of its members in marital disarray, Jackie saw from her earliest years that marriages were often impermanent relationships, that husbands and wives did not live together, that men blithely pursued their own fortunes and fantasies. Her father sought escape in liquor and affairs, while her mother rode and hunted, pursuing the trappings of wealth and status with fierce determination. The Bouviers and the Lees were families who took appearances gravely indeed. But behind the respectable, polite masks were frightened people with a tenuous grasp on reality. They all loved horses, dogs and every kind of animal life, but they were not terribly skilled at dealing with the problems of adults in a society that placed the highest value on mere presentation.

This ethos included astonishingly formal parties for well-bred children, for this was a way of publicizing the parents. Hence, on her second birthday, Jackie was tendered an entertainment that had almost the embellishments of a theatrical garden party. That summer of 1931, Jack and Janet leased a house far more modest than Lasata—a place that had once been a wild hostelry frequented by gin-swilling poker players. Moved several times on its foundations, the aptly christened Rowdy Hall was finally installed at the corner of David's and Egypt Lanes, East Hampton. Rejuvenated and redecorated, it was the setting on July 28 for an event documented in the *East Hampton Star* under the heading FUTURE DEBUTANTE HOSTS SECOND BIRTHDAY BASH:

> Darling little Jackie Bouvier, daughter of Jack Bouvier and the former Janet Lee, will not make her bow to society for another 16 years or more, but she was a charming hostess at her second birthday party given at the home of her parents, Rowdy Hall, on Egypt Lane. The party featured games and pony rides for the children, followed by Jack Horner pie and birthday cake.

In fact, the precocious hostess was already, thanks to her mother's tenacious training, amazingly adept on horseback, and that summer marked a kind of formal, if amusingly premature, entrance into the world of dressage, for she did more than ride a pony: she put the animal through some pretty paces—and continued to do so in the coming years.

"Mother and daughter, riding their mounts side by side at these events, made a charming impression," recalled Jackie's cousin John Davis. "Here was the impeccably attired and unfailingly spunky Janet in her high black homburg, ascot tie, coat with contrasting collar and jodhpurs to match the collar, and tall leather boots, trotting alongside this miniature of herself, the confident little Jacqueline. I remember all the cousins sitting on the rails were in awe of Jacqueline's self-assurance on horseback." From childhood, Jackie's alliance with horses taught her to maintain her composure, to maneuver carefully, to strike the proper blend of gentleness and strength, when to demand and when to reward. These skills she learned from her mother and perfected through repetition; as is so often the case, they became a complex of talents not irrelevant in her dealings with human beings.

The following month, Jackie was encouraged by Janet to take Hootchie, her shaggy black Scottish terrier, to a local dog show. Again the press was on hand to record Jackie's advance into society, for her mother was tremendously busy that summer, hauling reporters and photographers from offices, clubs and beach blankets. "Little two-year-old Jacqueline Bouvier," according to the local newspaper, "toddled to the show platform and exhibited with great pride a wee Scotch [sic] terrier of about her own size."

A photo taken of Jackie that day reveals all the striking characteristics of the woman she would become: the direct, serene gaze from wide-set eyes; the dark hair and high cheekbones; the uncommon poise. She had, in other words, her father's features and her mother's polish, and she was neither abjectly shy nor annoyingly pretentious.

Perhaps to her mother's frustration, there was no mention of Janet, but Jack's name was inserted into the same article: "Mr. Bouvier is so deeply tanned with East Hampton sunburn that he much resembles one of those handsome Egyptians you see careening along in their Rolls-Royce cars in Cairo, in the land of the Nile!"

HER PARENTS' MARRIAGE was certainly troubled, its future uncertain as the arguments and name-calling, recalled years later by cousins, reached critical mass. But in the unpredictable nature of intimacies, Janet and Jack informed their parents in the early autumn of 1932 that a second child was expected. On March 3, 1933, Caroline Lee Bouvier, named for her paternal great-grandmother and her maternal ancestors, was born in Doctors Hospital, Manhattan. Jackie clearly relished the idea of a sister, and at once she wanted to share the supervision of the infant with Miss Newey. The newborn was, from the start, called by her second name.

The day after Lee's birth, Franklin D. Roosevelt took the oath of office as president and delivered a message of determination and hope to a country crippled by unemployment: 13 million were jobless, one of every four heads of household. Scores of banks had failed, factories were shuttered, farmers were evicted. In nearby Central Park, Jackie and her nurse, pushing Lee's stroller, saw hundreds of families living in tar-paper shacks and foraging for food in trash bins. On the city sidewalks, once-dapper businessmen, now dressed almost in rags, sold apples.

But of Depression-era soup lines and suicides, Jackie knew nothing. Among some Wall Street prophets, there was even a rush of confidence. Jack Bouvier, never one to languish, decided to gratify his wife by tossing a lavish party for two hundred guests that summer; the event marked their fifth anniversary, Jackie's fourth birthday and Lee's baptism.

One day that autumn Bertha Newey took the girls to Central Park, as she so often did. Somehow Jackie wandered away and became separated from her nurse and sister. An hour later the telephone rang at 740 Park Avenue.

"Is this Rhinelander 4-6167?" asked a man. Janet said that it was. "We have a little girl here," he said, adding that he was a police officer calling from the local station house. "She gave us this telephone number, but not her name. Could she be yours?" Janet rushed to the police station, only to find Jackie completely at ease, observing the activities of the officers and, at the tender age of four, asking questions from her perch on a high stool. Clearly, she had instantly become the darling of the precinct. The duty officer recited the facts. Jackie, strolling alone in the park, approached a patrolman and calmly announced, "My nurse and sister seem to be lost."

The child's sangfroid and refusal to dramatize often created disconcerting moments for her mother. One such incident occurred a few years later when Janet and her daughters returned one afternoon to the apartment. The uniformed elevator operator had a crest of red hair that sprang up, bold and recalcitrant. "Hello, Ernest," said Lee politely. "You look nice today." Just as Ernest cleared his throat to thank the child, Jackie, who was about eight, turned to her sister: "How can you say such a thing, Lee? It isn't true! We all know perfectly well that Ernest looks just like a rooster!" Janet, for once embarrassed to silence, whisked the girls into the apartment; Ernest's reaction has not been recorded.

It should be added that Janet tried carefully to monitor the children's speech, wardrobe and manners, and so Jackie and Lee matured with admirable diction and with the pronunciation specific to a certain Northeast class of families. *Literature* was pronounced "lit'ra-tyoo-ah," *mayonnaise* was "my-oh-nez," the vowel sounds of words like *heard* and *skirt* were much softened. There was little of New York in the tone, and more of what was later called the Bryn Mawr accent.

With proper elocution came, of course, reading. By the time she was five years old, a year before attending school, Jackie was able to read. As early as the summer of 1934, she recited from memory brief passages from L. Frank Baum's *The Wonderful Wizard of Oz,* A. A. Milne's *Winnie-the-Pooh* and Frances Hodgson Burnett's *Little Lord Fauntleroy*. She found a volume of Chekhov among her mother's books and stayed with it long enough to ask, "What's a midwife?"

In addition, Janet scattered books on art history and ballet around the apartment and occasionally escorted her daughters to museums and dance recitals. Neither child took to ballet as a participant, but both developed a passion for it as spectators. As for art, Jackie early on demonstrated a remarkable ability as a quick sketch artist: throughout her life, her pen swept across pads, notebooks and foolscap, and her representations of people, events and travels delighted family and friends.

Each of these sketches revealed not only an impressive interpretive skill but also, and often, a devastatingly trenchant wit. One of her earliest cartoons was of the Wall Street All Stars, the baseball team her father formed in East Hampton during the summer of 1934. Jackie drew stick figures with hilariously accurate personalities: a short-tempered catcher, a dazed pitcher, a too-eager baseman. The bodies were merely suggested, but the faces were highly individualized.

Her interest in art was much advanced in the spring of 1935 when Grandfather Bouvier took Jackie to visit her great-uncle M. C. Bouvier, on whose wealth virtually the entire Bouvier fortune depended. At the time, he was quite frail and confined to his opulent brownstone on West Forty-sixth Street. Every antique was described for her, every tapestry, bibelot, chandelier and clock, and she was given a detailed tour of an amazing collection of paintings—among them, two canvases each by Corot and Millet. When she returned home, she recited virtually the entire inventory to her astonished father.

Not long after, a critically important event took place. On July 29, 1935, the day after Jackie's sixth birthday, old Uncle Michel died at eighty-eight. A lifelong bachelor, he had no direct heirs, a circumstance that brought every remote cousin of the Bouviers to New York for the reading of the will. After taxes, the estate was valued at $3.25 million, of which Jack received only $5,000. But he did inherit, via his father, M. C.'s business. In short order, Jack opened the brokerage company Bouvier, Bishop & Co. That year, he took home more than $35,000 in profit, but his lavish lifestyle produced bills of over $40,000. Nor did the $35,000 please Janet, who had become something of the proverbial fisherman's wife: too much was never enough. Arguments echoed in the Bouvier home. Life at home was a confusion of realms, a strange mixture of polite appearances to outsiders and emotional disorder in private.

But order, discipline, new friends and a certain predictability suffused Jackie's life that autumn when she entered school. Whatever questions the child had about her parents' disputes, her mother shrewdly deflected. At six, Jackie therefore learned that any bewilderment or fear she felt about life at home was to be kept to herself. Discussion about unpleasant, private things simply was not done.

JANET BOUVIER HAD attended Miss Chapin's School for Girls, which she selected for her daughter and to which she delivered Jackie that crisp October morning in 1935. It was a venerable institution, as true to the ideals of civilized society as to those of a first-rate academy. That season three hundred girls were registered in twelve grades and a year of college prep, a faculty of thirty constituting an impressive ratio. All students were expected to be in place at 8:45 each morning; the dismissal bell rang at noon for those in grades one through four, at 1:15 for those in five through twelve. The girls were not, therefore, overburdened with a lengthy scholastic day. But during those few hours, a great deal was accomplished, for nonsense was not tolerated.

At Chapin, Jackie studied from first through sixth grades, from the ages of six to twelve. Grandpa Bouvier underwrote the annual tuition of $575 per year (which also covered lunch, books, tennis and bus service), much to her father's relief. This total amount was, it should be noted, higher than the annual income earned by millions of Americans during the Great Depression.

Chapin girls all wore the required blue uniform—a custom introduced decades earlier to equalize the dress of all students and therefore to obliterate the most obvious distinctions between the finery of the rich and the simpler garb of those less affluent students on scholarship. A black-uniformed maid greeted visitors to the school.

No less an arbiter than Virginia Gildersleeve, dean of Barnard College and a tough judge of educational institutions, their values and curricula, observed in 1928 that Miss Chapin's School for Girls was "one of the pillars of women's education in New York City." From its founding in 1901, the pillar was an elegant one that retained, both in genteel ideals and in its choice of students, "truest to the *Social Register*," as an impartial evaluator wrote years later, although she hoped it would "eventually attract a more varied clientele."

For its time, however, the school was unique in several aspects. Maria Bowden Chapin, the founder, born in 1863, came from a family whose fortunes had suddenly failed, and she was denied a formal education beyond the age of ten. From that time, she became something of an autodidact who handily absorbed languages, art and history. At the age of thirty-eight, Miss Chapin—by now a prematurely white-haired and stern woman of grave beauty—joined a friend named Mary Cecelia Fairfax, and together they opened Miss Chapin's School for Girls at 12 West Forty-sixth Street. Several moves followed between 1905 and 1928, when the new building was completed on East End Avenue.

At the same time, the standards at Chapin altered dramatically. Schools for wealthy young ladies during the first quarter of the twentieth century were, for the most part, little more than day-care centers that prepared an alumna to be a housewife or hostess. But Miss Chapin, an ardent suffragette, devised a program that not only included instruction in the crafts of housewifery, called rather grandly home economics, but also imparted the fine points of academic subjects. "It is not safe," the Chapin bulletin proclaimed,

for the average girl to take it for granted that after she has left school with as little as possible in her head, and has a good time for a year or so, she will marry some nice young man, and her worries will be over. The recent crash has shown us that almost anything may happen, and that the wife may have to become the breadwinner for the family.

Bold words for an elite girls' school, even during the Depression. Miss Chapin was of hardy stock.

She herself taught a class in history, poetry or Latin to every upper class; visited the lower grades each week to survey both teachers and students; and introduced her notorious "character reports," in which were detailed the development of each girl for the edification of her parents. Only the best available instructors were employed, all of them college graduates and not merely holders of teachers' certificates. More remarkably, Miss Chapin never hesitated to subsidize, from her own salary, the advanced education of staff who could not afford a summer of study in Europe.

One of the teachers she subsidized was Miss Ethel Grey Stringfellow, whom Miss Chapin sent abroad to consider the new so-called progressive movement of education. Miss Stringfellow returned flush with excitement over the principles of Maria Montessori, and soon after, Chapin and Stringfellow were attending Madame Montessori's New York lectures.

By 1933, a program of summer study was required of students, to be dispatched on their own time when they were not frolicking at the beach or negotiating mountain trails with their families. Every day included a planned lesson or project, and serious results were expected in October. Perfect spelling, as Jackie learned even in the first grade, was a hallowed tradition: "She could see a misspelled word through the cover of a book," said one student of Miss Chapin. In failing health, the founder resigned in 1932, turning over joint directorship to Miss Fairfax and Miss Stringfellow. Fairfax and Chapin died in 1933 and 1934, respectively, and at that time the school's board unanimously appointed Stringfellow and, as the founder had wished, legally changed the name of the academy to the Chapin School.

When Jackie arrived, primary-grade students attended classes in more than reading, writing, geography, arithmetic and athletics, in each of which she routinely excelled. Fierce about culture, Miss Stringfellow also arranged for famously creative people to visit: Pearl Buck and Robert Frost came to read and discuss their work, for example, and musicians from symphony orchestras played instruments and answered questions. There were, as well, occasional "roundtables" with experts in the fields of politics and foreign affairs, for Miss Stringfellow had inherited her predecessor's insistence that the girls not study history or government in isolation from current events. By 1939, every graduate of the Chapin School was accepted to the college of her choice.

These credentials were impressive, and the school liked, with some reason, to consider itself in the avant-garde. But during the 1930s, it also inculcated the same kind of quaintly simulated, faintly stuffy English manners that prevailed among the upper echelon of Long Island society. The same Dean Gildersleeve who had proclaimed Chapin second to none in academic seriousness added that the finest boys' schools in America—she mentioned St. Paul's, St. Mark's, Groton and Exeter—had, as prototypes, the hallowed halls of Eton, Harrow and Rugby in England. "May we not hope," concluded Gildersleeve, "that as [those British boys' academies] have trained the selected youth of England in brain, in character, in vision, to be the leaders of a great empire, so the Chapin School may train women who will be a true aristocracy of leaders in this vast and perplexing city?"

WHEN CLASSES ENDED in May, Jack, Janet and the girls repaired for the summer of 1936 to East Hampton, where they settled into Wild-moor, on Appaquogue Road—the six-bedroom residence of Grandpa Bouvier before Lasata, and still owned by him. Wildmoor was set on ten acres of lawns and fields, and appearances suggested that Black Jack's fortunes had not been at all affected by the worst year of the Depression. Two elegant cars were in the driveway; prize horses (Step-aside, Pas d'Or and Danseuse among them) were still taken out by Janet and Jackie; and thoroughbred dogs leaped and cavorted around the property.

But the trappings of wealth belied the financial pressures Janet and Jack felt more uncomfortably that summer. His expenses, as always, exceeded his commissions (the bulk of his income), and he could no longer provide his wife with the many comforts she now saw as her right—a surplus of servants, for example, and a lavish household budget. Jack's father, whose wealth was fading fast because of the enormous inheritance taxes on Uncle M.C.'s estate, saw no chance of his son's repaying the considerable debts he had accrued. As for James Lee, he felt that it was more than enough that he had provided his daughter's husband with a rent-free Manhattan home.

Still, Black Jack was a Hurrah Harry, as the English would say: jolly, courtly, generous with time and money, full of fun—and, to his credit, a doting and devoted father. But that year he turned forty-five and began to show, physically and emotionally, the signs of a piteously thoughtless life. The merriment too often had a desperate quality; the courtliness, a frank expectation of sexual response; the youthful high spirits, a distasteful hollowness. Of all this he seemed blissfully oblivious. "Jackie," he told his daughter that summer, "you never have to worry about keeping up with the Joneses, because we are the Joneses. Everyone has to keep up with us!" But few people could match him on the level of debt: he had a $64,000 tax bill and considerable debts to his father and the estate of his late great-uncle.

For Janet, the issue was rather one of surpassing the proverbial Joneses. She, too, was unfailingly charming and attentive to her children's needs, insofar as she perceived them. But she was also mannered, her charm was cool and superficial, and to her girls she gave every comfort and social advantage but not, by all accounts, much tender affection. She was also a material pragmatist, an adamant realist; and regarding Jack's financial future, she discerned the inauspicious handwriting on the wall.

What had happened to this marriage, once so full of marvelous promise? Whither their supposedly impregnable estate in life? Would the *Social Register* continue to include their names? What would become of Janet and her children if they were forced to scale down their lifestyle? She did not require furs and diamonds, but she had become accustomed to servants, to breakfast in bed, ironed sheets and French cologne. Now all that was in jeopardy. And there was the matter of Jack's rampant infidelity, which did not diminish with his bank account. This, too, was an increasingly public embarrassment she was no longer willing to endure merely for the sake of the girls and for appearance's sake.

During the late summer of 1936, Jack and Janet quarreled more violently than ever, and the walls of Wildmoor echoed with recriminations and the sound of Jack's whiskey tumblers, smashed to the floor by either husband or wife. During such altercations, Jackie calmly picked up a book, took Lee into a room at the other end of the house and read to her sister—loudly, if necessary.

Janet and Jack finally formalized their differences, and as of October 1, as the legal papers read, "the parties [agreed] to live separate and apart from each other for the period of six months." Jack had to pay his wife $1,065 each month, plus medical and educational fees, for the support of their daughters, whose custody was assigned to Janet. For his part, he could visit his children "at all reasonable times and places and on Saturday afternoons and Sunday mornings at his own home or elsewhere as he may wish." But at his wife's insistence, he quit 740 Park Avenue, where Janet and the girls remained; Jack was reduced to a room at the Westbury Hotel on Madison Avenue. The wounds to his ego and his bank account were deeper than ever. For a man who sought solace in drink, this new set of circumstances was disastrous.

The situation was also, of course, traumatic for Jackie; at three, Lee understood and absorbed little of the ordeal and was much protected by her older sister, who told her that Daddy was away on business and could see them only on weekends. When he did, he gaily squired the girls to the zoo, museums and movies, and to lunches and skating at Rockefeller Center. He also escorted them to the floor of the Stock Exchange one afternoon, where they impressed the gentlemen with their formal curtsies and patrician manners.

But for a seven-year-old, the sudden absence of a father because of parental discord was deeply disturbing. Jackie began to experience the pull of both factions and to exhibit behavior patterns that were, however predictable in such situations, profoundly difficult to resolve for several years.

Janet indoctrinated Jackie and Lee in social refinement, the necessity of suitable behavior and appropriate attire; most of all, the girls were to cultivate a code of ladylike restraint and coolness. Public displays of emotion or temper were not acceptable: there was always a correct way to walk, act, speak. Miss Stringfellow and her colleagues at Chapin reinforced this code with their venerable rules and regulations, designed to produce the ideally cultivated, poised, proper young lady.

Jack's visits and outings brought a contrary spirit. He took them out in their play clothes, let the girls race and tumble through Central Park and (horrors!) allowed them to lick ice-cream cones while strolling on Fifth Avenue. He did not require them to wear white gloves, nor did he react with something like near hysteria if strawberry ice cream dripped on a white blouse. According to Berthe Kimmerle, who had succeeded Miss Newey as nanny, Jackie and Lee often cried when they had to return to Janet after a capricious day or weekend with Jack. Their mother, after all, was neither demonstrative in her affections nor prodigal with treats.

But there was greater conflict than varying styles and directives of deportment. When Jackie visited Grandpa Bouvier and the clan at his Park Avenue home for parties and holidays, she was alone among her cousins in being deprived of her mother's presence. Contrariwise, to counter the Bouvier influence and the Bouvier outlook, Janet took her daughters more often to visit *her* family. But this was problematic, too, for Janet's parents were separated, her grandmother was never mentioned, and old Mrs. Merritt was still treated like a servant. Jackie grew to prefer the Bouviers, a fondness that had the predictable effect of disappointing, then hurting, and finally enraging her mother. With this, Jackie unconsciously acquired a skill often found among children of broken homes: she learned to pit her parents against each other for her own benefit. "She succeeded admirably," according to her cousin John Davis, "especially with her father, [and] she learned the great lesson of her life: that with a little charm, and a little cunning, you could get almost anything you wanted out of a man."

The precocious charm and cunning had little effect at school, however, and this, as so often, was the locus of Jackie's trouble. Bright, alert and attentive, she was also becoming high-strung and difficult to manage, for here, of course, was an opportunity to defy Janet in the person of her teachers. Jackie was now a contrary and mischievous pupil, argumentative with her classmates and sometimes downright prankish with her teachers. Criticized and corrected by her mother, pampered and praised by her father, she had no equilibrium in her life. Rebellious acts, however venial, are the standard childish result.

Her conduct led often enough to Miss Stringfellow's office, which the headmistress did not, for the time being, report to Janet. But it was mentioned offhandedly to Janet one day by one of Jackie's schoolmates.

"I hear you are summoned to Miss Stringfellow very often," Janet said to her daughter when they were alone. "What happens when you're sent to Miss Stringfellow?"

"Well," Jackie began slowly, "I go to her office, and Miss String-fellow says, 'Jacqueline, sit down. I've heard things about you.' I sit down. Then Miss Stringfellow says a lot of things, but I don't listen."

That season, Janet and the headmistress conspired about a mode of correction. "I know you love horses and that you yourself are very much like a thoroughbred," said Miss Stringfellow on Jackie's next visit to her office. "You can run and you have staying power. You're well built and you have brains. But if you're not properly trained, you'll be good for nothing. Suppose you owned the most beautiful horse in the world. What good would he be if he weren't trained to stay on the track, to be still at the starting gate, to obey commands? He would be useless to you and you would have to get rid of him."

It took some time, according to Miss Stringfellow, for the logic of this argument to work. As one of Jackie's teachers said, the child was "very clever and very artistic [but] full of the devil." By the third grade she was, according to the headmistress, "the most inquiring mind we'd had in the school in thirty-five years—otherwise, I mightn't have kept her."

In any case, a lifelong friendship took root at Chapin. "She was very funny [and had] a vivid imagination," according to Nancy Tuck-erman.

> While she could be strong willed and stubborn, at the same time she was always fair and willing to compromise. Beyond this, Jackie held the distinction of being the naughtiest girl in the class, and this was in the days when good manners and proper behavior were key factors in our education. We were in awe of her escapades—escapades that invariably ended with

Jackie being sent to Miss Stringfellow . . . for a stern warning to "behave or else." . . . Whatever she did—however naughty she was—she was never mean. Just full of spirit, boundless energy and humor.

But slowly and subtly, a change occurred as Jackie approached adolescence. Whereas she was always popular with classmates, she was often, over the next several years, reserved and introverted, with a shy, almost embarrassed manner.

This is not difficult to understand. She wished neither to displease her elders nor to risk the loss, in summertime, of her beloved horses, as Miss Stringfellow threatened to recommend. But there were deeper worries, for Janet constantly feared they would all be hauled off to the poorhouse—by which she meant pitchforked from the *Social Register*— and thus Jackie absorbed her mother's anxieties about money and possessions. The love of privilege was accompanied by a terror of losing it; and the longing for acceptance and approval encouraged her to rely on the formalities of good manners and the repression of an immediate emotional reaction to anything. As her mother often reminded her, the impression a real lady makes depends on her refined demeanor, cultivated style and polished deportment. With these, a girl could go anywhere.

At the same time, Jackie was more and more indoctrinated in the faith of the Bouviers. Sensing her diffidence and withdrawal, Grandpa Bouvier, at Christmas 1936 and during many meetings thereafter, not only showered her with attention, affection and education but also read and explained the fine points of *Our Forebears*, that flamboyant little book that placed the Bouviers, the Vernous and their progeny in a noble line. From the formal gardens, the gently splashing fountains and the summer morning mists of Lasata to the family legend, Jacqueline Bouvier grew up drenched in myths worthy of Mallory or Tennyson. Her life, her history, her ancestry—all of it might have been sprung from engravings by Gustave Doré, who had so romantically illustrated the story of Lancelot and Guinevere. Jackie pored over the engravings in the art books Grandpa and Janet bought for her.

At this point, she began to sketch even more prolifically and seriously—seaside images when she was at East Hampton, scenes from fairy tales, from stories, from life in a favored quarter of city life. Every-thing was passed through the prism of a keen imagination.

The principal effect of all this precocious aestheticism and romantic mythology, both from Grandpa Bouvier and from books, was not only the healthy development of an artistic sense and a vivid imagination; it also provided an escape from the sadness and confusion of Jackie's family life. Her true history, she believed, was a noble one: so much was she taught. Her real self, therefore, belonged to the stuff of fairy tale, not soap opera. But then reality intervened, with the proximity of family struggle and the inevitable loneliness of a girl whose adored father was mostly absent.

To be sure, life was real, life was earnest. But somewhere, in time past and perhaps future, lay the deeper truth every child, however preconsciously, covets—the myth of being unique, especially in light of such instability at home. She told her mother that someday she wanted to go to France, where she would learn about her noble past. Janet, sheepish about her own heritage, could hardly suggest that Jackie make a detour to the Irish countryside to trace the lineage of the Lees.

CHAPTER THREE

1937-1943

$\mathscr{T}$he trial separation of Jack and Janet Bouvier ended on March 31, 1937, when he prevailed upon her to attempt a reunion. For a brief time, there was an effort at harmony. "I'll never forget," Jackie recalled years later,

> the night my mother and father both came into my bedroom all dressed up to go out. I can still smell the scent my mother wore and feel the softness of her fur coat as she leaned over to kiss me good night. In such an excited voice she said, "Darling, your father and I are going dancing tonight at the Central Park Casino to hear Eddy Duchin." I don't know why the moment has stayed with me all these years. Perhaps because it was one of the few times I remember seeing my parents together. It was so romantic. So hopeful.

And, alas, so short-lived.

That summer on Long Island, husband and wife had little contact or connection. To Janet's distress, Jack was obliged to take an even more modest rental than Wildmoor. "Relations between [the couple] were strained and irritable," according to Nanny Kimmerle, who added that Janet "was generally engaged in doing what she wanted [and was often] not home, and the children, consistently without their mother, were always in my company." There was, as it turned out, no sinister or salacious explanation for Janet's absence. She was simply looking elsewhere for social diversion. There were no rumors of affairs—although it soon became clear that she was on the lookout for whatever or whoever might improve her circumstances.

But in Jack's attention to his daughters that summer there was no interruption. "Both [daughters] were devoted to him," according to Miss Kimmerle,

> and both sought his company whenever it was possible. This was particularly so when Mrs. Bouvier, day after day, would leave him alone in the house. He seemed to get a real pleasure out of the children's companionship, and it was equally clear that they got the same pleasure in romping, playing and talking with and to him. I did notice a certain reserve when the children were in the presence of their mother that they never showed when in the presence of their father.... This was particularly so in the case of Jacqueline, who was an unusually bright child, with a passionate fondness for horses. Little Lee was a lovable little mouse, not as high-strung or as alert as her sister, but strong, sweet and affectionate.

There was at least one happy event. Both parents celebrated Jackie's achievement when, just at the time of her eighth birthday, she won the riding events at the Southampton Horse Show in the division for children under nine.

Otherwise, the time was full of tension, and as the term of the second separation drew near, the atmosphere of disappointment and suspicion hung thick in the air. Janet asked Jack to summon a lawyer to initiate formal divorce proceedings, but he failed to do so. On Sunday, September 26, she summoned her father to the house to confront her husband. The three adults were soon arguing loudly, and Jackie burst into tears and ran to Miss Kimmerle for comfort. "Look what they are doing to my daddy!" she cried. Following that rare display of emotion, Jackie fell into a gloomy silence for days. She rode in silence, she walked in silence. Only Lee's need of companionship drew Jackie out, and in this regard, she was often a surrogate mother to her four-year-old sister.

Back in New York for the new school term, Jackie watched quietly as the divorce suit began its protracted course, according to the law of the time. Now Janet began her search for a new husband—an enterprise, she felt, that would take time, patience and great prudence. During the autumn and winter of 1937–38, she was often away on weekends with one gentleman or another, but none of them was brought home to meet her daughters. Jack, on the other hand, entertained a series of ladies in his room at the Westbury, but the weekends were unfailingly reserved for Jackie and Lee—horseback riding in Central Park, lunch at the Westbury's Polo Lounge or at Grandpa Bouvier's apartment.

At Christmas, everyone tried to put a smile on the holidays. But there was nothing merry about the last evening of 1937. That afternoon, Janet left the girls with Miss Kimmerle and, in the company of a handsome and rich older man, spent New Year's Eve and the following day in Tuxedo Park, just north of the city. "If Lee cries for her father while I'm gone, spank her," Janet advised Miss Kimmerle. Lee wept, but the nanny forswore corporal punishment.

THE YEAR 1938 began similarly, with Janet on a constant whirl of dinners, card parties, fashion shows and late nights with various candidates for her slim, firm, receptive hand. At the same time, Jackie was among the top students of her class in school, and there she always remained.

That summer, Janet found a modest cottage for herself and her daughters in Bellport, west of the Hamptons. This village was in the less fashionable holiday precincts of Nassau County, but it was on the Great South Bay, opposite Fire Island, where at least one of Janet's beaux was in residence. Jackie turned nine in July, an occasion that again coincided with her acquisition of a blue ribbon in riding. By this time, she had the basic look that would be hers until death: the thick, dark hair; the lean body and long, muscular legs; the intense eyes.

Over the next several years, in addition to her love of horses and dogs, Jackie continued to read voraciously quite apart from school assignments: among her favorite characters were Margaret Mitchell's

Scarlett O'Hara and the nameless, beleaguered heroine who succeeds Rebecca in Daphne du Maurier's Gothic romance. She had no interest in dolls or paper cutouts, preferring instead movies with Irene Dunne, Katharine Hepburn and Greer Garson.

When she was really amused by something, Jackie's smile lit up a room, and she could spread a sense of fun everywhere—as, for example, when she mocked the pretensions of classmates or the snooty airs that sometimes characterized activities at Chapin. For the most part, however, Jackie was a grave, sometimes unhappy and always secretive girl, embarrassed by her family and, to complicate matters, guilty for feeling so.

But there was a sense of new beginnings that autumn. At James Lee's insistence, Janet and her daughters vacated 740 Park Avenue for a smaller but still choice apartment at 1 Gracie Square, farther to the north and east, near the mayor's mansion and the Chapin School. From here, while Lee attended nursery school and Jackie went off to Chapin, Janet pursued her social life, was often out until the small hours, slept until noon, and for a time—according to her maid, Bernice Anderson— drank excessively and began to rely on sleeping pills.

"She was, once upon a time, a good mother," according to John Davis, "but she got bitchier and bitchier—there's no other word for it."

Janet's irresponsible and uncontrolled behavior so alarmed her father that he came several times each week to discuss, among other things, the state of her health and the progress of her divorce. Eventually, Janet had the good sense and courage to resolve these dangerous habits, but for much of 1938 and 1939, she was more than ever a distant shadow of herself, and hence less present to her daughters.

About this time—again, according to Bernice Anderson, who had no reason to prevaricate during the subsequent divorce proceedings— Jackie confided to the maid and to her father "that she hated her mother." This statement and the angry shouting matches that often marked the conversations between Jackie and Janet are not rare occurrences in the emotional development of young girls. But in this case, the cold war endured for several years with only the rarest thaw; the reason, it seems, was Janet's single-minded insistence on separating her daughters from their father. To Jackie, this was an intolerable stratagem that forever deepened the disaffection between her and her mother.

Her solace, as often, came at the shore during the summer of 1939—an unusually rainy season during which Jackie frequently huddled in a corner of the cottage with a book. Reading, sketching, writing short lyrics: these were her recreation and restoration during times of family strife. That winter, Jackie presented to her father a sheet of artist's paper on which she had drawn a beach scene and written a very brief poem. Surrounded by a border of vines and starfish was the figure of a girl on the strand, her hair windblown, her gaze fixed on soaring gulls. In the neat handwriting that never altered in the decades to come, she wrote that her only wish was to live "by the booming blue sea" for the rest of her life. The little lyric was signed "Me—1939."

AS SHE APPROACHED adolescence, Jackie became a girl for whom privacy and seclusion were neither depressing nor lonely. She seemed to require hours and sometimes days to retreat from the world. She joined her sister and mother or father for meals or family events, she worked with classmates on projects, she engaged in athletics and continued to ride with a few friends. But she could never renounce the need to be alone.

For Janet, her daughter's tendency to solitude, poetry and sketching was fine as far as it went, but such pursuits did not go far enough in furthering the socializing process. In addition to the activities at Chapin, therefore, Jackie was sent to ballroom and ballet exercise classes at the Colony Club on Park Avenue. With boys, Jackie was often aloof: she was far more mature (not to say brighter) than most, and she did not suffer gladly their awkwardness. As for ballet, she was too tall and muscular of leg to be partnered easily, although in the spring of 1939 she did manage a sprightly little solo turn to the merry music of Debussy's "Golliwog's Cakewalk." Golliwog, she learned, was an exotic Caribbean or West African rag doll, and Jackie's impersonation astonished parents and teachers.

IN EARLY 1940, Janet sued Jack for divorce on grounds of adultery. Photos of the couple and their daughters appeared in newspapers

around the country under the syndicated headline SOCIETY BROKER
SUED FOR DIVORCE:

> A line in the Social Register will be cracked right in two if
> Mrs. Janet Lee Bouvier of 1 Gracie Square has her way. Mrs.
> Bouvier asks alimony and custody of two children, Jacqueline
> and Caroline. Mrs. Bouvier claims the society broker was over-
> friendly with another socialite, Marjorie Berrien, as well as with
> unnamed women in his summer home in East Hampton.

Janet ought not, however, to have provided the press with these
details before she went to court. By an odd stroke of irony, she and
her lawyers could not prove adultery: Jack had been discreet in covering
his amorous tracks. Nevertheless, the damage had been done, and there
were unfortunate repercussions on his social life and on the children.
In 1940, a sex scandal did not have the distinction of naughty glamour
it later assumed, and the children in such families were pitied, scorned
and sometimes rudely avoided. Girls at Chapin often giggled in Jackie's
presence and whispered to one another details both real and imagined.
This, to no one's surprise, made her all the more wary, withdrawn and
retiring.

As for her father, he simply wanted the entire matter of the divorce
resolved—hence, he agreed to a swift Nevada decree, often, at the time,
the only route that could be taken by people of means to avoid a lengthy
procedure. The final decree obliged him to pay $1,000 each month for
alimony and child support, as well as all educational and medical expenses. His visitation rights were now restricted to alternate weekends,
one day each week, half the school-term breaks and six weeks each
summer.

JACKIE AND LEE spent that summer of 1940 with their father in East
Hampton, while Janet resided with her parents. By this time, Jackie's
reputation with horses was widespread. She had mastered much with
Danseuse, her favorite steed, and that season she scored a double vic-
tory, winning the Alfred Maclay Trophy for horsemanship and the
Good Hands competition. This was "a rare distinction," noted the

Times, "[because] the occasions are few when a young rider wins both contests in the same show."

For a reason that was not yet clear to the children, Janet decided to treat Jackie, her sister and the maid to a holiday in the nation's capital—the cost cheerfully borne by Grandpa Lee. During Easter week 1941, they strolled with other tourists, admiring the cherry trees in bloom and snapping photos of one another at the great monuments. After a visit to the White House, Jackie felt, she said years later, "strangely let down. It seemed rather bleak; there was nothing in the way of a booklet to take away, nothing to teach one more about that great house and the presidents who had lived there." It lacked, in other words, even an elementary sense of history. Her reaction at the time may not have been as sophisticated as her later analysis, but there is no dispute that the young girl was unimpressed.

The National Gallery was an entirely different experience. "My love of art was born there," she said.

> We had lunch with the chief curator [and then] looked at the paintings and sculpture together. It was then that I first discovered one of my greatest delights—the deep pleasure experienced in looking at masterpieces of painting and sculpture. After all, a child of any age gets his own message, his very own important emotional response from looking at a work of art.

Jackie was also delighted when she was fingerprinted during the tour of FBI headquarters.

But tourism was not Janet's only interest that spring of 1941. In the evenings, she left her daughters and the maid at the hotel and slipped away to meet her new beau, introduced to her once briefly in Manhattan the previous winter. Hugh D. Auchincloss Jr. was a lawyer and investment banker with both a pedigree and a portfolio that were impressive. He already had three children by two previous wives, but now he was single, available, and wealthier by far than any Bouvier; he was also ten years Janet's senior.

Born August 28, 1897, at Hammersmith Farm, the family estate overlooking Narragansett Bay in Newport, Rhode Island, Auchincloss descended from an old Scottish family. He had served in the navy during World War I, graduated from Yale, studied in England and then had received a law degree from Columbia University. His family fortune began with his grandfather, a founding partner of Standard Oil. And the wealth accumulated considerably as the Auchinclosses married upward into America's wealthiest families.

"Hughdie," as Hugh D. was affectionately addressed, had been a special agent with the Commerce Department before joining the State Department as an aviation specialist in 1927. Four years later, he resigned government service and used some of the enormous inheritance from his mother to found the Washington brokerage firm of Auchincloss, Parker & Redpath. In this profession he went, as the saying goes, from strength to strength, making his own substantial additions to inherited wealth. The second wife of Hugh Auchincloss had been Nina Gore Vidal, daughter of an Oklahoma senator. By *her* first husband, she had a son who became the eminent writer Gore Vidal. Contrary to a widespread misconception, then, Jacqueline Bouvier was not even remotely related to Gore Vidal. They certainly knew each other over many years, however.

A calm, sober multimillionaire, Auchincloss enjoyed his wealth without hesitation or vulgarity. In addition to Hammersmith Farm, he was master of the resplendent Merrywood, a vast estate in McLean, Virginia, an idyllic place with a view of the Potomac and a stable of horses he rode and shared with friends. At Merrywood and Hammersmith Farm, two of America's grandest estates, Auchincloss maintained a score of servants. As long as everything was perfectly arranged, the cost was almost inconsequential.

In any case, finances were rarely discussed within the family. Were they rich? They would have thought the matter too indelicate for conversation. As that sharp old statesman Everett McKinley Dirksen said, "A billion here, a billion there, and pretty soon you're talking about real money." In the New York *Social Register,* there were two full pages and forty-seven listings under the Auchincloss name, compared with forty-two Rockefellers, eight Vanderbilts and a mere two each of those named Astor and Bouvier.

Hughdie's preeminent social status and vast wealth more than compensated in Janet's estimation for his humorless, dull, unimaginative personality. She saw him as respectable and sober—nothing like that flashy boozer Black Jack, whom Janet now considered a repellent remnant of Jazz Age license. "I regret to say," recalled John Davis, "that Janet's bitchiness reached its heights when she met Auchincloss. Now she became the ultimate snob, and this, I think, is why Jackie really didn't like her mother." Of this time, Janet simply said, years later, that Jackie had "enormous individuality and sensitivity, and a marvelous self-control that perhaps concealed inner tensions."

Marrying Auchincloss was almost immediately Janet's goal, Catholic proscription to the contrary notwithstanding. The courtship proceeded slowly, with no whisper to the press of the friendship between Mrs. Bouvier and Mr. Auchincloss. Immediately after the end of the school term, however, Janet whisked her girls away for another trip—this one to a ranch outside Reno, where, after a six-week residency, she was granted an uncontested divorce, which was trumpeted in vast numbers of society news columns.

At Christmas, just as America entered World War II, the girls met Hughdie, who took them all to lunch amid a nervous and preoccupied Washington populace. Janet suggested that her daughters call Auchincloss "Uncle Hugh" or "Uncle Hughdie," which they did forever after. In time they grew fond of him: he treated them like his own children, but he never tried to replace their father.

While the adults discussed adult matters during that first meeting, Hughdie's son Hugh—nicknamed Yusha by his Russian-born mother—accompanied the girls to Arlington National Cemetery. "Row after row, she went to see the generals' graves," Yusha recalled, adding that Jackie was particularly "impressed with the guards at the Tomb of the Unknown Soldier, and their precision. Then we stood high on the hill below the Custis-Lee Mansion. That was the first full vista she had of Washington. How impressed she was with the sweeping view!"

BACK IN MANHATTAN, Jack Bouvier sank into a terrible depression. Living now in a four-room apartment at 125 East Seventy-fourth Street, his daughters absent at Christmas for the first time, his business prospects failing, Jack, then forty-nine, felt that his life was slipping by. He had the occasional evening tryst, but there were no serious relationships and never a thought of remarriage. Most of all, he dreaded the loss of

Jackie and Lee to Janet and Hughdie, about whom he learned at once from his daughters. Pride now collided with guilt, devotion with anxiety, benevolence with a fearful reliance on drink, which of course offered nothing except a renewal of the cycle of anguish and remorse.

As it happened, he need not have worried about the loyalty of his daughters. But they were, after all, growing up and therefore, inevitably, psychologically if not emotionally as far away from him as from Janet. But they were living with Janet, and whatever their conscious or repressed feelings about her, she was supervising their lives, and on her approval they had naturally to depend. For a man so reliant on the adoration of his girls, their maturing was a poignant fact Jack never really faced. Hence he saw betrayal in the presence of Auchincloss, a situation out of his daughters' control; and he perceived rejection where there was only the natural evolution of girls' sensibilities. Jackie and Lee would not, in other words, be his little princesses much longer— not because they ignored him or he them, but because of a permanently broken home and the normal transition of children into adults.

Additionally, the girls may have had to rely on their parents for necessities, but they were learning that little in life is permanent—not material circumstances, not family life. In the past two years, luxuries had often been curtailed; the stability of home, mother and father had been shaken beyond repair; men and women had entered and departed the lives of their parents. Life was adventurous, to be sure, and never dull; it was also unpredictable, and nowhere could there be found steadfast love, much less commitment. The Bouvier girls had every comfort, and they enjoyed privileges given to few other children. But *things* were no substitute for deeper needs.

ON JUNE 21, 1942, Janet married Hughdie in Washington. All the children were shipped in for the reception at Merrywood: Jackie and Lee along with Hughdie's Yusha, Nina and Tommy. The family tree grew more limbs in 1945 and 1947, when Janet bore Hughdie a girl they named for her, and then a boy, Jamie.

Jackie's primary residence for almost a decade, the Georgian-style Merrywood was set on forty-six acres of rolling, thickly wooded land where all the amenities were in place: an Olympic swimming pool, tennis courts, stables, riding trails, lush gardens. Chandeliers sparkled,

Aubusson tapestries and carpets muffled noise, white-gloved servants appeared and vanished, leather-bound classics lined the library walls. "It was a peaceful, golden life, a bit Henry Jamesian, a world of deliberate quietude removed from twentieth-century tension." Such was the description of Gore Vidal, who had lived there when his mother was married to Auchincloss. "It was a life that gave total security, but not much preparation for the real world. Most of us broke away. Jackie surely rejected the Great Lady tradition. But we all [i.e., residents of Merrywood] in one way or another have tried to re-create Merrywood's heavenly ambience in our own households."

Lasata had certainly been lavish and 740 Park opulent. But Merrywood seemed more enduring, and life there was far more formal, more mutedly elegant.

More to the point, Merrywood was Jackie's opportunity to release some of the unhappiness of the past. To be sure, she had known great joy on the Long Island shore. Riding and running with her animals, she had come close to nature in ways that city life disallowed. But in recent years, the predominant tone of life there had been neither cheerful nor easy. Negotiating the contours of family life seemed to require so much effort.

Thus, Janet's marriage to Auchincloss did, in a way, sever Jackie from something in her early life—and it happened just as she turned thirteen, a strategic time in everyone's life. At Merrywood, there was even greater space for walks in the woods, for riding. She had her own room and could all the more benefit from silence and cultivate solitude, which came so naturally to her. Here, as she threw herself into the currents of adolescence, she could also read, write, reflect and— precisely because she was now one of five children—it was paradoxically easier to find the quiet without which she seemed unable to live agreeably.

In important ways, then, East Hampton and what it represented began to fade, like one of Jackie's delicate watercolors exposed to daylight.

BECAUSE IT WAS summertime, the Auchincloss caravan did not remain long at Merrywood but repaired instead to Hammersmith Farm. Set on a high, lush hilltop with a wide view over Narragansett Bay, the estate consisted of seventy-eight acres, a carriage house, stables, an animal cemetery, and vast gardens designed by Frederick Law Olmsted, who, with Calvert Vaux, had designed New York's Central Park. The twenty-eight-room house, with ten bedrooms, a dozen full baths, more than a dozen fireplaces and a profusion of gables, cupolas, balconies and loggias, was something of a Victorian hodgepodge, but that had been all the rage when the mansion was completed at the end of the nineteenth century.

Inside was an accumulation of dark and heavy Victorian furniture and furnishings, with the stuffed heads of elk protruding from the walls and bearskins laid ominously on the floors. Jackie quickly decorated her third-floor bedroom in yellow and white, to complement the flower-painted frieze and caned furniture.

She was not idle that summer, for it was wartime: the complement of servants had been reduced from sixteen to one. Under Janet's practical tutelage, Jackie learned to cook, keep house and act as telephone receptionist, for the war limited them to one receiver. There was also a real danger that the gardens would fail from neglect, and so the new mistress of the farm at once put her daughters to work pruning, clipping, watering and cutting. With the exterior allées and the five enclosed hothouses, this was an enterprise requiring muscle, energy and patience, but Jackie and Lee cheerfully pitched themselves to the task; two of the three Auchincloss children were too young, and the oldest was away at camp. Prudently, Janet decided to scale back the gardens, and soon there were plows and tractors churning up the earth.

Hammersmith Farm was really that—the last working farm in Newport—and it supplied the naval base there with poultry, vegetables and dairy produce throughout the war. During the summers from 1942 through 1945, Jackie also fed chickens, tended calves, collected eggs, milked cows and picked apples.

According to Yusha, Jackie read widely about the war and the history of Japan and Germany. Consistent with her adolescent idealism, she also fell in love with the idea of the French resistance, and she idolized the great American and European generals of the war.

When she was not dispatching chores that summer, Jackie preferred to stroll to the bay and sit alone, watching battleships, destroyers and aircraft carriers enter and leave the naval base. She and Yusha heard that sailors frequented a red-light backwater in town, and once or twice they stole into the neighborhood. Curious about the sexual high jinks of the sailors, she engaged them in conversation in her low, flirtatious voice.

But most of her free time was quieter, more contemplative, for Jackie really preferred to be alone, working with her artist's pad and poet's notebook.

A FEW TEENAGE boys were smitten with Jackie, whose height and form were rapidly advancing, but while they found her polite, she was also timid about expressing her opinions, much less her knowledge. Years later, Janet recalled that Jackie feared being thought pedantic, and in the presence of others she usually toned down her learning. "Oh, I'm terrible at math, too," she said to a dispirited boy who had confided a recent failure and had no way of knowing that Jackie was a whiz at the subject, as she seemed to be at everything else required of her. While Lee was considered the prettier of the two, Jackie was certainly the brighter and more artistic, but she never broadcast her talent, nor did she compete with her sister.

In September, they were all back at Merrywood, whence Jackie went forth each day to the staid, proper and serious rooms of the Holton-Arms School on S Street in Washington. Founded by Jessie Moon Holton and Carolyn Hough Arms, it offered instruction from grades one through twelve and two years of junior college; at that time, more than four hundred students were enrolled, eighty of whom were in residence. Here Jackie spent, as she said later, "two happy and rewarding years."

That is as it may be, but while she loved her classes in French, Spanish and art history, Jackie also developed her skills as a hilarious mimic. During her eighth- and ninth-grade classes, from 1942 to 1944, this sometimes got her into trouble. In the midst of acting out a send-up of one of her teachers, for example, the woman, unseen by Jackie, suddenly stepped into the room while Jackie continued, blissfully unaware as her audience held their collective breath. She also had great fun overusing a vaguely rude Spanish word, and to this new affectation, Grandpa Bouvier had a magisterial reaction:

Caramba is agreeable to the ear, and if my knowledge is correct means nothing more than an innocuous "damn it." But if, at the time you are expressing it, you stamp your foot impatiently, pirouette slightly, throw your arms upward and heave your bosom, the whole makes for an impressive ensemble and lends a certain amount of weight and dignity to the word which otherwise would be practically meaningless. But I see no particular virtue in cultivating *caramba,* however adorned.

The word, a tame little malediction unlikely to shock any Victorian maiden aunt, remained in her vocabulary for several years; in her refined, breathless tone, it sounded comically unsuitable (as she doubtless knew), especially at school.

Among her teachers were Mildred Brown and Sally Evans Lurton, two women of astonishing beauty and refinement. Miss Brown, aptly nicknamed Queenie, instilled in Jackie a lifelong passion for art history, while Miss Lurton's English classes communicated not only the fine points of grammar but also the right combination of poetry, drama and fiction. Laura Crease Bunch, a grave-looking woman, managed the guidance department and arranged for students to visit Congress, the Supreme Court, concerts, plays and art shows. Jackie never missed an outing.

To her great surprise, Jackie loved Latin, although she never admitted it at the time. Helen Shearman, a stickler for accuracy and stylistic elegance, "expected and tolerated only solid effort," as one student recalled. "For laziness or obvious lack of preparation, we got disapproval, disgust and sometimes a blackboard eraser well aimed at our heads or navy blue–blazered shoulders." Yet Miss Shearman was not an unsympathetic instructor, and she earned not only the admiration but also the affection of her students.

But life at Holton-Arms was no idyll from the sweetly scented pages of *The Secret Garden.* Two facts were far from amusing.

First, there had been a dark moment in the history of the place, and precisely because the details were unclear, it was fodder for the imagination and whispers of adolescents. Mrs. Holton, still the director, only rarely and in the most oblique, wistful tones referred to her former pupil, friend and cofounder, Miss Arms. There was good reason for

Mrs. Holton's reticence. Miss Arms, the poor soul, after a series of breakdowns, had gone permanently mad and was confined to a lunatic asylum for almost a quarter century, until her death in 1935.

Mrs. Holton refused ever to consider separating the name of her late friend from that of the school; hence the identity and fate of the hapless Miss Arms introduced a subtle note of almost Gothic horror into conversations. No student, however transient at this cultivated academy, was unaware of the cloud of illness and untimely death that had once darkened the school and still, at odd moments, passed over everyone.

As Jackie read Charlotte Brontë that year, it was perhaps inevitable that the demented and confined Bertha Rochester reminded her of the tragedy of Carolyn Arms. The literary convention of the mad heroine thus had a real-life resonance right there at school. To Jackie's poetic, sensitive nature, with its sometimes melancholy complexion—the latter formed by the memories of her father's frequent lapses into alcoholic stupor—the story of Miss Arms was redolent of the tragic and the unpredictable in life. She composed at least two short lyrics, now lost, which reflected on this sad chronicle.

The second element shading her school days was Washington itself, a tense, crowded town during World War II. Regardless of age, Americans were aware of the savagery abroad and terrified of attack at home, especially in the nation's capital. Everywhere were the signs of military missions and the enjoinment of loyalty, prudence and constant alertness against any idle chatter that might weaken the national defense. Students sold war stamps and bonds, learned first aid and shared rations. There was, in other words, a general atmosphere of anxiety to which no one was immune.

AS SHE HEADED for another school in 1944, Jackie wrote to Yusha, who had joined the marines. At the age of fifteen, she had already developed an impressive epistolary style, and her notes and letters were, forever after, full of acute, astonishing observations and the dashes that became so distinctive of her writing:

> *I always love it so at Merrywood—so peaceful—with the river and the dogs—and listening to the Victrola. I will never know which I*

*love best—Hammersmith with its green fields and summer winds—
or Merrywood in the snow—with the river and those great steep
hills. I love them both—whichever I'm at—just as passionately as
I loved the one behind.*

*I began to feel terribly homesick as I was driving—just like a
dream—I started thinking of things like the path leading to the
stables at Merrywood, with the stones slipping as you ran up it—
and Hammersmith with the foghorns blowing at night—all the
places and feelings and happiness that bind you to a family you
love—something you take with you no matter how far you go.*

Rightly, Janet believed her elder daughter had "the temperament and
talent of a writer, that perhaps she could write novels, poetry or fairy
tales."

But of the "happiness that [binds] you to a family you love," she
remained forever unsure. "I've always felt an outsider," she said years
later when alluding to this time. The feeling of estrangement, of course,
is common to many people, but in Jackie's case, it had perhaps many
roots. There was no affection between her and her mother, and while
Hughdie was a pleasant surrogate, he was not her father—for whom
her feelings of devotion were always commingled with anxiety for his
health and, perhaps, a resentment that his habits had broken up their
home.

Creative and perceptive, she was at the same time wrenched from
one tradition and family to another, from one school to a new one.
Torn between loyalty to a father she adored but whose problems she
clearly saw and gratitude to a mother who provided everything but had
pitchforked her into a new family, Jackie felt at home with neither
parent—hence her constant need for intervals of solitude.

For all the luxury and privilege, then, there was a profound sense
of insecurity. Where did she belong? Who were the people who really
loved her? How would she know, and how would she respond? Whom
could she trust? And, in the final analysis, what would become of her?
The only way through the muddle was to find the true self, the core
of her being—the "Me" she so often put as a signature to her poetry.

CHAPTER FOUR

1944-1949

"All my greatest interests—in literature and art, Shakespeare and poetry—were formed because I was fortunate enough to find superb teachers in those fields." So recalled Jackie years after the end of her formal education.

The instruction at Chapin and Holton-Arms was followed by three years at Miss Porter's School, in Farmington, Connecticut, an expensive academy in a picturesque suburb of Hartford. Jackie might have stayed on at Holton-Arms or chosen Foxcroft, an exclusive girls' school in Middleburg, Virginia, close to Merrywood; Foxcroft was famous for its virtual obsession with riding. But she wanted to go to boarding school, to put some distance between herself and the Auchinclosses; besides, Miss Porter's headmasters, Mr. and Mrs. Ward L. Johnson, who had just taken over in 1943, had trumpeted a new emphasis on college preparatory courses, and college was Jackie's goal.

Arriving in Connecticut in the autumn of 1944, at the age of fifteen, she began her last three years of high school in a slightly rarefied country atmosphere that might have come straight from Norman Rockwell's easel. "If you were a Farmington girl," said her cousin the younger Edith Beale, who had graduated in 1935, "you were trained not only in the classics and all kinds of literature, language and so forth—it was also a training for life. You were bred with deportment and elocution—

how to move, how to speak, how to behave." There was, in other words, a joining of the old "finishing school" ethos with academics.

A girl at Miss Porter's was expected to rise to the occasion, to put her best foot forward, to do what was right—even in times of crisis—and to display, as the chaplain often said at the nondenominational Sunday services, "guts and gumption." These were not mere clichés, accumulated and announced like school cheers. Uncle Hughdie's married cousin Annie Burr Auchincloss, for example, was an alumna of Miss Porter's and lived with her husband, the historian and literary scholar Wilmarth Lewis, in Farmington. When Jackie met them in Connecticut during the fall of 1944, Annie had given up the dainty life of a suburban socialite and had pitched herself zealously into war work. "No previous education or training had prepared her for this," as the biographer and social historian Stephen Birmingham noted, "no provisional year, even, with the Junior League doing volunteer work. She simply *was* prepared, and did what needed to be done, providing, in the process, leadership for others."

Among those so inspired was Jackie, who learned at once that, as Emerson counseled,

When Duty whispers low, Thou must,
The youth replies, I can.

But Jackie's social service, if such it may be called, did not take the route of Annie Lewis or of those inspired by Eleanor Roosevelt to such practical endeavors as rolling bandages, a popular charity work at the time. Instead, Jackie found her own way of following the injunction to assist in this particular cause. She added to her reading list several volumes of Jefferson, Franklin and Diderot, borrowed from the Lewises' library. And what she learned, she incorporated into short articles published in *Salmagundy,* the school newspaper: essays on American political philosophy's roots in the French Enlightenment, and observations on the war, the scourge of Nazism, the survival of democracy and the heroism of resistance fighters.

The individualism and self-determination urged by Miss Porter's were revealed in other ways, too. In the matter of dress, for example, Jackie lived up to no one's expectations. She never wore the popular fur coat in winter (she preferred a cloth garment), nor did she own the white slicker that was all the rage among schoolgirls during the 1940s.

In more important ways, she developed a keener social conscience during these three years: Jackie objected most of all to the absence of nonwhite students. Did the administration recruit only Caucasians? Were there no scholarships for minorities?

As for her social life, she was regularly invited to parties, dances and athletic events at the fashionable boys' academies—Hotchkiss, St. Paul's, Phillips Exeter, Groton and Choate. But Jackie was particular when it came to accepting offers. Schoolwork came first, her poetry and art second, riding and sports third. Whatever time was left for dating usually bored her, for the fact is that she was far more mature than most of her contemporaries of either sex. "I just know that no one will ever marry me, and I'll end up as a housemother at Farmington!" she complained one day—not because she believed it, but because she had something to say about some of the women in that position as rather narrowly focused. As Arthur Schlesinger Jr. said years later of this time, "She observed the conventions, but underneath a shy exterior [she] developed [a] cool judgment of people and an ironical slant on life."

BY A HAPPY coincidence, Nancy Tuckerman, Jackie's best friend from Chapin, had already matriculated to Miss Porter's, and after the first year, they shared a room. "Jackie was an avid reader," according to "Tucky" (as Jackie called her), who added that her favorite courses were English literature and art history. Tucky recalled that when other girls socialized after evening study hall, "Jackie seldom joined in, happily staying in her room, reading, writing poetry or drawing. Popular among her classmates, by nature she was a loner."

This popularity was nourished by her father's visits, when Jackie invited a few girls to join her and Jack for lunch. "All my Farmington friends loved Daddy. He took batches of us out to lunch at the Elm Tree Inn. Everybody ordered steaks and two desserts. We must have eaten him broke."

But if Jackie loved her solitude, she was certainly no cloistered nun. School records indicate that while maintaining a consistent A-minus average, she was also busy in the drama and riding clubs and helped edit the newspaper. She also wheedled her father into shipping her favorite horse, Danseuse, from Long Island to Farmington, and the Major subsidized the animal's boarding fee.

In the snowy Connecticut winters, Danseuse pulled Jackie and her friends in an old-fashioned sleigh; when the weather was more temperate, she rode to her heart's content over the countryside. Jackie soon put Tucky, who had never mounted a steed, to the test, despite the school regulation forbidding students to ride without parental permission. When Tucky fell and injured her arm, she feared the headmaster's discipline, but Jackie simply advised her to report that she had fallen from a tree. The ruse worked, and nurses bandaged the arm without suspicion.

Soon thereafter, this little escapade found its way into one of Jackie's cartoons for *Salmagundy*. She had begun contributing occasional entries about the antics of a madcap character called Frenzied Frieda, a dizzy girl who manages to get into all sorts of trouble.

There were less dangerous pranks in the polite dining hall. Since 1843, Miss Porter's had trained young ladies in the most exquisite manners; speech was modulated, conversation refined. Linen napkins were thrice ironed, tablecloths pressed to perfection. Here girls alternated waiting on tables, the better to prepare them for the details of hosting dinners. And here, on a dare, there emerged signs of Jackie at her most playful. She deliberately and artfully dumped a slice of chocolate cream pie into the lap of a particularly fastidious teacher. This trick Jackie executed so convincingly as an "accident" that she incurred no one's wrath. Similarly, the dean never imagined that the soft-spoken Miss Bouvier was the culprit responsible for the weekly theft of freshly baked cookies from the larder—cookies that kept the looter and her roommate munching happily after curfew for days after.

It was also bold of her to start smoking, a habit discouraged at Farmington but seen everywhere outside school precincts, and one that she indulged for decades. Speaking facetiously about her passage to maturity, she said later: "It happened gradually over the three years I spent trying to imitate girls who had callers every Saturday. I passed the finish line when I learned to smoke in the balcony of the Normandie theater in New York from a girl who pressed a Longfellow upon me [and] then led me from the theater when the usher told her that other people could not hear the film with so much coughing going on. Growing up was not so hard."

IN EARLY 1945, Jackie learned that her mother had given birth to a girl, named for Janet, as Jackie had been for her father. Soon after, there was news of a death that in some ways affected her even more deeply: that of President Roosevelt, in April. "I'm still so dazed," she wrote to her stepbrother:

> *I don't know what to do. Isn't it awful about the president? I'm so worried about what will happen now that Roosevelt is dead. I think he was really great, and I know the only reason I didn't like him was because Daddy was always moaning about what he did to the stock exchange. Did you have a memorial service or something like that for him at school? Do write and tell me that everything won't be so bad. . . . I feel sorry for poor Mrs. Roosevelt. It will be awfully hard to leave the White House after all those years.*

The death of the president struck her more poignantly than that of Grandmother Lee, who had died in 1943.

AS THE SUMMER of 1945 drew near, Jackie's studies in art history and French introduced her to one of the most fascinating characters in history, a woman whose spirit influenced her as much as any of her teachers, Juliette de Récamier.

One of the leaders of French society, she was born in Lyon in 1777 and was married at fifteen to a wealthy banker. A dark-haired beauty of remarkable wit and elegance, Madame de Récamier established a salon in Paris that very quickly became the gathering place for the most important literary and political figures of her time.

Jackie's study of Madame de Récamier then led her to consider the most famous members of her salon, among them Madame de Staël, a writer who exerted enormous influence on literary women in Europe and America; François Chateaubriand, the writer and statesman whose works pioneered the Romantic movement and celebrated the land and people of North America; and the generals Jean-Baptiste Bernadotte and Jean Moreau, both violently opposed to Napoleon's government.

Madame de Récamier's portrait was famously rendered by Jacques-Louis David in 1800 and again two years later by his most eminent pupil, François Gérard. Exiled in 1805 for her royalist sympathies, she returned to Paris after Napoleon's downfall, and there, despite her severely reduced financial situation, her revived salon attracted notables until her death in 1849.

For weeks, Jackie could not get enough of this colorful and courageous woman. Gifted and sensitive people always have inspirational mentors, as well as those from the past who affect their identities and their goals. In this case, Madame de Récamier became for Mademoiselle Bouvier a shining guide. Beautiful, educated, her life devoted to art, literature and the best traditions of the aristocracy, this historic Frenchwoman personified everything Jackie admired. She shared her enthusiasm with a few classmates, who noted with a combination of amusement and a little irritation that, at the end of term, Jackie spoke French whenever she had the opportunity, a development that led one young wag to ask one morning, "Who are you *today?*"

IN JUNE 1947, Jackie graduated from Miss Porter's near the top of her class, winning the Maria McKinney Memorial Award for Excellence in Literature, a prize that included a leather-bound book of poetry by Edna St. Vincent Millay, who remained one of her favorite writers. The yearbook profile noted that her favorite song was "Lime House Blues" and that at weekend dances she often said, "Play a rhumba next!" She was, the entry concluded, best known for her wit, could usually be found "laughing with Tucky" and had a chilly aversion to people who asked if her horse was still alive after so much exertion. Asked her ambition, Jackie wanted this goal inscribed: "Not to be a housewife."

That summer, Jackie marked her eighteenth birthday—the time for girls to observe the quaint custom of "coming out" in society, the time when wealthy families spared no expense at their city or country clubs, where they held lavish parties and formal balls.

There were two presentations of Miss Jacqueline Lee Bouvier that July. The first was a reception at Hammersmith Farm: a joint celebration of Jackie's imminent birthday and the christening of her half brother, Janet's newborn baby, Jamie. This tea party Jackie much preferred to the second event, which she said seemed too expensive.

Janet and Hughdie then introduced her to several hundred guests at the end of Tennis Week, when everyone on the prime list was in Newport. To the richly paneled rooms of the venerable Clambake Club, poised atop rocks that afforded a dramatic view of the water, came Hugh Auchincloss's business colleagues and Janet's society friends. Jackie greeted them in a formal receiving line, clutching a nosegay of white bouvardia and red sweetheart roses and wearing an off-the-shoulder, but not immodest, floor-length gown of white tulle, selected off the rack for less than sixty dollars, instead of the chic made-to-order Dior creation her mother had advised her to wear and had offered. Jackie was, however, glad for the required white gloves, since several fingers bore cigarette stains (soon after, she learned the cosmetic techniques for preventing them: one of the popular methods of the time was scouring the hands with white vinegar and lemon juice).

She had made a prudent choice, for the gown suited her perfectly, accentuating her best features and somehow diminishing what she thought a trifle awkward. She had now reached her full physical maturity, and although her hair was later shortened and straightened, her appearance altered only slightly, with a deepened, almost classic beauty, over the coming decades. At five feet, seven and a half inches and a weight that remained between 120 and 130 pounds, she had long, dark eyelashes, a slim nose, sharply defined features and a high waist, and wore size 10A shoes she chose with particular care. Her eyes and her smile were perhaps her best features; her carriage was so unselfconsciously straight that she projected a rare, natural elegance.

But she was a reluctant debutante, present only to please her mother and stepfather—and even, from afar, lonely Jack Bouvier, nursing the wounds of perceived rejection. Jackie merely tasted the clam chowder, lobster and apple pie; she sipped ginger ale and slipped into the ladies' room for a quick smoke. There, she giggled conspiratorially with Lee, then fourteen, who played the novice vamp with her daring pink, strapless, rhinestone-studded gown and fingerless black satin gloves.

Jackie disliked the obligation to dance with every boy, to make empty, polite chatter with his parents and generally to stand statuesquely while society matrons assessed her wardrobe, posture, smile, demeanor, diction and prospects for assuming her rightful place among them. Most of all, pretenders, poseurs and prigs simply did not survive in her presence: they might have awaited a glance or gesture that would admit them to some degree of intimacy, but eventually they crept away disappointed. But it took a keen observer to note these qualities, for she was charm itself, flattering male egos when necessary or simply sustaining them with a distant aloofness until, mystified and despairing, they moved along, taking away whatever impression of themselves they needed.

FROM THAT TIME forward, virtually to preserve herself, Jackie refined a sense of apartness, even aloofness. Jim Symington, a senator's son, felt that many were uncomfortable in her presence: she seemed, he said, to be almost breakable, so that one did not come too close. Some regarded her as a person they longed to protect, which often evoked maternal qualities in women and, in countless men, that fascinating alloy of paternal and erotic instincts. Others registered or even criticized what they saw as her moody diffidence. But as the contours of her life became more public, more demanding and eventually more dramatic, the tone and tenor of her deportment were a way of safeguarding her integrity and inner clarity.

There was no doubt, however, that she made an instant impression, as that keen-eyed social chronicler Igor Cassini, who wrote as Cholly Knickerbocker, observed in his syndicated newspaper column several weeks after the somewhat stuffy secular liturgy at the Clambake Club. To him fell the assignment of identifying the nation's new royalty.

America is a country of traditions. Every four years we elect a President, every two years our congressmen. And every year a new Queen of Debutantes is crowned. This year, for the first time since our predecessor selected Brenda Frazier as the Queen of Glamour, we are ready to name the No. 1 Deb of the Year— Jacqueline Bouvier, a regal brunette who has classic features and the daintiness of Dresden porcelain. She has poise, is soft-spoken and intelligent, everything the leading debutante should

be. Her background is strictly "Old Guard." . . . You don't have
to read a batch of press clippings to be aware of her qualities.

Thus the prophecy of the *East Hampton Star,* which in 1931 had proclaimed her a "future debutante" on her second birthday, had come
true.

But Jackie was not entirely enthusiastic about all this. "Newport,"
she said years later, with a sigh. "I knew I didn't want the rest of my
life to be there. I didn't want to marry any of the young men I grew
up with—not because of them but because of their life. I didn't know
what I wanted. I was still floundering."

"Young men were constantly trying every kind of trick to make
her go out with them," according to Letitia Baldrige, who was ahead
of Jackie at Miss Porter's and later in college and whose life would
intersect with hers in important ways. "Her classic good looks were
complemented by her sense of style, which had been apparent from her
early teens." Tish Baldrige added that Jackie put on a simple dress or
skirt or pants and shirt, added the right belt—and made the whole
outfit look superb with her posture and bearing. "Nothing ever looked
wrong on her."

But although she accepted dates with young men that summer and
the following year—dates that took her to New York, Yale, Princeton
and Harvard—Jackie found it hard to take any young man very seriously. Nor did she test the waters of sexual experience. Typically, returning from a date with a young man in a taxi, she told the driver,
as they approached her door, "Hold your meter." Optimistic escorts
knew they would not be admitted beyond the front door.

This did not indicate, some disappointed gallants notwithstanding,
that Jackie was anything other than a healthy young woman with normal desires. But it must be recalled that at the time, sexual urges did
not lurch, especially in polite classes, into full throttle, nor did young
people race, as it was said, "all the way." Sophisticated methods of
contraception were not readily or widely available—certainly not to
single women—and the fear of pregnancy, venereal disease and an
indecent reputation kept the reins on conduct. And penicillin, newly
used to combat sexually transmitted infections, was only recently available to the general public at the end of World War II.

This is not to say that the standards of Queen Victoria and Mrs. Grundy were everywhere observed; it is simply to state the obvious, that sexual intercourse for most young, single Americans half a century ago was neither as casual nor as commonplace as it would later become. In this regard Jacqueline Bouvier was no undersexed prude; to the contrary, the flirtations that she raised to a high art, and her later passional life, characterize a robust woman with a suitable appreciation for the then deferred but relatively imminent joys of carnality.

WITH A SUMMER of parties and a visit to her father behind her, Jackie packed her trunks and went off, quite naturally enough, to Vassar College, where her rank in the top 10 percent of applicants had won her immediate acceptance.

Matthew Vassar's success as a rural brewer made possible the realization of his socially prescient goal, a distinctive institution for women that would offer as fine an education as those of the best men's colleges. This he established in 1861, in the town of Poughkeepsie, on the Hudson River, seventy-five miles north of Manhattan. Resolute though the college was in its insistence of women's rights, every president was a man until the arrival, from the faculty of Cornell University, of the formidable Sarah Gibson Blanding in 1946.

By the fall of the following year, there were sixty-one buildings on 950 acres, a $10 million endowment and extraordinary prestige at Vassar College. The enrollment listed just over a thousand undergraduate women and, as a foretoken of the decision twenty years later to become coeducational, about a hundred men, war veterans then studying on government grants. The main building on campus, built at the end of the nineteenth century, was patterned after the palace of the Tuileries in Paris, which had been destroyed in 1871 during the Commune. Discovering this bit of institutional Francophilia, Jackie was naturally delighted, for it corresponded to her passion for French history and culture. For the time being, she was right at home.

"Progress is my watchword," said Miss Blanding in her opening address, quoting Matthew Vassar as she welcomed the new collegians. Her aphorism, reported at home by one student, was taken by her father to his company's advertising agency. After some corporate fiddling, the motto of General Electric became "Progress is our most important product," which sounds deep but is completely meaningless. Miss Blanding was not amused.

Jackie was one of about two hundred first-year students that autumn. She decided to join the college newspaper staff, the art club and the drama group (as a costume designer). Students liked her, but the consensus was, as one recalled, that "she was very secretive—you never knew what she was thinking or what she was really feeling."

Among her classes, in which she maintained a high average each term, her greatest achievements were in some of the most demanding courses—Helen Sandison's class on Shakespeare, for example, and Florence Lovell's on the history of religion. That year she memorized lengthy passages from *Antony and Cleopatra,* always a play close to her heart. As for Professor Lovell's lectures, they, too, gave her enormous intellectual pleasure and stimulation.

Jackie was certainly not a traditionally pious Catholic. Faith had not been a matter of primary importance in the Bouvier and Lee households, and she had little religious education except for the standard catechetical preparations for First Communion and Confirmation. In addition, it must be said that many people found the language and traditions of American Catholic piety uncongenial. After all, it was articulated mostly by and for immigrants, most of them Irish. Faith, in other words, often seemed a set of cultural traditions rather than an attitude about reality. The sentimental forms of piety were like a collection of funny hats bequeathed by a deceased maiden aunt; keeping them is the condition of inheriting her vast legacy. And so the funny hats remain in the wardrobe. But they were for the most part neither acknowledged nor worn by the Bouviers or the Lees.

Still, if Catholicism was attacked in conversation, Jackie was an ardent defender, and was known as such among other students. Her classmate Joan Ellis, for example, recalled that after a philosophy class on authoritarianism, she was angry at the rigidity of the Catholic Church and said so to Jackie. While they sat informally on a parlor floor, Jackie "roamed wonderfully through the fields of philosophy, religion and history and quietly talked about her faith. I remember thinking, 'She is reading things I haven't even heard of!' "

Dissatisfied with many of the empty forms of social life, dedicated to her intellectual and aesthetic growth and enchanted with the beauty of the physical world, Jackie had the sort of spiritual life typical of the English mannerist poets, the French symbolists and the American transcendentalists. Later, these would prove insufficient to her needs: they were fine as far as they went, but eventually they would not take her deeply enough. But for now, at eighteen, her primary concern was no longer the care and feeding of horses.

Invited to weekend football games and social events at northeastern colleges, Jackie attended them once or twice a month. In the spring of 1948, she met, on a train ride from Washington, a "tall, thin young congressman with very long, reddish hair, the son of a [former] ambassador," as she wrote home. He had flirted shamelessly with her, to no avail, and the encounter had, she thought, no significance at all: she did not even mention his name in the letter.

IN JANUARY 1948, Grandpa Bouvier died at the age of eighty-three. In stories and style, he had been an important influence on Jackie, on the development of her taste and sense of history. Their visits to M. C. Bouvier's house on West Forty-sixth Street, his encouragement of her poetry, his generosity to her while she was at school—all this made his death singularly poignant for her. That winter, Jackie read and reread a letter he had written, one among many she saved for the rest of her life.

"The capacity to adapt oneself to his or her environment," her grandfather wrote,

> *not only marks evolutionary progress, but discloses a practical philosophy which is more wise to cultivate. With you, happily, this process of adaptation has not been in the remotest degree difficult. . . . I discern in you more than passing evidence of leadership, but before leading others we must guide and direct ourselves. . . . Don't be pretentious or labor under [the] false impression of indispensability. To do so spells the prig, either male or female.*

Bouvier's death not only marked the end of an era in the clan, it also threw the family into a turmoil of anticipation and subsequent accusations over the disposition of his will. First of all, this man with (it had been presumed) such a vast fortune left an estate valued at a mere $824,000, of which $225,000 was taken in taxes. The loss of the several millions he had inherited was due to an enormously expensive style of living and the payment of debts incurred by various relatives. Very soon, Lasata was sold, and an entire way of life remained only in the family albums.

Jackie's father received $100,000 tax-free and was forgiven a $50,000 loan. Jackie and Lee received $3,000 each. This seemed like a great deal of money, since they were both living on a monthly allowance of fifty dollars from their father, a sum that the rather parsimonious Uncle Hughdie considered sufficient for a boarding student and hence did not supplement. Nor did Grandfather Lee feel obliged to help defray his granddaughters' living expenses. But the $3,000 never went into the girls' pocketbooks: Jack deposited the money in trust accounts for them.

The small monthly allowance, it must be added, went toward paying for Jackie's clothes, recreation, transportation, cosmetics, incidentals at school and whatever meals were taken off-campus; even in 1948, $12.50 a week did not go that far. No one suggested that Jackie take a part-time job at Vassar or in town: this simply was not done among young women of her class. There was only one thing to do. If Jackie wanted to be free of anxiety in the future, she would have to follow her mother's lead and marry a rich man—no, not merely a rich man, but a man of substantial wealth.

Later, Jackie wrote an account of her grandfather's wake at home. "I was sitting beside my grandfather's coffin, looking at him as he lay in his dark blue suit with his hands folded. I had never seen death before and was ashamed that it made no more of an impression on me. . . . I was glad he couldn't see how his children behaved [about their various inheritances] once he was dead."

She then described the arrival, at the wake, of one of Lasata's former gardeners, who offered the family a simple bunch of violets. A thoughtless aunt took them rudely, tucked them into a larger bunch of flowers and asked everyone to leave the room while the coffin was closed. But Jackie was not to be intimidated: "I knelt on the bench beside the coffin and put the violets down inside, beneath my grandfather's elbow, where the people who came to close the coffin could not see them."

ON JACKIE'S NINETEENTH birthday that summer of 1948, she was in Europe with three other young women: Julia Bissell and the stepdaughters of Edward Foley (Undersecretary of the Treasury), Helen and Judy Bowdoin. Chaperoned by Helen Shearman, Jackie's Latin teacher at Holton-Arms, the girls departed New York aboard the *Queen Mary* on July 9.

According to Helen Bowdoin, Jackie prepared for the trip as if for a university degree. She had read history books, polished her French, learned some German and Italian, and memorized a good deal of European history and art scholarship; clearly she regarded the summer as an educational experience, not merely a vacation.

They landed at Southampton, stopped in Stratford, visited a few of the great English country estates and finally arrived in London. After the visit to Shakespeare's home and the loveliness of the countryside in full summer bloom, the state of the capital was shocking. The city had not recovered from the bombings and terrible deprivations of the war, and the four young women and their chaperone were upset and bewildered at the sight of massive poverty, buildings in disrepair and homeless old people sleeping under bridges. Tickets to a Buckingham Palace garden party, obtained through Mr. Foley's influence, did not raise their spirits: rain poured down and they had only a distant glimpse of King George and Queen Elizabeth.

But Paris, spared the bombs, was radiant. They visited Notre-Dame and La Sainte-Chapelle, walked to the point of exhaustion, sipped coffee at Les Deux Magots and bought berets, which they wore every day. Standing before David's painting of her idol Madame de Récamier at the Louvre, Jackie told her companions the story of the historic hostess who had become a kind of tutelary spirit for her.

At Versailles, Jackie was bedazzled by the palace's grand scale, its opulence and its gardens; she spoke good French with the guards and guides; and she asked pointed questions about its history and its relics. The visit to Versailles was prolonged because they could not persuade Jackie to depart until closing time. "She was also much more private than any other person I've ever known," said Aileen Bowdoin, of another journey. "She was always standing back watching the scene and sort of recording it in her mind—looking at people, seeing how they acted toward one another. She was a born observer." From there, the group proceeded to the Riviera, and then on to Lucerne, Milan, Venice, Florence and Rome. Their grand tour ended back in Paris, and by August 25, they were home.

JACKIE'S SUBSEQUENT ANNOUNCEMENT, made casually to her father later that summer and to her mother in a letter from Vassar, should have surprised no one. After the coming sophomore year, she said, she would like to spend her junior year abroad—a tradition popular at the time among young women of background and breeding. Vassar did not have such a program, but Smith College did, and students with exceptional grades from other institutions were sometimes accepted into it.

Jack, Janet and Uncle Hughdie were, at first, cool to the idea, each for a different reason. Jack was now living in modest circumstances and, his judgment clouded by alcohol and his standard of living suddenly reduced, he feared the deprivation of his last great satisfaction, the presence of his elder daughter. "I suppose it won't be long before I lose you to some funny-looking gink," he wrote to her that autumn, "who you think is wonderful because he is so romantic-looking in the evening and wears his mother's pearl earrings for dress-shirt buttons because he loves her so." The Auchinclosses, however, feared both the extra expense to them and the further alienation of Jackie from their world—not to say the possibility that she just might settle down forever in France and marry a bearded, impoverished poet.

Her family might have succeeded in dissuading her from applying for foreign study, but Jackie knew how to play her hand. Well, she said in the soft, slightly breathless voice that could sound innocent, flirtatious or importunate, she could always quit Vassar, move to Manhattan and become a fashion model. That would pay well, she added. Such an idea, for Janet and Hughdie, was too terrible to contemplate.

In the spring, Jackie was allowed to transfer her Vassar credits to Smith, and after writing an essay and passing a French examination, she won a place in the foreign-study program. On August 24, 1949, she left America for a year in France.

PROFICIENT THOUGH SHE was in French, Jackie still had only an American student's command of its finer points. Hence, she and a handful of other applicants were first sent to an intensive six-week language course at the University of Grenoble. About three hundred miles from Paris and southeast of Lyon, Grenoble has been famous as a center of higher learning since the fourteenth century. In addition to the daily eight hours of lessons and conversations, Jackie had the opportunity to visit the rich collection of manuscripts at the library, which houses most of the works of Stendhal, born there in 1783. And with great admiration, Jackie met some heroes of the French resistance, which had been particularly active in Grenoble.

IN OCTOBER, JACKIE arrived in Paris to begin courses at the Sorbonne—all of them in French, and most in French history and art history. Instead of residing at Reid Hall with other American students, she and two others decided to rent rooms in a large apartment or town house owned by Parisians. The addresses of many such places were posted at the university, for almost everyone in the city needed money after the war, and people were thrilled to welcome responsible Sorbonne students. After she went to the home of a woman whose husband was executed by the Germans in retaliation for his work in the resistance, Jackie knew she belonged there.

At once she rented the room, on the avenue Mozart, in the heart of the fashionable sixteenth arrondisement, not far from the Trocadéro and the Palais de Chaillot. The Comtesse Guyot de Renty, a handsome woman who wore her long white hair in an elegant chignon, owned the apartment. She had two daughters—Claude, who was about Jackie's age, and Ghislaine, who was divorced and raising a four-year-old son. The large apartment had no central heating and only one bathroom with an antique tub. But despite postwar rationing, the countess somehow managed to cook hearty meals for everyone: as the weather turned cold late that autumn, Jackie learned to appreciate thick soups and hearty French stews.

Until December, she had a fairly fixed routine: classes, study and a total immersion in the life of the arts in Paris—opera, theater and ballet—and all of it costing little. Occasionally, she spent a few extra francs on coffee or a glass of wine at a famous venue like the Ritz Bar, the Café de Flore or La Coupole. Young men found it annoying that her attention was not fixed on them, their party or conversation, but rather on someone else two or twenty feet away. Craving interesting people connected to interesting things, she always seemed disappointed, and because both parents made it clear that she would not be supported forever, she knew that her maturity must somehow, and relatively soon, mean finding an appropriate husband. That meant, as her mother cease-lessly reminded her, a wealthy one.

Jackie's landlady had married a member of the old French aristoc-racy and had thus become a countess. Never mind her reduced circum-stances in old age: once life had been magical, as the countess liked to tell her American boarder. "Putting on a fur coat and being swanky at the Ritz Bar" was certainly part of Jackie's social agenda for a quite specific purpose.

As it happened, her most serious beau that year was the son of a French diplomat. They roamed the Left Bank, had late suppers in smart little boîtes, met for coffee and, huddling under an umbrella, strolled through the Luxembourg Gardens in the rain. For several months it was not unlike a sequence from Metro-Goldwyn-Mayer.

And then it was over.

Of the young man, we know nothing, and it is of course possible that they were friends and not lovers. Whatever the dynamic, Jackie was certainly in Paris as she was in Poughkeepsie: she refused to give herself too readily. There are no extant love letters, no evidence of stolen weekends in the country with the diplomat's son. Whether Jackie re-turned from Europe as a *virgo intacta* may never be known: on this matter, she kept her counsel.

One clue, however, may be in remarks she made years later: "I was galled," she said of this time, "at the patronizing attitude toward Amer-icans, annoyed by the compliment 'But no one would think you were American!' if one showed a knowledge of literature or history." The sort of man she sought, in other words, may have eluded her precisely because she was a young American woman—a pretty artifact, but hard-ly to be taken seriously. And if she was not readily, sexually available, there would have been, the same men would presume, no reason to pursue her.

She seemed that year to meet mostly intellectual students of dubious sexual orientation, and although other friendships flourished, there was "nothing romantic at all" that year, as she confided to Yusha and, years later, to a few close friends. And there is no reason to assume that she was prevaricating. Instead, she nourished her intellectual and aesthetic life in Paris, adding to her Sorbonne courses some art instruction at the École du Louvre and study in diplomatic history at the École de Science Politique.

Winter arrived prematurely in Europe that year, and the apartment on avenue Mozart was invariably damp and cold. Then a letter from Janet arrived in mid-December, announcing that she and Hughdie were arriving in Paris during her term break in February: they wanted her to join them on a holiday. Jackie did not have to think twice. Under other circumstances, she would perhaps have found an excuse not to accompany them, and to pursue her own leisure in and around the city. But by Christmas she could think only of heated hotel rooms and plenty of hot water on demand. She complained to no one about the spartan life with Madame de Renty, but she would not deny herself a cozy interlude.

CHAPTER FIVE

1950-1952

*I*n February, Janet and Hughdie swept into Paris with the wintry winds, which may have seemed appropriate for the temperature of their reunion with Jackie.

While her stepfather muttered about the price of everything, Jackie and her mother scrutinized each other warily. Janet required assurance not only that her daughter was behaving like the Perfect Lady but that she was refining all the skills and poise necessary to acquire the Right Man when she returned to America. For her part, Jackie wished to please but also to present herself as an independent young woman who had absorbed a new (that is, an old) world of Real Culture. The well-worn phrase "Oh, Mother, really" may have been the antiphon that concluded many exchanges that winter.

And that is how their conversations went: the issues were outlined in phrases as if they bore capital letters; and Jackie wanted to show she had learned so much that she inevitably took on airs. But for those clichés (Perfect Lady, Right Man, Real Culture), the visit was like something from the pages of Henry James. Here was the once naive American girl, now happily accustomed to the intellectual and cultural life of Paris; here, too, was the ambitious mother, full of stratagems and wiles; and here was the stuffy stepfather, who knew the price of everything but the value of little. To complete the analogy with James, we must picture the scene that first evening in February when Hughdie's complaint about the cost of dinner provoked Jackie's suggestion that they offset the hotel fees by traveling second-class on trains. Janet's horror was overcome by Hughdie's enthusiastic endorsement of the idea.

They departed Paris for Vienna, Salzburg, Munich and a side trip to Dachau, which Jackie insisted they see and which appalled and outraged her. But she did not, according to Yusha, who joined her for another holiday that summer, condemn the entire nation of Germany, nor did she speak of Germans negatively. Rather she saw the Nazis as distinct from the people, and she could praise the good in the rest of German history and culture. As for the Holocaust, she wanted to know about it in all its horror: it was a part of history, and history was her passion.

So, apparently, was traveling about like a native. "It's so much more fun traveling second and third class and sitting up all night in trains, as you really get to know people and hear their stories," she wrote to her stepbrother. "When I traveled before, it was all too luxurious and we didn't see anything."

After three weeks, the Auchinclosses returned to America and Jackie to her studies in Paris, a period that ended when she received a certificate of high achievement in May. "I never worked harder in my life," she said later.

AFTER A TOUR of southern France with Madame de Renty's two daughters, Jackie joined Yusha for a visit to Ireland and Scotland in July. Like her spiritual mentor, Madame de Récamier, she was turning into something of a royalist, her third-class accommodations notwithstanding. Along with literature, culture and the arts, her interests focused on the ancient castles, counts and conflicts of the titled families, and she was passionate to learn everything she could about royalty— in this case, the Irish kings.

In late August, Jackie docked in New York and visited her father. He had endured a difficult operation for cataracts, and she found him withdrawn, bitter and uncharacteristically depressed. Lonely and sometimes confused, he begged Jackie to return to Vassar so that she would be closer to him; he said he could easily find her a job in New York after graduation. She promised to consider it.

Back at Merrywood, Jackie told her mother about Jack's offer. Janet, of course, saw dragons there: she did not want her daughter under Jack's influence, nor did she think that a promise of Wall Street employment would take her daughter any further than the typing pool. Janet and Hughdie prevailed upon Jackie to transfer all her Vassar and Paris college credits to George Washington University, which had a superb French department, Jackie's chosen major. Within easy commuting distance from Merrywood, in the heart of the District of Columbia and just four blocks west of the White House, the university's forty-five buildings were an urban sprawl that still preserved its hundred-year-old campus trees and a sense of distance from the city's increasing noise. Her late application for immediate acceptance might not have been considered but for the influence of Auchincloss, who had had business dealings with several members of the university's board and administration.

That autumn of 1950, Jackie began her last year of college, dashing from Merrywood to her downtown courses in French language and history and classes in art, in which she took a strong minor. She dated a few young men, but there was still no serious romance. "I look at a male model and am bored in three minutes," she said. "I like men with funny noses, ears that protrude, irregular teeth, short men, skinny men, fat men. Above all, he must have a keen mind. And he must weigh more and have bigger feet than I do." It appears that the young men she met that year were in some ways too attractive and in others not nearly appealing enough.

As winter approached, Jackie became restless and nostalgic for Paris. And then, as if on cue, a hairdresser handed her a magazine to read under the dryer one afternoon. Her eye caught a notice in *Vogue* announcing its annual Prix de Paris contest, which awarded a six-month junior editing job in its Paris offices, followed by a New York assignment and some choice perks. She clipped the application and quietly began to prepare the required data.

First, she had to compose a self-portrait. The result was a refreshing and amusing piece, not at all typical of those usually found on the desk of *Vogue*'s editors.

Jackie began with a physical description of herself: five-foot-seven, brown hair, "a square face and eyes so unfortunately far apart that it takes three weeks to have a pair of glasses made with a bridge wide enough to fit over my nose." She did not have a fabulous figure, she added, but she knew how to pick the right clothes.

As for hobbies, she mentioned her love of painting original works that her mother "doesn't put in the closet until a month after I have given them to her at Christmas." She had also, she said, written for her younger siblings a children's book complete with fairy tales she concocted and illustrated. She also adored riding; and she would drop "everything, anytime, to read a book on ballet."

In the final part of this first section, she said that her year of study abroad had been the happiest year of her life thus far. "I learned not to be ashamed of a real hunger for knowledge, something I had always tried to hide, and I came home . . . with a love for Europe that I am afraid will never leave me."

Jackie also had to submit an essay about three people she wished she had known, and her choices—Charles Baudelaire, Oscar Wilde and Serge Diaghilev—must have sealed the impression of those at the magazine that here, indeed, was a remarkably unorthodox young woman. Baudelaire's poetry she had read that spring; Wilde's poems and plays she rightly thought remarkable, and she had been sufficiently moved to visit his tomb at the Père Lachaise cemetery in Paris; and Diaghilev's contribution to the history of dance was already familiar to her. Her essay was certainly a masterpiece of perceptive improvisation.

"Baudelaire and Wilde were rich men's sons who lived like dandies," she began, "[and they] ran through what they had and died in extreme poverty." The first "used as his weapons venom and despair," while the second "could, with the flash of an epigram, bring about what serious reformers had for years been trying to accomplish."

As for Diaghilev: "Though not an artist himself, he possessed what is rarer than artistic genius in any one field—the sensitivity to take the best of each man and incorporate it into a masterpiece all the more precious because it lives only in the minds of those who have seen it and disintegrates as soon as he is gone. . . ."

At the age of twenty-one, Jacqueline Bouvier had learned something about the history of ideas. Her education, in other words, had not been simply a matter of absorbing languages, names, dates and facts. She was going deeper—bringing things together within herself, making connections between them even as she was making personal links between them and herself. Whatever assessment one makes of her young life, the gravity and depth of Jackie's explorations into the relationship between art and life, and between events and ideas, cannot be doubted.

Demonstrating further imagination, she composed a brief reply to a question about a marketing campaign for a new perfume. Compare it to wine, she suggested: call them both "intoxicating liquids—the petal and the grape"—and print not the typical photo of a cologne bottle, but rather a wine cellar with a perfume labeled "Lentheric, Numéro 6/1950," just as wines are cataloged. For good measure, she included an entire artistic layout.

The editors also wanted to know her opinions about the methods of presenting new fashions: the magazine offered photos of professional but anonymous models, of celebrities or "ladies of distinction," and also simple line drawings. Which did Jackie prefer, and why? As for the professional models, she replied:

> A model's job is to efface herself and call attention to her dress. A woman is well dressed if people say, 'She looked heavenly but I can't remember what she had on.' . . . But *Vogue* would be a bore if it offered nothing but poker-faced mannequins posturing through its pages. It would have the commercial deadness of some wholesale buyer's magazine.

As she prepared for graduation in the spring of 1951, Jackie received word that she had won the *Vogue* Prix de Paris, and the announcement, along with her photo, was to be a major story in the magazine dated August 15. How soon, the editors wanted to know, would she able to move to Paris?

As she did so often, however, Janet swung into action.

"I didn't want her to go," she admitted years later. "She had already had a year in Europe and had fallen in love with Paris, and I was afraid that if she returned there, she would become an expatriate. I hoped I could persuade her to turn the prize down."

The exhortation was effective for two reasons.

First of all, Janet had only to point out to Jackie that she was not qualified for such a sophisticated position. It was one thing to be a good student enjoying life in Paris; it was quite another to work there. Did Jackie want to risk making a fool of herself? That, of course, was highly unlikely. But as Carol Phillips of *Vogue* recalled, Jackie at this stage of her life lacked self-confidence and readily believed her mother's politely phrased but firm abasement. "I guess I was too scared to go," Jackie said years later. To the disappointment of Jackie and the editors of *Vogue,* she declined the honor—which passed to the second-place winner, a senior at Vassar. As a consolation prize, Janet and Hughdie offered to send Jackie to Europe for several weeks that summer as a graduation gift, and to send Lee, who was now eighteen and would graduate in June from Miss Porter's.

But there was another reason for the pressure on Jackie not to accept a European job—and as frequently happens in making great decisions, it had to do with romance, or at least a romance encouraged by Janet. Single-minded in her pursuit of a good mate for her daughter, she parlayed Jackie's disappointment over *Vogue* into a potential triumph in matters matrimonial.

Through Hughdie's complex web of business and social connections, Jackie had been introduced to a man named John G. W. Husted Jr., who worked on Wall Street and came from a family listed in the *Social Register*. In fact, the Husteds knew Jack Bouvier, and when Jackie told her father that she was dating John Husted and would be traveling frequently to visit him in New York, Jack could not have been more delighted. In this matter, at least, it seemed that her parents were united.

And what of Jackie's feelings in all this? Husted was an attractive man, and clearly he was enamored of Jackie. But she seemed to allow the courtship to be pursued and propped up by him and her mother: she did little to encourage it. Her visits to Husted in New York, it must be added, had the advantage of allowing her to see more of her father and to revisit her favorite rooms in Manhattan's museums.

That spring, Jackie dashed to classes at George Washington University, wrote for the campus newspaper a few short stories based on her European travels and then sped over to Union Station and boarded the train for weekend dates with Husted in New York, where she duly spent the nights in her father's apartment on East Seventy-fourth Street.

The summer journey was not expected to interrupt the courtship of Jackie by John Husted, for he and his family had also scheduled a European trip, and they were to meet the Bouvier sisters at several points. Alas, the Husted family plans were scrapped; Jackie and Lee, however, proceeded.

But there was one evening before Jackie's departure that was, in the end, of enormous significance.

Early in the summer of 1948 and just before she departed for her first journey to Europe, Jackie had been one of several Bouviers invited to a Long Island wedding. There, she had met the groom's brother, Charles Bartlett, Washington correspondent for the *Chattanooga Times*. Bartlett, then twenty-seven and single, thought Jackie was pretty and personable, and he wanted her to meet his friend, a thirty-one-year-old congressman from Massachusetts who appreciated pretty, personable young women. But Bartlett could not wrest her away from her conversation with prizefighter Gene Tunney, and so the meeting of Miss Bouvier and John F. Kennedy did not occur that summer.

But as it happened, Charles Bartlett met Jackie again when she was at George Washington University. By this time he was married, and he and his wife invited Jackie to a small dinner party at their home in Washington. "She was no longer the little girl who lived next door," he recalled. "She was more exotic. She had become gayer and livelier." Among the other few guests at the Bartlett home that May evening was the clever and appealing Jack Kennedy, now in his third term as representative from the Eleventh Congressional District of Massachusetts.

War hero and politician, Jack was three weeks shy of his thirty-fourth birthday; Jackie was not yet twenty-two. She knew immediately, she said later, that this man "would have a profound, perhaps disturbing influence" on her life. She also realized, from his conversation and the talk about him, that "here was a man who did not want to marry," perhaps for the simple reason, well known in Washington even then, that he routinely enjoyed the company of a platoon of attractive women and showed no particular interest in selecting one of them for a permanent commitment. In addition, Jackie had the distinct impression that while Kennedy found many women sexually gratifying for one or more rendezvous, he had not, thus far, met the sort of woman who had what he needed politically. And any such candidate would have to be approved by his formidable father.

At the end of the evening, Jack escorted Jackie to her car: "Shall we go somewhere for a drink?" he asked, opening the door. Josie, Bartlett's fox terrier, leaped past them and jumped in, yapping loudly at someone in the backseat. Jack then peered in to find none other than John Husted, who had arrived in Washington too late for dinner but had come to drive Jackie home. Jack at once withdrew, and that, everyone thought, was the end of that.

ON JUNE 7, 1951, the Bouvier sisters boarded the *Queen Elizabeth;* their itinerary included stops in London, Paris, Venice, Rome and Florence. They documented the entire summer meticulously and hilariously in *One Special Summer,* a collection of drawings and poems by Jackie and detailed descriptions of their adventures written by both, which they presented to Janet on their return. The title was apt, for little about the summer was conventional.

Aboard ship, at first they had to share a cramped, third-class cabin with a strange creature named Miss Coones, a nonagenarian who slept stark naked and who, for reasons the Bouviers preferred not to consider, turned her bed-light on and off throughout the night. A sympathetic purser arranged for the girls to be transferred to their own private, but still third-class, quarters.

Their next introduction was to a Lebanese gentleman eager to do their every bidding; Jackie put a stop to this flirtation by warning Lee about "quirks in the sex lives of Near Easterners," about which her knowledge was presumably derivative. They then decided to ignore the signs urging passengers to PLEASE OBSERVE SOCIAL BARRIERS between classes, and in this breach of rules they succeeded for the time it took to enjoy a dance or two each evening.

Jackie's accompanying drawings reveal not only her artistic gifts but also her delicious sense of satire. In its bold exaggeration, the style is partly that of cartoonist William Steig; in deadpan humor, it resembles the wonderfully lunatic world of James Thurber; and perhaps most of all, there is the whimsical influence of Ludwig Bemelmans and his fanciful Madeline. *One Special Summer* is, in short, a witty report whose original artwork suggests Grandma Moses reworked by Raoul Dufy.

They bought a cheap car in London, which turned out to be not such a good idea since they spent most of their time in the city. This vehicle they took on the boat-train to Paris, where they sold it to a man who said he was a missionary "but looked as if he had just escaped from Benny Goodman's String Quartet." As it happened, the fellow was on his way to do charity work in Africa, and he asked the Bouviers to sell the car cheaply "because $5 could keep an African child alive for a month and every $5 he spent on himself meant one more would starve to death. We were for slaughtering the whole tribe, but his conscience would only let him starve 206 of them."

The weeks were indeed full of the kind of adventures that perhaps happen only to winsome, brave young women, long on class but short on cash. Jackie and Lee pitched themselves into every day, rather like Cornelia Otis Skinner and Emily Kimbrough on the European excursions they memorialized in *Our Hearts Were Young and Gay*. Once, the sisters were nearly caught in the crossfire of antitank guns on maneuver in the south of France.

"I guess you must be a little worried about us driving all over Europe by ourselves," Jackie wrote to Janet and Hughdie, "but really you shouldn't be. We never speak to strangers. . . . I know you are right about us representing our country, and that we must never do anything that would call attention to us and make people shocked at Americans. We do sew on all our buttons and wear gloves and never go out in big cities except in what we would wear to church in Newport on Sundays." But adjacent to this disclaimer was a contradictory photo of Jackie in pants and sandals, and Lee in short shorts.

In Venice, Jackie took art lessons from a painter, and Lee singing instructions from the head porter at the Danieli Hotel. When he took her to meet a famous Italian soprano in her studio on the Grand Canal, Lee froze with fright and could barely croak out a scale, much less the grand arias la signora wanted to hear. Jackie, shaking with laughter on a nearby divan, kept urging Lee, "Why don't you sing something from *Call Me Madam*?"

WINSOME AND WITTY though she was, Jackie knew when something significant was offered.

At his Tuscan villa, they spent a memorable afternoon with the great humanist and art critic Bernard Berenson, the world's leading authority on the Renaissance. Physically frail at eighty-six, he was still sharp, profound and wise. "He is a kind of god-like creature in the way that he doesn't fit in with the hurly-burly, busy pattern of our present world," Jackie wrote that evening. "He had lived every vein of life so fully and yet not thrown anything away. He is such a genius, such a philosopher, such a pillar of strength and sensitivity, and such a lover of all things. He is a man whose life in beauty is unsurpassable. Most of his conversation was about Life-Diminishing and Life-Enhancing People, the two terms he created in his last book. 'Don't waste your life with diminishing people who aren't stimulating,' " he counseled.

Brief though it was, the time with Berenson gave Jackie a mentor whose words and ways impressed her so deeply that it was one of the formative, deeply influential experiences of her life. Thus far, the wisdom of older men was manifest mostly in observations about the stock market; here was a sage who lived on another plane entirely. Jackie preserved his words forever in her spirit, as she did in her memoir of that day. "He set a spark burning" in her, Jackie added. Although it would not have enough fuel or air to burn brightly for years, the eventual flame inside her would blaze brightly.

It was the difference between living and existing that he had spoken of, and both of us [she and Lee] had simply been existing in our selfish ways far too long. "The only way to exist happily is to love your work [he said]. Anything you want, you must make enemies and suffer for."

In Spain, the Bouvier sisters were—again, thanks to family connections—welcomed at the office of the American ambassador. He asked about the health of Janet and Jack, and Jackie replied, "Fine, thank you—and how are Franco and Don Juan?" who were, for her, variants of her mother and father. The ambassador was unamused.

The same day, they attended a cocktail party for visiting senators, one of whom, named Wiley, clasped Lee's hand, kissed it loudly and said, "How'm I doin'—real Spanish, huh?" Near Jackie stood a Spanish journalist "whose hair looked as if he had just finished conducting Berlioz." Moments later, Senator Wiley asked Jackie and Lee if they were Republicans, adding, "I hope, I hope, I hope"—to which Lee replied, "Oh, yes, but we thought you were a Democrat!"

The next evening, they were in the home of minor German-Spanish aristocrats whose sons they had met at the embassy. The family home had once been a monastery, and it was full of rare and precious artifacts. The Bouviers sat in a chair once belonging to Christopher Columbus; they gaped at curio cabinets filled with crown jewels and (said Jackie) "at pictures signed 'Love, George V.'" They felt they should be taking notes for an art history course, "but all [the young men] wanted to do was make Ma and Pa change the [record player] while we jitterbugged to 'Wave the Green for Old Tulane' underneath the Flemish primitives."

ON SEPTEMBER 15, Jackie and Lee arrived home. Lee at once began studies at Sarah Lawrence College. Meantime, Jackie—armed with a college degree and the experience of three extended European sojourns—did not have the remotest idea what the future held for her. All the more reason, Janet said, why Jackie ought to consider settling down with a good (by which she meant rich) husband who could provide her with the means to travel, to indulge her aesthetic appetites, to retain the standard of living that was her due and to which she had become accustomed. After all, Hughdie had three children of his own to look after: he believed each should be self-supporting by legal age. Inheritances were one thing, but until they came through...

Autumn in the Virginia countryside can be a bracing, dazzling time. With little else on her horizon, Jackie rode, read and went out with John Husted, whose ardor had not cooled. Taking the line of least resistance, Jackie resumed the courtship, for she tried to see, as Janet urged, the advantages of such a union. At the same time, Auchincloss took other steps, as Jackie had asked, to secure for her a good, temporary job in Washington. Auchincloss rang his friend Arthur Krock, Washington bureau chief of *The New York Times,* who sent Jackie over to his friend Frank Waldrop, editor of the *Washington Times-Herald.*

Contrary to received tradition, Jackie did not begin a glamorous career in journalism. Instead, in late autumn she was hired as a part-time receptionist at the *Times-Herald* offices on H Street. But a week later, she approached Waldrop and asked for something more challenging.

Evidently, he had asked Krock a question or two about Jackie's intentions, for the boss was blunt with her: "Do you want a serious career in journalism, or do you just want to hang around here until you get married?"

"No," she said in that thin, deceptively demure voice, "I really want to write." Waldrop said he would consider the matter.

Then, just before Christmas, he had an idea. For years the newspaper had featured a weekly column written and photographed by a man, "The Inquiring Photographer," in which eight or ten people replied briefly to topical questions and were photographed. The aim of the column, which in those days was always polite and journalistically soft, was to present the way people felt, not what they thought about world or national news. But Waldrop thought it would be daring, in 1951, to have a female on that job, and he sent Jackie over to Sid Epstein, the city editor.

Did she know how to use a camera?

Well, Jackie replied, she had taken snapshots in Europe.

His staff didn't use Brownies or Leicas, Epstein said, narrowing his gaze. Only professional equipment like Speed Graphics. Did she know anything about flash attachments, correct lighting? Could she handle it?

Jackie asked for a few days to work on it, and Epstein and Waldrop were impressed when she returned with some passable headshots of various people she had collared outside the office. "She could see around corners," Waldrop said years later. "She was just getting right into things." She got the job, which paid the royal sum of $42.50 a week for putting together "Inquiring Camera Girl," which soon appeared with her byline. "She was soft-spoken and shy, attractive and really cute as hell," according to Epstein, "but she wasn't afraid to go out into the street and get her columns."

At Christmastime, over dinner at the Polo Lounge of the Westbury Hotel in New York, John Husted gave Jackie a brightly wrapped small box containing a sapphire-and-diamond engagement ring that had once belonged to his mother. The gift was magnificent, the meal first rate, the wine warming, the atmosphere quietly romantic, Husted's manner ardent. And perhaps Janet's voice came to Jackie through the air, urging, beseeching, recommending. Jackie accepted the proposal, and on January 21, 1952, *The New York Times* announced their engagement and a forthcoming wedding in June.

BY THEN SHE was back at work, coping gamely with the Washington winter, negotiating slushy streets and icy sidewalks, snapping photos and asking questions she had formulated. Over the next year and a half, Jackie put to the known (congressmen and cabinet members) and the unknown (a college boy, a Senate page, a housewife) a series of amusing, fey questions, a sprinkling of more sober inquiries, and even one or two on sports:

- "Do marriages have a better chance of survival when the spouses don't breakfast together?"
- "Are men braver than women in the dentist's chair?"
- "Is your marriage a 50-50 partnership?"
- "Can you spot a married man?"
- "Are men as inclined to fall for a line as girls are?"
- "Do the rich enjoy life more than the poor?"
- "What do you think women desire most?"
- "Would you like to crash high society?"
- "What prominent person's death affected you most?"
- "Should a candidate's wife campaign with her husband?"
- "Would you like your son to grow up to be president?"
- "Which first lady would you most like to have been?"

❖ "Do you think the [Washington baseball team] will pull out of their hitting slump?"

"She was a businesslike little girl," according to Waldrop, "quiet, concentrated, obviously very, very earnest in wanting to be a professional." By March 1952, her pay had been raised to $56.75; still, Waldrop continued, she was always somewhat short of cash. "She worked, and she earned a living. She knew she wasn't going to get anything from her father." According to Robert Denny, Jackie's colleague on the newspaper, she was "rather naive and almost touchingly trusting—an exotic innocent."

But she was having serious second thoughts about her engagement. Around mid-March, Janet, Hughdie and Jackie went to dinner at the Washington home of her stepfather's relatives. After dessert, Jackie withdrew to a quiet corner with Louis Auchincloss, whose father was a cousin of Hughdie; Louis himself was already well embarked on a double career as an eminent lawyer and respected author of fine novels and first-rate literary criticism. To him, Jackie confided that her future as the wife of a respectable New York businessman would certainly be peaceful, but it would also be dull. As it happened, Louis had just published his novel *Sibyl,* whose title character bore a striking resemblance to the kind of woman Jackie feared becoming. "That's it!" she said, almost vehemently. "That's my future. I'll be a Sibyl Husted."

Soon after, before Washington's cherry trees bloomed that spring, Jackie had returned the engagement ring to John Husted. She was not ready for marriage, she said; she enjoyed her job, and she felt she needed a little more independence, a bit more of the world, before she moved straight from a father's home to a husband's. According to Mini Rhea, who made dresses for her and her mother, "Jackie seemed more relieved than unhappy about it."

After a year in Europe and a few months with a major urban newspaper, Jackie preferred the company of entertaining, creative men to the traditional type of dependable, perhaps unimaginative fiancé, which for her was a fair description of John Husted. What she wanted, in other words, was a man who spoke of a larger world than Wall Street and who had a Park Avenue portfolio. It was a tall order.

———

BUT IT MIGHT be filled, thought the Bartletts, by the formidable Massachusetts congressman. When they learned that the Bouvier-Husted engagement had ended, they invited Jack and Jackie back for a dinner in May, almost on the anniversary of their first meeting. In the interval they had engineered another brief encounter in Florida, when the Bartletts were visiting the Kennedys in Palm Beach and Jackie, Janet and Hughdie were staying nearby. But that meeting occurred amid an enormous cast of supporting players: Kennedys were there in great abundance, political advisers crept about with briefcases and vast reams of paper, socialites drifted in and out. Jack's father, Joe, liked Miss Bouvier at once; Jack's mother, Rose, was not present.

But the Bartletts were there, "shameless in their match-making," as Jackie said.

On May 8, 1952, they conducted a reprise of the intimate dinner party of the previous year. This time, according to his brother Ted, Jack saw not only her graceful good looks, he was also fascinated by her intelligence. Within days, he invited her to dine and dance in the Blue Room of the Shoreham Hotel. He also invited his brother Robert and Robert's wife, Ethel, to join them at the movies.

At six feet one inch and 170 pounds, with an unruly shock of reddish brown hair and alluring gray-green eyes, Jack resembled nothing so much as a lanky postgraduate student. He had a keen, quick sense of humor, which Jackie found enormously appealing, and he knew precisely how to flatter when it was necessary and to withhold when it was alluring. Although known to be sexually aggressive, he was not an emotionally demonstrative man, and for Jackie this had an element of safety. Unsure of her own emotional depths, she would perhaps have been put off rather than swept away by an ardent, articulate lover who offered too much too enthusiastically and therefore deserved or demanded the same in return.

Over the next several months, Jackie learned a great deal about Jack and his family. Her romantic, idealistic spirit was touched and fascinated by the accounts of his great-grandparents' emigration from famine-stricken Ireland to America in the nineteenth century. His mother's father, John Fitzgerald, had been mayor of Boston, and Jack's father, Joe, had become an enormously successful businessman, an adviser to President Roosevelt and ambassador to Great Britain from 1938 to 1940. After graduating from Harvard in 1940, Jack had written a book, *Why England Slept,* about the turmoil leading to the war; Jackie, of course, was hugely impressed, and she read and reread it.

Of the nine Kennedy children, two had died violently: the oldest boy, Joe Jr., was killed when his plane crashed in Europe during military maneuvers; Kathleen went down in a plane crash in France four years later.

Jackie was astonished at Jack's courage and bravado, too, for he endured virtually constant pain from a serious injury he suffered during a school football game—a condition much aggravated by graver damage to his spine and legs during navy duty in World War II and from unsuccessful surgery thereafter. In addition, he withstood the debilitating effects of Addison's disease, a deficiency of the adrenal glands that was diagnosed in 1947 and that could so impair his immune function as to endanger his life. Since their first meeting, Jack had almost died from this condition during a trip to Asia with his brother Bobby.

Jack's sense of humor would naturally have aroused her interest. Ironic, with a sense of the absurd, he loved a play on words and a good joke, and he smiled broadly at Jackie's barbs against pomposity. Jack had access to a huge fortune, but he never dressed or acted like a rich man. Part of that, of course, was calculated bonhomie; but it was also consistent with a man who believed that at any moment, health, good fortune and even life itself could be taken away.

Money, it also seemed, was more of a convenience than a prime value to Jack. At his maturity, in 1938, he began to receive the annual income on a trust fund of $10 million. "I fixed it," said Joe Kennedy to anyone who would listen, "so that any of my children, financially speaking, could look me in the eye and tell me to go to hell." Which was scarcely something anyone, much less a beneficiary, would say to the man who had amassed something like $500 million from his interests in liquor, movies and the stock market.

Jack Kennedy was, Jackie came to see, a fatalist whose experience led him to believe that life was short and painful, that little should be taken seriously but the opportunity for—there was no other word for it—fun. "He was always able," according to Theodore Sorensen, one of his speechwriters, to relax as intensively as he worked, to catch up on his sleep or his sun or his golf, and to laugh at the world and himself. Nor did he, in his moments of utmost pride and solemnity, ever pretend to be free from human vices and imperfections . . . his language could be as coarse in private conversation as [it was] correct on the public platform [and] he followed Franklin's advice of "early to bed, early to rise" only when he could not otherwise arrange his schedule.

But this was, it seemed, nothing like a serious romance that was going to lead to marriage; Jack, after all, was devoted to the pleasures of the bachelor's life. He had another preoccupation that year, too: the uphill battle for a Senate seat. "He spent half of each week in Massachusetts," Jackie said later. "He'd call me from some oyster bar up there, with a great clinking of coins, to ask me out to the movies the following Wednesday in Washington. He loved Westerns and Civil War pictures. He was not the candy-and-flowers type, so every now and then he gave me a book—*The Raven,* which is the life of Sam Houston, and also *Pilgrim's Way,* by John Buchan." Jackie, meanwhile, spent an exhausting May and June hauling around heavy camera equipment in the humid Washington heat. Her occasional gifts to him were a book on French history, art or poetry.

By all accounts, Jackie hatched no ambitious plan to ensnare Jack Kennedy. She had liked his wit, his ironic understatement, his refusal to take seriously the foibles and silliness of so much about politics—and, of course, his undeniable appeal. He also seemed, to Jackie, to project a quality not immediately evident to others, but one that touched her protective instincts, much as earlier in her life she had cared almost obsessively for dogs and horses and, during their summer in Europe, her sister Lee. She thought, Jackie said, that Kennedy "looked a little lonesome and in need of a haircut and perhaps a square meal."

These, of course, were not unattractive characteristics. But as she freely admitted soon after, Jackie was frightened. Jack was, in many important ways, subject to his family's expectations: "I think my destiny is what my father wants it to be," he often said with a rueful smile.

That was a powerful burden, and it showed in a sort of rebellious diffidence, an apparent refusal to take anything, himself included, terribly seriously. In addition, he had a reputation as a cheerful, often irresponsible rake. And to this Jackie had an odd reaction: any hope she might have about herself and John Kennedy portended only disappointment and heartbreak, "but just as swiftly [I] determined that such heartbreak would be worth the pain."

This is a curious statement indeed, for the negatives are doubled; there is no payoff for any effort. One would have expected Jackie to say that "love would be worth the accompanying heartbreak," or "heartbreak would be offset by love." Jackie may simply have misspoken, uttered a verbal blunder. But her remark was made for the record, in an article printed just after she became First Lady, and the author, a friend, gave her the opportunity to correct the interview before it went to press. This was too important, too intimate not to be emended if it was misleading, but Jackie let her statement stand: "heartbreak would be worth the pain." Other changes in the text were made, but this assertion remained: in it, she perhaps half willingly disclosed the dark side of a marriage to a man she loved without dilution.

What exactly was going on here?

To understand how much she loved and perhaps how little she expected to be loved in return, we must perhaps take seriously Jacqueline Bouvier's own emotional history. She had been raised properly, educated well, given privileges and advantages. But the Bouviers and the Lees were not remarkable in the give-and-take of basic human love. Her father's emotional life was dissipated in shallow flirtations and the escape of alcoholism; her mother filled life with money, possessions, property and social status. Janet and Jack adored animals and things, but they were not terribly good with people. Whatever the finer points of their parents' characters—points known, perhaps, to a few intimate friends—it is no exaggeration to say that the Bouvier daughters were denied the primal nourishment of parental affection.

It cannot be surprising, then, that Jackie grew into a young woman who had no realistic appreciation of her own assets and virtues. She eagerly pursued her intellectual and artistic life and was serious about her career as a journalist but, as colleagues noticed, was not particularly confident of herself. She knew what she could do but was entirely unsure of how well she was doing it. Janet, after all, had successfully dissuaded her from accepting the *Vogue* assignment by pointing out what she considered her daughter's weaknesses and her need of a wealthy man to care for her. According to Yusha Auchincloss, who was living with Jackie and the clan at Merrywood that year, Jackie never fully appreciated her own charm, or even her own beauty. "She didn't know whether anybody was going to be attracted to her. She was insecure in this respect."

It is, of course, fairly common for people with such insecurities to select as the object of their affection those they think they can nurture, even (and sometimes especially) those unable fully to return the devotion. Unaccustomed to love and unaware of it in her family, Jackie had no expectation of it for herself. The great women of legend, the illustrious ladies of history, the noble queens of the past—these were her models, not the lovers, courtesans or mistresses. And in this regard, the slightly unkempt Jack Kennedy, always burdened with a responsibility to his family and often contorted in pain, was like a wounded colt needing the best attention of *la belle dame avec merci*.

The roots of love, after all, are often watered by one who simply feels needed. His bravado and sexual exploits notwithstanding, there was a terrific vulnerability at the heart of Jack Kennedy, and a sensibility that a quick laugh and an easy conquest tried to mask. Not once during his many confinements to school infirmaries for illness was he visited by his mother. "She was on her knees in churches all over the world," he said later, with ill-concealed bitterness. To this Jackie responded with instinctive sympathy for a man she saw as a "little boy, sick so much of the time, reading in bed, reading history . . . reading the Knights of the Round Table."

Nor was this diminished by the fact that she was dealing with "a man so vain you can't believe it." This perception was admitted by others in Jack's circle (Ted Sorensen, for example) and was one that, along with his loneliness and sense of life's fragility and swiftness, doubtless had something to do with a rampant promiscuity.

As she came to understand, Jack's early life had been in some ways as bruised as her own. His parents remained married for the sake of politics, business and the appearance of piety, but it was an arrangement, a loveless union not unlike that of Jackie's parents. Like Black

Jack Bouvier, Joe Kennedy was a notorious womanizer; like Janet, Rose Fitzgerald Kennedy took comfort from her wealth and her wardrobe. But unlike Janet, Rose was most of all sustained by her religious faith.

As for Jack, he saw Jackie as something of a kindred spirit. They had each endured a lonely and difficult childhood with emotionally distant mothers and philandering fathers. Both had learned a great deal from living abroad, both had taken less than ideal circumstances from their youth and refashioned their temperaments to something fresh, youthful, alive, classy and determined. In addition, Jack valued Jackie's wit, intelligence and refinement, and they could both be still and find something restorative at the seaside, for which they had a need that almost matched that for air and food. "I always go to Hyannisport to be revived," said Jack, "to know the power of the sea. . . . I always come back here and walk on the beach when I have tough decisions to make. It's the one place I can think and be alone." Jackie, even as a child, had walked for hours on the Long Island shore, and she, too, instantly fell in love with Hyannisport.

But Jack and Jackie were affected by their pasts in complex ways. Each had cultivated a certain solitude, a distance from others, and they did not find it easy to disclose themselves.

In addition, he was proud to escort this attractive woman and sought her taste in clothes and her opinion about arts and letters, occasional references to which he needed in his speeches. And her background was Catholic and distinctly upper-class: with Jackie the Kennedys might move into a higher echelon than even money provided.

Jack's religion was nominally Catholic, too, but he was first and foremost a devout Democrat. Until the summer of 1952, Jackie was a Democrat only when President Roosevelt died. Never much concerned with politics, she considered herself a Republican, like her forebears. That changed when she went with Jack to spend not merely an afternoon with his family (as she had before, in Florida) but a long weekend that summer.

The Fourth of July holiday was full of typical Kennedy activities: touch football on the lawn of the sprawling compound at Hyannisport and much talk of family lore, of sports, of races and games, of movie stars, of excelling. "We don't want any losers around here" was Joe Kennedy's mantra. "Mother and Dad put us through rigorous training in athletics," said their daughter Eunice. "Dad wanted his children to win the sailing and swimming races—I remember racing fourteen times a week when I was twelve years old." To which her mother replied with a smile that "the main point of the whole exercise was not winning *per se*. It was rather that we wanted them to do their absolute best." This was a whimsical cover, but it was also unconvincing in light of Joe's motto: "Don't come in second or third—that doesn't count. Win!" Or else, it was implied.

At first, Jackie tried to refrain from joining in the rough-and-tumble: "Just watching them wore me out," she said. "It was enough for me to watch them at tennis. It wasn't necessary for me to be the best." This, of course, was an alien language to any Kennedy. Hence Jack's brothers—and especially his sisters, whom Jackie quietly nicknamed "the rah-rah girls"—found her a trifle too delicate, too sophisticated, too intellectual and too shy, characteristics they wrongly interpreted as airs and graces, a superior attitude they felt they had to demolish. For her part, she found their indifference to the arts astonishing. This was not an easy beginning.

To her credit, it must be said that Rose did her best to make Jackie feel at ease amid this big, boisterous clan. "She was terribly sweet to me," Jackie said years later. "I had a sort of special dress to wear to dinner. I was more dressed up than his sisters were, and so Jack teased me about it, in an affectionate way, but he said something like 'Where do you think you're going?' And [Rose] said, 'Oh, don't be mean to her, dear. She looks lovely.' "

Although Jack continued to have an avid romantic life, or at least a busy sexual one, with a fleet of eager, peppy women, they were pleasant diversions; he never gave any sign that he took them seriously, nor should his partners. At the same time, he treated Jackie differently. "Never once," according to their journalist friend Laura Bergquist, "did this suitor propose they go off for a night or an [unchaperoned] weekend." More to the point, Jack had introduced few of his other intimate lady friends to his family.

That July weekend, however, it was his father who told Jack that his political future required a wife—that his career depended on projecting an image of ideal American family stability—and Jack, of course, knew the truth of it. "His chariness of marriage was being superseded by the political need for a wife," said Betty Spalding, the wife of Jack's close friend Chuck Spalding. After all, Joe and Rose had an unspoken agreement that gave Joe license to pursue casual and even sustained amours elsewhere while Rose had access to unrestricted spending, travel and the social influence that came from being the wife of Joseph P. Kennedy.

Joe told Jack that he must consider taking an appropriate wife who would be a political asset; Jack's private life could be continued without much interference, for Jackie would essentially be happy to live within the sublime light that shone from the Kennedys. In one way, father and son correctly assessed that Jackie incarnated the old-fashioned ideas about a woman's place, her complaisance, her understanding that men were different and that one just had to put up with some things. At the same time, they woefully underestimated her essential independence, as well as the fact that some people changed and that one day Jackie might be among them. Jackie added an important element that weekend when she declared, "I guess I'm a Democrat now!" after hearing Jack speak in Quincy and Fall River.

Until the election in November, Jack and Jackie were not often together, for he doggedly campaigned for the Senate seat. But as the returns showed a Republican landslide for Eisenhower and Nixon, it seemed that Kennedy's chances of replacing Henry Cabot Lodge were dim indeed. At about three in the morning of November 4, the tide began to shift, and before dawn it was clear that John F. Kennedy, against all expectations, had beaten the odds. He had done so by a margin of 70,737 votes out of a total cast of 2,424,548.

Before Christmas, Frank Waldrop sent his Camera Girl to Capitol Hill to interview the statesmen and young pages about the experience of observing one another at close range. Hearing the rumors of a budding romance between Kennedy and Jackie, Waldrop called her in. "Don't get your hopes up," he told her. "This bird is older than you are and far more experienced. Besides, he doesn't want to get married. Mind your step."

Jackie smiled and went off to the Senate chambers to ask her question. Kennedy's young page, Jerry Hoobler, replied in words drafted by Jackie: "Senator Kennedy is always being taken for a tourist by the cops because he looks so young. The other day he wanted to use the special phones, and they told him, 'Sorry, mister, but these are reserved for senators.' And he always brings his lunch in a brown paper bag and eats it in his office."

Then Jackie trotted over to Richard Nixon, the vice president–elect. He intoned a solemn, orotund reply about future statesmen coming from the ranks of noble young pages. Kennedy, who joined Jackie's pretense that they were just now meeting for the first time, replied with a wry smile, "I've often thought the country might be better off if we senators and the pages traded jobs. I think Jerry Hoobler might be just the fellow to help me straighten out my relationship with the cops. I've often mistaken Jerry for a senator, because he looks so old."

As the year ended, two decisions were made. Jackie decided to prepare nutritious gourmet lunches for Jack, which she sent over to his office: no more paper bags, no more peanut-butter sandwiches. Even more astonishing, Jack invited Jackie as his guest for the Inaugural Ball. Another private campaign was beginning. "Jackie was different from all the other girls Jack had been dating," said his lifelong friend Lemoyne (Lem) Billings. "She was more intelligent, more literary, more substantial" and had "a certain classiness that is hard to describe." These qualities combined to make her "a challenge for Jack, and there was nothing Jack liked better than a challenge."

Part Two

❦

Mrs. Kennedy
1953-1968

CHAPTER SIX

1953-1955

*O*n January 20, 1953, the notoriously eligible bachelor Senator John F. Kennedy was seen for the first time escorting Miss Jacqueline Bouvier to something more public than a movie. The occasion was the Inaugural Ball of President Dwight D. Eisenhower, and Jack and Jackie were widely noticed.

After that, however, it was back to work; he in the Senate, where he was appointed to the Senate Commission on Government Operations, and she at the *Times-Herald*. With his devotion to the Senate (and his other amours), Jackie began to fear that "he couldn't be less interested in me." She was as eager for love, protection and security as Jack was for sex, independence and the fulfillment of his family's ambitions for him.

In 1953, a twenty-three-year-old woman from a good family had to "marry well." Although Jackie coveted her career and her independence, she knew that she had to make a decision, and soon, about Jack Kennedy. That same season, Jack's beloved sister Eunice was planning her elaborate springtime wedding to Robert Sargent Shriver Jr. Jackie's sister Lee, who turned twenty in March, was preparing to marry Michael Canfield, whose father was the New York publisher Cass Canfield. Jackie was maid of honor at the wedding, held on April 18 at

Merrywood. These events must surely have colored her thinking about her own prospects.

Hence she shrewdly devised ways of attracting Jack's attention during those early months of 1953—and one way was in her weekly column, in which the questions shifted to matters like

❖ "The Irish author Sean O'Faolain claims that the Irish are deficient in the art of love. Do you agree?"

❖ "Should engaged couples reveal their pasts?"

❖ "What is your candid opinion of marriage?"

❖ "What is your worst fault as a husband?"

❖ "Can you give any reason why a contented bachelor would want to get married?"

She knew, too, how to get a response from him if she felt ignored. She simply contradicted him about something or did not return his telephone calls or went away for a weekend without informing him. This, of course, had the predictable effect of making Jack feel he was losing control over the woman his father wanted him to marry. This, he might have been startled to realize, bruised his pride, enhanced his desire and spurred his determination.

In February, Jackie introduced him to her father at a New York restaurant. Since hearing of the growing mutual interest between the pair, Black Jack had only grumbled about the son of his sworn enemy, that hated Democrat Joe Kennedy. Old Joe, he reminded her, was chairman of the Securities and Exchange Commission during the 1930s; Old Joe had instituted various regulations that had much diminished the fortunes of the Bouviers.

But according to Jackie's cousin John Davis, she was delighted and astonished when the meeting went brilliantly. Her father and Jack Kennedy were, after all, quite similar. With the exception that Jack drank only moderately, the two men had much in common and shared the same passions for women, politics and sports. Both Jacks were surprised how much they liked each other.

At this point, as might be expected, Janet—perhaps precisely because her ex-husband countenanced the galloping if unofficial courtship—decided that she had certain misgivings. These Irish upstart Kennedys, she said (as if her own family had different roots), were beneath the dignity of the Lees and Auchinclosses. Her daughter ought to marry a Mellon, a Rockefeller or a Vanderbilt—as if they were vegetables available for the picking. But Jackie, perhaps for the first time, turned a deaf ear to her mother. Here was a man, she was certain, who needed her, and what else is more flattering to anyone's ego?

HAVING RUN FOR the Senate, Jack Kennedy now campaigned relentlessly for Jackie's vote at every place they met—from Georgetown dinner parties to art galleries and museums to movie theaters showing foreign "art films," as they were then called. Jackie visited Jack's Senate office, where she was duly impressed by the amount and complexity of his work. There were also gentle but ultimately futile attempts by both: Jackie tried to interest Jack in the arts, he attempted to draw her into the world of smoke-filled, backroom politics.

On his own, however, his conduct was unaltered; it was as Harriet Beecher Stowe said of Aaron Burr: "He never saw a beautiful face and form without a sort of restless desire to experiment upon it and try his power over the inferior inhabitant." Aware of the tenor of his life, Jackie was imperturbable. "Both of us knew [our relationship] was serious, I think, but we didn't talk about it then."

That spring of 1953, there was an event that pushed the matter of her marriage to the crossroad of decision, and one that for sheer pomp and circumstance outranked anything Janet Auchincloss or Rose Kennedy could stage. At the end of May, Jackie was dispatched by the *Times-Herald* to cover the coronation of Queen Elizabeth II. Her friend and former traveling companion, Aileen Bowdoin, accompanied her. She recalled that Jackie talked much about the lives of queens past: how much the wives of Henry VIII endured, and what changes Queen Elizabeth I experienced during her long reign. Jackie's cartoons of the trip—satirizing pretentious shipboard passengers and sketching Humphrey Bogart dancing with his wife, Lauren Bacall, at a party thrown by Perle Mesta—so delighted the editors that they were included along with her reports.

Just before Jackie's departure, Jack had proposed marriage. More concerned than coy, she simply smiled and said she would give him a reply very soon. According to Aileen Bowdoin, Jackie was concerned about losing her own identity, fearful of being swallowed up by politics and terrified of being overwhelmed by the ever overwhelming Kennedy family. A week later, after reading her dispatches in the *Times-Herald,* Jack fired off a brief wire: ARTICLES EXCELLENT BUT YOU ARE MISSED. LOVE, JACK. Not terribly ardent, but as much as he could muster and perhaps as much as he thought prudent in a transatlantic cable.

Jack was at the airport for her return, and that evening he presented a two-carat diamond-and-emerald engagement ring from Van Cleef & Arpels, which she accepted, unaware that Joe had selected it. He knew from the start that she was the right woman, Jack said, but he had wanted to wait awhile. Now that he was ready, his choice fell on her. "How *big* of you!" she said in that innocent voice. The next day she resigned from the *Times-Herald.*

News of the engagement, however, had to await the imminent publication of a major magazine article on Jack and his political future: it had already been titled "The Senate's Gay Young Bachelor." That done, *The New York Times* published photos of the couple to accompany the story on June 25:

SENATOR KENNEDY TO MARRY IN FALL
Son of Former Envoy Is Fiancé
of Miss Jacqueline Bouvier, Newport Society Girl

Engagement parties were tendered at Hyannisport and Hammersmith Farm, the event at the former, as usual, more lively than the one at the latter.

Since the death of his older brother almost a decade earlier, Jack had been the focus of his family's ambitions. Now that he was about to marry, the Kennedys feared, as Lem Billings said, "that he'd be drawn away from them, taking the center away from their lives. It wasn't true, of course, but they didn't know that at the time, and as a result, they perceived Jackie as a threat. This was particularly true for Jack's sisters, who called her 'The Deb,' made fun of her babylike voice and worked relentlessly to engage her in the family's physical activities, where they knew she could never excel. And it was even true for many of Jack's friends, who saw in Jackie a serious rival for his time and affection."

There was, however, no ribbing from Joe, who liked Jackie's feisty spirit, even when he was the target. Had the situation been different, she might well have been the convenient object of a sexual proposition. But as it was, he settled into a comfortable father-daughter relationship with her. His view of life was one of extremes—people and things were either wretched or wonderful. But Jackie would have none of that. Life was complicated, she told him, shifting the topic of their chat from finance to fine arts while the rest of the clan threw the football on the compound's spacious greens.

Rose's initial warmth, meanwhile, was appreciably altered. Was Jackie good enough for her son? Wasn't she too independent, with her own ways of dressing, her refusal to engage in family sports, her unorthodox opinions about things? Never mind. Jackie did her best to improve their relationship, calling Rose "Belle Mère," which is French for "mother-in-law"; Rose was convinced that it ought to be rendered literally as "beautiful mother." In any case, the final judgment on the bride-to-be went forth from Joe to all their friends: "We are all crazy about Jackie." He spoke mostly for himself.

And then, in early July, it happened: the beginning of the aggressive adoration of the press, responsive to a public eager to know about and follow a charismatic couple from the world of money, politics and high society. First to be invited to the Hyannisport scene was a crew from *Life* magazine. The carefully staged piece—a story titled "*Life* Goes Courting with a U.S. Senator"—featured Jack and Jackie on the magazine's cover, windblown and smiling as they sailed with the bay breeze.

Accompanying the story was a photo of Jack tossing stones into the surf and improbable pictures of Jackie swinging a baseball bat, Jackie running with a football, Jackie examining portraits of the Kennedys visiting with royalty, and Jackie "between games," relaxing on the verandah of the main house. "We hardly ever talk politics," she said of her conversations with her fiancé. That was the only accurate representation in the article. *Vogue,* on the other hand, simply published a full-page photo of Jackie ("a young woman of almost extravagant beauty") with a few lines about the upcoming wedding; less, they believed, was so much more.

From Cape Cod, the caravan proceeded the short distance to New-port, where the two mothers were to meet and discuss plans for the September wedding. There they were, according to Jackie, "the two mothers sitting there in their hats and pearls and white gloves, chat-tering away about the wedding," while she and Jack went for a swim. At lunchtime, the ever punctual Rose called loudly to Jack, who was on the beach: "Jack! Ja-a-ack!!" It was, according to Jackie, "just like little ones who pretend not to hear their mothers calling"—until even-tually he had to scurry up to Rose, saying obediently, "Yes, Mother." The situation amused Jackie: "Here was Jack, thirty-six at the time, grown up and a senator! I'm sure it was one of his least favorite days."

She was, as usual, right on the mark. To his navy buddy Paul "Red" Fay, Jack wrote that same month:

> I gave everything a good deal of thought—so am getting married this fall. This means the end of a promising political career, as it has been based up to now almost completely on the old sex appeal. I hope you and the bride will be able to come. . . . Your special project is the bride's mother . . . who has a tendency to think I am not good enough for her daughter.

AS IT HAPPENED, the appearance of the *Life* article had been critically timed—not only for Jack's publicity, but also because he had been feel-ing wretched all during late June and into early July. On the fifteenth, while attending the final session in the Senate before the summer hol-iday, he collapsed and was taken to a hospital, suffering another bout of the malaria he had first contracted during the war. Joe's influence kept this episode from the press.

According to the official record, Jack recuperated on the Cape after Congress began its summer holiday and until the time of his wedding. But he was far away, sailing along the French Riviera, having a last bachelor fling with his old college buddy Torbert Macdonald and ca-vorting with a girl or two or three in every port.

One of them was a bright and attractive twenty-one-year-old Swede named Gunilla von Post, who was spending part of the summer at Haut-de-Cagnes, about twelve miles north of Cap d'Antibes, in earlier days a favorite trysting place for Joe and his lady of the moment. They had a romantic dinner high above the Mediterranean, and then Jack made his romantic move. "He was such a wonderful, exciting person to be with," she recalled years later. "He spoke of his parents, his late brother, his sisters and brothers—but for the moment, there was no mention of a fiancée."

After dinner, they went to a nightclub, and there Jack was suddenly taken by spasms of back pain. They left, and from there they drove down to Eden Roc, where Jack now declared to Gunilla that he had fallen in love with her. Just as he was about to move on to more persuasive lovemaking than the kisses and hugs that had been exchanged so far, Jack announced that he was about to be married. "If I had met you one week before," he said, "I would have canceled the whole thing." Not likely, but perhaps few impressionable young women would object to the words. He took her home, paused at the front door, and asked if he could come in for a while. This he was denied, whereupon he departed, and that—for the time being—was that.

WHAT WAS JACKIE'S reaction to her fiancé's departure for a Riviera holiday just weeks before the wedding, while she and their families were in the mild hysteria of preparations? Most of all, of course, she was confused and hurt—but she was also angry, and to deal with her anger at this stage, she decided she would have to make some concessions. This, she told herself and others, was the way some men act— her own father first among them. By now, she had also heard about Joe's past. But she loved her father, and she loved Joe, too. "Kennedy men are like that," she told the young woman who would marry Jack's brother Teddy in 1958.

According to her closest friends, Jackie simply decided that a certain profligacy was part of a man's character. Infidelity had nothing to do with love—she would provide that—and perhaps in time, once they had settled down, constancy was not an impossible dream.

In this hope, alas, she was doomed to disappointment. But somehow she found a way to soldier on, to find elsewhere the distractions she needed not to plunge into a dark and terrible despair. That she kept her promises, her confidence and her dignity for so long may be one of the most remarkable testimonies to her character.

In a way, Jackie was becoming more like the great ladies of bygone eras and the heroines of a certain type of romantic fiction. Before she was a teenager, she had read and reread Daphne du Maurier's bestseller *Rebecca* and had seen the movie. In some perhaps unacknowledged corner of her soul, Jackie saw herself as someone similar to the shy, unnamed English rose of a girl, overwhelmed by the suave, older Maxim de Winter. Although treated cavalierly by him, she is bedazzled by her great fortune to win his attention and apparent love, and she marries, only to find that she must confront the ghosts of his past. She does so, of course, and wins forever Maxim's love.

In addition, there was, for both Jackie and for du Maurier's heroine, the not negligible buffer of money—a great deal of money. Jackie did not have her mother's obsession with luxury, but she was terrified of poverty, for this threat had been put before her far too long as the logical result of her father's dissolute life. At the same time, she knew that the Kennedy fortune would provide for her and her children, that it would assuage her anxiety. In a light moment, Jack said he wanted to produce ten heirs, and given the number of his own siblings, Jackie believed him.

Over all this, however, is the witness of everyone present at what journalists called the wedding of the year: the assertion that Jackie was truly and deeply falling in love with Jack Kennedy. "She did all the things a young, beautiful girl does when she is in love and the man she loves is with her." Thus said Red Fay, recalling Jackie's glances and gestures; Fay's perception was echoed by many others.

BY SEPTEMBER 2, Jack the cruiser was home. The first of two bachelor dinners was held at the Parker House in Boston, where Joe, Jack and his brothers welcomed 350 men—cronies and colleagues, campaign workers and congressmen, all crowded in for the usual shenanigans. A week later, Hugh Auchincloss hosted the Newport rendition, and as might be expected, it was a much more sedate affair. This event took place at the Clambake Club, where Jackie had been presented in 1947. In a witty speech, Jack explained why he was giving up bachelorhood: he wanted to ensure that Jackie would not have a career with the press. She had, he said, simply become too good at her work, and too smart, and she just might endanger his political future if she continued to have a voice in the newspaper.

To everyone's surprise, Jackie's father was not at either party. This was a deliberate slight orchestrated by Janet, who was afraid that her ex-husband would do something embarrassing. He was, however, scheduled to escort his daughter down the aisle.

The wedding, on Saturday, September 12, at St. Mary's Church in Newport, was without question national news in a way that royal nuptials are in England. The following day photos of the couple appeared in countless American newspapers, including *The New York Times,* which featured Jackie and Jack front and center on page one, cutting their wedding cake beneath the headline NOTABLES ATTEND SENATOR'S WEDDING. He gave her a gold-and-diamond bracelet, while her gift to him was a silver money clip with an image of Saint Christopher, the patron of travelers. This present was perhaps more symbolic than either of them realized, for it represented the odd conjunction of money, religion and travel.

The event, gushed the normally sedate *Times,* "far surpassed the Astor-French wedding of 1934 in public interest." Indeed. At the church, a crowd of more than three thousand broke through police lines and nearly crushed Jackie as she arrived, resplendent in an heirloom lace veil and a gown of ivory silk taffeta with a deep portrait neckline and a bouffant skirt. Inside, eight hundred were crammed in a space designed for less than half that number. Governors, senators and congressmen were applauded as they arrived; the atmosphere began to resemble the Academy Awards. The nuptial Mass was celebrated by Archbishop (later Cardinal) Cushing of Boston, who was assisted by a team of bishops, monsignori and clergy of lower rank who managed to finagle a position in the sanctuary.

Lee was Jackie's matron of honor, and Bobby Kennedy was his brother's best man. But as it turned out, the bride was not escorted by her father but by Hugh Auchincloss. Janet learned that Jack Bouvier had had one or two drinks to drown his anger over the earlier snubs (although he was certainly capable of performing his duty that morning). But fearing that he would fall on his way down the aisle, Janet seized her excuse, swinging into action and threatening that if he came to the church, no one in his family would ever speak to him again. To ensure that her bidding was done, she dispatched two relatives to hold Bouvier hostage in his hotel room, which was easily accomplished by pouring another beaker or two of whiskey down his throat. At the church, Auchincloss presented Jackie to her groom "because of the illness of her father," as the *Times* noted.

As so often, therefore, Janet got her way, never mind her daughter's deep disappointment. Jackie was on the verge of tears as the organist began to play the processional march, but then she rose to the occasion. The eyes of the press, and therefore the nation, were upon her, and she would do what was asked of her. A moment later, she may have been jolted from sorrow by the sight of Jack, who the previous evening had played touch football with his buddies, plowed into a rosebush and now sported a line of scratches down one cheek.

Only when the vast throng of twelve hundred guests made their way over to Hammersmith Farm for the reception did Jackie manage a few moments alone with her bridal party, giving way to tears over her father's absence. But when she descended to meet her guests for the wedding banquet and the hours of posing for photographs, she was radiant and ready to do her duty. It took over two hours for all the guests to pass through the receiving line and shake hands with the newlyweds. "It was just like the coronation," said one enthusiastic guest.

Mr. and Mrs. John F. Kennedy spent two nights at the Waldorf-Astoria Hotel in New York City and then flew to Acapulco. From there, Jackie wrote to her father, expressing not only forgiveness but also compassion for the way he had been treated. The letter has not survived, but according to a colleague of Jack Bouvier named John Carrere, who saw it, only "a rare and noble spirit" could have expressed the sentiments Jackie did. Jack, meantime, fished, tanned himself and flirted with the young women at poolside, all this despite nearly incessant back pain, which he relieved only marginally by three hot baths daily and regular cortisone injections. From there, they drove north to California to visit Red Fay and his wife, Anita, who recognized at once that both the pressures of public life and a visit to one of his old navy buddies "intruded on the kind of honeymoon any young bride anticipates." But the intrusions, from every quarter, were only beginning.

WITH THE WEDDING trip behind them and the Senate about to resume session in October, the Kennedys returned not to their own home—a rented house in Georgetown that was not yet ready for occupancy—but to Hyannisport and the Kennedy compound, where Joe had a small house for them. This was the first problem: Jackie was being totally absorbed by her husband's family, everywhere surrounded by them, dominated by the raucous intensity with which sons and daughters, children and grandchildren, servants and house pets constantly came and went, an atmosphere which the revered patriarch and matriarch imperially observed, on which they commented and about which they decreed.

Jackie chafed against her forced attendance every evening at her in-laws' dinner table, especially because Rose and Joe were so obsessive about punctuality. One evening, Jackie arrived late and Joe needled her. "You ought to write a series of grandfather stories for children," Jackie said sweetly as she took her place. "Like 'The Duck with Moxie' and 'The Donkey Who Couldn't Fight His Way out of a Telephone Booth.' " The rest of the diners fell silent and turned to look at the old man's face. It went red for a moment, and then he burst out laughing. And only Jackie could have gotten away with the drawing she gave him, which showed a crowd of Joe's children on a beach, looking forlornly out to sea. "You can't take it with you," ran the caption. "Dad's got it all."

Most of the week, of course, Jack was in Washington, attending to government business—and to affairs of no governmental import at all. Suddenly, Jackie realized just how much she had to share her husband, and in every way. The lame little boy was now, thanks to his father's training, an ambitious politician who courted and wooed voters as well as congressional colleagues. To further complicate matters, his seductive tactics were used constantly with women, and with considerable success. Despite anxiety about her marriage, Jackie as usual found a measure of serenity on the windswept Cape Cod seashore that October.

Finally, in November, Jackie and Jack moved into their rented house in Washington, a small, dark and narrow house at 3321 Dent Place. Here, the full, dull burden of life first fell upon her, for Jackie was a curiosity, the youngest Senate wife, completely ignorant of politics and yet expected to host cocktail parties and small, politically advantageous suppers. She had given up any ambition for a professional life of her own and had only the responsibility of managing a household and somehow helping Jack's high-powered career—which, she quickly learned, included presidential ambitions. The main problem was that politics bored her to distraction. Indeed, she had not yet been inside a voting booth.

The woman who had said that one of her life's ambitions was not to be a housewife now found herself just that and little more, and she feared that her intellectual and aesthetic life was grinding to a halt. For a brief time, they were living together each day, but then Jack began to spend most weekends in Massachusetts or on the stump, making himself known to as many people as he could meet. He was also seen at chic New York nightclubs, squiring movie queens or British aristocracy, among them Lady Jean Campbell, the daughter of the duke of Argyll. Jackie was alone in Georgetown, welcoming her husband home, only to watch him depart again the next morning. "I found it rather hard to adjust," she said later.

Often he arrived unannounced, with a crew of political cronies who sprawled themselves around the house as if her home were their fraternity house. They broke glasses and ashtrays, spilled drinks, dropped cigarette and cigar ends in vases and generally made themselves a nuisance. Her husband could not fathom the reasons for her displeasure. "I married a whirlwind!" she said without amusement. Of this period, Jack said only, "It was difficult. I was thirty-six, she was twenty-four. We didn't fully understand each other."

Socializing did not help her at all. "They talked about their children and grandchildren," Jackie said, "and I talked about my little half-brother [Jamie, then age six]." Betty Beale, columnist and reporter for the *Washington Evening Star,* recalled years later that Jackie "hated the artificiality of the scheduled meetings of congressmen's wives, and the annual luncheon for Senate wives. This was in the tradition of Mrs. Truman and Mrs. Eisenhower, but she could not endure it."

As for his sexual escapades, Jackie was aware of her husband's promiscuity from the start. "Jack kept assuring us that she didn't suspect," said Jim Reed, another buddy from Jack's navy days. "But it was obvious that she knew exactly what was happening. He was so disciplined in so many ways. Discipline was, after all, the secret of his success. But when it came to women, he was a different person. It was Jekyll and Hyde." What she did not suspect, however, was that Jack's compulsion for multiple partners matched the intensity of his political ambitions. Nor did she expect that he would so blatantly ignore her feelings—even in public, even at a party, as Lem Billings recalled, when Jack often suddenly disappeared with some pretty young thing and left his wife stranded.

As 1953 drew to a close, the radiant bride had become a nervous, chain-smoking, nail-biting woman who often wandered around Washington looking more like the survivor of some terrible accident than the wealthy young wife of an ambitious and popular senator. It is easy to imagine that she thought often of her parents' marriage, an icy accommodation that caused misery for many people and ultimately ended in divorce.

Perhaps inevitably, she took refuge in redecorating the house, shopping, spending money, buying clothes—anything that might appeal to and attract her husband and encourage him to spend more time with her. She had the house refurbished and repainted, preferring pastel colors to lighten the darkness of the interior, and she took special pains with Jack's study. But he complained about the skyrocketing bills; apparently he had never taken into full account that his cost of living would include a sophisticated woman who believed that it was her duty to make her husband proud.

The issue was further complicated by their radically opposite tastes. Jackie liked French antiques, velvets and silk, high art, classical music and great literature, pâté de fois gras with a good Bordeaux and dinner parties for four or six, maximum. Jack, on the other hand, was a lounge-chair or rocker type of man whose preferences ran to pop songs, Irish airs, boiled beef and beer with a large crowd of boisterous buddies. To Jackie, it was ironic that the incalculable Kennedy wealth had been obtained through financial dueling no one could quite remember, or at least openly discuss, and that the wealth bore with it no discernible taste.

AT THE START of 1954, Jackie sought distraction by trying to enrich herself and learn about one of her husband's two consuming interests. In addition to reading the *Congressional Record* and attending his Senate speeches, she enrolled in a course in American history at Georgetown University's School of Foreign Service, just four blocks away; Foreign Service was, at that time, the only school of the university that admitted women. This activity was duly exploited by Jack's staff and Joe's friends, with the inevitable result of a photo story in *McCall's* later that year ("The Senator's wife goes back to school . . ."). But most valuable of all to her husband was Jackie's translation of passages from Talleyrand, Voltaire and Rousseau, selections with which he began to pepper his speeches. As for Jackie, she absorbed the works of Samuel Eliot Morison and Henry Steele Commager, among others.

BUT BOOKS ARE a poor substitute when one has expected the presence of a husband. "I was alone almost every weekend," she recalled. "It was all wrong. Politics was sort of my enemy, and we had no home life whatsoever." Throughout the year, she returned frequently to Merrywood, where she rode her horses to exhaustion through the Virginia countryside.

Meantime, Jack could not dismiss the memory of the young Swede he had met in the south of France. On March 2, he wrote to Gunilla von Post at her home in Stockholm, using his official stationery from the Senate Office Building. He was soon planning another trip to France, he said, and hoped they would be reunited, sailing the Mediterranean "for two weeks—with you as crew." Several amorous notes were followed by telephone calls that springtime. During one of them, Gunilla said that when she was a child, a neighbor told her she would grow up to be very dangerous to men—to which Jack replied, "I don't know if you are still dangerous, but I'm trying like hell to find out!"

Their reunion was scuttled, however, because the senator's back pain became so severe, and his mobility so compromised, that he was a semi-invalid. Dragging himself to Capitol Hill on crutches, trussed into a steel corsetlike brace, often carried up and down stairs by friends, Jack had to be attended more and more by Jackie at home. After consulting with specialists from Boston's Lahey Clinic, Jack and his family learned that he might well be confined to a wheelchair for the rest of his life unless complicated surgery was performed. Amid this pain and apprehension, Jackie, at first joyously pregnant, miscarried. The romantic young couple, darlings of the Washington press corps and of a nation that now doted on the extension of Hollywood glamour into politics, was privately engulfed in anxiety.

The procedure recommended as Jack's last hope to resolve his back problem and prevent permanent quadriplegia was a lumbar fusion, which would have been difficult and perilous even for a much healthier man, especially in those days before microsurgery. But for Jack Kennedy, who suffered the debilitating effects of Addison's disease, the operation was life-threatening: doctors told him, Jackie and his parents that in his case there was a 50 percent chance that he would not survive. He chose the risk rather than a passive acceptance of possibly permanent disability.

On October 10, Jack entered the New York Hospital for Special Surgery, and for the next ten days, specialists treated him with experimental medications to prepare him for the operation, which was performed on October 21. Within three days thereafter, he developed severe infections resistant to antibiotics. By the night of October 24, he was on the hospital's list of critically ill patients. Rose, Joe and Jackie were told that death was imminent; at their request, a priest arrived to administer last rites. For the next week, no one thought he would survive. Jack's parents, almost speechless with the fear that they might again lose a child, could do little but stand by helplessly and, it may be presumed, pray mightily in private. Jackie prayed, too—"for the first time in my life," she said later.

But she also displayed extraordinary practical strength and surprising nursing abilities, remaining at her husband's bedside virtually around the clock. She held Jack's hand, reading newspapers, poetry, jokes and movie reviews to him while he lay immobile, silent, sometimes almost comatose. When he rallied slightly, she was there, spooning ice chips and bland liquids into his dry mouth, then helping to bathe him and change his hospital gown.

The film actress Grace Kelly, hearing of the handsome senator's illness, asked if she could visit. Jackie thought this a marvelous idea, and she asked Kelly to wear a nurse's uniform, for Jack had complained that all the nurses were homely old crones. The actress arrived to find Jackie and a squadron of bustling nurses hovering over a bone-thin, frail, and ashen patient. He was only thirty-seven, but he looked much older, nothing like the picture of glowing energy Grace expected. Probably just as unforeseen was the large movie poster of an alluring Marilyn Monroe taped on the ceiling over Jack's bed, as if she would spring magically to life and cure him with miraculous caresses. Alas, Jack was medicated and unable to recognize Kelly. "I must be losing it," she whispered as she departed.

For two months, Jack remained confined in the hospital, gradually more alert but enduring intractable pain and unable to take more than two or three steps before slumping against the crutches and sometimes fainting from the agony and exertion. During this entire time, his life was in constant danger from debilitating infections. But just as no one ever heard him complain, so no one ever saw his wife weep or become angry, impatient or exacting of doctors or nurses.

Four days before Christmas, his physicians permitted Jack's transfer to the Kennedy winter retreat in Palm Beach, where perhaps the Florida climate and the familiar surroundings would encourage recuperation; to Jackie, Joe and Rose, however, the doctors said that he might not even survive the journey, let alone the coming weeks. He arrived safely, but gravely weakened, weighing a mere 115 pounds and requiring constant adjustment of his medication: infections constantly recurred, fevers made him delirious, and the eight-inch wound was so deep and suppurating that the dressings had to be changed every few hours. It was, said the doctor who would soon care for him, "an open, gaping, very sickly looking hole" in his back.

"Jackie cleaned the wound skillfully, gently and calmly," according to Rose, "and made no comment about it to anyone." Nevertheless, and despite her quiet ministrations and endless invention of cheerful distractions, Jack's friends—Dave Powers and Lem Billings, among others—were so distressed by his bitterness, depression and occasional confusion that they feared his loss of mental equilibrium as much as they feared for his life.

By early February 1955, it was clear that a second operation was necessary if John Kennedy were ever to walk again. On the fifteenth, in New York, he submitted to the surgery—a bone graft in his spine and the removal of the metal plate that been installed in October.

DURING JACK'S SEVEN-MONTH ordeal, Jackie often helped with Senate tasks and relayed information to and from Jack's secretary, Evelyn Lincoln. One afternoon while they were discussing great past senators,

Jackie said that Jack ought to write a book about the ideas of political leaders who ran against the current for a higher national good.

She at once set to work, scouring her history notes from Georgetown, bringing books and articles to the hospital and enlisting the help of her former professor Jules Davids. "She asked me," he confirmed years later, "if I could suggest for the senator the names of individuals who demonstrated outstanding examples of political courage in American history." And with that, a book indeed took shape, but Jack himself was not in any condition to do much of the actual writing.

While he certainly read all the background material, discussed the issues and vetted every word of the final typescript, Jack was not the actual author of the text. That task fell to others—principally, Theodore Sorensen (who always minimized his contribution) and Jules Davids (who researched and wrote five chapters, for which he was paid the sum of $700). The latter's work was explicitly acknowledged—at least privately—by Kennedy, who sent Davids a letter of gratitude "for your assistance in the writing of the book."

To each page, Jackie applied her critical eye and her editorial red pencil. During her lifetime, the extent of her contribution was not discussed, but Mary Van Rensselaer Thayer, whom Jackie appointed to chronicle her White House years, confirmed that the book "couldn't have happened without Jacqueline. She encouraged her husband, read to him, carried out independent research and on yellow-lined copy paper wrote down parts of the book."

"In private, there was nothing shy or quiet about Jackie," said their friend William Walton, a journalist and artist. "She was involved in all the conversations, and actively. She was very talkative. She had opinions on everything." Jack recognized her work in the preface to the finished book, which contains a note that is entirely his own composition: "This book would not have been possible without the encouragement, assistance and criticisms offered from the very beginning by my wife Jacqueline, whose help during all the days of my convalescence I cannot ever adequately acknowledge."

Years after Kennedy's death, his severest critics took aim at what they considered the subterfuge of publishing a book under the name of a man who did not actually write it. But as the eminent historian

Garry Wills has said, "This kind of political production is normal, not only for an officeholder's speeches but for his books. There is no deception in this, because there is no pretense that the man signing his name did all or even most of the writing."

When it was published in 1956, *Profiles in Courage* became an instant bestseller, received the Pulitzer Prize for biography and greatly increased Jack's political and public standing. But there remains the nagging coda to the story: Jack allowed his father to have the Pulitzer board improperly lobbied by his friend Arthur Krock, and thus did Jack eventually win the prize.

BUT THERE WAS an even more important development in Kennedy's thinking during his recuperation, and his wife had much to do with it.

Jack invited William David Ormsby-Gore, the British statesman he had known since his time in England before World War II, to meet with him and Jackie at Hyannisport. (From 1957 to 1961, Ormsby-Gore was Britain's minister of state for foreign affairs and, for the next four years, British ambassador to America.) Together, the trio took a hard and, in the end, disapproving look at the then-popular notion of massive retaliation during international conflict.

The record of this meeting, set down in Jackie's hand and preserved in the archives of the John F. Kennedy Library, expressed their belief that tactical nuclear war was an illusion and that disarmament was the only sane road to lasting peace. The conversations, laced with references to history, poetry and drama, reveal the enormous impact of Jackie's learning on these discussions.

Her role was not that of mere secretary at an important meeting. Jackie's wide, profound reading in French intellectual history, for example—particularly the theories of colonial warfare articulated by Gallieni, Bugeaud, Lyautey and de Lattre—significantly contributed to the development of Kennedy's intellectual life, the notion of a "flexible response" doctrine and his eventual commitment to arms control and the Nuclear Test Ban Treaty. The Kennedys and Ormsby-Gore agreed on the imperative of nuclear disarmament, and while the political evolution of the so-called Kennedy Doctrine was left to Jack, much of the historical, literary and philosophical support for it came from his wife.

The fundamental influence Jackie played in her husband's life was articulated by none other than the scholar, writer and educator Arthur M. Schlesinger Jr., a friend and confidant of the Kennedy family since his college days. At Harvard, he had been a classmate of Joseph P. Kennedy Jr., the eldest son of Joe and Rose, and subsequently became a trusted confidant to Jack when he went to Congress after the war. (Schlesinger was later special assistant to President John F. Kennedy.)

"Jackie played a very interesting role in the development of Jack's thought," Schlesinger said years later. "She was not only interested in the larger issues, such as human rights, she also quite enjoyed the nitty-gritty—she was amused by politicians fighting one day and appearing as close friends the next. In more serious matters, Jack could not read French, and when it came to his thinking about Vietnam, for example, he valued greatly her reactions and judgments about things."

FINALLY, THE LONG-AILING senator was able to return to work. On May 23, 1955, six days before his thirty-eighth birthday, he and Jackie flew from Hyannisport to Washington. He jauntily dismissed the nurses waiting with crutches and wheelchair, posed for cameramen in front of the Capitol and then—flashing his trademark smile—strolled to the Senate Office Building. But he was not long in Washington. Three days later Jack quietly left the capital and, unknown to the press, traveled to New York City.

On Thursday the twenty-sixth, accompanied by Dr. Ephraim Shorr, an endocrinologist who had attended Kennedy during his surgeries, Jack went to the offices of Dr. Janet Travell at 9 West Sixteenth Street. "He was thin, he was ill, his nutrition was poor, he was on crutches," said Dr. Travell years later. At the time, she was a fifty-three-year-old pharmacologist on the staff of New York Hospital.

There were two steps from the street into my office and he could hardly navigate these. His major complaint was pain in his left low back with radiation to the left lower extremity, so that he couldn't put weight on it without intense pain. But he also had an old football injury to his knee. . . . He could walk on the level putting his weight on his right leg, but he couldn't step up or down a step with his right foot. We could hardly get him into the office.

That same afternoon, Jack was admitted to New York Hospital for muscle stimulation and passive exercises over the long Memorial Day weekend. He remained there until Wednesday, June 1, and by that time Dr. Travell and her colleagues had found a protocol for the management of Jack's pain: the regular injection of procaine and novocaine. Thus began Dr. Travell's care of John Kennedy, which continued into his presidency and up to the time of his death. To her hands and those of specialists fell the complications of dealing with a man who had recurrent malaria, Addison's disease, a chronic spinal condition that was never resolved and severe allergies to milk, horses and any shedding dog. Most delicate of all, both from the public-relations and orthopedic standpoints, was the fact, in Travell's words,

> that he was born with the left side of his body smaller than the right; the left side of his face was smaller; his left shoulder was lower . . . and his [left] leg was appreciably shorter. . . . This was true all his life, and not just following surgery on the left side of his back. This was not secondary to surgery.

As part of her treatment, Travell measured Kennedy for a heel lift.

It is worthwhile to document these details of Jack's health precisely because they give some indication not only of the burdens he had to overcome as he anticipated running for the presidency but also of the complex medical situation that confronted Jackie. In many ways, she had to cope with as much as he did: she had to guard the secrecy of his fragile health, monitor his medications, supervise his diet, decide when his anxiety derived from pain and when from matters political. These were practical, daily concerns.

There were more difficult matters. She had, as well, to exercise an enormous amount of patience, to subjugate all her own desires and preferences to the issue of her husband's wellness, and to consider his health relative to the issue of what their children might inherit. This tangle of responsibilities, concerns and sacrifices, along with Jackie's profound respect for Jack, her appreciation of his physical if not moral courage, and, yes, her love for him, may partially account for her tolerance of his almost frenetic infidelity when he could take more than a step or two.

In some ways, loving Jack Kennedy was not unlike loving Jack Bouvier. She sustained a man's sometimes deeply embarrassing faults precisely because she saw them as coming from weakness rather than from malice. In addition, she had never known anything like the undiluted devotion of anyone—never had she been the object of anyone's unvarying, attentive love. Her mother was a chilly social climber, and even her more demonstrative father, a drinker and philanderer, was too often emotionally unavailable to her. Some part of her may never have expected love: even as a teenager, she neither spoke nor wrote romantically about that.

"No one will ever marry me, and I will end up as a housemother at Miss Porter's," she had frequently said to classmates while in school. Until the last years of her life, she seems to have had a vague conviction that she might never be partner to a commitment that was fixed, firm and forever. Marriage to Jack Kennedy, with all its conciliations, had material advantages and the benefit of a witty, bright companion who, she thought, at least did not abuse or humiliate her.

But her patience and tolerance were soon pushed to the limit.

ON AUGUST 5, Congress adjourned for a two-month summer holiday. Jack and his friend Torbert Macdonald boarded the liner *United States* for Europe. The purpose of the journey was to meet unofficially with NATO allies, to survey conditions in postwar Poland, to meet French leaders in Paris and Pope Pius XII in Rome. There would even be time for relaxation. Jackie remained in Washington to look for a house they might purchase, for they were both weary of hotels and of Merrywood, where they had stayed since the expiration of the lease on Dent Place. She was to join him in the south of France a few weeks later.

Kennedy and Macdonald landed at Le Havre on August 10. Before disembarking, Jack had sent a cable to Gunilla von Post, with whom he had not lost contact over the past two years: À BIENTÔT—JACK. As it was, the romantic reunion had been planned for months. He sped off to Båstad, a peninsula of southwest Sweden, where Gunilla awaited when the men arrived on the twelfth. Macdonald discreetly withdrew to his own room.

An intensely amorous week followed. The trio traveled across southwest Sweden, and Jack made himself more than merely agreeable to Gunilla's family. But obviously he was too rigorous in his various activities that week, for afterward he required crutches and emergency doses of major painkillers, obtained from lenient European pharmacists. While Jack rested one afternoon, Macdonald—on his own or coached— told Gunilla about "Jack's unhappy marriage." Kennedy had, Gunilla learned, sacrificed most of his life to please his father, had married to please his father, was working to please his father, and now he wanted (so he said) to make a clean break with the past and begin a new life— away from his father.

On the eighteenth, Jack and Macdonald left Sweden. Gunilla, excited, hopeful and perhaps too credulous, told her mother about Jack's plans to divorce his wife and marry her. Mamma was gently realistic: "Our Jack wants to be president of the United States someday, and his father wants that for him, too. Do you really suppose he would divorce Jackie now? For a Swedish girl nobody in his country has ever heard of?"

She was, of course, on the mark. Had Kennedy left his pretty young wife, there would have been an immediate negative reaction from the general American electorate in those postwar days of Eisenhower and *Father Knows Best*. More to the point, John Kennedy would immediately have lost the support of most Catholics—a substantial percentage of the American population and precisely the constituency he required in order to overcome the presumption that anyone loyal to Rome (whatever that meant, which was not much to Jack) could not be trusted to serve as president.

In any case, Jack wrote to Gunilla on August 22 from the Hôtel du Cap d'Antibes on the French Riviera. Jackie and her sister were due to arrive at any moment, and they were proceeding together to Capri and the rest of the European journey. He followed this letter with a telephone call, but Gunilla was not at home, and her mother answered. Politely but firmly, she reminded Jack that he was a married man.

As the Kennedy party moved through Italy, France and Poland, Jack somehow found opportunities for telephone calls to his Swedish lover. "I talked to my father," he told her one evening. "It wasn't a very pleasant conversation. It's impossible to bring up my troubles with my wife to him. He doesn't even want to hear about it, because she likes him and he responds to that." He had told Joe, he said, that he wanted to end his marriage, and his father, predictably, had been furious. "You're going to be president someday. . . . Divorce is impossible. . . . Can't you get it into your head that it's not important what you really are? The only important thing is what people *think* you are!" Telephone calls, letters and promises followed, but from that point on, they both knew the affair was really over. The following summer, Gunilla von Post married.

JACKIE PERSEVERED, SERVING as Jack's translator in Paris and winning points from the European press for her sophistication and knowledge of the country's history and art. In Rome, the situation took on an irony worthy of a political satirist, for Jack's back and legs were so painful that he could not observe the custom of the time, a genuflection to kiss the symbolic Fisherman's Ring on the Pope's hand. Toward the end of the journey, the party was invited to join a company of vacationers aboard Aristotle Onassis's yacht *Christina*. Lee's marriage to Michael Canfield had not been successful, and she and Onassis—always called Ari—were thought to be romantically involved, although he was much older and married. In addition, Jack wanted to meet Winston Churchill, also a guest onboard. But Churchill would have none of Kennedy, perhaps because of his contempt for Joe's earlier isolationism. Jack complained of the snub to his wife, who pointed to his white dinner jacket and said with deadpan humor, "I think he thought you were the waiter, Jack."

On October 11, they returned to New York on the *United States,* and Jack was at once taken to Janet Travell's office. She increased the doses of painkilling injections, and once a week for the rest of the year he slipped out of Washington to her office for treatment.

The season's routine was interrupted by two events.

In October, the Kennedys found a house called Hickory Hill, in McLean, Virginia. With stables, a swimming pool and space for a large family and servants, the house cost the then-astronomical sum of $125,000. Extensive remodeling was to be done, for Jackie insisted that Jack's bathroom be fitted so that he need not lean over to open drawers or stand uncomfortably to shave. She also worked on plans for the nursery.

Her work was subverted by the second development that autumn. On Sunday, November 13, while Jack and Jackie were in Hyannisport for the Veterans Day weekend, the family went out for its usual scrimmage. Good sport that she tried to be, Jackie joined the game; moments later, she tripped and fell, crying out in pain. Taken to New England Baptist Hospital with a broken ankle, she was confined for five days and left wearing a plaster cast from below the knee to her toes. So that she could be well looked after, she and Jack lived at Merrywood during her recuperation, while work continued at Hickory Hill. Ted Sorensen drolly suggested that Jackie write an article, "Profiles in Athletic Courage."

Her marriage, too, limped along that season. Jackie endured terrible periods of depression, doubtless because her husband was again absent much of the time—preparing for a possible presidential candidacy in 1956, or at least a run for the vice presidency with the Democratic presidential favorite, Adlai Stevenson. Quite understandably, Jackie also felt as if she had regressed: she was living in her former room, again subject to her mother's counsel and approval, once more feeling like a dependent child. Then twenty-six, she did not find this a congenial situation.

In mid-December, she and her husband joined the Kennedys in Palm Beach, where she joined no activity more dangerous than a round of carol singing. While in Hyannisport, Jackie had privately told Joe how miserable she was, and how she wondered if her marriage was doomed to the same fate as her mother's and her sister's. Her father-in-law, probably as shaken as he had been by Jack's calls from Sweden, offered Jackie $1 million, carefully and quietly invested in sheltered trust funds, not to divorce Jack.

But a shattered ankle had interrupted the discussions about a fractured marriage, and the matter came up again in Florida and early in the new year 1956. By that time, Jackie had flatly declined Joe's offer. The reason was soon clear: she was again pregnant, and the child she yearned to have—the child that might change and seal her marriage— would not be submitted to the fate Jackie herself had endured, the confusion and unhappiness of a broken home.

CHAPTER SEVEN

1956-1960

*I*mmediately after *Profiles in Courage* was published in January 1956, its author of record was in demand as a guest speaker around the country—a development that brought him instant national exposure and a strong measure of popularity.

While Jackie rested at Merrywood and supervised, from there, the continuing work on Hickory Hill, Jack conferred with his father, his advisers and Democratic Party leaders. Ought he to challenge Adlai Stevenson for the presidential nomination, or seek the vice presidential position on the ticket? By late spring, he had wisely chosen not to aim for too much too soon—but perhaps the second spot was realistic? Joe, however, weighed in with a wise bit of advice against it. He rightly predicted that President Eisenhower would win a second term, and he said that if Jack was Stevenson's running mate, the loss would be blamed on Jack—by which he meant Jack's Catholicism. But Jack's team proceeded to canvass the public, the pollsters and the party about the sound of "Vice President John F. Kennedy."

Joe's wisdom prevailed, but not, for once, because of his influence on his son. Jack's name was put forward for the vice presidency, but he was defeated. The venerable Eleanor Roosevelt, among others, went on record against Kennedy's nomination for anything, because he had failed to speak out against Senator Joseph McCarthy, whose witch-hunts and spurious Red-baiting both capitalized on and had fed an almost lunatic paranoia in America. Democrats, she said, referring implicitly to *Profiles in Courage,* ought not to nominate "someone who understands what courage is and admires it, but has not quite the independence to have it." Such comments virtually killed his chances of winning the nomination—but not, after all, his future, which was nourished by the enormously favorable impression Jack made that August.

As Kennedy historian James MacGregor Burns has pointed out, this convocation put John F. Kennedy's name and face on the national map. His dramatic run, his near victory, the winsome smile and the collegiate good looks that television lights and cameras beamed so cooperatively all went straight to the heart of America in the 1950s. That August of 1956, his campaign for the presidency was unofficially launched. His many subsequent public appearances became more and more polished, more spiced—thanks to Ted Sorensen, Jackie and a few others—with touching, witty, apposite quotations from Shakespeare, Jefferson, Lincoln and American poets. "His clothes and hairdo," observed no less a careful observer than James Reston of the *The New York Times,* "are a masterpiece of contrived casualness [and] his influence with lady politicians is almost naughty."

The party had asked Jack to stand behind Stevenson, and he did so—by reading a statement drafted by his wife in her own hand:

In recent months, I have been questioned frequently as to the candidate of my choice for the Democratic presidential nomination. My position can be stated simply. Adlai Stevenson was my choice for the presidency in 1952.... His intelligence, farsightedness and reasonableness have neither diminished nor been matched by any other potential nominee. Consequently, Adlai Stevenson remains, in my opinion, the most outstanding choice for the presidency in 1956.

Some have accused him of being too liberal—others have charged him with being too conservative. But Adlai Stevenson is beholden to no man and to no section—only to the welfare of our nation at home and abroad.

It might not be an exaggeration to say that Jackie's admiration for Adlai Stevenson—and not only her loyalty to her husband—aroused, for perhaps the first time, her interest in politics. Sorensen, among others, felt that among politicians, Stevenson's wit, eloquence and intelligence singularized him in Jackie's estimation. Hence it was not really party politics per se that she found fascinating, or to which she could dedicate her time and energy; rather, it was specific people—people of conviction and discernment.

Eight months pregnant, Jackie nonetheless traveled to the convention, quite against her doctor's recommendation, because Jack's sisters and sisters-in-law were present, applying gentle pressure on her, too. She mostly rested in her hotel room, reading, telephoning family and friends and reviewing the short list of names she and Jack had discussed for their baby. Hoping for a girl, Jackie had a definite choice—Arabella. She did, however, manage to attend the sessions in which Jack formally nominated Stevenson for president and in which Jack lost the vice presidential spot to Estes Kefauver. For the rest of the time, her husband was so busy that Jackie "never had a chance to talk with Jack all week," as even Kenneth O'Donnell and Dave Powers—close aides and probably his most ardent defenders—frankly admitted.

From that time forward, she became involved in his political activities only when she felt (not because she was told) that her presence was crucial to her husband, or when he specifically asked for her.

IMMEDIATELY AFTER THE convention, the Kennedys retreated to Hyannisport. Within days, Jack—angry and frustrated, according to O'Donnell and Powers—was off to join his father on the Riviera, where they cruised the Mediterranean. Teddy went along, as did Florida senator George Smathers—but not Jackie, who went to Hammersmith Farm. Some might consider it odd, or even inappropriate, for a man to sail away when his wife was near the term of her pregnancy.

And then something terrible happened while the rising political star was relaxing off the Italian coast, removed from anxiety, pressure and any sort of responsibility. On August 23, Jackie collapsed in agony. She began to hemorrhage and was rushed to Newport Hospital, where an emergency cesarean section was performed. When she emerged from the anesthesia, her brother-in-law Bobby had to give her the sad news that a baby girl was stillborn. For days, Jackie was withdrawn and inconsolable, especially in the absence of her husband, who was blithely drifting in the Mediterranean. Finally, he learned the news when he docked at Genoa on August 26 and put through a telephone call home.

At first Jack saw no reason to return, since what had happened, he said, had happened. The kinder interpretation would be that he was too shocked and saddened to travel, that—as often when tragedy struck—he wanted to deal with it in solitude. And surely no one would suggest that John Kennedy was without feeling for his wife and for their loss. Smathers, frequently Jack's companion on his rounds of local and distant wenching, convinced him that remaining abroad would be a bad decision. Kennedy finally arrived back home two days later, only to find—could he have expected otherwise?—a cool reception from his wife, who had begged him not to leave the country in the first place. On their third wedding anniversary, September 12, she was still confined to bed.

From that point on, the marriage went into its darkest and most perilous period. According to Washington columnist Drew Pearson, "For a long time, she wouldn't listen to his overtures for a reconciliation. He blamed himself for the estrangement."

JACK AND JACKIE were not people with extravagant emotions, nor did they express their deepest feelings easily. In public they struck a dignified pose together—which was not, it must be said, anything phony or misleading, for such was the demeanor expected at that time. In the 1950s, Americans did not expect people to disclose their thoughts and emotions for the scrutiny of the press and the documentation of cameras. Hand-holding, kisses and hugs performed on cue, tears and sobs—all the characteristics of "letting it all hang out" introduced by the reactive 1960s and expected of just about everyone by the 1990s—none of this came naturally to most people outside their homes half a century ago.

The background, breeding and personality of both Jack and Jackie Kennedy italicized this emotional reserve. They went about their lives, they endured pain, they took their private pleasures—many more in his case than in hers, it seems—and asked for no one's approval. More to the point, they took to the grave the details of their private moments with each other—hence we must be cautious about imagining, much less reconstructing, the give-and-take that characterized their marriage.

One thing can be confidently asserted, however. From the time of the loss of their daughter Arabella, a chilly distance was established between them. "We didn't fully understand each other," Jack had said of their first year of marriage. By the autumn of 1956, their fourth year, the mutual incomprehension had deepened, and Jackie was close to clinical depression. Hence, she could not proceed with the move to Hickory Hill, with its cheerful nursery all in readiness and its numerous rooms redecorated not for a couple essentially isolated from each other but for a happy family. Jack did not object. The house was quickly sold to Bobby and Ethel, who had five children at the time and would eventually produce eleven.

Instead, as if it were a sign of the conditional nature of the marriage, they took yet another rented house, this one at 2808 P Street, in Georgetown—once again, a place furnished and decorated by others, the rooms dispiriting, the atmosphere alien and unwelcoming. There Jackie's life seemed to slow to a halt. She seemed often in a haze of grief and uselessness, and to friends she confided her fear that perhaps a miscarriage and a stillbirth were signs she would never be a mother. Meanwhile, Jack rushed around the country, giving speeches, doing his political duty, almost fiercely enjoying his present even as he shaped plans for the future.

It would be easy to oversimplify this period of time—to accuse Jackie of emotional vacuity and Jack of an almost pathological callousness. But by all accounts, there was no malice—only a terrible sadness with which each of them coped differently. The marriage that had promised her security and him respectability, the marriage Joe Kennedy had in effect stage-managed, was now close to collapse. Wounded by their pasts, Jack and Jackie had few resources to cope with their present.

Perhaps no one has the right to say that they themselves did not feel the sense of failure and grief most acutely. Their deepest feelings ought not to be gauged by their silence on these matters—particularly in the case of Jackie, who never courted the public's fickle adoration by telling her story to the world.

Why, then, did the marriage endure?

For Jack's part, divorce was obviously unthinkable: it would have meant the end of his career. For Jackie, it was primarily, before she had children, a matter of sheer, dogged duty; later, after she became a mother, it was a matter of honor. Whereas earlier she had perhaps idealized John Kennedy out of all proportion to reality, now she clearly realized that the object of her love was full of weaknesses—but not, for all that, unworthy of love. The reconciliation that Drew Pearson had spoken of was not a refusal to be a wife: it was a refusal to return to the earlier romantic notions. "Look, it's a trade-off," Jackie said years later to a woman trying to cope with her husband's extramarital affairs:

> There are positives and negatives to every situation in life. You endure the bad things, but you enjoy the good. And what incredible opportunities—the historic figures you meet and come to know, the witness to history you become, the places you would never have been able to see that now you can. One could never have such a life if one wasn't married to someone like that. If the trade-off is too painful, then you just have to remove yourself, or you have to get out of it. But if you truly love someone, well . . .

"My mother thinks that the trouble with me is that I don't play bridge with my bridesmaids," Jackie remarked with a wry smile early in 1957. She preferred, instead, to spend her solitary time reading, and that year she took a subscription to *History Today*. It was, she said, the best way to understand the link of the political present to the past.

In March, Jackie was told that she was pregnant again—news she could hardly receive with unalloyed happiness, since she feared a repetition of the previous summer's sadness. Nevertheless, with her customary optimism she took Jack to see a lovely house nearby, and later that spring they sealed the purchase of 3307 N Street N.W.—the first place she and her husband would own together. "My sweet little house leans slightly to one side, and the stairs creak," she told the noted designer Dorothy Parish, known to all as Sister Parish, a nickname bestowed on her by her three brothers. Jackie brought her in as consultant, and together they set about the task of redecoration.

The house was a three-story redbrick building, Federal in style, with a backyard planted thick with magnolia trees. Kennedy paid $82,000 for it, and Jackie's remodeling cost another $18,000. As she proceeded, Jackie had the floors painted in a white-and-green design, chose Louis XV armchairs and porcelains, Louis XVI dining chairs, and an antique carpet—it was as if Madame de Récamier was returning after exile. Even before they moved in later that year, Jackie decided the precise locations for fresh flowers, to be placed in French copper cooking pots. There would be servants, but not one detail of house management escaped her eye or was planned without her approval.

Jackie was also insistent that however lovely some of the furnishings, there must be no museum atmosphere. "There have to be big, comfortable chairs," she told Sister Parish, "and tables where politicians can put papers, coffee cups, ashtrays. And I don't ever want a house where I have to say to my children, 'Don't touch.'" She never did.

Thus the spring and summer proceeded. Then Jackie took a telephone call from New York on July 27, 1957, the eve of her twenty-eighth birthday. At first she thought the call was a surprise greeting from her father; indeed, it would have been a surprise, for in recent years there had been little communication between them. As Jackie dealt with the vagaries of her own life, Jack Bouvier felt, with all the neurosis of a guilt-ridden alcoholic, that his daughters were abandoning him. He had become more and more difficult, reclusive, dependent on the ministrations of whichever woman was in his life at the time.

But it was a physician calling to say that her father was ill—just how gravely, no one was certain, but he was in Lenox Hill Hospital for tests. Jackie made arrangements to travel to New York the following week, but on August 1, the poor man slipped into a coma and two days later he was dead. The once suave, confident playboy, the promising broker, the doting father, the man in summer whites who always held a trinket for his children in one arm and, it seemed, a new girlfriend on the other, was dead of liver cancer at the age of sixty-six.

"He never created another life for himself [after his daughters' childhood]," said Lee years later. "He always felt that he was a failure in some way. In the end, he was a heartbreaking figure." At the time, however, Lee was in London, and so to Jackie, then six months pregnant, fell the burden of handling the details. The funeral was held at St. Patrick's Cathedral: Bouvier was, after all, the father-in-law of Senator Kennedy, and an ancestor had donated an altar there. Instead of the traditional floral sprays, Jackie arranged for white wicker baskets of daisies and bachelor's buttons in the sanctuary and around the coffin. There were only a few mourners from the glory days, when everyone at least had seemed so carefree.

For years, little happiness had come to John Vernou Bouvier III— or rather, he seemed to disallow it in his life. He had fled into his own misery; he had become detached, suspicious and demanding, which, of course, is a blueprint for desolation. At his burial in East Hampton, Jackie arranged for white baskets of flowers to be banked around her father's coffin. She wanted, she said, to represent—however briefly and modestly—the loveliness of Lasata in the full bloom of high summer.

JACK BOUVIER HAD stipulated that after taxes and a few small bequests, his estate be equally divided between his two daughters. Each received a check for $79,708; it was the first family money they had received since the $3,000 bequest from Grandpa Bouvier, and it was the last.

Jackie's pregnancy proceeded healthily, but not without further distressing interruption. In September, Jack suddenly spiked a high fever, with severe back pain and swelling appearing along the site of his earlier surgery. For this, he had to be admitted once again to the hospital, where a virulent staphylococcal infection was diagnosed. He had to be treated under general anesthesia. "The appearance," said Dr. Travell, not mincing words, "was what might be called a mess." He responded to antibiotics, however, and insisted on proceeding with his scheduled appearances in Canada that October. But Jackie was having none of the travel this time. She remained at her father-in-law's New York apartment that autumn, awaiting, as calmly as she could, the first labor pains.

They came a few weeks early, and this time Jack was present when the doctor emerged from surgery to tell him that his wife and baby daughter, born by cesarean section, were just fine. Caroline Bouvier Kennedy, named for her aunt and great-grandmother, was born on

November 27, 1957, the eve of Thanksgiving Day. Archbishop Cushing, by now a close friend to Jackie as to all the Kennedys, traveled from Boston to baptize the infant at St. Patrick's on December 13.

Perhaps to the surprise of many who knew them, Caroline's birth restored her parents' marriage, at least partly and temporarily. Before Christmas, they moved—along with the newly employed nursemaid, Maud Shaw—into the new house on N Street. Soon a butlervalet, a cook and a housemaid were added to the staff.

While boxes and crates were still being unpacked, Jack and his buddy George Smathers flew off to Havana for a few days of stag fun. Kennedy gave the trip the patina of business by addressing the American embassy staff, but for the most part he played golf, sailed, visited various nightspots and generally disported himself with his usual abandon. "We were just going, frankly, for a vacation," Smathers admitted later.

Back in Georgetown in the role of husband and father for Christmas, Jack found his wife happily immersed in caring for Caroline; henceforth, motherhood gave her a full-time distraction from the constant disappointment of her husband's frequent absences. With good cheer and a kind of insouciant generosity, she had taken a major share of her inheritance and purchased a white Jaguar as a Christmas present for Jack. But advisers persuaded him that this extravagance made for a bad public image, and he exchanged it for a more sensible Buick.

THE ABSENCES WERE only beginning.

"If I decide to run for the presidency in 1960," Jack Kennedy said as he began his campaign for reelection to the Senate in early 1958, "I will at least have been around and met a lot of people in different parts of the country." That was certainly an understatement. In the first half of 1958, he received 2,568 invitations to speak and accepted 96, which were obviously selected to give him the widest possible national exposure. By year's end, he had given more than 210 speeches and had shown up, in fair weather and foul, in the two Dakotas, Oregon, West Virginia, Wyoming, Montana, New York, Wisconsin, Connecticut, New Jersey, California, Michigan, Arkansas and of course Massachusetts. He did not neglect to appear in the Senate; he simply dashed in and out of Washington when necessary.

The variety of Kennedy's audiences was astonishing: he addressed, among other groups, the National Conference of Christians and Jews, the Overseas Press Club, college commencements and symposia, the American Jewish Committee, the Friendly Sons of St. Patrick and the American Gastroenterological Association. It is easy to understand why he was invited to address other Irish Americans; it is difficult to determine why he was asked to address doctors specializing in digestive problems.

The combination of John Kennedy's peripatetic life, his hectic schedule and his enormous political ambition provides much of the explanation for the deepening, inexorable gulf separating him from his wife during those years. "The senator was not often to be seen," said Caroline's nanny, Maud Shaw, with characteristic English understatement.

But for the public, precisely the opposite impression was meticulously staged: photographers from national magazines and news groups were regularly invited to document the blissful happy family at home in Georgetown, and Jackie agreed to appear on the occasional television interview. At least, she said, these engagements allowed her to stay at home, although they made her profoundly uncomfortable. "She was as nervous as a kitten about it," remarked Nanny Shaw about the typical on-camera conversation with Jack and Jackie.

"Nothing disturbs me as much as interviewers and journalists," Jackie told her stepbrother Yusha that year. "That's the trouble with a life in the public eye. I've always hated gossip-column publicity about the private lives of public men. But if you make your living in public office, you're the property of every taxpaying citizen. Your whole life is an open book." Perhaps not the whole life at that time, but enough of it to make Jackie uneasy. She became even more so as the invasion of privacy intensified with time.

AS ELECTION DAY 1958 approached, however, Jackie decided to close, at least temporarily, the almost constant geographic gap between her and her husband: she dutifully accompanied him on a vote-getting swing through Massachusetts—and beyond, for he accepted invitations wherever it could benefit his presidential ambitions. Whatever could be accomplished by smiling and handshaking, Jackie was willing to do.

At this point something was forever changing in the style of American campaigns, and it had to do with the Kennedys. This was never planned, but it is true that their manner more and more resembled that of the British royal family. They knew how to convey, in dress and manner, something of the appearance of ordinariness while maintaining a wary distance, thereby creating an aura of something mysterious, magical and otherworldly. Like royals, they met with ordinary people but did not draw too close to them.

Much of this had to do with their personalities. They knew how to make themselves agreeable to people, and they smiled, nodded and waved amiably. But both had been denied the primal experience of any demonstrative parental devotion; both had been sent away to school. Jack was not a naturally warm or empathetic man; Jackie did not make emotional demands. They were handsome in the way no other political couple was, but there was something almost statuesque about them. The point at which their personalities were slightly elusive, their manner evasive, was the point at which they fascinated a public increasingly eager to touch, to address, to know.

In this regard, it may not be going too far to say—just as the brief Kennedy era was dawning—that Americans were perhaps hankering, in some deep, disarticulate way, for the royals they booted out over two hundred years ago. Celebrity was the ultimate aphrodisiac, fame almost an erotic four-letter word. Closer to our own time, it is interesting to watch the mad scramble of supposedly democratic, antiroyalist Americans to welcome, to interview and to associate with the divorced Duchess of York (once a title held by the mother of Queen Elizabeth II), the former wife of Prince Andrew. Nor may it be irrelevant to point out that Americans like to designate a great female movie star a "queen." Clark Gable was "the king;" John Wayne, "the Duke;" there were also "Duke" Ellington and "Count" Basie. Later there were Queen Latifah and pop figures who put on and took off such titles as "Prince."

Jack and Jackie, in other words, adopted precisely the style of the modern British monarchy. As the constitutional historian Walter Bagehot observed in the nineteenth century, it was crucial for the royal family not to let too much light stream upon the magic, not to risk dispelling the charm. "The idea of a family on the throne is a good idea," Bagehot wrote in the time of Queen Victoria—for the obvious reason that the humblest subject can identify with a family. One might add, more than a century later, that even a fractured, dysfunctional royal family is not entirely irrelevant, for many families are fractured and dysfunctional.

JACK COULD NOT ignore his wife's growing importance, for as O'Donnell added, "When Jackie was traveling with us, the size of the crowd at every stop was twice as big as it would have been if Jack was alone." Without being coached, she knew instinctively that to help her husband's cause with ordinary folks—and hence to solidify her own value to him—she must not appear too rich. Like a postrevolutionary, nineteenth-century Frenchwoman, she maintained her naturally elegant sophistication while appearing in a simple wardrobe with little jewelry and makeup. Here, indeed, was Madame de Récamier, wondrously brought back to life in the twentieth century, wearing a Chanel suit.

According to O'Donnell, Jackie was "always cheerful and obliging, never complaining, and to me a very refreshing change from the usual campaigning candidate's wife because she did not bother to put on a phony show of enthusiasm about everything she saw and every local politician she met. The crowd sensed that and it impressed them."

That could have been a perfect description of England's twentieth-century royal consorts—Queen Alexandra, wife of King Edward VII; Queen Mary, wife of George V; Queen Elizabeth, wife of George VI. In all these cases, the crowds sensed just enough that was human, but not so much that they lost interest or respect. And if Jackie felt she were being pushed too far, she could suddenly retreat. Newspaper and magazine executive Ben Bradlee recalled that as Jack so often rushed to meet the crowd, Jackie could equally often stand frozen, "staring resolutely straight ahead, daring anyone to make conversation with her."

Like her husband and his advisers, the people could neither predict nor entirely understand everything about her, but as Arthur Schlesinger observed after his introduction to Jackie, "underneath a veil of lovely inconsequence, she concealed tremendous awareness, an all-seeing eye and a ruthless judgment."

The economist John Kenneth Galbraith, one of Kennedy's campaign advisers and later his ambassador to India, saw Jackie's influence at close range and agreed with Schlesinger's assessment of her extraordinarily keen judgment. "It was assumed," Galbraith observed, "that she was not politically involved. . . . There could have been no greater error: Jacqueline Kennedy was *deeply* involved, [but] she had chosen her own role carefully."

To illustrate, he recalled that during campaigns, Jack traveled with a briefcase full of speeches, political notes and biographical material on politicians he had to meet. Jackie's reading matter could not have been more different: "She had the *Mémoires du Duc de Saint-Simon* in French. She would take no part in the day's political persuasion, [but] she had a deeper purpose: it was she, not the more trusting J.F.K., who would observe, hear and render judgment on the politicians they would encounter." And for Galbraith, Schlesinger and others, this was an important element of Jackie's influence on her husband. She came to know and observe those on whom Jack had to rely, and she was able to distinguish between those who were working for him and those who labored for themselves. She was particularly adept in recognizing the frauds and phonies. "Her wise and astringent analysis," according to Galbraith, "was especially important to John F. Kennedy . . . [and] Jackie's view of people was essential. She made no conscious decision to analyze them; she simply took it for granted that it was her job." Her judgment was invaluable, as even her husband admitted: "She breathes all the political gasses that flow around us," Jack said in 1959, "but she never seems to inhale them."

IN OTHER WAYS, Jackie brilliantly accommodated herself to her audience. On their fifth wedding anniversary, in September, she and Jack were in Omaha, where Jackie scored points by asking keen questions about Nebraska's pioneer history. She spoke French at a Cajun festival in Louisiana, Italian to immigrants in Boston, Spanish to Puerto Ricans in New York. "You couldn't tell the Italian Americans of the North End [of Boston] that the Kennedys were Irish," said one New England politician. "No, the Kennedys were Italian because Jackie spoke the language so well." In such situations, people rushed to kiss her, and old women chatted away with her in their dialects as if they were welcoming one of their own. In such situations, of course, Jackie garnered her husband much-needed votes. On November 4, 1958, Jack was reelected to the Senate by 73.2 percent of the voters.

But as her mother-in-law coolly observed, "she was not a natural-born campaigner. We knew she had plenty of spunk and courage, but we also knew that she was a rather shy person who found a lot of public attention uncomfortable." And not only the public attention: even after five years, Jackie and Rose Kennedy were not entirely at ease in each other's company; only several years later did shared grief draw them together in a sympathy that would never thereafter be broken.

THE WHIRLWIND CONTINUED in 1959, when Jack swept through fourteen states; as for Jackie, she insisted on extended withdrawals from the travel, if only to spend more time with Caroline. She also urged Jack, in the interest of his unannounced but obvious campaign for the White House, to improve his wardrobe. That spring, he managed a few weeks at home, and he let his wife guide him to a new and improved selection of tailored suits. He did, however, stick to his own taste in reading: political tracts, of course, but also espionage novels. Jackie that year was reading Kerouac and Proust. From this period of time to early 1961, her eclectic book purchases included at least eight titles on the history of French design; books by Churchill, Colette, Cocteau, Lampedusa and others; the *Memoirs* of Casanova; and more than two dozen children's books. She also subscribed to *The Spectator,* the London *Times Literary Supplement, Connaisance des Arts, Réalités* and *Vogue Paris.*

But Jack's sojourns in Georgetown always seemed too brief, almost like intervals, and friends, passersby and the press often caught sight of the lanky senator dashing, like Dagwood Bumstead, from his front door or office to the airport. His staff was always on high, nervous alert when Jack took over the driving from his chauffeur and raced through the capital, defying traffic lights, honking motorists and whistle-blowing policemen. From July 1959 onward, he was rushing to catch his own plane. After forming the Ken-Air Corporation, Joe bought a Convair he then leased to Jack for $1.75 a mile. The plane was christened the *Caroline,* and Jack logged 110,000 miles aboard it over the next fourteen months.

"He was fighting hard, and running, just running," said Jackie about this time. Sometimes, to catch up with him, she had to attend a political luncheon—precisely the sort of event she loathed. Seated six places away from Jack, she looked over at him, then turned to the man on her right: "This is the closest I've come to lunching with my husband in four months!"

But Jackie did not always run with him, sometimes to Jack's disappointment. "Jackie is superb in her personal life," he told a friend one day, in her presence, "but do you think she'll ever amount to anything in her political life?" His wife at once turned to the friend and asked calmly, "Jack is superb in his political life, but do you think he'll ever amount to anything in his personal life?" As Charles Bartlett then said, "She loosens Jack up, deflates him when he gets too serious or pompous. But hers is a wry, offbeat humor, not the rough razzing of the Kennedys."

Jackie was not, after all, always as shy as people gauged. When a member of the Democratic National Committee asked her where she thought the 1960 convention should be held, Jackie, who was watching her husband dash off for yet another speaking engagement, replied at once, "Acapulco." As for his anticipated announcement of a run for the presidency, Jackie was frank: "It's not the right time of life for us," she told a reporter wistfully, drawing her daughter close to her. "We should be enjoying our children, traveling, having fun."

IN MARCH 1959, Jackie's sister was married a second time, in a Virginia courthouse. The ceremony was quiet and unattended by the press, but the bride and groom were not shy about their identities. This time Lee's favor had fallen on a London businessman named Stanislas Radziwill, who was more than twenty years her senior and twice divorced. His dark coloring, mustache and somewhat stately manner reminded Jackie of their father.

Radziwill's family had for three hundred years been using a princely title once bestowed upon them by the Holy Roman Emperor. The groom's father had been Polish secretary of state before World War II, was interned in a concentration camp, and eventually died penniless. His son Stanislas (always called "Stash") escaped the rape of Poland, fled to Switzerland and eventually settled in London, where he entered the real estate business. By the time he met Lee, he had become so successful that he owned a London mansion, a country house and a large Fifth Avenue apartment. Although British law required him to renounce his title when he swore loyalty to the crown, Radziwill continued to style himself "Prince."

This was obviously immensely appealing to Lee, who—no matter that the title no longer existed—at once chose to be called the Princess Radziwill, as she was so designated in *The New York Times* on March 19. Reporters were also hilariously and incorrectly informed that "the prince is a descendant of kings of Poland." But the prince, however self-styled, was just folks, it seemed: five months after the Virginia wedding, Lee gave birth, at full term, to a baby boy. A noble title was not among the gifts offered to the infant.

That August, Jack and Jackie joined Joe Kennedy on the Riviera— not only for a holiday, but for a more productive meeting with Winston Churchill than in 1955. The topic addressed was Jack's Catholicism as a stumbling block to election, and the discussion was held aboard Aristotle Onassis's fabulous yacht, the *Christina*. Of this trip, Jackie remembered only Ari's generosity and casual courtliness. He spun colorful tales of Greek mythology and the Greek Isles, and he invited the Kennedys for a cruise on the *Christina* at their convenience.

At Christmas, they were at Hyannisport, where Jack drafted his speech announcing his candidacy for the Democratic presidential nomination, which he delivered in Washington on January 2, 1960. "If Jack didn't run for the presidency," Jackie said with a hint of resignation, "he'd be like a tiger in a cage." That danger averted, they took Caroline and Nanny Shaw and stole away for a holiday at the Half Moon Hotel in Montego Bay, Jamaica.

Although she shared her husband's idealism and supported his ambitions, Jackie also knew that their lives were taking a critical and perhaps perilous turn. On January 11, she took a sheet of hotel stationery and quickly drafted a temporary will, which she mailed to Evelyn Lincoln, Jack's secretary. "If we don't arrive back from Jamaica, will you please send what's below to Jack's lawyer. Otherwise, tear it up!" Mrs. Lincoln was helpful but disobedient, and almost forty years later the letter turned up for auction:

My Last Will and Testament

I, Jacqueline Bouvier Kennedy, wish to make provision for my daughter Caroline—that in the event of her parents' death she should go to live with her father's youngest brother Edward M. Kennedy and his wife Joan—to be raised as one of their own children. She should spend as much time as possible with my sister Caroline Bouvier Radziwill, vacation & summer holidays—with her husband Stanislas Radziwill & their son Antoni—as I wish her to be as close to them as to her father's family. Everything I have should be left to her—money, furniture, jewelry, etc.

BY THE TIME Jack began his arduous race for the nomination and then for the presidency, it was clear that Joe Kennedy—who eventually spent almost $30 million to realize his ultimate ambition—saw that Jackie was an invaluable asset in the quest. Her dignity, beauty, style and intelligence could be enlisted in an entirely fresh approach to politics and in the presentation of a political family. Jack, too, appreciated everything his wife brought to him and his campaign: she ought, he said, to appear all over the country, but "subliminally, in one of those quick flash TV spots."

Jackie had inherited her mother's sense of fashionable propriety and her father's awareness of the value of appearances—precisely the qualities, it should be noted, that Rose and Joe Kennedy prized, too. But she was not and never would be a social or political climber, nor would she create a false self to serve anyone's ambition, least of all her own, which was modest in any case. She wanted to make, first of all, what her own parents could not: a good marriage, with all its complex compromises, and a good home for the children she and her husband wanted. These she did not see as subservient or humiliating.

The role of campaigner's wife and then First Lady were bestowed on her, not actively sought. But when a responsibility was inevitable, she saw it, as did her heroines from history, as her destiny. She rose—some would say sublimely—to what the occasion required. Her favorite Corneille heroines, in neoclassical French drama, had taught

Jackie that duty itself was her glory. With them, she could have spoken of *ma gloire* not to dramatize or exalt herself, but rather to discern her calling, her place in history, and then to find the courage to meet it.

In this regard, Jackie was not at all passive. She refused to believe—in the fashionably bogus humility that began to characterize so much in American life—that she was unimportant or that her life was negligible, that she could do little, that she bore no responsibility. Her attitude and actions counted, she believed; her inner stance determined what contributions she could make—not only to the lives of those she loved but also to a larger world. This was indeed something of a religious conviction, although she never expressed it in the traditional language of religion.

As 1960 began, then, Jackie not only wrote a will about tangible goods, she was developing a volition about the intangible. Now she would discover how best to live out a destiny that she saw, without apology or self-aggrandizement, as a vocation. She took up, to the mute astonishment of her husband's buddies and counselors, the writings of the American Protestant theologian and ethicist Reinhold Niebuhr. He had been writing for years, in books such as *Moral Man and Immoral Society* and *Christianity and Power Politics,* about the profoundest kind of faith. This would not, according to Niebuhr, be simply a call to a moral life: it would work to create a system of justice that would save society from its own selfishness. Unassailably honest in his radical concern for social ethics, he refused to separate love from the most active expressions of human solidarity. His work, not incidentally, was at the same time having a profound effect on the Christian activism of the Reverend Dr. Martin Luther King Jr.

What did Jack think of his wife's recondite interests? "I never know what she's going to do," he replied, but with genuine wonder rather than disapproval. He liked her because she was different, unpredictable, never dull—and most of all because she wanted to please him and his family. One of the reasons she did so had to do with one of Jack's most attractive qualities: his complete lack of pomposity and his willingness to learn. Whatever recognizable human failings were his, an exaggerated ego and an overestimation of his intellectual capacity were not among them; indeed, one of Jackie's decade-long goals was to encourage her husband to take himself just a bit more seriously.

Part of her technique was to subordinate her essential distaste for politics to her husband's needs, which also, she felt, gave her the opportunity to make her own mark. For the first half of 1960, she accompanied him on much of his campaign, and her impact was far from negligible at events from whistle-stops to long dinners in a dozen states. Kenneth O'Donnell and Dave Powers, with Kennedy at every public moment, for years after told stories about Jackie's work that January and February, climbing out of cars in snow and wind to meet people on one side of a street while her husband worked the other. "Jackie's drawing more people than I am, as usual," Kennedy frequently muttered that year.

Prior to the Wisconsin primary, for example, she filled in for Jack when he had to rush back to Washington for a Senate vote. In small towns from La Crosse to Stevens Point, from Marshfield to Neillsville, she spoke of her husband's goals for America, and while her remarks were mostly cast in general terms, she uttered them with such conviction that Kennedy pollsters could see the numbers rise almost by the minute.

"You shake hundreds of hands in the afternoon and hundreds more at night," she said later.

> You get so tired you catch yourself laughing and crying at the same time. But you pace yourself, and you get through it. You just look at it as something you have to do. You knew it would come, and you knew it was worth it. The places blur after a while, they really do. I remember people, not faces, in a receiving line. The thing you get from these people is a sense of shyness and anxiety and shining expectancy. These women who come up to me at a meeting—they're as shy as I am. Sometimes, we just stand there smiling at each other and don't say anything.

In Kenosha, she went to a busy supermarket and heard the announcement of bargains over the loudspeakers. A moment later she found the manager, bedazzled him with her smile and took over the microphone: "Just keep on with your shopping," she said, "while I tell you about my husband, John F. Kennedy. He served his country during the war and has done the same thing for fourteen years in Congress. He cares deeply about the welfare of our country, so please vote for him." The roll of shopping carts seemed to cease throughout the store and, according to a member of the press corps not remarkably sympathetic to the Kennedys, "while she was talking, you could have heard a pin drop."

Most of all, however, people everywhere liked her lack of guile and pretense: she resolutely refused to address topics she knew nothing about, nor would she disparage opposing candidates like Hubert Humphrey. When she visited schools, she told reporters that the youngest boys and girls there made her feel homesick for her daughter. *The New York Times* chronicled her visit under the headline KENNEDY'S WIFE CHARMS VOTERS.

What she most insistently did not like, however, were political cocktail parties or mere fund-raisers. "She didn't want any part of it," recalled Elizabeth Gatov, former U.S. Treasurer and a Democratic leader from California. "She made an enormously favorable impression, [but] she didn't want to be present when political matters were being discussed."

Jack returned from Washington in time to introduce himself and his wife in a Polish American community, where Jackie surprised everyone by saying a few words in elementary Polish. Then, in Madison, a newsman gave him trouble, during a private interview in their hotel suite, about Kennedy's religion. Getting nowhere and frustrated with the man's sarcasm, Kennedy snarled, "Well, write what you want, you vicious anti-Catholic son of a bitch"—to which the newsman replied, "Yeah? Well, up your ass!"

With that, Jackie stood up, put aside the book she was reading— the second volume of General de Gaulle's memoirs—and at once smiled and extended her hand: "Good-bye, Mr. McMillan. It certainly was nice to see you again."

As it turned out, Mr. McMillan's published account of his meeting with Kennedy was largely flattering. As for the national debate about a potential conflict between Jack's loyalty to his Roman Catholicism and to his possible oath of office, Jackie was forthright: "I think it's so unfair of people to be against Jack because he's a Catholic. He's such a *poor* Catholic. Now, if it were *Bobby,* I could understand it!"

For three weeks that April and May, Jackie toured West Virginia with Jack. "It's the only way I can see him," she told an interviewer. She went into the poorest sections of the state, and here for the first time she came up against the kind of deprivation she had thus far in her life only read about. To everyone's surprise, she prolonged her visits in miners' shacks, talked with their wives, and on one cold, damp day asked her driver, Ed King, to stop the car near some railroad tracks. There she saw a group of forlorn, striking railroad workers and spent an hour discussing their grievances. "I just can't believe it," said Jack. "I am so proud of Jackie." In a note to his staff he wrote, "We need to promote her more."

As for Jackie: "In all the places we campaigned," she wrote later to a friend, "those are the people who touched me most." The readings from Niebuhr, henceforth no less an influence than her conversations with Berenson and her love for France, were bearing fruit. At her request, Jackie was seated with Niebuhr at a Liberal Party dinner in New York that season. Expecting to be supremely unimpressed with a woman he had thought offered glamour and little else, Niebuhr virtually staggered from dinner: "She's read every book I ever wrote!" he announced to anyone who would listen.

The opposition, of course, soon retaliated. When she appeared for the first of many times on the fashion critics' list of Ten Best-Dressed Women that year, there were reports about the amount of money she spent on clothes, as if anyone had the remotest idea of what that figure might be. Was it really $30,000 that year? "I couldn't spend that much unless I wore sable underwear," she told a reporter from the *Times.* When that remark appeared on page one, Jack was adamant: "That's the last thing Jackie's going to say in this campaign!"

Some also tried to attack her privileged background and patrician tastes, but as usual she used humor to disarm the enemy. "When you are First Lady," a reporter said, "you won't be able to jump into your car and rush out to go fox-hunting."

"You couldn't be more wrong. That is one thing I won't ever give up."

"But you'll have to make some concessions to the role, won't you?"

"Oh, I will. I'll wear hats." Almost immediately newspapers and magazines reported that milliners were beating a path to Mrs. Kennedy's doors.

FOR A WHILE, however, the press was held at slightly more than arm's length. In early spring, Jack and Jackie learned that she was pregnant, and by June, she all but withdrew from public life. While he continued to campaign, she retreated to their house in Hyannisport, safely secluded now behind a stockade fence. There she read Henry Adams's novel *Democracy*. First published in 1880 and perhaps the first American novel about political corruption, the book tells the story of the young widow Madeleine Lee, who comes to Washington to learn about the government. "What she wanted was POWER," wrote the author, subordinating style to emphasis. Jackie showed to a few Kennedys a passage she had marked:

> The old is going: the new is coming. Wealth, office, power are at auction. Who bids highest? Who hates with most venom? Who intrigues with most skill? Who has done the dirtiest, the meanest, the darkest, and the most political work? He shall have his rewards.

To which Jackie added in the margin: "What? Nothing about the press?"

On the morning of July 14, Jackie awoke on Cape Cod to hear the news that late the previous night in Los Angeles, Jack had won the Democratic nomination. Only ten days before, because of her absence from the convention, the official news of her pregnancy had been announced.

Within days, Jackie called a school chum—Letitia Baldrige, who had been three years ahead of her at Vassar and whose parents were friends of the Auchinclosses. Tish Baldrige, as she was called, at once joined the Kennedy bandwagon as a public relations consultant; after the November election, she became Jackie's social secretary, a position she held with distinction until 1963. But in July, when Jack and Jackie formally engaged her, some eyebrows were raised, for Baldrige was an ardent Republican who had worked for ambassadors in Paris and Rome and was then public relations director for Tiffany's.

When he returned to the Cape, Jackie welcomed her husband with a gay, comical painting of herself, Caroline, Nanny Shaw and a brass band on a dock, cheering the arrival, by canoe, of the victorious Jack, like Washington crossing the Delaware. Crowds line the shore, gun-boats set off celebratory fireworks and a small plane circles above the tiny figures of Joe and Rose (who were on holiday in Europe), with the trailing legend "You've done it again, Johnny—Call us at Cap d'Antibes."

Turning to more serious support, she won immediate approval from the Democratic National Committee to write a series of syndicated columns called "Campaign Wife," which addressed, even from her confinement, issues of special interest to women. These half-dozen brief essays, which were published between September 29 and November 1, were like Eleanor Roosevelt's earlier "My Day" columns, and they did more than praise her husband. She addressed hard topics of educational funding, medical care for the aged and voter registration, and she did the writing herself.

On September 29, 1960, she made her international television debut with Jack on *Person to Person,* filmed and later beamed around the world by CBS. "What should be the major role of the First Lady?" asked Charles Collingwood.

"To take care of the President," replied Jackie, as if this were a silly question, "so he can best serve the people. And not to fail her family, her husband and her children." In 1960, that was not considered a weak or old-fashioned reply.

In her seventh month of pregnancy, Jackie bravely accompanied Jack to a Manhattan ticker-tape parade on October 19. More than a million New Yorkers lined an astonishing thirty-mile route, from lower Broadway north to Yonkers, in Westchester County, and back again. Their car was frequently halted when people broke through police barriers eager to meet them, to shake their hands, get autographs, touch them. The crush was so overwhelming that at times, Jackie said that evening, "it felt like the sides of the car were bending." Concerned for the safety of her unborn baby, she left the motorcade after lunch.

That same day, the Reverend Dr. Martin Luther King Jr. was

arrested for participating in a peaceful civil rights demonstration at a luncheon counter in an Atlanta department store. The charges were dropped against him and the other protesters, but six days later, King was sentenced to four months of hard labor on a Georgia prison farm. The matter was at once trumpeted in the news, especially because President Eisenhower did nothing, nor had he a word to say.

Harris Wofford, a lawyer with a special commitment to civil rights, had been counsel to Reverend Theodore Hesburgh's Commission on Civil Rights in 1958 and 1959, the first such commission. Hesburgh, president of Notre Dame University, then brought Wofford to that school to teach law, but in April 1960, Wofford joined the Kennedy team as speechwriter and point man on Asia, Africa and Latin America.

When it became clear that the campaign was having trouble winning over black voters, Jack asked Wofford to head the special civil rights section of the campaign. It is important to detail these developments precisely to see the difference of perspective between Jack and Jackie on such an important matter. Wofford, it should be noted, was later the associate director of the Peace Corps, a U.S. senator from Pennsylvania, an author and one of the most committed American statesmen in the areas of human rights and national service.

Wofford prepared a public statement for Kennedy that criticized King's arrest and called for his release. Then, perhaps to no one's surprise, politics intervened. Kennedy was informed that if he made this statement, he would lose the support of three southern governors, one of whom said that if Kennedy supported Khrushchev or King, his state would be thrown over to Nixon. That delayed the Kennedy statement, and when nothing happened after a few days, Wofford received a call from Mrs. King, who was terrified and six months pregnant. Through a series of maneuvers, Kennedy was convinced at least to call her while an attempt was made to resolve the situation.

At the same time, there was another force of moral suasion acting on Jack. As it happened, Jackie had been reading King's book *Stride Toward Freedom* (which had been cowritten by none other than Harris Wofford), and she, too, weighed in on the case. Jack must work to release King, she insisted: King's book had acknowledged explicitly the spiritual mentorship of Reinhold Niebuhr, who had just thrown his support to Kennedy—thanks to Jackie. Niebuhr, Jackie pointed out to her husband while he temporized, had enabled King to recognize, in King's words, "the complexity of man's social involvement . . . the glaring reality of collective evil [and] . . . the illusions of a superficial optimism concerning human nature and the dangers of false idealism."

Her philosophical and social positions, and Wofford's urgent moral and political pressure, were immediately taken into Kennedy's decision-making process. He telephoned Mrs. King with a message of sympathetic support, and on October 26, Robert Kennedy appealed to the sentencing judge for King's release. He was freed on bail, and the favorable reaction of the black community to Kennedy's intervention could be measured a few days later, when they cast their votes for him in huge numbers.

Years later, Harris Wofford was not at all surprised to learn that there is evidence of Jackie's private moral intervention in the matter. "I was and am a great fan of John F. Kennedy," he said,

> but I don't think he had any kind of passionate moral vision about politics. He believed in applying reason to solve public problems in good spirit, with excellence and skill and with a sense of humor. Unlike Bobby, who was passionate when he was pursuing Hoffa and passionate when he was pursuing the Communists and even more passionate when he was convinced about black rights, the poor and the Vietnam War, John Kennedy was cool. I would say that yes, Jacqueline would certainly have been the source of moral warmth on these issues, because John was not. He had a comic approach to politics and the human condition. He was bored with earnestness and piety. I'm sure he was rationally and morally offended when he learned about the mistreatment of blacks, but it was a detached reason that generated him to action.

Just as she did with her commitment to nuclear disarmament, Jackie brought academic learning—in this case, familiarity with the work and principles of both Niebuhr and King—to bear on issues of critical human concern. To say that she was disinterested in politics is sheer nonsense: politics was for her more than personal; it was the arena in which the profoundest values could be worked out for the public good.

ON TUESDAY, NOVEMBER 8, 1960, Jackie, Jack and 68 million other Americans voted. Ignoring candidates for all other offices, Jackie cast only one vote: "It is a rare thing to be able to vote for one's husband as president of the United States," she said, "and I didn't want to dilute it by voting for anyone else."

They spent the day and evening at Hyannisport, where there was a general mood of quiet anxiety: a Kennedy victory was by no means certain. Nor was the issue resolved by three o'clock the next morning, when Jackie finally went to bed. An hour later, Kennedy himself fell asleep. At noon on Wednesday, the first announcements were made, and the numbers began to take on some clarity. John F. Kennedy was indeed elected the thirty-fifth president of the United States—but by the slimmest margin in history. Although he won 303 of 537 electoral ballots, he received only 49.72 percent of the votes; Richard Nixon had 49.55 percent. Kennedy had won by a plurality of only 114,673 votes and fewer than half the states had thrown their support to him.

Jackie, now close to giving birth, was uncomfortable with the clattery celebrating of the Kennedy clan, as Jack's parents, brothers, sisters and in-laws bustled about. As usual, their somewhat aggressive communality clashed with her quiet introspection and need for frequent retreat from the madding crowd. "She seemed dazed as people rushed up to congratulate her," recalled photographer Jacques Lowe, who had documented the campaign and was on the scene. Then, as so often since childhood, Jackie sought peace and quiet by taking a solitary walk along the shore, where she could assess what had happened and consider what lay in the future. Jack found her, walking slowly, her head bowed, far down the beach.

The press naturally blared every element of newness about John Kennedy's victory. He was the youngest man ever elected to the White House, the first Catholic, the first who had been a millionaire since his teens. At thirty-one, Jackie would not be the youngest wife of an American president—that distinction went to the wives of John Tyler and Grover Cleveland—but she would be the first one born in the twentieth century.

She had been a photographer, she had grown up with the movies and fan magazines, and she had traveled with her husband—just when the word *paparazzi* was invented and their potency was first being felt. (The word itself comes into English via Italian. In 1959, the Italian filmmaker Federico Fellini gave the name Paparazzo to the character of a greedy photojournalist in his film *La Dolce Vita; paparazzi,* of course, is the plural from. Fellini had taken his cue from his cowriter, Ennio Flaiano, who had come across the name of a character, Coriolano Paparazzo, in a nineteenth-century novel by George Gissing titled *By the Ionian Sea.*)

The world and those who documented it, Jackie realized, were changing so swiftly that no one could take its full measure. Jackie knew about polls and popularity contests, about the press and reporters, about the inexorable erosion of privacy, and she distrusted the waves of adulation that so often encircled her for the wrong reasons—her beauty, for example, or her glamour or even her apparent passivity. Just as she never sought the roles destiny apportioned her, neither did she ever court the celebration of those roles.

Most of all, she told a reporter two days after the election, she was thinking about the problem of raising her children amid the relentless glare of publicity. "I have thought about that more than anything," she told Nan Robertson of *The New York Times.* "I don't want my young children brought up by nurses and Secret Service men." That, it would turn out, was essentially a veiled warning to potential intruders. "I feel," she added a few days later, "as though I have just turned into a piece of public property. It's really frightening to lose your anonymity at thirty-one." She would never regain it.

ON FRIDAY, NOVEMBER 11, three days after Election Day, Jack, Jackie and Caroline left Cape Cod. The president-elect, en route to the Kennedy compound in Palm Beach to confer with his father and a team of strategists, stopped in Washington, where Jackie and Caroline proceeded to the house in Georgetown. Her baby was due in early December, travel was awkward (not to say painful), and probably thinking of the loss of Arabella, she became naturally anxious and wanted to spend the remaining time near her doctor. It was, perhaps, all the more astonishing that her husband did not arrange to have his meetings in Washington—not necessarily at home, but perhaps by taking over a floor at a nearby hotel. The Auchinclosses, who had converted to the Democratic Party for this one campaign and election, even offered Hammersmith Farm for this purpose, and among other benefits, it was easy to maintain security there. But no, Palm Beach it was, for whatever other reasons one may never know. From there, Jack flew to Texas for a meeting with the vice president–elect, Lyndon Johnson.

In the meantime, Jackie decided not to wait idly for her baby. She summoned Letitia Baldrige, and they conferred with members of the White House staff about the standard protocols for receptions and dinners. In light of those discussions, Jackie came up with some new ideas about entertaining at the White House. "Mrs. Kennedy will have so much news to impart," Baldrige announced exuberantly during a brief press conference. "The entire entertainment program will be revamped. At first, it will be experimental." They really could not tell, she added, what might appeal: they intended to try things out and see what worked. A larger number of guests could be accommodated, for example, at an informal reception.

To some, that sounded like a royal garden party: many people would be unable even to get near the hosts. But to most, it seemed as if fresh winds were beginning to stir in Washington "after eight years of Eisenhower tranquility," as Helen Thomas, White House correspondent for United Press International, put it, "after eight years of feeling older than we should have."

On Wednesday the twenty-third, Jack returned to Georgetown for Thanksgiving and an early celebration of Caroline's third birthday, which was the following Sunday. At 8:20 on Thursday evening, Jack rose from the dinner table, kissed Jackie and Caroline and again departed for Florida aboard the *Caroline*. Their dinner guest, the artist Bill Walton, with whom Jackie was discussing the issue of art in the White House, left a few moments afterward.

Two hours later, Jackie was reading in bed, and her daughter, a maid and Maud Shaw were asleep.

Suddenly she felt sharp pains. A few minutes later, according to the hospital report, Jackie began "hemorrhaging a little," and the pains worsened. She called out to Nanny Shaw, who at once rang the obstetrician, Dr. John Walsh. He said that he would arrive soon but that Shaw must call an ambulance at once.

David Kipps, the night dispatcher at the Hospital Ambulance, Oxygen and Equipment Company, took the urgent message and relayed the details to Willard Baucom, the driver on duty: "Emergency call," he said. "Go to 3307 N Street N.W. and pick up a Mrs. Kennedy, going to Georgetown University Hospital."

"*A* Mrs. Kennedy?" repeated Baucom over his two-way radio. "Don't you know who *that* is?"

"At first it didn't register at all," Kipps said the next day. "When it did, I got really excited."

Not as excited as the press.

In what seemed the space of a heartbeat, word went out from the ambulance company and over the wire services. Helen Thomas, exhausted after days of Kennedy-watching, was just settling down for the night when a call came from her office: "Get over to Georgetown Hospital!" Like other key members of the Washington press corps who were receiving similar messages, she bolted from her apartment and hailed a taxi.

Meanwhile, Jack's plane was en route to Florida, but efforts to get through to him were to no avail in the heavy rainstorm battering the Eastern seaboard.

Ambulance driver Baucom muted his siren but flashed the emergency beacon as he sped through the quiet streets of Georgetown. He and medical attendant Walter Myers were admitted by the maid. Moments later, Dr. Walsh arrived. They found Jackie in her second-floor bedroom, pale and a little shaky. She had managed to put on a white sweater and socks and a tweed coat over her nightgown. She tried to smile, but everyone saw the anxiety on her face. "Will I lose my baby?" Jackie asked Walsh, who, acting quickly, assured her that all would be well. They tucked Jackie into the ambulance and headed for the hospital, ten blocks away, where she was prepared for a third cesarean section.

In Palm Beach, Kennedy's press secretary, Pierre Salinger, was the first to step from the plane as it touched down just after midnight. A messenger pulled him aside: there was an urgent call from Washington—from Georgetown University Hospital. Jack spoke briefly with Dr. Walsh, who was about to scrub and dress for the surgery, and then he ordered the crew of the *Caroline* to prepare for the return flight.

But that would require some work on the plane, and therefore a DC-6, usually used by the press, was commandeered.

At 12:22 A.M., the operation began. Shortly afterward, on that early morning of November 25, 1960, Jackie bore a six-pound boy. At 1:14 Jack entered the plane's cockpit, drew on earphones and hunched over the flight engineer. A moment later, Salinger took the plane's public address system and announced the news to the reporters on board. Soon someone had figured out that this was the first baby ever born to a president-elect.

The plane landed in Washington a little after four that morning, and Jack was soon at his wife's bedside. "I'm never there when she needs me," he muttered to Kenny O'Donnell, who would not have been so bold as to express hearty agreement. Leaving the hospital at the day's first light, he encountered a squadron of reporters who asked about the baby's name. "Why, it's John F. Kennedy Jr. I think she decided—it has been decided—yes—it's John F. Kennedy Jr." Western Union's lines were clogged over the next week with more than three thousand telegrams pouring into Washington with congratulations for the family that, it seemed, America was about to embrace more completely than any other First Family—much less a First Family to be.

THE NATIONAL OBSESSION for and adulation of the Kennedys was only beginning—to the point that it was almost a royal anointing. The slightest detail about the family was picked up and exploited as the basis for a major news story. On December 3, the Associated Press declared solemnly that the baby was out of an incubator and had been taken to his mother's hospital room for the first time. "He has been put in a bassinet with a lightbulb underneath for warmth."

By the time he was baptized in the hospital chapel on December 8, the event had been anticipated by three days of stories about what would occur and who would be present in which capacity. Like his birth, the baptism merited front-page coverage in *The New York Times* and hundreds of other newspapers, complete with a three-column photo of the baby and his parents. With reverence for every detail, the *Times* let it be known that the infant had gained almost two ounces in nine days.

Adoration, when offered to humans, encourages strange kinds of imitation. Within twenty-four hours of the Kennedy birth, national newsmen reported that a mother in Massachusetts named her newborn boy John Kennedy McInnis, and one in Dallas named hers John Fitzgerald Endsley. Similarly, a John Kennedy Spann was christened in Louisiana, a John Fitzgerald Saddler in New York, and among the girls, a Jacqueline Bouvier Trotta in Westchester County.

In all this, Jackie rightly foresaw the inception of an alarming and not at all flattering trend, one that would soon rob her of the privacy she so coveted. Her suspicions were confirmed when another patient at the hospital recognized her, shuffled right up and asked, "You're Mrs. Kennedy, aren't you? I recognize you from your pictures!" To which she replied with a sigh, "I know. That's my problem now."

After two weeks of recovery in the hospital, Jackie took her baby to N Street on December 9, the day after the christening. But the return to Georgetown would not be for long. She left John with a nurse and, although still weak and easily tired by any effort, braved subzero temperatures for a two-hour tour of the White House. Her hostess was Mrs. Eisenhower, who up until Election Day had fully expected to welcome her old friend Pat Nixon as the new First Lady. Told in advance that Jackie would require a wheelchair for her walk through the long corridors, Mamie replied that if Mrs. Kennedy wanted one, she could ask for one—and had the chair stashed in a closet. "I didn't know if there was one or not," Jackie said later, "but I was too embarrassed to ask."

Jackie's subsequent exhaustion only aggravated her negative reaction to the mansion itself: "Oh, God," she told her secretary wearily after her departure, "it's the worst place in the world! So cold and dreary—a dungeon like the Lubyanka [the Russian prison]. It looks like it's been furnished by discount stores. I've never seen anything like it. I can't bear the thought of moving in! I hate it, hate it, hate it!" And to Tish Baldrige she confided that the place looked like "a hotel that had been decorated by a wholesale furniture store during a January clearance." Mamie Eisenhower, who shortly afterward minced no words, must have noticed Jackie's instant reaction: "Well, she's awfully young! And she's planning to redo every room in this house! There certainly are going to be some changes made around here!" Well might she have guessed.

As for Jackie, her warmest words about former First Ladies were reserved for, of all people, Bess Truman. "She brought a daughter to the White House at a most difficult age, and managed to keep her from being spoiled, so that she has made a happy marriage with a lovely child of her own. Mrs. Truman kept her family together in spite of White House demands, and that is the hardest thing to do."

Two hours after posing at the White House with Mamie, Jackie returned to Georgetown, collected her baby and, with her husband and his transition team, boarded the *Caroline* and headed for Palm Beach. Kenneth O'Donnell recalled that Jack sat with his family, chatting with his staff about the implementation of his so-called New Frontier and blowing cigar smoke around the baby until Jackie objected and pushed the president-elect and his men to the forward cabin.

The Kennedy villa provided warmth, seclusion and the chance for some rest—but not much serenity. "It was so crowded," Jackie said, "that I could be in the bathroom, in the tub, and then find that Pierre Salinger was holding a press conference in my bedroom!" In search of tranquility, she moved from one part of the house to another with her notepads, planning for the relocation from a snug house to a vast public mansion, outlining her wardrobe needs for Oleg Cassini, whom she had selected as her personal wardrobe designer, and jotting down ideas for the family's private rooms at the White House. "There are," she told Baldrige in a phone call, "many things that can be done to make [the White House] warmer, more gracious, more distinguished." Even before the inauguration, Jackie had decided just how she would stake her own new frontier. During these weeks, she curled up with dozens of volumes—on White House architecture and on the history of interiors.

But for a moment, it almost seemed as if there would be no inauguration of John F. Kennedy as president. Jackie, not feeling well enough to attend Mass one Sunday that December, bade her husband farewell while he headed for his car to drive to St. Edward's Church. Nearby, a man named Richard Pavlick parked his car, which he had loaded with dynamite and planned to drive into the president's vehicle.

"I believe that the Kennedys bought the Whitehouse [*sic*]," he later wrote on a scrap of paper, "and it was my intention to remove him in the only way available to me."

Seeing Jackie and little Caroline in the doorway, however, Pavlick decided to try again at another time. Alerted by the Massachusetts State Police that the man had been making threats, the Secret Service forestalled his second attempt. Virtually nothing was released to the press about this ominous incident. It was thought negligible, an anomaly, a nonevent. And no one made much of the poor madman. After all, nothing had actually happened. And as one of Kennedy's old friends said, things like this are always, somehow, prevented.

CHAPTER EIGHT

1961

*I*mmediately after Jack's victory was announced, the Kennedys' Georgetown house at 3307 N Street, which Jack had purchased in 1957 for $78,000, was listed for sale, and just as immediately it was sold for $110,000. At the same time, because Jackie wanted a weekend getaway, she and Jack asked their friend Bill Walton to help find a country retreat not too far from the capital. It had to be, they added, a place they might lease for the president's first term and one where Jackie could ride at ease, far from the press. "She guarded her privacy more than any occupant of the White House I ever knew," recalled Alvin Spivak, for many years a White House correspondent for United Press International.

Jackie's growing conviction was that the press had to be avoided at all costs. She accepted their inevitable presence in her husband's life, but she resented even honest reporters in the case of herself and her children—and she seemed, at least to some, to resent, most of all, women reporters. "Jackie referred to the women in the press corps as Harpies," recalled Helen Thomas, also a White House correspondent for United Press International, who had been covering First Ladies since Eleanor Roosevelt. "There was no question that she was brilliant and always ten jumps ahead of us. But Jackie was also very wary—in fact, I don't think she liked those of us in the press."

Helen Thomas was right on the mark. And her colleague Gwen Gibson, White House reporter for the New York *Daily News*, added that while Jackie was "chic and sharp, quotable and stubborn—in other words, good copy—she began, as early as the time of the Inauguration, to carve out an independent life for herself." This Jackie accomplished by insisting that there be a country retreat for herself and the children, where she could look forward to spending astonishingly long weekends—on average, two of every four weekends lasted from Thursday afternoon to Tuesday morning. If she had tasks—the restoration of the White House, for example—the calls, meetings and paperwork could be referred to her rural getaway. "It's true," Gwen Gibson continued. "She was not there to be only a First Lady. She had her own life to live—and some of that had to do with the problems in her marriage, of which we in the press were aware, but about which, of course, we all kept quiet."

Walton went out to see his old friend Gladys Tartière, who owned Glen Ora, a four-hundred-acre estate near Middleburg, Virginia, about an hour from the White House. Jackie, who saw photos while she was in the hospital, liked the French-style mansion, the gardens, lawns, woods and pastures and the expansive acres for riding. She judged the place even more appealing than Merrywood and convinced her husband to apply for the lease. But Mrs. Tartière was not at all enchanted with the idea of the First Family as tenants: she foresaw the Secret Service, the press and vast numbers of visitors roaming all over, and hence all sorts of potential damage to her estate. Already, wherever the Kennedys went, the Secret Service was sure to go, sending messages back and forth about "Lancer" (the president-elect), "Lace" (Jackie), "Lyric" (Caroline) and "Lark" (John): each of the family's code names began with the letter after *k*.

Eventually, after considerable coaxing from Walton and Clark Clifford, one of Kennedy's attorneys and advisers, Mrs. Tartière agreed—but only to a one-year lease. The Kennedys took it sight unseen and furnished. At Glen Ora, Jackie escaped the pressures of Washington; there, she trained Caroline to ride, too, and there she was, as nearby residents said, "just one of the fox hunters."

But she was most emphatically not one of that rarefied social set. Jackie rode, she played with her children, she took long walks with a few friends and neighbors, she shopped in country stores. She always took her meals at the house on those weekends: she saw enough people during the week, she said, and if it seemed antisocial to restrict her life at Glen Ora to the parents of Caroline's playmates, then so be it. At the end of the year, the Kennedys bought thirty-nine acres on an isolated mountain, where they designed and built their own home, named Wexford, after the Irish county of the Kennedy forebears. The president and his family spent only four weekends there prior to his death.

CONTRARY TO THE image given to the press and the public in the first weeks of the New Year—an image of Jackie's robust health, energy and radiant glamour—the truth was different. Oppressed by the details of moving and surrounded by a huge White House staff, an international crew of reporters, various Kennedys rushing in and out, designers and craftsmen offering plans for fabrics and furnishings, Jackie was on the verge of collapse. "PROTECT ME, as I seem so mercilessly exposed and don't know how to cope with it," she wrote plaintively to Oleg Cassini, who was busy night and day designing a new wardrobe. "I read tonight [in a magazine] that I dye my hair because it is mousy gray!" Like almost everything else about her private life, the allegation about her hair was far from true.

Nor did she recover from her surgery quickly. "John was born prematurely because of all the excitement," she said. "He was sick that winter. I was sick. They were painting the quarters we lived in, which was like a big drafty hotel." Hence she summarized the early months of 1961: "The period was not the happy time in my life that it looks like in all the pictures." And as if all that were not enough to concern her, Jackie had to find ways of dealing with the fact of her husband's sexual escapades, which were not much diminished by his new role and responsibilities.

In addition to his long-time affair with Ben Bradlee's sister-in-law, the painter Mary Pinchot Meyer, various White House personnel were the talk of the mansion—two recent college graduates who had worked in the presidential campaign, for example. Priscilla Wear now worked for Evelyn Lincoln, and Jill Cowan was on Pierre Salinger's staff. These two winsome young ladies were known among the gossips as Fiddle and Faddle. In addition, Jackie once introduced a visitor to Pamela

Turnure, formerly the receptionist in Jack's Senate office, as "the woman my husband is supposedly sleeping with." There was also a small company of Hollywood blondes who visited the president in Florida or Los Angeles, or in Washington when Jackie was away; the purported affair with Marilyn Monroe was a matter of only one afternoon in March 1962, at Bing Crosby's home in the California desert.

Throughout all these furtive liaisons, Jackie had to cope with the inevitable feelings of rejection, humiliation and frustration—but she could not let them affect either her own job performance or her husband's loving relationship with their children. Quite unlike her own mother, she never took the slightest step to alienate their affection from their father, nor would she, forever after, do anything but guard their high estimation of him. Privately, she at least needled him, and only rarely did she slip and use in anyone else's presence her nickname for Jack—"Bunny," which referred to his astonishing sexual energy and appetite.

Several decades later, many find it difficult to understand why Jackie simply sustained so much, from her husband's political ambitions in the 1950s to his blatant cavorting with women. The answers are readily found.

For one thing, she had a profound sense of duty—to Jack's vision, which she endorsed, and to her marriage. She would not fail where her mother had, nor would she turn away simply because she was wounded. She would not subject her children to the consequences of a broken home.

In addition, there was a real insecurity in Jackie, who never considered herself particularly beautiful or desirable and was always surprised when others did. This trait, combined with her admiration for Jack's wit, the rank to which he had risen and his evident ease in the corridors of power, made her easily feel subordinated to him. "She must have made reference to her husband no fewer than a dozen times," recalled the novelist and critic Diana Trilling after spending time with Jackie after a White House dinner in 1962; she added that the First Lady confessed "how Jack had been very angry at her, how Jack had told her to stop reading in bed and put out the light." It was as if a dependent, insecure girl sought desperately to please her father and feared that she was terribly inadequate. In this regard, it is interesting to discover that all during her husband's years as senator and president, Jackie always addressed Evelyn Lincoln as "Mrs. Lincoln," both in person and in writing, but she always signed herself "Jackie."

It is not likely that she was the first woman in history to feel that if her husband strayed, it must at least be partly her fault. It was at this time that articles began to appear in American magazines about what a woman ought to do, in and out of the bedroom, to "keep her man."

The candor that began in the early 1960s in such publications as *Good Housekeeping, Woman's Day* and *Cosmopolitan* increased astonishingly over the next decades, to the point that one could count on at least one essay on sexual therapies each month in all of them. But as the 1960s dawned—and as television brought cosmeticized, fabricated glamour into homes, and movies became ever bolder—many people, women perhaps especially, were led to feel that they compared poorly with celebrities. Young mothers, of course, feel unique pressures in this regard, and Jackie was not immune.

Regarding their marital life, the private exchanges between Jackie and Jack are, of course, entirely unknown to historians, and therefore it is impossible to guess what compromises were explicitly arranged, or even if any were ever discussed. What can be known for certain is that, like the women she admired from the past, Jackie braved the situation by learning to take infidelity as an unpleasant but perhaps unavoidable element of the marital equation. Indeed, what else could she do if she wanted to avoid dreadful publicity for her children and perhaps a ruinous life for herself?

More to the point, Jackie knew that her husband's many acts of adultery were not emblematic of new, deep relationships; she knew all too well that they were, on the contrary, passing fancies. She also knew that Jack could not leave her, and this gave her a certain moral supremacy and even a kind of control over him—not a conscious suasion, perhaps, but at least he owed her as a result of the hurt and humiliation they both knew she felt. In turn, Jackie could demand, however plainly, her own independence. And most of all, she knew that Jack really loved and admired her.

In the final analysis, of course, no one can ever really understand the terms of a marriage, nor can one entirely plumb the depths of how people establish certain accommodations between each other. "I have no doubt that they loved each other," said Arthur Schlesinger, who, as the president's special assistant, was certainly in a position to observe the couple. "Jackie was a realist, and she must have accepted certain problems in the marriage. But remember: JFK admired her, adored her and was enormously proud of her. She loved Jack in spite of all his infidelities, and he loved her—in spite of all his infidelities."

Here was a challenge to which she could bring her own independent spirit and make her own unique contributions. And in this regard, Jackie was not merely a passive woman, a relic from preliberation days, who stood for everything later contested by more strident voices. As she told J. B. West, the White House chief usher (general manager or executive major domo), she most emphatically did not wish to be referred to as the First Lady. The title reminded her of a saddle horse, she said. Rather, she wanted to be called Mrs. Kennedy, and everyone on the staff was to be so instructed.

Her demand may well have been a way of taking a stand against the unpleasant reality that her marriage was, at the time, little more than a formality. West put it delicately: he, for one, felt that "Mrs. Kennedy was trying to grope through the maze of differences between [her and her husband]—differences in interests, background and personality." Gwen Gibson summarized the marriage at this time as "a partnership, an arrangement for their mutual benefit. Later they became closer, but that happened so near to the end."

JACQUELINE BOUVIER KENNEDY was a woman committed to many values of an Old World, a world of elegance and refinement, of serious purpose, of wit and intelligence, and of style—style that was both respect for tradition and for oneself. But she was Old World grafted onto the New. The Old World she adored in Europe enriched the fading old world she had known, the vanishing style of the Long Island aristocracy. Her spirit, in this regard, was in marked contrast to that of the Kennedys, for she respected the art of Old Masters whereas they coveted the craft of new power.

Jackie represented the roots of historic American idealism more than any politician who uttered fancy phrases about it. Respectful of history, she was ever poised between past and present. Eager to preserve the past, she was also a woman of fashion and a mother who wanted the best of the new for her children.

In a way, then, her silent acceptance of what others considered intolerable offenses freed her to explore precisely where she could flourish, and to discover to which life she could bring the best of herself. Not wishing to be known as First Lady suggested just how deeply she would carve out her own individual image. "I don't want to go down into coal mines or be a symbol of elegance," she said. "I will never be a committee woman or a club woman, because I'm not a joiner." She had to be herself, not Eleanor Roosevelt. "What do you suppose they want me to be?" she asked wistfully. "I've always been the same person. I always felt I was myself, but with so many reporters watching, listening, how can anyone not seem like someone you're not?"

Thus she brought her interests and abilities to projects that benefited the White House and affected both the style of her husband's administration and the standards of American culture. Through her commitment to the arts, and in her restoration of the executive mansion—an enterprise she supervised during 1961 and 1962—Jackie indeed made dramatic, unprecedented statements. Despite her husband's warnings about not singularizing herself, she decided in some ways— perhaps because he was not the loyal husband—not to play the obedient wife. She struck out on her own, making it possible for subsequent First Ladies to strike out on their own, too.

In this regard, she did, in her way, as much for the life of the nation as did Eleanor Roosevelt, who had gone where her husband could not because of physical disability. Jackie's contributions were not merely about style and appearance: they were about a commitment to excellence, which had less to do with her own taste than with introducing the nation and its leaders to the best the culture had to offer.

The Kennedys could not have accomplished any of this on their own. After Jackie, as historian Garry Wills pointed out, "a President's wife could no more afford to be without her project than a President could afford to be without a wife." Somehow, she managed to add style to democratic ideals. Her extraordinary alchemy fascinated Americans, drew them to her and finally won her their undying loyalty—but her glamour never alienated people.

Most remarkably, Jacqueline Kennedy understood that the White

House represented an important tradition that was beyond politics. Why, she wondered, should it not inspire all visitors—Americans and foreigners alike? Ought it not to make everyone feel proud of the nation's cultural heritage, and not merely be a kind of hotel where heads of state dined and official entertainments were held? "I was warned, begged and practically threatened" not to undertake the restoration, Jackie recalled. But she did. She wanted, as she said, "only the best" for the White House.

Jackie rescued the White House from dreadful neglect. She restored furniture and furnishings from past presidential eras, located paintings and artifacts appropriate for each room, refreshed the private quarters and altered the style of formal and informal entertainment.

"She made the whole country aware that the White House is a legacy, a historic residence that needs to be taken care of," said Clement Conger, a curator of the White House. Her love of antiques, her appreciation of the finest craftsmanship, her refusal to worship at the altar of sheer modernity for its own sake—these were values and lessons, as well as historic details, she had absorbed from her family as early as her days at Lasata.

When the nation tuned in to watch her televised tour of the restored White House, millions heard her discussing, with newsman Charles Collingwood, the background and history of major pieces she and her committee had brought to 1600 Pennsylvania Avenue. Every detail of the project was summarized in a new White House guidebook, which Jackie herself edited and for which she did the photo layout. At last, the White House was a true repository of the nation's history. Among hundreds of items, Thomas Jefferson's inkwell was returned to its rightful place; Van Buren's Empire chairs reappeared, as did Washington's armchair, Mrs. Grant's writing desk and china that had been chosen by Mrs. Hayes, Mrs. Harrison and Mrs. Polk. "The detail and organization was basic to her personality," said Helen Thomas. "Jackie was the most organized planner I ever knew in my life—she was the sort of woman who began planning in July for the coming Christmas. At every moment, she was thinking ahead."

Respectful as she was to the members of her Restoration Committee, she had her own mind. When she hung a still life in a drawing room, the collector and expert Henry F. du Pont entered the room and said to her and Susan Mary Alsop, who was also on the committee, "Ladies, surely you are aware that still lifes are only for dining rooms?"

"Oh, Mr. du Pont," said Jackie in her breathless tone, "it just shows how little we know. Goodness, we are lucky to have you to teach us what to do. The still life will come down immediately." And it did.

But only for the time being. Several months later, du Pont returned for another function, and again Jackie was in the same room with some guests. Du Pont noticed the still life, brazenly returned to its former spot, and at once revised his earlier opinion. "Jackie really does have a remarkably good eye," he admitted to Alsop. "Everything looks splendid."

Margaret Truman, who had once lived there, much admired Jackie's achievements—and a kind of benevolent but subtle wiliness. She also recognized Jackie's brilliance in using the word *restoration* rather than *redecoration,* for the former term suggested disinterested authenticity rendering the project immune to criticism. As Miss Truman noted, there was, of course, "no previous perfect White House in the past which diligence and research could restore. For most of its long career, the place had been an unnerving mixture of the elegant and the shabby. . . . [But] Jackie hurled herself into her task with a passion that swept away obstacles and enlisted enthusiasts everywhere." And this she accomplished by the gentle imposition of French taste on the project—not least by engaging the French decorator Stéphane Boudin, whom she supported unequivocally, despite his arrogance and incivility during the project.

Jackie was also, to the surprise of many, no commandant of a project; rather, she was willing to undertake the physical work, too. James Roe Ketchum, curator of the White House from 1961 to 1963, recalled her dressed in sweater and jeans, helping movers lift heavy mirrors and furniture. But Ketchum was most impressed by the fact that Jackie, originator and guiding force behind the entire project, neither gave herself credit nor put herself in the limelight: she directed the praise to her committee, to donors, to everyone but herself.

To the exterior, she was just as attentive: "The White House lawns are a disgrace," she wrote to the chief usher early on. "Something truly drastic must be done." She used those same last six words the following year, when her intervention saved historic Lafayette Square from demolition. At a time when so many people seemed hot to want to destroy the old, Jackie insisted, with a cool and precise respect for tradition and history, that much should be retained—otherwise, there would never be a history upon which to reflect in the future.

Although she had no mind to install formal French gardens, the new Madame de Récamier was always inspired by Versailles. At the state dinner for Pakistani President Mohammed Ayub Khan in July 1961, Jackie supervised every detail of a candlelit dinner in Mount Vernon that would have impressed the court of Louis XV. Poulet chasseur, couronne de riz clamart, framboises à la crème Chantilly, petits-fours secs and demi-tasse appeared on the menu. René Verdon, the White House's new French chef, was obliged to follow every instruction even as he led the new Gallic taste—to which, it must be said, the president was monumentally indifferent.

But all this attention to detail was part of Jackie's realization of an ideal, an ideal that represented something important about her own complex spirit. In a way, she was restoring something of her own past—the lost ideals represented by Lasata, Hammersmith Farm and Merrywood, where happiness had been so anticipated but was, in the end, so elusive.

In this regard, the White House project was not unlike the obsession of Queen Mary (consort of King George V of England from 1911 to 1936), who commissioned an intricate and fantastic dollhouse to enable future generations "to see how a King and Queen of England lived in the twentieth century and what authors, artists and craftsmen of note there were during her reign." Mary had always had a fondness for miniatures, and the famous architect Sir Edward Lutyens was engaged to design and execute a four-story Georgian dollhouse. It eventually contained literally tens of thousands of tiny pictures and pieces of furniture, made to scale by sixty well-known artists and three hundred craftsmen.

The dollhouse, three years in preparation and nine feet long when completed, could have accommodated a family of six if none was taller than half a foot. They would have arrived at their luxurious residence in any of six miniature, expensive reproductions of the royal Daimlers. Then they would have gone to dinner and eaten minute portions of real foodstuffs and drunk from tiny bottles of expensive wine, served on small gold or Royal Doulton plates. After dinner, they would have chosen their favorite music on the gramophone, which played real thumb-size recordings, or might have chosen to select a book from the two hundred postage-stamp-size volumes in the dainty library, which was festooned with hundreds of infinitesimal watercolors and drawings. They could have ridden in tiny mechanical elevators to their little bedrooms, washed in real water that spouted from miniature taps, and then climbed into beds covered in the finest miniature swatches of linen and silk.

But despite all this effort to achieve the quintessence of accurate and adorable daintiness, there was one significant and eerie omission: there were not actually any dolls to represent the royal inhabitants— no stand-ins for humans, just real little *things*. This project, the closest enterprise to Queen Mary's heart in her entire lifetime, was a perfect miniature representation of her own existence. There were grand living quarters and meticulous attention to the details of elegant props and supports, but at the heart of it, there was nothing warm and alive.

Just as in the case of old Queen Mary, who died in 1953, the year Jackie married Jack, the First Lady lavished on the White House all the loving attention that might otherwise have been reciprocated by her husband. She put all her unrequited devotion into her project of restoring a house, when all she really wanted was a home.

Likewise, the issue of her extensive wardrobe suggested a similar compensation: her painstaking attention to the details of style, coiffure, and elegant, refined presentation were certainly what the public wanted—but she wanted it all, too. In 1962 Jackie spent $121,461.61 on "family expenses"—which her personal secretary, Mary Barelli Gallagher, knew were clothing costs; this amount was $21,000 more than the president's salary. "Is there such a thing as Shoppers Anonymous?" Jack asked after reviewing the bills one day. In a way that was perhaps more poignant than reprehensible, Jackie was perhaps asking mere things to fill the terrible emptiness in her inner life.

IN ADDITION TO the White House project, Jacqueline Kennedy was, of course, known for importing guest artists and performers. If the president had his way, there would have been little more than jazz quintets for entertainment. But beginning in 1961, Jackie made certain that it was no longer considered undemocratic to feature high culture in the executive mansion. Why, she asked, was it presumed necessary to always have the lowest common denominator of talent and entertainment? Ought not the White House set the standard, not merely follow one?

She began her new plans five days after the inauguration, when George Balanchine, the choreographer, was in town with his New York City Ballet, inviting him to tea and asking what she could do for the world of classical dance. Soon thereafter, he wrote her a letter, urging Jackie to become a kind of aesthetic savior of America—to enable people

> to distinguish between material things and the things of the spirit—art, beauty. No one else can take care of these things. You alone can—if you will. Your husband is necessarily busy with serious international problems and cannot be expected to worry too much about the nation's art and culture.

In a sense, Jackie became the nation's unofficial minister of arts; she thought it was appalling, in this regard, that billions of dollars were spent at the Pentagon, but there was no budget for a Ministry of Culture, no governmental support of the arts on any significant scale (as there was in Europe), no educational television. All these concerns she expressed to the president, and as she affected these areas, she never wanted it known how important her influence was. Later, New York City's Shakespeare Festival, for example, owed its considerable success to her support, but she never used her name nor took credit for her donations or lobbying on its behalf.

Regular concerts were offered and ballets were staged in the East Room as after-dinner entertainment. Violinist Isaac Stern lunched with Jackie and helped plan numerous concerts. Cellist Pablo Casals, violinist Alexander Schneider and other musicians performed. Members of the American Shakespeare Festival enacted scenes from *Hamlet* and *A Midsummer Night's Dream*. Composers such as Leonard Bernstein and Aaron Copland led orchestras in performances of their works. Excerpts from musicals like *Brigadoon* were put on, and actors (Ralph Richardson, Basil Rathbone and Fredric March, among others) read excerpts from classic drama and fiction. "What a joy," said John Steinbeck dryly, "that literacy is no longer *prima facie* evidence of treason." America's creative community was routinely represented at White House dinners, where guest lists regularly included the likes of Igor Stravinsky, Carl Sandburg, Elia Kazan, Gian Carlo Menotti, Andrew Wyeth, Robert Frost and others.

The spirit of Madame de Récamier—not to the extent of a formal salon, but with complete dedication to a serious and joyful cultural life—was alive and well in Jacqueline Kennedy. Anything commonplace, rude, coarse, or even merely folksy was repellent to her. If America was to be a great civilization, she reasoned, it would have to pursue what was fine and beautiful and not remain forever confined to the cultivation of mediocre achievement.

But she was not unrealistically immersed in the past. Jackie prized her recordings of jazz, Latin American bossa nova and Chubby Checker, and later she was an avid collector of the Beatles' albums. When she wanted good movies shown at the White House, she asked for European films by Truffaut (*Jules et Jim*), Resnais (*L'Année dernière à Marienbad*), and Fellini (*La Dolce Vita*).

WHATEVER HER GRAVITY of purpose, Jackie was a study in apparent contradictions—but perhaps they were not really contradictions after all: they were marks of inclusion, for her character and personality conjoined the courtesies of one world and the directness of the other. To the outside, she seemed courtly, remote, stately; and indeed, she projected these qualities because they were part of what she owed the public.

This came naturally to her as part of her sense of appropriate manners. It was not hypocrisy—it was the proper way of behaving, of honoring the fact that she was watched for example, and example she would provide. She withheld displays of emotion from the world not because of contempt for that world, but precisely because she respected it. Her private feelings were for private situations; she was in no way a contributor to the lamentably imminent culture of letting it all hang out.

In private, Jackie was nonchalant, playful, even irreverent. She rarely wore dresses in the White House except for when she had appointments: her normal habit was to don slacks and sweaters. "Relaxed and uninhibited," as J. B. West added, she could most often be found "sitting on the floor, kicking off her shoes, her hair flying in every direction" while she worked on various projects. "We all had fun along with her." But lest nothing get done, and lest she lose her ability to lead and to achieve results, "she also drew a line against familiarity." That, too, was part of her ability to unite the Old with the New World.

Jackie teased and satirized everything, her husband and herself included—indeed, this was a habit they shared. It was just as difficult for Jackie as for Jack to take with utter gravity every matter and every person who wanted to be taken with utter gravity. A smile seemed so often about to break out on the president's face, and on hers, too. What *did* they know that we did not? Only that little was really of supreme consequence. War and peace, surely, and the health of their children. There was more, but the list was short.

Her humor was quick and irrepressible. The Eisenhowers' bedroom curtains she described as "seasick green," the first-floor hallway like "a dentist's office in a bomb shelter." Told that the White House engineers could not fine-tune the thermostats, she wondered why "the greatest brains of army engineering cannot figure out how to have this place heated like any other normal rattle-trap of a house." And when a newsman wanted to know what her German shepherd puppy ate, she replied with a smile, "Reporters."

Serious though she was about her restoration project, Jackie was not above self-mockery. Ketchum had worked up a good impersonation of Stéphane Boudin, who worked with Jackie on the formal, grand state rooms at the White House. Boudin was the venerable French decorator who had restored Versailles and counted the Duchess of Windsor among his clients, and he evoked awe and sometimes fear in people. In addition, there was a staff member who could do herself up like Jackie and turn in a good imitation. "She insisted we do a kind of Nichols and May routine of redecorating a room," Ketchum recalled. "She didn't mind being mocked. She seemed to be able to bring out the child in every one of us. You saw the wit every day."

But her humor never bruised, and she would have done anything to avoid hurting anyone's feelings. "She was so soft-spoken, so deft and subtle," said West, "that she could even impose her will upon people without their ever knowing it." Whereas Mrs. Eisenhower simply commanded, issuing orders as if she, not her husband, had been Supreme Allied Commander during World War II, Jackie quietly asked of White House employees, "Do you think you could . . . ?" or "Would it be too much trouble if . . . ?" Along with Ralph Waldo Emerson, she believed that "life is not so short but that there is always time enough for courtesy." And she agreed, too, with Hilaire Belloc: "the Grace of God is in courtesy." When she learned that Secret Service agents had to guard the First Family even at Christmas, she insisted that they be permitted to bring along their wives and children. Similarly, Jackie invariably sent handwritten notes of thanks to the White House chef and kitchen staff after a formal dinner.

Her courtesy extended especially to the vice president and his wife. On state occasions, the tradition was to play "Hail to the Chief" and then to announce the president of the United States and Mrs. Kennedy to the assembled guests. "Will you tell whoever it is," Jackie wrote in a memorandum to the chief usher, "at *every* occasion when they play 'Hail to the Chief'—to please also say, 'The Vice President of the United States and Mrs. Johnson.' It is so embarrassing to have them not announced and just disappear like maids." This gesture was much appreciated by the Johnsons, who grew enormously fond of Jackie. Their warm relationship was never interrupted, whatever the shifting fortunes of the Kennedy-Johnson symbiosis.

Part of Jackie's fundamental courtesy was her awareness that most people who come to the White House are almost rigid with awe. To put people at ease, she established a completely new atmosphere. "The entertaining is going to be very important to us," she told Letitia Baldrige. "I want to make it warmer, more gracious, more distinguished." Jackie quickly abandoned the traditional U-shaped dining table used for state dinners and substituted a group of round tables for eight or ten: except for a few state occasions, the traditional formality was to be replaced by a kind of cultivated but unconfined warmth, with flowers, candles and live music—usually a string quartet. "Really, she had the enthusiasm of a young girl," according to Betty Beale, who had the impression that Jackie wanted to please.

The First Lady created, as Baldrige said, "the intimacy and conviviality of smaller groupings." No one was to feel intimidated, and to this end Jackie replaced the formal receiving line with casual mingling by her and her husband. As for the food, there were major differences from the Eisenhower banquets. Ike and Mamie had entertained with six courses and twenty-one items at a meal; entertainment afterward was almost invariably music by Fred Waring and the Pennsylvanians. The Kennedys had four courses and eight items served; eighteenth-century music was played by a quartet, and the entertainment afterward was opera, dance, theater and recitals. And to the horror of some, cocktails and wine were now routinely served, in defiance of the mavens of temperance who still influenced social protocol, even at the executive mansion.

"We used to have to come to the White House when Jack was a senator and the Eisenhowers were here," Jackie told Diana Trilling. "It was just unbearable. There would be Mamie in one chair and Ike in another. And on Mamie's right side would be the guest of honor, male, and on Ike's right side would be the guest of honor, female, and everyone stood, and there was nothing to drink. During that regime, there was never *anything* served to drink, and we made up our minds, when we came to the White House, that nobody was ever going to be as bored as that. We do try to make it a good party."

JACKIE WANTED, IN effect, to make the White House not a museum or a forbidding temple to democracy but a home in which guests felt comfortable. It would be, in other words, what she had always wanted for herself. If she didn't have the marriage she had hoped for, at least she could have a dwelling for herself and her children, however temporary their residence there. And she was always aware that she was living in a rented house. Like Glen Ora, the White House was not hers: she was temporary custodian. And as with Lasata, Hammersmith Farm and Merrywood, she managed to find at the mansion a space for herself—a private room for reading and writing, a nook to which she could escape.

Jackie met with designers and historians, architects and refurbishers. She set up a committee to locate, as she said, "authentic furniture from the time of the building of the mansion" and "to raise funds to purchase this furniture as gifts for the White House." Then she scoured government storage halls, canvassed antiques dealers and gently importuned wealthy collectors in her search for authentic but usable Americana. All the while, she insisted that everything "must have a reason for being there. It would be sacrilege merely to 'redecorate' [the White House]—that's a word I hate. It must be *restored*—and that has nothing to do with decoration. That is a question of scholarship."

To the surprise of many reporters and photographers during the Kennedy years in the White House, Jackie turned the attention away from herself. "Don't take pictures of Jack and me," she often said. "Take pictures of what we are looking at and what we're doing. That is what's important." And in pointing to what was important, she took a stand, then and forever after, against the minimizing of everything. She was, in effect, a role model for a new kind of American woman—not only a housewife and mother, but a woman with her own mind, performing a difficult and exacting task with style and intelligence.

IN THE PRIVATE quarters, Jackie again worked with Sister Parish. The family rooms were accordingly redone in a warm, relaxed style, a fire blazing at autumn's first chill and fresh flowers always adorning the corners, the tables—in each room. From her earliest days with Grandma Bouvier's tours of the gardens at Lasata, Jackie knew the buoyant effect of flowers on interiors.

She was constantly aware of the greatness of her husband's destiny. But he was also the father of her children, and they deserved his presence and attention. Here, she had to achieve a delicate balance. Jackie had to ensure that there was time for him to spend with Caroline and John during the day, not at night, when they would have to be shuttled away and when he was often too busy or too tired for a children's hour. Before she sent Caroline off to the schoolroom she had set up in the White House, Jackie encouraged her daughter to accompany her father to his office each morning.

The lives of Caroline and John were to be as normal as possible. "I don't want them to think they are 'official children,' " she told J. B. West. "When I go out with them or when they go out with their nurses, please ask the doorman not to hover around to open the doors for them." What did the president think about all this? It was difficult to know. When Jackie asked his opinion or guidance, "he tells me, 'That's your province.' And I say, 'Yes, but *you're* the great decision-

maker. Why should everyone but me get the benefit of your decisions?'" Touché.

Whenever he could, the president lunched alone with his wife and
children. Then he took a short nap and headed for the White House
swimming pool. If possible, he made time late in the day for the children. This was the primary reason why Jackie refurbished the family's
private quarters, to create a style that was both warm and informal
("Off to the dungeons with these hideous Victorian mirrors!"). The
president relished the role of father, with the family spending no less
than ten of the first sixteen weekends of 1961 at Glen Ora. These times
were hallowed, for she considered them essential to her children's
healthy upbringing. "No matter what else I might achieve," she said
memorably, "if my children turn out badly, I would feel that I had
failed."

Guarding Caroline and John's privacy was Jackie's primary concern. "I feel strongly," she wrote in a memorandum to press secretary
Pierre Salinger, "that publicity in this era has gotten completely out of
hand—and you must really protect the privacy of me and my children."
After one magazine published unauthorized photos of the children
playing, she wrote to Salinger angrily, "*I mean this*—[I] want no more
and if you are firm and will take the time—you can stop it. So please
do. What is a press secretary for—to help the press, yes—but also to
protect *us*."

But there was another issue at stake in this protection and this
privacy. As Robert Kennedy and many others noted, Jackie had an
extremely independent spirit: part of the paradox concerns her dependence on men and her simultaneous independence. Even as she derived
her sense of self from associating with powerful men, so something in
her yearned for independence and took steps to establish it—just the
way she had sought solitude even in childhood.

JACKIE NEVER HAD many intimate friends. "Mrs. Kennedy didn't
seek out the companionship of other women," J. B. West recalled. Unlike Eleanor Roosevelt or Mamie Eisenhower, "she had no clique who
came by for [card games], no confidantes in the outside world," and
neither her Kennedy sisters-in-law, the Senate wives, nor even Mrs.
Lyndon Johnson came to lunch. When she did invite guests to tea, they

were usually older men interested in the arts, for to Jackie socializing meant learning, and in her capacity as hostess, she preferred to engage men in conversation. "She knew how to flatter men," according to observers like Betty Beale, "and she fluttered her eyelashes like a debutante—of course they all adored it."

This tendency, which became a firm habit, alienated some of the most talented women she might have attracted to the White House. Many women would have agreed with the most respected and influential among the press—like Helen Thomas, who felt that Jackie tended to ignore them, that she had a "desire to have it both ways. When she was creating the image of a concerned First Lady, she wanted press coverage. When she was flying off on her Friday-to-Tuesday weekend trips, she wanted to pull the velvet curtain closed."

When they wanted dinner companions, Jackie chose *Newsweek* bureau chief Ben Bradlee and his wife, Tony, who may have been unaware of her sister's continuing affair with the president; Charles and Martha Bartlett; columnist Joseph Alsop and his wife, Susan Mary; Texas oilman Charles Wrightsman and his wife, Jayne, who were donors to the White House restoration; and ever available bachelors like Bill Walton and Lem Billings. "Jackie was great fun at those dinners," recalled Charles Bartlett, "because she could keep the president gay and tease him a little bit."

Robert Kennedy agreed: "She's poetic, whimsical, provocative, independent and yet feminine. Jackie has always kept her own identity and been *different*. Jack knows she'll never greet him with, 'What's new in Laos?' " Bobby was probably unaware of the blithe condescension in his remark, but after all, the Kennedy family excelled when it came to male chauvinism, and they gave not much thought to Jackie's intelligence. "In their eyes," according to Margaret Truman, "she was, like all the other women in their lives, strictly for relaxation."

But as time went on, Jack had reasons to appreciate his wife's acute intelligence. "My wife is a very strong woman," he once said, "romantic by temperament, sensitive, intuitive, [with a] fantastically retentive memory." As his presidency continued, he developed an enormous respect for her political savvy.

First of all, she was more informed than most people thought: she plied Deputy Defense Secretary Roswell Gilpatric with questions about the Pentagon, about who wielded what power, about the motivations of those who had the president's confidence. Before a visit from Morocco's King Hassan, Jackie wrote him a five-page personal letter and then asked for a transcript of his appearance on *Meet the Press*. According to Letitia Baldrige, Jackie found international politics intriguing and knew a great deal more than she let on. "I'm sure she discussed things with President Kennedy," said Baldrige. "She is like a sponge— she absorbs everything she hears. She may not say anything, but she always listens very intently."

Baldrige was absolutely correct, as Major General Chester Clifton, an administration military aide, confirmed. "JFK turned to his wife for advice whenever a crisis arose: the Berlin Wall, the Cuban Missiles, the Bay of Pigs. She wouldn't advise his staff, she would advise him— that's why nobody knew about it." The nature of the advice was, to be sure, general, and based on the principles of peacemaking and, where possible, the avoidance of conflict: this was, after all, the standard that had guided Jack and Jackie ever since the 1954 meeting with Ormsby-Gore, when the Kennedy Doctrine, a commitment away from the Cold War and toward the goal of nuclear disarmament, began to take clear shape.

AS FOR FAMILY, they saw the president's relatives mostly in Palm Beach or Hyannisport, although of course Robert Kennedy was not only attorney general but also his brother's closest friend and confidant. Jackie also saw her father-in-law as often as possible—they shared the same somewhat cynical wit. When he came to the White House, "she fairly danced down the halls, arm-in-arm with him," recalled West, "laughing uproariously at his teasing. Her face was animated and happy, as it was when she was playing with her children." After Joe suffered a permanently debilitating stroke in December 1961, Jackie took every opportunity to provide for his comfort and to attempt encouraging diversions. Indeed, she was closer to Joe Kennedy than to her own mother and stepfather, with whom her relationship was formal, polite but never warm.

At Palm Beach parties, too, Jackie knew some trying moments. Gwen Gibson clearly recalled a party at which Jack danced rather too ardently with one woman after another, completely ignoring his wife. After a while, Jackie simply rose and swept out. "She did her duty," according to Gibson. "She had greeted the people she had to greet, and then she left."

Essentially, this added up to a somewhat sequestered life, although Jackie's proclivity to mining richness from solitude forestalled the depression that might have come from the feeling of being, remarkably often, profoundly alone. Especially in modern times, with the constant emphasis on social distraction, noise and idle chatter, many mistake reflective, introspective personalities for aloof, detached or patronizing people. Jackie was often wrongly considered snobbish, enigmatic and mysterious when she was simply pensive and private. She would not turn herself into public, accessible property simply because she had swiftly become the most famous woman in the world. Nor would she apologize for preferring the company of poets, musicians and artists to that of athletes or mere celebrities.

Why, she often wondered then and later, did a false sense of democracy mean one had to court the favor of the most popular instead of the most accomplished? Perhaps the most ironic of all aspects of her White House years was that from 1961 to 1963, Jackie's picture was seen more and more often than any internationally renowned movie star. The word *star* was first used to describe Jackie by *The New York Times* on March 22, 1961: "A guest star at the New York City Ballet last night never left her seat," began the story. And so it went.

PART OF THE stardom derived from her beauty and from her exquisite taste in clothes, which was supported by the talents of Oleg Cassini, the designer she most favored. Cassini had been married to movie star Gene Tierney (once one of Jack's conquests), and he had designed costumes for her and others in a series of Hollywood pictures before he opened a design studio. In early December 1960, while Jackie was still in the hospital, Cassini had been invited to visit her and to submit sketches for her consideration. "I talked to her like a movie star and told her that she needed a story, a scenario as First Lady." They spoke about the history of fashion, and he learned of her passion for French elegance. "You have an opportunity here," said Cassini, pausing for dramatic effect, "for an American Versailles." Henceforth, when they discussed her wardrobe, it was "in terms of Italian masters and eighteenth-century France," as Cassini said.

This Jackie found enormously appealing, of course. But she had a caveat for Cassini: "I know that I am so much more of fashion interest than other First Ladies [and] I refuse to have Jack's administration plagued by fashion stories of a sensational nature [and] to be the Marie Antoinette or Josephine of the 1960s." But as Cassini said, she had "a great sense of history and a keen historical perspective," and as time would reveal, Marie Antoinette and Josephine were, however indeliberately, the models she took as she assumed her new role. So was the court of Napoleon: Cassini and Jackie discussed "the French courts of Napoleon . . . and how Eugénie, wife of Napoleon III, always had the most beautiful and intriguing men and women present because it amused the emperor."

From this time forward, according to Cassini, Jackie wanted to be "the best-dressed woman in the world without appearing to be the best-dressed woman in the world." And that required enormous funds for a lavish wardrobe. On instructions from Joe Kennedy, Cassini was not to send his bills to Jack or Jackie: "Just send me an accounting at the end of the year. I'll take care of it," Joe instructed the designer, reminding him not to discuss the cost in public "as it might be used politically against the president."

With her choice of Cassini, the idea and image of the First Lady's couturier were dramatically altered. He became her production designer, making Jackie the first non-Hollywood star in American history.

All other previous stars had come from the movies. But now *Photoplay* ran her picture on its cover and called her "America's Newest Star." *Modern Screen, Screen Stories, Teen Tempo* and *Movie World* followed. *Motion Picture* magazine featured Caroline on the cover of its December 1962 issue.

This development is not hard to understand. Since the Great Depression of the 1930s, fashion had presented images and ideals of the so-called American *girl*—a kind of fantastic golden child who disported herself through magazines and movies with a tennis racquet, perfect lipstick, a man in black tie. The press declared that Jackie's youth and beauty made her a new kind of First Lady, which was rubbish, for there had been younger and more vivacious women in that position. But after Eleanor Roosevelt, Bess Truman and Mamie Eisenhower, as Margaret Truman said, "Jackie was new in capital letters."

For a brief time, before the 1960s really began with the president's death and the rise of the hippie and drug cultures, there was now, with Jackie's patrician bearing, a heady sense of *class* in American life. For a brief time, Americans knew that their First Family, thanks to their First Lady, could be favorably compared with British royals and French diplomats.

Jackie conformed to no set standard; indeed, she broke the public mold of what had come to characterize the ideally desirable American woman. The buxom blonde had been America's fantasy in the 1940s and 1950s, but here was a tall, almost flat-chested brunette whose features were slightly out of proportion. She rode horses; she discussed classical history, music and French novels. And none of this was mere tokenism: she read voraciously with astonishing retention.

Mrs. Roosevelt had certainly dedicated herself to matters of humanitarian concern, and there is no question that she greatly contributed to the formation of America's social conscience. But Jackie projected the idea of the First Lady as a young mother of the twentieth century, a woman who could wear high fashion, discuss matters of the mind and spirit and clearly present an image of unofficial diplomacy and independence. Nothing about her conformed to her predecessors' styles, or, it may be suggested, that of her successors. And she, too, contributed to the formation of moral consciousness—most of all in her influence on her husband's policies. Henceforth, all kinds of rules were broken by the new star and her costume designer—as together they projected a bold and exquisite new sense of fashion. Soon Jackie could easily do what no other First Lady in memory had been able to do: she appeared, to breathtaking effect, with one and then both shoulders bare. The famous and trend-setting pillbox hat, first worn by Jackie on Inauguration Day and wrongly credited to the designer Halston, was actually created by Oleg Cassini and Diana Vreeland and executed by Marita of Bergdorf Goodman.

The everyday wardrobe was just as impressive but never flashy. In consultation with Cassini, Jackie had, according to Mrs. Gerald Ford, "such marvelous taste that all women in Washington, all the women across the country, copied her. We wore the same things she wore, the little pillbox on the head, the sleeveless shift. It was epidemic, that wardrobe." In no time, the famous and the unknown imitated the Jackie look, from Mary Tyler Moore's television character on *The Dick Van Dyke Show*, with her Jackie-like hair, pants and flat shoes, to advertising and fashion mannequins.

And not only, as it happened, was the style an epidemic—so was the documentation of the woman who wore it. *Life* magazine proclaimed her, as early as Inauguration Day, "the nation's No. 1 fashion influence—a deserved compliment to a very young and very poised First Lady." Ten days later *Newsweek* declared that the national topic of conversation was "not the new American President, but what his wife was wearing." By the end of 1961, Jacqueline Kennedy was voted "Woman of the Year" by the editors of no less than one hundred international periodicals, from the Polish *Swiat* to the Russian *Trybuna Ludu*. And Latin America's Public Opinion Research Institute proclaimed that she and Pope John XXIII were the two outstanding models for the world. From January 1961 to November 1963, letters of praise poured into Jackie's White House office at the rate of six thousand to nine thousand a week.

Thereafter, every detail but the most intimate was reported by *The New York Times,* which in December 1961 descended to the level of monumental silliness:

> As it must to all women, a run came today to the stocking of Mrs. John F. Kennedy. It showed up on the First Lady's ankle when she mounted the speaker's stand at El Dorado Airport on her arrival in Colombia. She seemed unaware of it.

And again in August 1962:

> After dining out at the home of the Duke of Sangro in Amalfi, Mrs. John F. Kennedy and a group of friends went nightclubbing at Praiano near Positano. . . . Mrs. Kennedy danced the twist and other dances . . . and then went out for her routine swim.

That same month:

> Mrs. John F. Kennedy slept late today . . . [and then] returned
> to the [hotel] after having lunched.

Never was she more of a star than during her first international
tours with Jack in the spring of 1961. But before their journey together
to Canada, Paris and Vienna, she insisted that the president do his
homework. "She helped him very much to understand France," said
Hervé Alphand, that country's ambassador to the United States. "She
asked him to read the memoirs of General de Gaulle," whom they
were about to meet. Her stepbrother Yusha Auchincloss recalled that
Jackie went to France with the idea that Jack and de Gaulle were
continuing the historic association between George Washington and
General Lafayette.

Letitia Baldrige added that Jackie wrote long letters to de Gaulle
in advance of her arrival in Paris—letters about French art and culture
and about her family's French background. But the letters were in
preparation for conversations in person, which were also Jackie's way
of furthering American foreign policy: she worked out, in discussions
with the president, her own type of diplomacy, which appeared not to
be diplomacy at all.

The tour began in Canada in May, where the president met with
Prime Minister John Diefenbaker in what *Life* magazine called more
of a bull session than a summit meeting. Both Canadian and American
reporters, however, were more interested in Jackie, as even the Canadian Speaker of the Senate acknowledged in Parliament: "Her charm,
beauty, vivacity and grace of mind have captured our hearts."

The *New York Times* story about the diplomatic visit was entirely
about Jackie, except for an item about Jack's wielding a shovel rather
too enthusiastically during a tree-planting ceremony in Ottawa and
badly wrenching his neck and back. A man named Max Jacobson was
summoned to deal with the president's discomfort.

In 1961, little was known about the dangers of amphetamines, bar-
biturates and narcotic abuse and dependence. Heroin was thought to
characterize the lives of street addicts; marijuana was occasionally found

in the homes of celebrities; cocaine use was heard of among some musicians. But millions of people took tranquilizers or diet pills: it was almost a distinction that testified to their demanding, privileged, glamorous and therefore important lives. Countless deaths occurred, and an epidemic of costly misery, before the world at large took note of terrible new addictions.

At the time, however, men and women in artistic, political and social circles easily obtained Nembutal, Doriden, Luminal, Seconal, phenobarbital, Dexamyl and a cornucopia of other perilous drugs. There was little government regulation or control over them, and physicians could write prescriptions at will; the "scheduling" and classification of various types of dangerous substances was still to come. Hence, some doctors were only too glad to retain and expand their clientele by providing whatever made their patients feel good.

Among these dubious caregivers, none was more notorious than Max Jacobson, who was actually referred to in social circles as Dr. Feelgood. Ultimately, Jacobson was stripped of his medical license, but only after he had "treated" a cadre of men and women, some of whom became addicts and died.

The disgrace and downfall of Max Jacobson, who had already been the subject of government investigation, began on December 4, 1972, with a lengthy, front-page article in *The New York Times.* For years Jacobson had been making concoctions of vitamins, amphetamines, steroids and God only knew what else. The immediate effects of his injections were touted far and wide, and his reputation brought to his door a constant stream of the famous, the powerful, the insecure and the merely rich and bored—among them, Tennessee Williams, Eddie Fisher, Cecil B. DeMille, Congressman Claude Pepper, Otto Preminger, Alan Jay Lerner, Truman Capote and Marlene Dietrich.

Jacobson administered and even taught his patients to inject themselves with intravenous amphetamines, commonly known as "speed"— which gives a false sense of power, security, control and brilliance and which enable people to go without sleep, to remain, or so they think, alert and receptive for days on end. "It is known," reported *The New York Times,* "that Dr. Jacobson uses unusually large amounts of amphetamine in his practice. The doctor's office reported"—that is, he himself admitted—"that Dr. Jacobson buys amphetamine at the rate of

80 grams a month. This is enough to make 100 fairly strong doses of 25 milligrams every day." No wonder his fame spread quickly and that it was often difficult to schedule an immediate appointment.

Among Jacobson's patients was one of the Kennedys' closest confidants, Mark Shaw, also one of their favorite official photographers. Married to the singer and actress Pat Suzuki, Shaw published *The John F. Kennedys,* a cheerful photo-essay he dedicated "to my friend and companion Dr. Max Jacobson." Among Shaw's many pictures of the Kennedys at play, one shows the president on a Florida outing with Jacobson and one of his other patients, Prince Radziwill, the president's brother-in-law; a passage accompanying the photo notes that Jacobson "insisted on treating everyone in sight." It was, therefore, through Shaw and the prince that John Kennedy, who rarely had a pain-free day in his life, became a patient of Max Jacobson. Early in 1961, Jacobson began visiting the White House as well as Palm Beach. (Mark Shaw died of a drug overdose at the age of forty-seven.)

Janet Travell, the president's personal physician, later observed that Kennedy had, at the time, "a problem with the neck. He had stiffness in his neck muscles extending from the low shoulders. Owing to the difference in leg lengths, the left shoulder was appreciably lower than the right and this created stress and strain on the neck muscles."

This was much aggravated by the tree-planting incident that May in Canada. With the Kennedys scheduled to go on to even more important summit meetings in Paris and Vienna, Max Jacobson was summoned. During the rest of the journey, Jacobson was in constant attendance, and as he later admitted, he gave the president injections. It must be emphasized, however, that the precise contents of these injections cannot be known.

But it must also be emphasized that the president pointedly did not want Janet Travell to accompany him on this journey, making it known that his association with this circumspect woman was to be slowly but definitely diminished. "Travell was a real lady," according to Helen Thomas, "and the president simply didn't want her around anymore. The fact is, she knew too much—about everything." But he need not have worried: Janet Travell was, unto death, the soul of discretion.

The record is clear that in Europe and again in New York that September—when Kennedy addressed the United Nations—Max

Jacobson administered medications to the president's neck, injections so powerful that pain "vanished within minutes" (in the doctor's own words). Of this time, Jackie would later only admit that she, too, had been treated by Dr. Jacobson, but she declined to elaborate.

Another of the president's physicians, who had attended him in 1955, was upset about the Jacobson injections: "I made it very clear that I was not going to tolerate this," the doctor told the *Times*. "I said that if I ever heard he took another shot, I'd make sure it was known. No president with his finger on the red button has any business taking stuff like that." That this physician remained anonymous in the press of course proves nothing, although some would feel that it suggests he knew the injections were dangerous. But no one can ever prove this: there is no evidence to suggest that either the president or the First Lady received addictive drugs. If they did, they would have been among many innocent people who did so while trusting a well-known physician not yet disgraced. Furthermore, there is not a shred of evidence that either Jack or Jackie was ever addicted to anything at all.

IMMEDIATELY BEFORE HER arrival in Paris, Jackie read Marcus Cheke's exhaustive biography of Cardinal de Bernis, an aristocratic diplomat in eighteenth-century France who was also in the entourage of Madame de Pompadour. On behalf of Louis XV, this powerful churchman helped negotiate a treaty at Versailles between France and Austria. This kind of serious historical reading reveals not only the intellectual preparation Jackie made for the journey but also the gravity with which she took her husband's role, and by association her own, as aristocratic peacemakers. As First Lady she was more than ever spiritually immersed in the lives and fortunes of history's nobility. "Jackie was an inveterate reader," said Mary Barelli Gallagher, "[and she spent] many, many hours, when people thought she was having gay times, reading books on many subjects."

With their team of advisers, secretaries, security guards, Max Jacobson and Jackie's twenty steamer trunks, the Kennedys arrived in Paris, where they remained from May 31 to June 3. "The radiant young First Lady was the Kennedy who really mattered," declared *Time;* indeed, Jackie charmed President de Gaulle as well as the normally blasé Parisians. Cries of *"Vive Jacqui!"* were heard everywhere they went, according to Gwen Gibson, who covered Jackie during the entire European journey. "Paris simply went wild about her—she was *the* topic of conversation." Jackie's ambition was fulfilled: in her wardrobe and demeanor, she wanted, as she had instructed Cassini, with capitalized emphasis, about her clothes, to appear "as if Jack were President of FRANCE."

Aware that no stray thread or hair, no tiny flaw in hair or hemline would escape the French press, she had prepared her wardrobe to precise specifications and had sent ahead a lock of her hair to Alexandre, the city's leading hairdresser. Even Jack was impressed: "Well, I'm dazzled," he said privately—and to a gathering of journalists at the Palais de Chaillot, he said famously, "I do not think it altogether inappropriate for me to introduce myself. I am the man who accompanied Jacqueline Kennedy to Paris."

He was, for perhaps the first time, taking full stock of her importance to their image—which meant, primarily, *his* image. On that first day in Paris, Jackie completely overwhelmed General de Gaulle during an official luncheon at the Palais de l'Elysée. After chattering away with her in French about Louis XVI, the Bourbons and the geography of France, he turned to Jack: "Your wife knows more French history than any Frenchwoman!" With that, according to Kenneth O'Donnell, "de Gaulle turned back to Jackie and did not take his eyes off her for the rest of the meal." For Jackie, this must have been supremely complimentary: not only was she finding approval with the head of a country she adored, she was also being noticed by an older man she respected and who clearly respected her—"dazzling and cultivated," de Gaulle described her. This was not the sort of acknowledgment or attention she received with alarming frequency from her own husband. (Rose Kennedy and Eunice Kennedy Shriver, also on the trip, were virtually ignored.)

At the formal banquet, held at Versailles, Jackie continued to undergo an unmistakable transformation in the eyes of Europe. Her confidence also grew. Glittering in a Givenchy gown, her bouffant hairdo patterned by Alexandre after a Louis XIV favorite, the Duchesse de Fontanges, Jackie was losing her shyness and blossoming in her own estimation, too. It was this European trip in June 1961 that marked a new phase of her own independence: henceforth, she began to announce

an occasional excursion on her own or with her sister or other friends—
quite apart from her husband's duties or plans. After all, he made
frequent business and pleasure trips without her: why could she not
have the same freedom? That night, while he was settling into a hot
bath, the president told O'Donnell and Salinger, "de Gaulle and I are
hitting it off all right, probably because I have such a charming wife."

That June, all over Paris, she was mobbed, and her reactions were
everywhere documented. At the Jeu de Paume she viewed the great
collection of Impressionist masterworks, announcing that her favorite
was Manet's *Olympia,* a portrait of a reclining nude who just happened
to have been a courtesan. She loved, too, her visit to Malmaison, the
Empress Josephine's country retreat. From there, she went to La Celle
de St. Cloud, the hideaway of Madame de Pompadour.

Most of all, however, Jackie shone at the state dinner, held to great
effect at Versailles. Here, she dared to wear a diamond tiara—a touch
that would have been entirely inappropriate on the head of any other
woman who was not a legitimate European royal. *Elle s'en tient* was
the general reaction: "She can get away with it." And she did. She
wanted, she had told Cassini at the time of the inauguration, to appear
"pure and regal." The apotheosis was, by this time, proceeding nicely.

For her tours of the Louvre, Versailles and Malmaison, André Malraux, the Minister of State for Cultural Affairs, escorted Jackie. Just
days earlier his two sons had been killed in an auto accident. Still, he
insisted on hosting the feverish activities, and for this Jackie was forever
grateful. Vigorous but sensitive without being improperly familiar,
Jackie formed an instant friendship with this highly cultivated man.
Later he shipped the *Mona Lisa* on special loan to the National Gallery—not, he specified, as a tribute to the American people, but to their
First Lady. The following May, Jackie returned his hospitality in Washington.

The effect of this portion of her journey was felt as soon as she
returned to Washington. Inspired by the state dinner at Versailles,
Jackie decided to host the formal dinner for Mohammed Ayub Khan,
the president of Pakistan, that July at Mount Vernon, with historic
costumes, fireworks, marching bands—all of it as unprecedented as the
tiara. At the same time, she approached John A. Carver Jr., Assistant
Secretary of the Interior for Public Land Management. "Jackie wanted

the public monuments illuminated," he recalled, "but the Department of Parks didn't want a French *son et lumière,* and Jackie was frustrated" over the failure of her plan to bring a touch of Paris to Washington. After her tenure, the idea was eventually implemented.

IMMEDIATELY FOLLOWING HER triumph in France, she evoked much the same reaction in Vienna, where Kennedy met with Soviet Premier Nikita Khrushchev. Jackie and Mrs. Khrushchev smiled and held hands for photographers—Jackie looking as though she had stepped from the pages of a fashion magazine, Madame Khrushchev like a plump grandmother who once may have read one. The political climate was cool, but when the Soviet premier was asked to shake the hand of the American president, he winked at Jackie and said through his interpreter, "I'd like to shake *her* hand first."

During the state dinner that evening, Jackie and the Russian leader discussed the dog that had been put into a Soviet Sputnik flight. The dog recently had pups, Khrushchev said, and Jackie replied, "Why don't you send me one?" Eventually, he did. "Pushinska" arrived several months later, with a warm letter from Khrushchev. Jackie's self-assurance was indeed increasing. As they were discussing the Ukraine, he launched into a discussion about the number of teachers there. "Oh, Mr. Chairman," said Jackie, "don't bore me with statistics!" As he later said, "She had no trouble finding the right word to cut you short if you weren't careful with her."

From Vienna, the group proceeded to London, where the Kennedys stayed with the Prince and Princess Radziwill and dined with Queen Elizabeth—for which occasion Jackie went without her tiara. By this time, not even Max Jacobson's remedies could alleviate the president's constant discomfort, and Jack returned to Washington. Jackie, however, stayed on for several more days in London—and on June 7 flew off with the Radziwills for a week's holiday on the Greek islands. Stopping in Epidaurus, Delos, Hydra and Mykonos, Jackie swam, water-skied, danced with locals, sipped native wine and decided that, along with Paris, this was her favorite place in the world. "I have never been happier," she declared to a reporter.

Her husband, meantime, was not at all cheerful. A week in Palm Beach did little to alleviate his pain, and soon he was back on crutches.

When this information was given to the press as the true reason for his absence from Washington, reporters asked why Jackie was continuing her Grecian odyssey if her husband was in such difficulty. Well, said Pierre Salinger, improvising, she had no idea the problem was so serious, and her husband had happily waved her on to her holiday.

That was as it may have been, but the state of the marriage—a brilliantly successful formality by this time—required all manner of embellishments and arabesques. For once in her life, she discussed intimate details of her sexual life, which her confidant—no less a trustworthy father figure than Adlai Stevenson—found "most indiscreet." This was not the only hot spot for Salinger: asked if the president was taking medication for his pain, the press secretary responded, "I don't know if he is or not." But the press was, in those more polite days, not inclined to push Salinger for knowledge he most likely had, given that the purpose of speaking with reporters was to explain his employer's distressing condition.

A brief journey to Puerto Rico, Venezuela and Colombia took place that December; by this time it was clear that Jackie was rather enjoying the international approval that was everywhere evident. In Caracas there were anti-American placards everywhere: "Kennedy—No!" But when Jackie stepped up to a microphone to address a crowd in Spanish, she looked out over a contrary sentiment: "Jackie—Sí!" Her pleasure at moments like these was immediately obvious, and the American press, always in attendance, began to take note.

So did her most loyal allies. "She has a great flair for publicity and understands it even better than her husband," said Adlai Stevenson. "I hope she doesn't overdo it." For a short time, as First Lady, she did: from 1961 to 1963 many people detected a certain *folie de grandeur,* which, in light of her youth, inexperience and need to be distracted from the disappointments of her marriage, may have been unavoidable.

THE PRESS SENTIMENT was synthesized in a 1961 Women's Press Club show, when Gwen Gibson and Sidney Schwartz wrote the lyrics and music for a song called "That's Me, Jackie." It was sung by none other than Helen Thomas, who by all accounts performed it with great gusto and in good humor:

If I want to fly away,
Without taking JFK—
That's me, Jackie.

If I'm fond of French champagne,
If I'd rather not campaign—
That's me, Jackie.

If I want to give a ball
For just me and Charles de Gaulle,
I have absolutely all the gall
I need.

If I like to water-ski
And I want my private sea,
Don't look askance:
With half the chance,
You'd be like me—Jackie.

Si je suis très debonaire
Or wear sable underwear,
That's me—Jackie.

If I like to live in style
On my own Aegean isle,
That's me—Jackie.

If I use Mount Vernon's lawn
For amusing Ayub Khan
And we choose to dance till dawn,
Then c'est la vie.

If I rewrite history,
Name the White House "Chez Jackie,"
Am I to blame?
You'd do the same,
If you were me—Jackie.

For every formal appearance, Jackie was, said the press, "dressed, coifed [*sic*] and made up as elaborately as any princess." Indeed, her recent visit to Europe had brought out a streak of royal pretension in Jacqueline Bouvier Kennedy—a subtle attitude of noblesse oblige that was perhaps inevitable in light of all the adulation tendered to her. Usually quite prompt in keeping appointments, she quoted Louis XVIII: *"C'est la politesse des rois"*—punctuality is the politeness of kings. This Jackie said with a little laugh; it does, however, give some idea of the people in her mind, those in whose tradition she considered herself.

"My goal was to dress her like a queen," said Cassini, and Jackie's goal was to look like one; rarely has there been so perfect a symbiosis between the dresser and the dressed. The public went along with it all, and *Look* magazine designated the Kennedys "the new U.S. Royal Family"—a title ironically bestowed in the issue dated July 14, 1961, which is, of course, Bastille Day, celebrating the birth of French democracy.

Jackie's strong sense of the power of myth, and of her own position in history, made her think of herself as virtually the regal chatelaine of a new Versailles, and she often referred to the White House as "la Maison Blanche." French art, French cuisine, the emphasis on French influence in America, the presence of artists and the after-dinner concerts and recitals she supervised: all these led, by an inexorable logic, to the notion of a mythic, royal past she later took up as the idealized image of Camelot.

CHAPTER NINE

1962-1963

*O*n February 14, 1962, Jackie led CBS news correspondent Charles Collingwood and more than 60 million Americans (80 percent of those who owned a television) on a tour of the White House. The event was so unprecedented, so heralded weeks in advance by the press that it virtually stopped the nation in its tracks. CBS and NBC carried the broadcast simultaneously, and the reviews of her performance were ecstatic.

As it happened, the show had been taped over nine hours on January 15, when eight tons of equipment and fifty-four technicians invaded the mansion. Producer Perry Wolff and his sound crew were anxious about Jackie's thin voice, but, as he said later, "as soon as she saw that it was not a prison of lights and cables, she began to relax and enjoy herself." Seen almost forty years later, the program has a certain awkward formality, too carefully rehearsed and far too polite. "Is not this the famous East Room?" asks Collingwood, and Jackie replies coolly, "Yes, this is the famous East Room." A few moments later: "Oh, Mrs. Kennedy, this room has a very different feeling from the Red Room!" A slight pause, then Jackie's reply to Collingwood: "Yes, it's blue." Toward the end of the tour, the president, right on cue, strolls in, praises his wife and her scholarly restoration team and, for the first and last time, refers to her publicly as "Jackie." Whether in pain or otherwise distracted, he seems remarkably uncomfortable.

In fact, life in the White House showed signs of constant strain during 1962. For one, Jack's affair with their friend Mary Pinchot Meyer continued, with astonishing audacity, right in the tidily restored White House. From October 1961 to August 1963, the gate logs at 1600 Pennsylvania Avenue note that "Miss Meyer" or "Mrs. Meyer" was admitted no less than fifteen times—fourteen of them during Jackie's absences at Glen Ora or Hyannisport or when she was out of the country. This is not a complete list of her rendezvous with the president; it is only a summary of those noted by the Secret Service.

Meyer was not the only woman on intimate terms with John Kennedy, but she was certainly one of the constant visitors to his door. According to everyone close to what was going on, Jackie was well aware of the situation; nevertheless, as Pierre Salinger memorably said, "She dismissed it completely. She wouldn't talk about it; she wouldn't listen to it. If something came up like that [in the news], I'm sure she would have turned off the TV."

But she can scarcely be called a complaisant wife, indifferent to the disarray and emptiness of her marriage. Occasionally the strain was evident in their social life. Charles Bartlett, who had found the earlier gatherings with Jack and Jackie so relaxed and pleasant, recalled that a year later there was some tension when the conversation turned to the future. Where would the Kennedys live after his time in the White House? More to the point, as Jackie asked, "What are you going to do, Jack? I don't want to be the wife of a headmaster of a girls' school."

This was a significant, if uncharacteristically sarcastic, thing to say. Jackie did not, even for the benefit of her guests, mention that he might be head of a foundation or an ambassador, a Supreme Court judge, a university president, or head of a *boys'* school. No, when Jackie thought of her husband at work, it was as headmaster of a *girls'* school, and her suggestive implications could not have escaped anyone.

On March 9, the president visited his ailing father in Palm Beach, where he deposited Caroline and John with their nurse and the family servants. He then continued south to Miami Beach for the weekend. That same evening, Jackie and her sister left the country on a commercial flight for a three-week unofficial tour of India and Pakistan.

Accompanying them were aides, secretaries, personal attendants, a reporter and photographer and the usual Secret Service men and Signal Corps communications personnel.

As she had done after the European journey in 1961, Jackie was again striking out on her own, which she was doing more and more often, for both short and long periods. Even a cursory review of her schedule suggests some kind of hidden domestic drama. Jackie spent three- and four-day weekends at Glen Ora; she made more and more shopping expeditions to New York; and she went to Palm Beach when her husband was in Hyannisport and Hyannisport when he was in Palm Beach.

En route to India, the party stopped for one night in Rome, where Pope John XXIII received Jackie—without her sister—in a private audience. The eighty-one-year-old Pontiff was already known for his warmth and accessibility, and when his introduction to Jackie was detailed years later, it emphasized the affable humanity of the man who was about to astonish the world by summoning a council that would benefit both the Church and the world. For days the Pope had been asking his counselors the correct form of address he should use for the wife of the American president. Was she to be called "Madame" or "Madame First Lady" or simply "Mrs. Kennedy"? What was he to do?

When she was admitted into his presence, Jackie knelt before the Pope for the first of three traditional genuflections, an ancient and servile custom appropriately terminated by the forthcoming Ecumenical Council.

As she rose, stepped closer and prepared to kneel again, the stout old man would have no more of this deference. Rising from his chair, he threw his arms open wide and almost ran to her. "Jack-eee!!" he cried, and, shocking bystanders, threw his arms around his guest. Their smiles could have illuminated the Pope's dark, small private library.

The press was, of course, told only that His Holiness and Jack-eee observed the protocols, discussing, only generally, the struggle for world peace and justice. But according to the Italian journalist Arnaldo Cortesi, the Pope also turned the conversation to her children, for whom he had modest gifts. This could not have been the sort of formal audience Jackie anticipated, for it was nothing like her 1951 visit to the Vatican: then, the princely Pius XII drew near to no one and offered solemn blessings from his portable throne, borne aloft on attendants' shoulders. "He's such a good man," Jackie said later of Pope John XXIII, "so of the earth, and centuries of kindness in his eyes."

Eleven years earlier, Lee had been in the crowd at the Vatican with Jackie. This time, she was absent, hoping perhaps to avoid embarrassment while certain influential friends, it was said, worked to expedite the Vatican's approval of her marriage to Stanislas Radziwill. That could be accomplished only through the tortured mechanisms of an annulment, which was a complicated matter, for the prince and princess had marriages that could have come from the pages of Schnitzler's *Reigen* (better known as the film and play *La Ronde*). Radziwill had once been married to Grace Kolin, who had married the Earl of Dudley, who was once married to Laura Charteris, who then married Michael Canfield, who had been Lee's first husband. It is not likely that Jackie and the Pope had the time to list the relationships, much less discuss their legitimacy. The matter was not sorted out by the time the Radziwills divorced in 1974.

ON MARCH 12, the touring contingent arrived in New Delhi, where they were escorted by John Kenneth Galbraith, the economist, author and, at that time, American ambassador to India; Jackie, he noted, was "full of life and looking like a million dollars in a suit of radioactive pink." They were followed everywhere, from the Taj Mahal to Jaipur, by a riot of photographers and reporters, but Galbraith observed that Jackie "didn't seem to mind [it] and I think rather enjoyed it." In Benares, she showed "her excellent sense of theater," for she "had put on a lavender dress, which could be picked out at any range up to five miles." In Jaipur, she stood in the back of an open car and waved at the crowds. The visit, filmed by the U.S. Information Agency, was officially described as a private holiday, but Jackie turned it into a public-relations bonanza, both for herself and, by association, the president. A major New Delhi newspaper called her Durga, the Goddess of Power, and plain folk simply mistook her for the Queen of America.

Back in Washington, Jackie spoke enthusiastically of her journey to anyone who would listen (and who would not?) at virtually every social event that season, including the formal White House dinner that April for forty-nine Nobel Prize winners. Present that evening was novelist Pearl Buck, whom Jackie reminded of her inspiring visit, years earlier, to the Chapin School. This dinner was the occasion memorably described by John Kennedy as "the most extraordinary collection of talent, of human knowledge, that has ever gathered together at the White House, with the possible exception of when Thomas Jefferson dined alone." Diana Trilling, who was present, had the impression that the entire Kennedy clan "realized that the whole occasion we were having and the way the White House looked and how it ran were [Jackie's] doing—and this was not to mention the response of the public to her charm. She was their billion-dollar asset, and they were far too clever not to recognize it." Jackie was especially gratified by Jack's reference to Thomas Jefferson, for they had just recently been discussing him as the epitome of the eighteenth-century spirit.

Then, in May, Jackie shone when she welcomed André Malraux—novelist, art critic and politician—to Washington and, as she had the previous year in Paris, made such an impression on him that he would later publicly hail her as "ever present when it comes to uniting art, the United States and my country."

That August, Jackie was off to Europe again, this time with Caroline, where they stayed at the Radziwill villa in Ravello, Italy; among the other guests were Gianni Agnelli (of Fiat) and his wife. This time things were entirely casual, and there was not a whisper of official or unofficial diplomatic activity. Jackie was photographed swimming, on water skis, sunning herself, dancing and generally comporting herself like a jet-setting holidaymaker. She seemed to care little about the reaction of the press, the public or Washington to her husbandless vacation, but sufficient word got back to Kennedy that he cabled Jackie to spend less time with Agnelli and more time with Caroline. She may have thought that for once, the proverbial shoe was on the other foot, and there was little he could do about it. (It should be stressed, however, that Agnelli and Jackie were friends and nothing else.)

In addition, Jack Kennedy had to face the fact that his wife was, in important ways he never could have foreseen, an important political ally. She defused the tension between him and the difficult Prime Minister Nehru, whom she charmed quite against his expectations during his visit to Washington. And her friendship with Adlai Stevenson bridged a gap between him and the president. "Thank you for all that you did for my [United Nations] Mission," Stevenson wrote to her in early 1963, "and for better relations with the whole cockeyed world!"

Jackie also worked for better relations with that world when, as David Ormsby-Gore said, she encouraged Jack to join with Britain and Russia in the Nuclear Test Ban Treaty—the logical result of their 1955 conversations. As it happened, some of Jack's advisers were against it, but Jackie, who believed in normalizing relations with Russia, prevailed. It was she, according to Ormsby-Gore, who also pushed the president to approve the proposed sale of 150 million bushels of wheat to the Soviet Union. For her, this was simply the point at which politics was a matter of humanity.

THERE WAS, IN 1962, a momentary thaw in the family chill—and it occurred, with stunning irony, during a far more perilous moment in America's Cold War with Russia. At the time of the Cuban missile crisis that October, the survival of the Western world, and perhaps the entire planet, was not at all certain.

On Friday, October 19, the president was departing for a brief political trip to the Midwest. Janet Travell saw him stride from the West Wing toward the helicopter that would take him to the airfield. He entered, but before the steps could be drawn up, the president appeared in the doorway and descended. Then she saw why: Jackie was running from the South Portico. They stood embracing, silent and motionless for several moments.

Saturday morning, October 20, he telephoned Jackie from Chicago as he was about to return to Washington; by now she was at Glen Ora with the children, and he asked her to bring them and meet him at the White House so that the family could be together in case of an emergency. It was not for his sake, but for theirs: there was fear of an imminent surprise nuclear attack on Washington. This would definitely mean the complete destruction of Virginia—but not, it was wrongly believed, the inevitable deaths of those who were to be transported to a secret underground shelter just outside the capital. By that afternoon, Jackie, Caroline and John were back in Washington. "If we were only thinking of ourselves," Jack told his friend and confidant Dave Powers, "it would be easy. But I keep thinking about the children, whose lives would be wiped out."

That evening, when Powers went to the family living room to deliver some crucial papers to the president, Jack was sitting with Caroline on his lap, reading her a story. "I watched him sitting there with Caroline," Powers told O'Donnell, "and I thought of what he had been saying to me about the children everywhere in the world. I handed him the papers and got out of there as fast as I could. I was all choked up."

As the unimaginable horror seemed steadily more probable, Jack told his wife that she must take the children and go to a place closer to the assigned underground shelter. But according to Sorensen and O'Donnell, who were both present, she refused to leave him alone in the White House.

IN EARLY 1963, Letitia Baldrige decided to leave the White House staff. She was, as she wrote, "physically exhausted" from her twelve to eighteen-hour-a-day, seven-days-a-week job. Jackie replaced her with an old schoolmate, Nancy Tuckerman, whose first assignment was to issue a strong announcement about Jackie's decision to become even less available to the press and public. "I'm taking the veil," she said in a memorandum to her secretary. "I've had it with being First Lady all the time, and now I'm going to give more attention to my children. I want you to cut off *all* outside activity—whether it's a glass of sherry with a poet or coffee with a king. No more art gallery dedications— no nothing—unless absolutely necessary."

Instead, she supervised plans for the construction of Wexford, their new weekend getaway at Atoka, Virginia, located on 166 acres of Rattlesnake Mountain, just a few miles from Glen Ora. Jack, meantime, was perfectly happy spending weekends at Camp David, and he told Jackie that he was not at all keen on spending his own money for Wexford. But she wanted a better place for riding and hunting, and she got her way. He also complained loudly about her clothing bills, which for some reason were now coming to him, perhaps because of Joe Kennedy's serious paralysis after his stroke in December 1961. "Department stores—$40,000!" he exclaimed, "blowing his stack" at her, recalled Ben Bradlee, who was present.

In April, Jackie had a perfect excuse for further withdrawal from public view when she announced, after several weeks of public and private denial, that she was expecting a baby in early autumn. This would be the first child born to a president in office in the twentieth century. (President Cleveland's wife, married to him in the White House, bore him two daughters, in 1893 and 1895.) "He never wanted [his own children] all crowded together like Bobby and Ethel," Jackie said privately. "But he always wanted a baby coming along when its predecessor was growing up. That is why he was so glad" when he learned of her pregnancy.

Thus, in June, the president traveled without Jackie to Texas, Colorado, California and Hawaii—and then on to Germany, Ireland, England and Italy. After a meeting with Pope Paul VI, who had just been elected after Pope John XXIII's death, Jack returned to Washington on July 2, the day after Jackie and the children had arrived on Cape Cod. He had a gift for Jackie, one that was magnificent but that may well have made them both laugh: an ancient Roman artifact, the head of a young satyr.

That summer, Jack had rented a cottage on a peninsula of Hyannisport called Squaw Island, which was more secluded than the Kennedy compound; over the next few weeks, he flew back and forth from the capital to the Cape, where he cruised Nantucket Sound and played golf. Jackie was seven months pregnant and feeling very well indeed. She was proud and gratified when her husband announced a limited nuclear test ban treaty on July 26. He was with her two days later, for her thirty-fourth birthday.

While he was in a White House meeting on August 7, the president was told that Jackie, after collapsing in severe pain, had been rushed to the hospital at Otis Air Force Base. By the time he arrived at the base early in the afternoon, Jackie had delivered, again by cesarean section, a four-pound son who had such difficulty breathing that the chaplain did not wait to baptize him. Patrick Bouvier Kennedy was about six weeks premature, and at first it seemed as if there was no danger. But shortly after the infant was placed in his mother's arms for a few moments, his respiration worsened. That evening, the president accompanied the baby to Children's Hospital in Boston and then to Harvard's School of Public Health, which had a high-pressure oxygen chamber.

As his staff recalled, John Kennedy was white with panic, for by this time doctors had diagnosed hyaline membrane disease, a condition that prevents proper oxygenation of the blood. On August 8, after flying back to visit the bedridden Jackie at Otis, he returned to Harvard, where he spent the night at the hospital. At two o'clock on the morning of August 9, he was awakened and asked to come to the baby's bedside. Just over two hours later, the little heart gave out. "He was such a beautiful baby," the president said in a thin voice to Dave Powers. "He put up quite a fight." And then, for the first time anyone who knew him could remember, John Kennedy sat down and sobbed. His son had not lived forty hours.

By that strange prescience often vouchsafed to mothers, Jackie seemed to know even before her husband arrived back at Otis to break the news. This was the third tragedy they shared. Jackie was not well enough to attend the funeral and burial in Brookline, which were solemnized by their friend Cardinal Cushing. About the president, Cushing said soon after, "He wouldn't take his hands off that little coffin. I was afraid he'd carry it right out with him."

Before the tiny casket was interred, Jack placed inside it the gold Saint Christopher medal that Jackie had given to him when they married, which he always had with him. A month later, when they quietly celebrated their tenth wedding anniversary, Jack gave Jackie a catalog from Van Cleef & Arpels and told her to select any item she wanted. Her choice was easy: she gave him a gold Saint Christopher medal. It was with him, too, when he died.

From that sad summer day forward, John Kennedy was, by every account, a changed man.

He had always been, by common consent, one of the most insistently private, least confiding of public figures. Still, this man—whose emotional life may forever be inaccessible to historians—was never more attentive to his wife and children than during (as they turned out to be) the last three months of his life. He had always loved Caroline and John, who were never in any case neglected for state reasons.

"The loss of Patrick affected the president and Jackie more deeply than anybody except their closest friends realized," wrote Kenneth O'Donnell and Dave Powers. They saw a singular example of this some weeks later, when Jack had returned to Boston for a fund-raising dinner. Following the event, he and his aides attended a Harvard-Columbia football game, but after the first half, the president turned to O'Donnell. "I want to go to Patrick's grave, and I want to go there alone, with nobody from the newspapers following me." At the cemetery nearby, he gazed down at the simple headstone that bore only one word: KENNEDY. Turning to his two friends, the president said, "He seems so alone here." That would be remedied all too soon, when Jackie arranged for the transfer of the little coffins of Arabella and Patrick to their father's side at Arlington National Cemetery.

Jackie left the hospital on August 14 and spent much of the next six weeks in seclusion on Cape Cod. A survey of the president's schedule shows clearly that between that date and September 24, he spent no less than twenty-three days—more than half his time—with his wife in Hyannisport or at Hammersmith Farm. There was really no one— no, not even anyone in their own families—who could enter into this grief as could the couple themselves. Their parenthood bound and bonded them—their nurturing of those who lived, and their sorrow for those they lost.

The last decade was telescoped for them that summer of 1963, as if the glorious light of Jack's accession to the presidency now paled in the cold glare of death. Life seemed more fragile, more provisional. And now, for once at least, everything Jack did and said signaled his efforts to console his wife. Bill Walton, Ben Bradlee and others noticed that in the weeks after Patrick's death, Jack and Jackie seemed closer than they had ever been. For the first time, they embraced in public; they sailed together; they spoke on the phone several times each day.

Lee Radziwill was also solicitous of her sister's physical and emotional health. When she learned the sad news, she was in Athens with Aristotle Onassis. He would be happy, said the shipping tycoon, to put his yacht *Christina* at the service of the First Lady of the United States if a cruise might benefit her at this trying time. Lee relayed the invitation at once.

Jack was not terribly pleased with the idea, for Onassis had run aground, to the point of various indictments, in past dealings with the Internal Revenue Service and was widely considered something of a pirate on the grandest scale. In addition, Ari was known as ringmaster of a set of rich idlers who were just beginning to be known as the international jet set. But Jackie longed to go, and so her husband, only to please her, relented. On October 1, she flew from New York, with Undersecretary of Commerce Franklin D. Roosevelt Jr. and his wife as chaperones, to join the Radziwills, the dress designer Princess Irene Galitzine and a few others at the port of Piraeus, whence they boarded the *Christina*.

THAT SUMMER OF 1963, Aristotle Socrates Onassis was fifty-seven years old. Although he stood only five feet five inches and had dark and weathered features, he supplied in unaffected charm what he lacked in traditional good looks. Ari was also a sympathetic man, extravagantly generous to guests and friends.

Born in Smyrna in 1906 to a Greek family of Turkish background, Ari lost his mother when he was just six. His father remarried, and soon Ari and his sister, Artemis, had two half sisters. Fleeing Turkish intolerance of Greek nationals—he saw three of his uncles executed— Ari sailed to Argentina as a teenager, and there he supported himself at such odd jobs as dishwasher and telephone operator. By the time he was twenty-five, he had made his first million dollars by buying ocean freighters at bargain prices and then charging various governments exorbitant fees to ship supplies during World War II. In 1946, at the age of forty, he married seventeen-year-old Athina Livanos, with whom he had a son (Alexander, in 1948) and daughter (Christina, two years later). In the next decade he established homes in New York, Paris, Antibes, Athens and Montevideo.

By 1959 he was the major stockholder in a number of international companies—Olympic Airways among them—and his estimated worth was $300 million. He had also devised systems whereby he paid minimal corporate taxes in Greece, France, Monaco and America but contributed personal taxes nowhere. "My favorite country," he said, "is the one that grants maximum immunity from taxes, trade restrictions and unreasonable regulations. I call that business sense." But he was bright in other ways, too, and because it was also good business sense, Ari became fluent in French, Italian and English.

In that same year, his marriage was about to be dissolved, for Ari had become involved in a notorious affair with the opera singer Maria Callas, who was neither his first nor his last lover. In 1962, he bought the Greek island of Skorpios for $110,000 and was pouring more than

$10 million into "improving" it. His fortunes seemed to increase annually; as he said, "All that really counts these days is money. It's the people with money who are the royalty now."

For two weeks that October, Jackie sailed the sea with Captain Ari aboard his fantastic *Christina*—a 303-foot-long floating hotel for which luxurious opulence is too modest a description. With gold, silver and marble in lavish measure, enormous guest suites, a pool with a marble floor that could be electrically raised for dancing, a library, a movie theater, game rooms and a ballroom, the yacht had sixty servants to look after fewer than a dozen visitors. The most strenuous activities were swimming, card games, dining and pouring drinks; in other words, the idea was to have no occupation but pleasure and diversion. People as diverse as Greta Garbo, Winston Churchill and Prince Rainier and Princess Grace were imperially entertained, for Ari stocked the yacht with endless supplies of the finest caviar and champagne, lobsters, Scottish beef and crates of vintage wines and liquors.

Jackie, like everyone else, was bedazzled—not only by the extravagance but also by the host himself, who had provided two hairdressers just for her, as well as a masseuse and an orchestra for evening dancing. She found Ari "an alive and vital person who had come from nowhere" to become a stunning success. In a way, he might have reminded her of her parents and grandparents, and indeed, there was something warmly paternal about Ari, who was twenty-three years her senior and a solicitous host. As it happened, they had much more to discuss than politics, for Jackie loved ancient Greek art and history, and Ari was far from ignorant of his country's culture. From Athens to Istanbul, Lesbos, Ithaca, Crete, Smyrna, Skorpios, Delphi and Marrakesh, the party continued nonstop.

By the time Jackie returned to Washington, on October 17, she had acquired a substantial array of antiques, gifts for her family and ample additions to her wardrobe. She was met by her husband, the children and a gathering political windstorm. Some Republican congressmen publicly asked if it was appropriate for the First Lady to accept the hospitality of a man of checkered background who had dubious business dealings with European governments and American shipping companies.

Another problem for these same critics was the sight of Jackie in newspapers and magazines, dressed in glamorous cocktail dresses and in swimsuits, cavorting with the international social set. These objections, of course, vanished into oblivion when she stepped down the airplane ramp, tanned, stylish, embraced by Jack, Caroline and John; from that moment, she was, at least for the next five years, immune from even a scintilla of criticism.

"Jackie has stars in her eyes—Greek stars," said someone in the White House staff. To be sure, she seemed to have banished the summer's depression. But this she had achieved only by distractions, only by acquisitions, only by an almost total immersion in a world of luxurious indolence. In a way, she had floated, somewhat dazed, through those two weeks.

The Republican backlash and the minor murmuring in the press, however temporary, made Jackie somewhat remorseful about her trip during a White House supper to which she had invited Ben and Tony Bradlee on October 21. The president insisted that Onassis not visit America until after the 1964 election, lest there be even more political damage, and he told the Bradlees that "Jackie's guilt feelings" about the entire excursion might work to his benefit.

He explained how. He asked Jackie if she would do something he knew she loathed: would she accompany him on a trip to Texas in November? This would be her first political appearance since 1960. Eager to repent, anxious to please, she replied at once that she would go with him wherever he wanted, wherever it would be helpful.

A week before their departure to Houston, Fort Worth, and Dallas, Jack and Jackie invited Joseph and Susan Mary Alsop to dinner, and the conversation turned to the imminent journey. "She didn't enjoy political trips," recalled Mrs. Alsop, "but felt she had to do it for Jack. She put the best face on it by saying things like, 'I love the idea of going to Dallas!'" And then Jack, who personally supervised every detail of her wardrobe for the journey, asked his wife to show the Alsops the pink Schiaparelli suit he had chosen for Dallas. After it was brought down and everyone admired it, the Alsops rose to leave: "We said good night and wished them well."

A few days later, *New York Times* reporter Joseph A. Loftus broke the story of Jackie's forthcoming activism on behalf of the campaign: "It is the charm of her shyness that has made her a strong attraction wherever she has appeared. She will do all she can to help her husband." While many thought Jackie's shyness was charming, some thought it a less appealing barometer of her true character, as she acknowledged: "I am a very shy person, [but] some people take this for arrogance, and my withdrawal from publicity as a sign of my supposedly looking down on the rest of mankind."

CHRONICLED IN COUNTLESS books and on miles of documentary and investigative film, the events that occurred in Dallas, Texas, and in Washington, D.C., from November 22 through 25, 1963, are perhaps the most familiar and recognized moments in American history. It would be easy merely to process and to coordinate the details of John Fitzgerald Kennedy's dreadful death and the grief that engulfed the nation—indeed, the entire world—over that long weekend. But in a biography of his wife, perhaps it is better to stress her impressions and memories as she recalled them during the official government investigation into the president's assassination and during the few crucial interviews she granted on the subject in subsequent years.

There were, of course, lacunae in her reporting, precisely because what had happened was literally stunning to her. Some details, therefore, are properly supplemented by the comments of other eyewitnesses, especially Nellie Connally, wife of the governor of Texas, who wrote an account soon after, and Lady Bird Johnson, the wife of the vice president, who days later dictated comments into a tape recorder.

On Friday, November 22, after stops in San Antonio, Houston and Fort Worth, Jackie and Jack flew to Dallas. "It was terribly hot," Jackie said of the ride in the motorcade, "just blinding all of us." She and Jack sat in the rear seat of the topless car, Governor and Mrs. Connally in the "jump" seats close in front of them. As the Lincoln limousine moved through town, "We could see a tunnel in front of us. Everything was really slow then. And I remember thinking it would be cool under that tunnel."

According to Nellie Connally, all around were "great, surging, happy, friendly crowds. I could resist no longer and turned to the president and said, 'Mr. President, you certainly cannot say that Dallas doesn't love you.' He smiled in obvious pleasure."

They seemed to be surrounded by street noises, Jackie said—crowds shouting, motorcycles buzzing.

And then three blasts from a rifle.

"All I remember was seeing my husband," Jackie told the Warren Commission in June 1964. "He had this sort of quizzical look on his face, and his hand went up—it must have been his left hand." The first bullet had entered the back of John Kennedy's neck and passed through the front of his throat.

Mrs. Connally could never shake off the terrible image: "There was no utterance of any kind from him. There was no grimace."

Governor Connally was badly wounded, too, but eventually he recovered.

The second bullet to hit the president entered the back of his head and exploded the right side of it. A mass of blood, skull and brain tissue blew out. President Kennedy was dead almost immediately. "I turned and looked at him," Jackie said. "I could see a piece of his skull and I remember it was flesh-colored. I remember thinking he just looked as if he had a slight headache."

"I felt something falling all over me," recalled Mrs. Connally. "My sensation was—buckshot. My eyes saw bloody matter in tiny bits, all over the car."

"We saw pieces of bone and brain tissue and bits of his reddish hair flying through the air," said Kenneth O'Donnell and Dave Powers, riding in the car behind. "The impact lifted him and shook him sharply, as if he was a rag doll." The car suddenly lurched and sped away.

In her frenzy and to her peril, Jackie crawled onto the trunk of the car to retrieve a chunk of Jack's skull. She was then pushed back to safety by Secret Service Agent Clint Hill. "They have killed my husband!" Jackie screamed. "I have his brains in my hand!" And with that, she pressed the piece of skull to his head, as if by the gesture she could somehow save his life.

"I just remember falling on him and saying, 'Oh, no, no, no—oh, my God, they have shot my husband!' I was shouting. And just being down in the car with his head in my lap. And it just seemed an eternity."

It was just after twelve-thirty. John F. Kennedy—who had been the thirty-fifth president of the United States for just two years, ten months and two days—was dead at the age of forty-six.

AT PARKLAND HOSPITAL, Dave Powers raced to the car and, seeing Kennedy's eyes open, cried, "Oh, my God, Mr. President—what did they do?" And then, still holding her husband's head, Jackie slowly turned to Powers and said quietly, "Dave, he's dead." Only when a few men wrapped a jacket around the shattered head did Jackie allow him to be taken from her lap. Dr. Marion Jenkins recalled that "she was carrying one hand cupped over the other hand. She nudged me with her left elbow, and then with her right hand, she handed me a good-sized chunk of the president's brain. She didn't say a word."

Inside, Jackie was asked to wait while doctors expended efforts that everyone knew to be a futile formality. She wanted to enter the examining room: "Do you think seeing the coffin can upset me, Doctor? I've seen my husband die, shot in my arms. His blood is all over me. How can I see anything worse than I've seen?" She forced her way past a nurse and into the room where his body lay, and then slipped off her wedding ring and gently put it on Jack's finger. "Do you think it was right?" she asked Kenneth O'Donnell an hour later. "Now I have nothing left." Next morning, after the autopsy at Bethesda Naval Hospital, O'Donnell retrieved the ring and returned it to a grateful Jackie.

ON THE FLIGHT back to Washington, Jackie sat next to the coffin, dazed and dry-eyed. Lady Bird Johnson, who enjoyed a warm relationship with Jackie, approached her in the private rear cabin. "Oh, Lady Bird," Jackie said, "we've liked you two so much. Oh, what if I had not been there? I'm so glad I was there!" Lyndon Johnson, suddenly catapulted to the presidency, had to cope with (as so many thought that day) the possibility of some sort of conspiracy that might target him, too. And there was the question of the protocol for the succession. But by all accounts except for one or two fierce Kennedy loyalists, Johnson behaved toward Jackie with the utmost discretion, sympathy and respect. When he was asked, over the next weeks and months, what ought to be done in a matter relative to the Kennedys, Johnson invariably replied gently, "Whatever the family wants."

Lady Bird noticed that Jackie's gloves were thickly caked with drying blood, that one leg was almost completely covered in blood, and that her suit was splashed through. "I asked her if I couldn't get someone in to help her change, and she said—with almost an element of fierceness, if a person that gentle, that dignified, can be said to have such a quality—she said, 'I want them to see what they have done to Jack.' "

And the world did see. Jackie did not change from her pink suit until dawn the next day, after she returned to the White House from Bethesda. The photograph of her wearing the bloodstained suit, standing at Johnson's side as he was sworn in as president aboard *Air Force One*, and the film of her descending from the plane to the waiting hearse in Washington were beamed around the world along with the majestic services she devised that entire weekend.

"She was absolutely stoic during the entire time," recalled Muriel Dobbin, White House correspondent for the *Baltimore Sun*. "Most of us journalists felt that she knew about Jack's philandering, and the consensus was that there had been huge fights between them. But Jackie was crazy about him, and his death very nearly destroyed her."

On Saturday, the president's body lay in state at the White House, and at the Capitol on Sunday. That same day, the assassin was himself assassinated as he was being transferred from one holding place in Dallas to another, witnessed by countless millions on live television. It was the first time anyone could recall an event ever replayed instantly on television. The United States, bound perhaps as never since the death of Franklin D. Roosevelt in 1945, now seemed to be having some kind of nervous breakdown.

In the Capitol Rotunda there were eulogies, and President Johnson placed a wreath at the foot of the flag-draped casket. Then Jacqueline slowly approached, Caroline at her side. They knelt to pray, and as Jackie leaned to kiss the bier, the little girl slipped her hand beneath the flag, touching the coffin.

No one who saw these images, aired on live television and reproduced in countless documentaries and in books of photo-essays, could ever forget them:

. . . the view of Jackie, her veiled head held high with consummate dignity as she led a gathering of forty world leaders, marching behind the caisson . . .

. . . the pictures of Jack's beloved brother Bobby, holding her hand . . .

. . . Jackie, bending down to her son, whispering that yes, now he could say good-bye to Daddy, and then—perhaps most heartbreaking of all, the next instant, when little John, who would have his third birthday the day of his father's burial, stepped forward and raised his hand in a salute . . .

. . . the caisson drawn by six horses, with the flag-draped coffin atop, and behind that the riderless horse, with reversed boots in the stirrups, symbol of a fallen leader . . .

. . . the one moment when Jackie's composure cracked, as she stood in the chill, waiting for the awful, final procession to begin, holding the children's hands, and when she lowered her head, her shoulders shook, and she sobbed . . .

. . . the lighting of an eternal flame at the grave in Arlington National Cemetery—a flame inspired by the French, who keep one forever burning beneath the great Arc de Triomphe, at the Tomb of the Unknown Soldier; here, in privacy and under cover of night on December 4, Jackie attended the reburial of Arabella and Patrick, insisting they must be with their father.

Jacqueline Bouvier had, since her schooldays, been trained to rise to the occasion, to put her best foot forward especially in times of crisis, to display, as the chaplain at Miss Porter's had so often urged, "guts and gumption." This attitude was bred in her bones, and now, as General de Gaulle said after being with her that solemn weekend, "She gave an example to the whole world of how to behave."

WHO WOULD HAVE blamed this thirty-four-year-old woman with two young children if she had simply vanished into seclusion and let others—her husband's family, the new administration, the masters of government protocol, or even strangers—supervise the great funeral?

But that was not her way. Even from *Air Force One*, en route from Dallas to Washington, she telephoned Bill Walton and senior members of the White House staff about the ceremonies and the funeral.

Abraham Lincoln would have come immediately to her mind. "She had already known of the woodcuts in *Harper's Weekly* that showed the East Room during Lincoln's funeral," recalled James Roe Ketchum, "and that's what she asked us to work out with Larry Arata, the White House upholsterer. He already had the black cambric, and additional material was acquired throughout that Friday night and into Saturday morning. This was an attention to detail you saw from the very beginning."

She wanted the ceremony, added Arata, to be "very humble, the same as Lincoln's funeral." In this, too, her focus enabled her to take a stand against the madness that was darkening her world. What was more, this was indeed a colossal moment in history, and everything about the necessary ritualization, the marking of it, must give evidence that it was linked to other great moments in history. Hence the recourse to the traditions of the past, the ongoing rubrics by which a nation understands itself, the liturgy by which people both dedicate themselves and transcend their limitations. The frame of reference pointed to mysteries that were eternal, not merely of the moment—to what was tragic for the order of society.

Meticulously following Jackie's request to use the 1865 engravings as a guide, the staff draped black webbing over the East Room chandeliers and windows. The florist was sent to gather magnolias from the tree Andrew Jackson planted in Lincoln's memory on the South Lawn.

Who would have blamed her if she had permitted herself to be taken to a hospital, had collapsed in grief and asked for heavy sedation? But that was not her way. She had a duty to her husband and to her children and to the nation. With chaos raging all around her, she must apply what order she could. Sudden widowhood had become a terrible fact—which was known and somehow accepted. Anyone might be forgiven the complete withdrawal from all concerns, but that was not Jackie's way. On the Friday and Saturday after Jack's death, she went through his personal effects, selecting various small items. She then gave each member of the cabinet and of the White House administration an appropriate memento: a cigarette case, a cigar box, a pen, a tie bar, a small art object, a paperweight: "Jack would have wanted you to have this." . . . "Won't you take this as a keepsake for the wonderful times you had with Jack." . . . "Jack was so grateful for your help, I know he would want you to have this little memento."

But what of the unknown: what of her children? The fact that she celebrated John's birthday on the night of the burial and Caroline's two days later demonstrates not a blocking of grief but its opposite: these youngsters were Jack's legacy to her and to the world. To everyone, she spoke of their shared love for Caroline and John and of her dedication to them now and for the rest of her life.

That weekend, Jackie came to Pierre Salinger's office. "She looked like a ghostly apparition," he recalled; and then she said, "Pierre, I have nothing else to do in life now except to raise my children well, to help them move forward through this terrible thing—otherwise, they will be tied forever to their father's death. I have to make sure they survive."

A few hours later, she saw J. B. West in the Cabinet Room and asked to speak with him for a moment.

"My children—they're good children, aren't they, Mr. West?"

"They certainly are."

She gazed out at the sandbox, the trampoline and tree house built especially for the Kennedy children. "They're not spoiled?"

"No, indeed," West replied quietly.

Jackie turned slowly and gazed searchingly into the face of her devoted attendant. "Oh, Mr. West," she said in a voice thick with loneliness, "will you be my friend for life?"

Unable to speak, he simply clasped her arm and nodded.

DE GAULLE WAS right: she did indeed teach the world how to grieve.

"It's just like Versailles when the king died," said Stanislas Radziwill when he arrived for the funeral. Indeed, Jackie taught the world the real meaning of royalty, the deepest truth of aristocracy. Without uttering a public word, without calling a press conference, she lifted the country by not breaking down. When she held her children's hands during the weekend of services, it seemed as if she were clasping the hands and calming the hearts of hundreds of millions of people. "I had never understood the function of a funeral before," Arthur Schlesinger wrote. "Now I realized that it is to keep people from going to pieces."

Truly noble souls, of whatever station, have a profound sense of and regard for their own vocation, their function, and their destiny in the world. This is not to glorify oneself: it is simply to take with utmost gravity the significance of oneself, of what one is called not only to do for others but to be for them. It is to have a sense that life has depths.

It is to insist that there is meaning, even when it cannot be grasped, that the great sorrows in life can somehow be accepted in light of a great mystery, a great chain of being. "I have peace in my heart and hatred for no one," Jackie said to Janet Travell just days after the funeral, while they were watching the evening news report on television. Then a face flashed on the screen, and there was an interview with the wife of Lee Harvey Oswald. "Oh, I feel so sorry for her," Jackie said. "She is such a nice-looking woman."

Truly noble women and men have somehow learned how to speak and act in ways appropriate to the moment, no matter what their personal feelings or "needs." And that weekend, no one with an atom of decency can deny, Jackie was magnificent. The country had idolized her, and now the country needed her to hold all people together, to find a way to feel, to weep, to hold and yet not to hold. She let no one down. Her sense of history, her dignity, and her refusal to think only of herself: it was she who brought order to the chaos.

When she greeted each visiting head of state who came to Washington; when she never stopped being an attentive mother; when she lit the flame at her husband's grave; when she saw to the comfort of everyone, from kings, emperors and generals to the White House janitors; when she wrote personal notes to every one of 114 staff members that weekend, thanking them for their condolences; when she insisted on going forward with her children's birthday parties the following week; when she comforted those who wept in her arms—could anyone dare to say that she was merely escaping into the formalities of protocol?

AS IF GRIEF were not enough, Jackie and the children suddenly had no place to live—and what of Caroline's school, which now included a number of other children and was in full operation in several White House rooms? To Jackie's great relief, Lady Bird Johnson generously suggested that the school remain until Christmas. "I would to God," Mrs. Johnson wrote in her diary, "[that] I could serve Mrs. Kennedy's comfort; I can at least serve her convenience."

But White House regulations and those budgetary considerations strictly controlled by the government require that a supplanted family, under whatever circumstances, vacate the executive mansion immediately for a new president. Johnson's administration, therefore, had to take over the White House, his family the residence, his staff the personal and official duties. Although it caused him, his family and his personnel considerable complications, Lyndon Johnson gallantly remained at his Washington residence and made no attempt to hurry Jackie and her children from the White House. This, of course, was a logistical nightmare.

For obvious reasons, Hyannisport was not an appropriate residence for Jackie and the children; she had, after all, lived mostly in Washington since she was thirteen. Nor was it congenial to live in the new house the Kennedys had almost completed, way out in Virginia. What to do?

This was scarcely a matter of a widow and her children about to be tossed into the snow like characters in a Dickens novel. The president's will divided his large estate into two equal trust funds, the income from one assigned to Jackie and the other to be shared by his children. When he signed this document in 1954, it contained an additional bequest of $25,000 and all his personal effects to her. In addition, Congress voted to pay all Kennedy's funeral expenses; to provide Jackie with a $50,000 budget for two years of staff assistance; free mailing privileges; and a year of Secret Service protection. Under existing law, she was also entitled to a widow's pension of $10,000 annually for life or until she remarried.

But regardless of anyone's financial status, it is impossible to purchase and occupy a house on a few days' notice. In this case, space, security, proximity to friends and family—all these elements had to be taken into account.

"I didn't have anyplace to go," Jackie said years later during one of her few formal interviews. This was no exaggeration: her father had left her no property, the inheritance from Jack had to be shared with her children and would take time to sort out, and there was no room at Merrywood physically or emotionally for a new family of three. Jackie was, she added, "in a state of shock, packing up. But Lyndon Johnson was extraordinary. He did everything he could to be magnanimous, to be kind. It must have been very difficult for him. . . . It was such an awkward way [for him] to come to the presidency, wasn't it. There should be a dividing line; this was an unnatural division."

Left and below: At five, summer 1934, with her parents, Janet and John ("Black Jack") Bouvier, at the Southampton Riding and Hunt Club, Southampton, Long Island. *(Corbis/Bettman-UPS)*

The Inquiring Camera Girl in Washington, 1951.
(Globe Photos)

With Senator John F. Kennedy, Hyannisport, summer 1953.
(NBC/Globe Photos)

A whisper from her new father-in-law: wedding day at Newport, September 12, 1953. *(Corbis/Bettmann-UPI)*

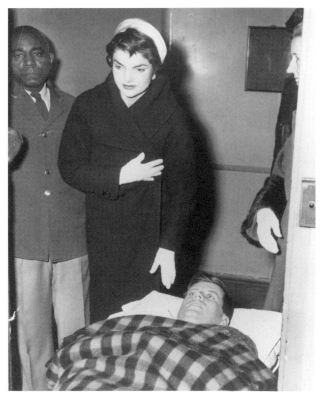

With JFK at the Hospital for
Special Surgery, 1954.
(Globe Photos)

At home in Georgetown, 1955. *(Globe Photos)*

At Hyannisport, with JFK and Caroline, 1959. *(J. Murphy/Globe Photos)*

At the U.S. Conference of Mayors, Miami, 1960. *(Globe Photos)*

On the stump with JFK, 1960. *(Globe Photos)*

Bobby, Joe, Rose, Jackie, JFK, and Eunice, 1960. *(Globe Photos)*

Pregnant but campaigning in
New York, 1960.
(Globe Photos)

With John F. Kennedy Jr. and Caroline, 1961. *(Globe Photos)*

In Paris, 1961. *(Globe Photos)*

In the Capitol Rotunda, facing the bier of JFK, November 24, 1963.
(Corbis/Bettmann-UPI)

With Cardinal
Cushing and Robert
Kennedy at the
burial of JFK,
November 25, 1963.
(Globe Photos)

Shopping—Greece, 1973. *(Globe Photos)*

(Globe Photos)

With Aristotle Onassis.
(Elio Sorci/Globe Photos)

With Lee Bouvier Radziwill in
New York, 1974.
(Paul Schmulbach/Globe Photos)

With Mikhail Baryshnikov.
(Globe Photos)

With John Carl Warnecke.
(Art Zelin/Globe Photos)

At a reception in her honor at the French
Embassy, New York, 1977. *(Globe Photos)*

With Caroline. *(Globe Photos)*

The working mother in
New York, 1977.
(Barrett/Globe Photos)

With Maurice Tempelsman, 1992. *(Globe Photos)*

(Corbis/Reuters)

Happily, Ambassador John Kenneth Galbraith had an idea to help Jackie. He asked Undersecretary of State Averell Harriman, who had several homes and traveled much of the time, if he might be willing to loan his Georgetown residence. Harriman rose to the moment, and Jackie prepared to move to 3038 N Street N.W. with her children on December 6. But she still had to depend on the hospitality of the government and of the Johnson family for more than two weeks, which was a highly irregular situation.

ON TUESDAY, NOVEMBER 26, the day after her husband was buried, Jackie invited the new First Lady for tea, to introduce her to the private quarters: "She was," recalled Mrs. Johnson, "orderly, composed and radiating her particular sort of aliveness and charm and warmth. Mrs. Kennedy is like an indescribably fresh flower—so I won't try to describe her, except that there is an element of steel and stamina somewhere within her to keep her going as she is. . . . She went on to say a lot of things, like 'Don't be frightened of this house—some of the happiest years of my marriage have been spent here—you will be happy here.' In fact, she repeated that over and over, as though she were trying to reassure me. Then we got up and walked around from room to room so that I could see how my furniture would fit into her bedroom. . . ." Before she and the children moved, Jackie rearranged some furnishings to cover bare spaces: she wanted, she said, to make the place more welcoming to the Johnsons.

That same day, Jackie wrote a long letter to the new president, in which she referred to his courage in walking, against advice, in the funeral cortege and to her decorations for the Oval Office. This letter alone demolishes the rumors of hostility between the Johnsons and Jackie:

Dear Mr. President:
Thank you for walking yesterday—behind Jack. You did not have to do that—I am sure many people forbid you to take such a risk, but you did it anyway.
Thank you for your letters to my children. What those letters will mean to them later—you can imagine. The touching thing is,

they have always loved you so much, they were most moved to have a letter from you now.

And most of all, Mr. President, thank you for the way you have always treated me—the way you and Lady Bird have always been to me—before, when Jack was alive, and now as President.

I think the relationship of the Presidential and Vice Presidential families could be rather a strained one. From the history I have been reading ever since I came to the White House, I gather it often was in the past.

But you were Jack's right arm—and I always thought the greatest act of a gentleman that I had seen on this earth was how you—the Majority Leader when he came to the Senate as just another little freshman who looked up to you and took orders from you—could then serve as Vice President to a man who had served under you and been taught by you.

But more than that we were friends, all four of us. All you did for me was as a friend and the happy times we had. I always thought, way before the nomination, that Lady Bird should be the First Lady—but I don't need to tell you here what I think of her qualities—her extraordinary grace of character—her willingness to assume every burden. She assumed so many for me and I love her very much. And I love your two daughters—Lynda Bird most because I know her the best—and we first met when neither of us could get a seat to hear President Eisenhower's State of the Union message and someone found us a place on one of the steps in the aisle where we sat together. If we had known then what our relationship would be now.

. . . Late last night, a moving man asked me if I wanted Jack's ship pictures left on the wall [of the Oval Office] for you (they were clearing the office to make room for you). I said no because I remembered all the fun Jack had those first days hanging the pictures of things he loved, setting out his collection of whales' teeth, etc.

But of course they are there only waiting for you to ask for them if the walls look too bare. I thought you would want to put things from Texas on it—I pictured some gleaming long horns—I hope you put them somewhere.

It cannot be very much help to you your first day in office to hear children on the lawn at recess. It is just one more example of your kindness that you let them stay—I promise they will soon be gone.

Thank you, Mr. President.
Respectfully,
Jackie

She wrote scores of personal letters at this time, many of them to foreign and domestic political leaders. Those to Nikita Khrushchev and to Richard Nixon, for example, are noteworthy for their warmth and genuine respect.

When Lady Bird Johnson went to her new quarters for the first time, she found a small bouquet of flowers and a note: "I wish you a happy arrival in your new house, Lady Bird—Remember—you will be happy here. Love, Jackie."

FROM THE TIME of the burial on Monday (her son's birthday) through Wednesday (Caroline's birthday), Jackie visited the gravesite no less than five times. After another trip to Arlington National Cemetery on Thursday morning, she joined the Kennedy family in Hyannisport for a somber Thanksgiving holiday. Heavy rains lashed Cape Cod all that weekend, the fog made driving dangerous, and an icy wind surrounded the compound. Jackie remained mostly alone, gazing out over the water and, once or twice, braving the weather to walk along the shore.

Then, on Friday morning, November 29—exactly one week after her husband's death—Jacqueline Kennedy did something that forever altered the seascape of American mythology. She telephoned Theodore H. White, who had published a book about Kennedy's presidential race, and asked him to come at once to Hyannisport. She had something to say to him and to the country, and she wanted to tell it through *Life* magazine.

He arrived late that night to find her in the company of a few relatives and friends, whom she at once dismissed. Tearless but ashen, Jackie sat with him for several hours. As if nature were providing the appropriate setting, a terrible storm raged: all that weekend heavy rain and strong winds pounded the Cape. There was a fire crackling, but not enough wood to last the evening, and the room became damp and cold. Still, Jackie spoke, her voice thin and dry.

"She wanted to make certain that Jack was not forgotten in history," White recalled, "to rescue him from all the bitter people. She did not want Jack left to the historians." Wandering back and forth through the events and times of her husband's life, she longed to memorialize the magic and grace she had seen in him. She described in detail the awfulness of his death. And then she came to her point.

"There's this one thing I wanted to say . . . It's been almost an obsession with me. I keep thinking of this line from a musical comedy. At night, before we'd go to sleep, we had this old Victrola. Jack liked to play some records . . . and the song he loved most came at the very end of this record, the last side of *Camelot:* 'Don't let it be forgot, that once there was a spot, for one brief, shining moment that was known as Camelot.' . . . There'll never be another Camelot."

On she went, while White scribbled in his notebook.

"Do you know what I think of history? For a while, I thought history was something that bitter old men wrote. But Jack loved history . . . this lonely, little sick boy . . . scarlet fever . . . this little boy, sick so much of the time, reading in bed, reading history . . . reading the Knights of the Round Table . . . and he just liked that last song.

"Then I thought, for Jack history was full of heroes. . . . Men are such a combination of good and bad . . . He was such a simple man. But he was so complex, too. Jack had this hero idea of history, the idealistic view, but then he had that other side, the pragmatic side. His friends were his old friends, he loved his Irish Mafia."

"What Jacqueline Kennedy was saying to me now," White later said, "was: please, History, be kind to John F. Kennedy—don't leave him to the bitter old men to write about."

At midnight, they concluded their four-hour conversation. White rushed to his typewriter and tapped out the story that ran in *Life* a week later. "She wanted Camelot to top the story," he remembered: Camelot, heroes, fairy tales and legends.

And so, in the fullness of time, the era of John F. Kennedy was called Camelot. At first, this was an undiluted honorific; later, many people decided that personal failings made the myth of Camelot a sham.

Most of Jack's ardent admirers admitted, years later, that his taste in music was pretty much limited to "Bill Bailey, Won't You Please Come Home?" and he had a particular fondness for "Hail to the Chief." Alan Jay Lerner, who wrote the lyrics for *Camelot,* had been a friend of Jack's since their schooldays at Choate. But when the president chose recordings for relaxation, they were usually Irish jigs and reels or beer-barrel tunes. This is not to say he may not have known and even liked Lerner and Loewe's Broadway hit, but Jack Kennedy was no romantic idler; never a dreamer about past legends, he was the toughest realist.

"There was no Camelot in the early 1960s," wrote his Secretary of State, Dean Rusk, "and John Kennedy himself would have been the first to kick such notions out the window. He was too skeptical for sentimentality." Arthur Schlesinger agreed: "The Camelot idea is a kind of mythomania. He may certainly have known of the show, but the notion that he identified with it was unheard until Jackie brought Teddy White to Hyannisport. Anyone who made that kind of connection would have been swiftly mocked by Kennedy himself."

But that day, Jackie was adamant: "All I keep thinking of is this line—it's become an obsession with me. . . ."

Eventually, as Jackie admitted to John Kenneth Galbraith and others, she realized that she had rather overdone the Camelot mythology. But she also knew how inadequate mere chroniclers can be, and how bitter. She was enough of a historian to know that it is easy to dilute the past, to rob it of the mystery and the complexity that are built into the truth. Oversimplifying is so easy. Little did she know that most would come to regard her Camelot that way.

This was hardly a grievous deception, an attempt to win for her husband what she thought he never deserved. For one thing, a grieving widow perhaps naturally wishes, for herself and her children, to recall only the best of times, the highest hopes. She refused ever to criticize John Kennedy, nor would she focus on anything except his concrete actions and goals for the country. No personal details of their life together, no morsels of gossip ever passed her lips, nor would she hear them from anyone else. She knew enough of gossip and the cult of celebrity to realize that cynicism, sarcasm and innuendo are the prelude to hatred, and it was hatred that took her husband from her and her family.

But for Jacqueline Bouvier Kennedy, life was incomprehensible without art, without story and legend; and to the creation of the grandest of all she dedicated herself when she edited the final drafts of Theodore White's elegy.

Her grandmother had taken her as a child at Lasata around the gardens, pointing out this flower and that plant and spinning out the folklore and ancient legends about each species.

And then there was her grandfather, with his flamboyant little book that placed the Bouviers, the Vernous and their descendants in the line of French nobility. From the gently splashing fountains of Lasata to the myths of *Our Forebears,* Jackie had grown up in an atmosphere worthy of Mallory and Tennyson. In school and at home, she had pored over the story of Lancelot and Guinevere, and those haunting engravings by Doré that captured the glory and the sorrow of Camelot. And during her European travels, Jackie had become passionate about the great legends—particularly after her visits to the ancient Irish and Scottish castles, to the rocky promontories of Cornwall, the cradle of the Arthurian legend.

Everything had come together when the press and the public called the Kennedys the American royal family. She was the chatelaine of the new Versailles, her Maison Blanche was the new castle in which the best of the past and the brightest of the present could shine. Throughout her life, the great and noble women of the past had been her models. How else could she see her brief and shining moment but as a kind of Camelot?

But if the story of Camelot is considered in all its fullness, was she not, after all, more accurate than the cynics were? Did not her time with Jack have, as perhaps its most precise and appropriate archetype, the story of Lancelot and Guinevere? After all, she knew the entire tale, with its great, tragic episodes of deception and death.

That stormy November night in Hyannisport, as wind and rain battered the cottage and the fire began to die in the hearth, Jacqueline

Bouvier Kennedy asked that posterity record only the best of her husband's legacy, to place it within a mythic tradition. Very soon after, she realized that this was a hopeless ambition. The shining moment, for her as for her forebears, had indeed been brief, and then clouds blotted out the sun.

CHAPTER TEN

1964-1968

For a long time, it was as if she lived in a gray haze of grief and confusion. She was only thirty-four, but Jackie felt much older, and she often told friends that her life was over, that she was simply waiting for the end. Only her loving duty to her children enabled her to survive. Complicated though her marriage had been, it had given her a structure for living, and now she was tossed onto the mercies of a world that adored her but waited to see how she would manage on her own.

As far as she was concerned, however, she was not on her own, she was merely alone, and so for a certain time she, like the public, turned to her ambiguous past for solace. "I know my husband was devoted to me," she told one of her interior decorators, Billy Baldwin. "I know he was proud of me. It took a very long time for us to work everything out, but we did, and we were about to have a real life together. I was going to campaign with him. I know I held a very special place for him—a unique place."

In addition, she had depended on him—not always for a confirmation of devotion, but because life with Jack had given her a reason for being. "I never had or wanted a life of my own," she said significantly. "Everything centered around Jack. Sometimes I wake in the morning, eager to tell him something, and he's not there. Nearly every religion teaches there's an afterlife, and I cling to that hope. Those three years we spent in the White House were really the happiest time for us, the closest, and now it's all gone. Now there is nothing, nothing."

Such sentiments were often expressed to friends and confidants, and they make even more comprehensible her creation of Camelot, which was not so much an achievement as a poignant wish. "I should have known that it was asking too much to dream that I might have grown old with him," she added in her own hand to the text of a memorial essay published in *Look* on the first anniversary of Jack's death. "But learning to accept what was unthinkable changes you."

A great part of her loneliness would be irremediable, even when she allowed herself the comforts of romantic attachments. Friends often found her pale and distracted, her eyes red with weeping, her fingernails bitten. There were, early in 1964, whispers about psychiatric help or medical treatment of some kind, for Jackie was often almost neurasthenic, smoking more compulsively than ever. (Her favorite brand of cigarettes during those years was, ironically, named Newport.)

SHE WAS NOT left to solitary grief, however. Robert Kennedy attended Jackie and virtually adopted her children, but he had his own large and ever growing family. He was also Attorney General of the United States and, at thirty-eight, had his own political ambitions—a Senate seat and, it turned out, the presidency.

President and Mrs. Johnson were warmly solicitous, too. They often invited Jackie and the children to visit the White House, but this she could not bring herself to do. "I explained that it was really difficult for me, and I didn't really ever want to go back. . . . It was just too painful. . . . Even driving around Washington, I'd try to drive a way where I wouldn't see the White House." She did not return to 1600 Pennsylvania Avenue until 1971, when President and Mrs. Nixon invited her and the children for a private supper and to see the official portraits of Jack and Jackie that were about to be displayed in the White House.

It was not easy to turn down the kind invitations from the Johnson family, for they were bound to her by a deep and true mutual affection. According to Pierre Salinger, the new president "was as grateful to Jackie Kennedy and her late husband as she was to him. Often, and in very emotional terms, he'd tell me how much he appreciated how kind they had always been to him. In early 1964, he told me he wanted to 'do something nice for Jackie—I'll name her ambassador to France.' I carried the message to Jackie, who appreciated the gesture but declined. LBJ was fond of telling people, 'She always made me feel at home' "— most of all, perhaps, because Jackie saw how patronizing the Kennedys could be toward the Johnsons.

Her mother and sister visited her almost daily at the end of 1963 and into early 1964, helping to facilitate the move to Georgetown and to comfort her through the long winter evenings. And Jackie's secretarial staff arrived daily and read a selection of the cards and letters arriving from all over the world.

On January 14, 1964, wearing a collarless black wool suit and no jewelry but her gold wedding band, she spoke before television cameras from the Attorney General's office:

> I want to take this opportunity to express my appreciation for the hundreds of thousands of messages—nearly 800,000 in all— which my children and I have received over the past few weeks. The knowledge of the affection in which my husband was held by all of you has sustained me, and the warmth of these tributes is something I shall never forget. Whenever I can bear to, I read them.

Her voice broke slightly for a moment:

> All his bright light gone from the world.
>
> All of you who have written to me know how much we all loved him and that he returned that love in full measure. It is my greatest wish that all these letters be acknowledged. They will be, but it will take a long time to do so, but I know you will understand.
>
> Each and every message is to be treasured, not only for my children but so that future generations will know how much our country and people in other nations thought of him. Your letters will be placed with his papers in the library to be erected in his memory. I hope that in years to come, many of you and

your children will be able to visit the Kennedy Library. It will be, we hope, not only a memorial to President Kennedy but a living center of study of the times in which he lived and a center for young people and for scholars from all over the world.

May I thank you again on behalf of my children and of the president's family for the comfort that your letters have brought to us all. Thank you.

The mention of her children was of supreme importance, for as Jackie had said to Pierre Salinger, among others, nothing took precedence over them. Additionally, it cannot be overemphasized that Jackie fiercely protected her children from unflattering perceptions of their father. They matured hearing about Jack's devotion to the common good, about his love for them, about his commitment to world peace. Of his infidelities she never spoke, hence Caroline and John grew to love him without dilution—precisely because they sensed how much their mother always did.

SHE WAS THIRTY-FOUR years old and would live another thirty years. Occasionally she would speak on behalf of favorite causes, and twice she addressed legislative bodies to save a historic building—but that broadcast was the last time she spoke of herself and her feelings to the world at large.

With that final statement, she rose and moved toward a group of reporters and technicians familiar from the White House—but they moved away, apparently thinking she wished to pass through the crowd and depart at once. "Why are you all running away?" she asked with a smile, stretching out her hands. "I wanted to say hello." Yes, it was true, she told them when one asked if the morning papers were correct: her lawyers had closed the contract for Jackie's purchase of a magnificent, eighteenth-century Colonial home with twelve rooms at 3017 N Street N.W. She made a down payment of $60,000 and took a mortgage for the balance of $115,000. And she told the group more about the plans for the John F. Kennedy Library in Boston. After making one public plea, Jackie raised more than $10 million for the project.

The Institute of Politics at Harvard's Kennedy School of Government also claimed her attention. Richard Neustadt, its first director, recalled that Jackie was serious about an academic place where students could meet for intense discussions about public service. She met with the young people there, seeing to it that they came not only from the ranks of the privileged at Harvard but from often ignored groups; to the professors she brought searching questions and by her frequent presence at student forums ensured that political debate engaged everyone. According to Neustadt, Jackie wanted the Institute to have the kind of exciting give-and-take she had known in Paris years earlier, when the cafés along the Boulevard Saint-Michel hummed with lively debate.

In early February, she and the children moved to the new house. At the same time, Caroline and her first-grade classmates, no longer installed in their White House schoolroom, were meeting in rooms that had been donated by the British embassy. After the term ended in May, the group disbanded, and in September, Caroline attended the Convent of the Sacred Heart in Bethesda, Maryland. John marked his fourth birthday in a cooperative preschool Jackie arranged; he and a few other children met alternately in their homes.

ALL THESE AND other details were breathlessly reported in the daily press, as the national idolization of Jacqueline Kennedy began. Sympathy and admiration for her in the first days of her widowhood now turned into an obsession. Reporters wanted to know everything about her—where she shopped, with whom she had lunch, which invitations she accepted and which were declined; she found all this ever more persistent prying offensive and alarming. Her press assistants were importuned, cajoled, bribed for interviews and for more, ever more news—anything!—about her, her outings, her habits, her gradual return to social life.

From 1964 forward, this dilemma was exacerbated until it reached epic proportions as Jackie became more and more something of a royal figure. In light of her experiences, education, personal tastes, aristocratic bearing—and what is called the temper of the times—this was perhaps inevitable.

Her childhood, while materially privileged, was spent in an emotionally bankrupt family. Her father was deeply wounded by his own frailties while her mother was obsessed with social status. Since Jackie had made her debut at eighteen, she had been destined for a kind of American queenship. Her marriage to John F. Kennedy and her subsequent accession to First Ladyship had fulfilled many of her mother's dreams and had confirmed that part of her character which had longed for a noble destiny.

Thus, a decent, serious, meditative young woman with a fine mind and a sharp sense of humor became, by accident, somewhat lost in an aura both imposed and accepted. The irony—and she was aware of it—was that she was required only to be and to appear at the proper place and time, smiling, waving, an ambassador of what-you-will. She did not have to accomplish anything of significance. People required only that she look magnificent.

But there was, of course, a movie-star schizophrenia to it all.

After her husband's death, Jackie had to distinguish between "what the widow Kennedy can or must do" and "what I think and feel in my privacy." She was becoming, as Shakespeare said of Hamlet, the observed of all observers, but she was also an observer of herself and constantly had to present the world with an idealized icon of herself as Mrs. Kennedy.

In light of that, she had perhaps no alternative but to offer the public a kind of mask and to retreat into her deserved privacy behind that mask. She was not a cold woman, but her image became that of someone predictable in her elegance and almost immutable in her character. The public had admired her as First Lady: now they wanted to adore her forever as First Widow and First Mother. The idea that she might remarry—or worse, ever again have a passional life—was simply unthinkable. At thirty-four, she was assigned the role of queen dowager—very much like the beloved Alexandra, Mary and Elizabeth, the queens consort and the widows of England's King Edward VII, George V and George VI.

The problem, of course, was that Jack and Jackie had to do what they had to do. When they had appeared on television, everything seemed to augur well: instant exposure meant free and positive publicity. But in this feigned intimacy, there had been enormous danger. Having once allowed the camera to enter, they had opened Pandora's box. The media machinery could never again be kept out or prevented from becoming more and more intrusive.

As a photojournalist and as wife of a senator on the campaign trail, Jackie had seen the gradual incursion of the press into the lives of private citizens. The several homey television interviews she and Jack had given had shown them off to remarkably good political advantage, but this sort of thing always made her profoundly uncomfortable, for she knew well the difference between image and reality. Still, the White House years, during which she and Oleg Cassini presented her as a new kind of First Lady, completed the impression that a resplendent new age had dawned with her as consort, empress and mother.

As the president's wife, she had been able to exercise a certain degree of control, especially regarding sheltering Caroline and John from a voracious and intrusive press. But now, suddenly, she was a private citizen again—and the most attractive sort of private citizen, a beautiful and photogenic young widow, apparently lonely and bowed with grief, brave, fragile and strong all at once. As popular culture was offering a greater profusion of melodramatic soap operas by day and by night, so, too, did the press scramble to find the right subjects for newspapers and magazines. Jackie fit the requirements perfectly.

These were, of course, major moments in the American culture's valuation of image, of glamour. More and more, public figures came to resemble movie stars and were so treated. Slowly but inexorably, life was expected to resemble entertainment, and even to surpass it. And what better figure than Jackie to capture the public's need for someone to adore?

WHEREVER SHE WENT, there were ubiquitous reminders of the assassination and its aftermath. "People tell me that time will heal," she told a friend later that year. "How much time? Last week I forgot to cancel the newspapers and I picked them up and there was the publication of the Warren [Commission] Report [on the assassination], so I canceled them for the rest of the week. But I went to the hairdresser and picked up *Life* magazine and it was terrible." Chronicles of Kennedy's death were unavoidable—indeed, they proliferated like mushrooms during 1964.

This public preoccupation led directly to an unfortunate episode.

Because Jackie and her in-laws were almost fanatically protective of the image of the late president, she joined Robert Kennedy in approving the choice of William Manchester to write, as they hoped, the official book on the events of November 1963. "Jackie wanted," recalled Edwin Guthman, who had been senior press officer in the Department of Justice, "an authoritative history of the assassination, and Manchester was a highly reputable and respectable writer." In addition, he had already written a laudatory book about John Kennedy.

But the arrangement whereby Manchester granted the Kennedys absolute approval of the final draft was not judicious on anyone's part. *The Death of a President* was finally published in 1967, but only after a lengthy and bitter dispute that extended from editorial offices to the courts.

For one thing, Jackie had granted Manchester extensive interviews, the transcripts of which she wanted edited before publication, in order to delete certain personal details, such as the fact that Maud Shaw was delegated to break the news of their father's death to Caroline and John while Jackie was still in Texas. She also wanted him to omit poignant details Jackie had mentioned regarding the sight of her husband's corpse, and the fact that before she left the hospital, she was so dazed that she performed the automatic act of freshening her lipstick. None of the matters she wished to expunge was any more indelicate than these, none would have shocked anyone. But it is easy to understand her anxiety about virtually everything that would appear in print for people to read—her children, most obviously—and perhaps misinterpret.

Second, Manchester's stance was decidedly hostile to Lyndon Johnson. Except for Jackie, the Kennedys had no affection for the man they generally regarded as a complacent usurper, and by 1967 Johnson felt similarly about Robert. But so frank a tone as Manchester adopted could only jeopardize Robert Kennedy's standing in the Democratic Party and thus his own ambitions, which were taking shape by 1967. And while he had his eye on the presidency, Jackie was focused on the past.

For editorial comments on Manchester's book, Bobby asked Ed Guthman, then national editor of the *Los Angeles Times,* and John Siegenthaler, also a former Kennedy aide and later editor of the *Nashville Tennessean,* to read the first draft of the manuscript. "John and I met with Manchester and his editor," recalled Guthman, "and we had identical reactions. The early chapters were so harsh on Johnson that we felt they would undermine the credibility of the entire book." Arthur M. Schlesinger Jr., once Kennedy's special assistant, agreed: "You will be under great pressure to tone down the LBJ passages in the book," he told Bobby. "Of course, everything that is petty and gratuitous should go."

Hence, for a complex of reasons both personal and professional, Jackie and her brother-in-law brought pressure against the author, who tried to be as cooperative as he felt his integrity permitted. But finally he felt too much compromised. At the same time, Jackie regarded the enormous serial-rights payment he was to receive—$650,000 from *Look* magazine, which would publish three installments—as inappropriate because such an enormous amount of money made the topic seem entirely too commercial a venture. A lawsuit against Manchester, filed on the basis that he had refused to acknowledge the Kennedy proprietorship, was withdrawn after he excised a few passages Jackie and Robert found offensive. Both Harper & Row, the publisher, and the author— with astonishing generosity of spirit, Jackie said—then signed over most of the book's income to the John F. Kennedy Library fund.

But no one could be said to have won the case. The struggle badly affected both Manchester's health and, if only briefly, public sentiment about Jackie and Bobby. The president's brother, eager only to stand by his sister-in-law, was wrongly judged a ruthless and arrogant manipulator, and many people incorrectly suspected that there were matters about her marriage that Jackie wanted to hide.

SERENE IN PUBLIC, Jacqueline Kennedy was, for most of the period from 1964 to 1976, restless as never before and, it may fairly be said, in a state of confusion. She met with Manchester, with Kennedy advisers and lawyers, with designers of the Kennedy gravesite at Arlington and the proposed Kennedy Library in Boston, but she was quietly regarded as no longer a Kennedy except by her brothers-in-law, Bobby and Teddy. There was no concerted effort to dismiss her from the family circle: rather, her inclusion in it had always depended on Jack. Rose was empathetic but dealing with her own profound grief, while

Joe, whom Jackie loved dearly, was paralyzed and speechless. Jackie felt she was tolerated among Kennedys only because of her children.

In this regard, she still much depended on the counsel and leadership of a strong man. For a remarkably long time, Robert Kennedy fulfilled this need, but there is not a shred of evidence to support the ugly rumors of an adulterous romance between them—contrary to those gossips who were eager to interpret spiritual alliance as erotic attachment. Jackie showed her devotion to Bobby by appearing at a reception during the Democratic National Convention that summer; this did not hurt his political fortunes. Bobby delivered a moving tribute to his brother before that vast throng and, the following November, handily won the race for senator from New York.

In 1964, Jackie began a long period of disturbing aimlessness, her date book a schedule of ceaseless wandering—"and shopping," as Helen Thomas reported years later. "She ran around to stores and boutiques buying things for which she seemed to have no need, as if she were trying to fill some emptiness inside herself."

During that same year, she took weekend ski trips to Vermont and recovered from that exertion by resting for eight days in the Caribbean. That was followed by a two-week cruise of the Adriatic, the Dalmatian coast and the Mediterranean, thanks to the generosity of wealthy friends. When she was not visiting chic European ports, she hopped, without much purpose, from Hyannisport to Virginia, from Palm Beach to New York, from Newport to Georgetown. The press, of course, followed every jaunt. But her iconic status was unthreatened. For the present, the American people considered her still the bereaved, noble widow, even if she now had a wardrobe even more glittering and expensive than that of the White House years.

One of the reasons for her almost breathless and somewhat frantically peripatetic life had to do with the situation in Georgetown, where, as it turned out, she found none of the privacy she had anticipated. Tour buses parked nearby at all hours, with their passengers climbing out to take photos and even ringing the doorbell in hopes of a visit with their favorite celebrity. "It's very upsetting," Jackie told her decorator, Billy Baldwin. "Women are always trying to grab and hug and kiss the children as they go in and out."

Thus, on July 6, her press secretary announced that Jackie was about to sell both the Washington house and Wexford. Mrs. Kennedy was moving to New York City, where she hoped to find privacy and anonymity. This, too, was not to be, for she was considered public property for the rest of her life. But at least tour buses would not be permitted to stop outside her residence, nor autograph seekers to camp out on her doorstep to accost her and the children for photos.

She purchased a fourteen-room apartment at 1040 Fifth Avenue, overlooking Central Park and the Metropolitan Museum of Art, so that she would be close to her sister and in a residential neighborhood where other wealthy sophisticates would not pester her in public. For the most part, New Yorkers are determinedly blasé about recognizing famous people: they might shout a greeting, stare and point and whisper to friends or strangers, but rarely would they approach someone outright. In Jackie's case, however, it happened often enough so that she learned to avert her gaze from oncoming pedestrians and simply walk swiftly.

"Going back to our childhood days, she always loved New York and everything about it—the museums, the parks, the people," said Nancy Tuckerman years later. "She was always drawn back to New York. She chose to bring up her children in the city." But also like other wealthy New Yorkers, Jackie could not abide Manhattan every month of the year. Just as she had been raised, she came to appreciate time outside the city—now not in East Hampton, but in a ten-room "badly made-over barn," as she termed it, in Bernardsville, New Jersey. Nearby were thousands of acres for foxhunting and many miles of bridle paths for her and the children.

The apartment, which she purchased for $250,000 and which required annual homeowner fees in excess of $15,000, was spacious but never ostentatious or museumlike. Her favorite colors were a yellowish green she called citron and a slightly faded red she termed raspberry. To no one's surprise, the rooms had the feel of a Paris apartment—its pieces were antique, valuable but not arranged to impress. Everything looked as if it belonged. There was something casual about the place, for Jackie avoided decorative pretense as if it were a virus. Books were everywhere. In this sprawling, fifteenth-floor apartment, Jackie lived from autumn 1964 to her death.

Over the next years, she gradually invited people she could trust. There were composers (Leonard Bernstein, Gian Carlo Menotti), politicians (Averell Harriman, Robert McNamara, Franklin D. Roosevelt Jr., Adlai Stevenson), writers (Arthur Schlesinger, Truman Capote, George Plimpton and, eventually, some of those whose books she edited), and the occasional aristocrat, financier or actor.

Guests saw the same favorite furniture and objects over the next three decades, for this was Jackie's base for almost half her life. There was always, for example, the leather-topped Louis XVI bureau on which Jack had signed the Nuclear Test Ban Treaty in 1963. She kept, too, her collection of seventeenth-century animal drawings and miniature paintings from India; the Empire desk that had belonged to her father; and her collection of ancient art, gathered over the years.

Designer Mark Hampton counseled her on some minor redecoration over the years, but he noted later that "everything in the room was essentially just as it had always been. It was that same incredibly consistent taste that made her stand out for thirty years, when everybody else was experimenting. Age didn't matter to her at all. She was ageless and her style was ageless."

Her home, in other words, was nothing like Versailles, nor had it the grandeur she had bestowed upon the rooms of the White House. More than anything, she wanted a home for her children and a refuge for her friends. "Unless you had some knowledge, you would never notice how fine the pieces were," said Richard Keith Langham, another decorator. "Her taste was so quiet. There were a lot of French and Italian Old Master drawings and watercolors. But it felt like a family apartment—cozy, warm, friendly." There she made a permanent home for Caroline and John: a place they could make their own, invite their friends, and most of all, enjoy privacy.

But once she had settled into it, by late autumn 1964, Jackie embarked on a period of almost desperate travel, as if by often leaving America she could shake off the terrible memories of what had happened there—and as if by a surfeit of exotic images, and even by exhaustion itself, she might be free of the images she could never escape.

It was the age of the glamorous jet set, the era of yachts and parties and expensive trips, the time of the mad excess of Richard Burton and Elizabeth Taylor. The 1960s, which in a way can be said to have begun that day in Dallas, quickly grew into a decade of heady liberations, new liberties and more than a little license.

"I never had a life of my own," she said frequently. Nor would she find one for the next ten years, when she was caught up in a whirlwind of distracting, ultimately disappointing travel. Had she not lived beyond those years, had she not after all entered into the final years with purpose and depth, this period would have been a sad, inept coda to a life of dignity and accomplishment. But celebrities and the trappings of their lives bedazzled Jackie, who never considered herself a famous person and could never understand the public's adulation.

In light of the vacuum of meaning caused by her husband's death and her loss of the White House, one might ask what else she could have done but be drawn to a life of travel. For a long time she may have seemed like the Flying Dutchman. She sought peace of heart, but she knew not what form it should take or even if it was her destiny.

She began, toward the end of 1964, to give small parties and to host receptions and dinners at various museums and chic Manhattan restaurants. Her guest lists were eclectic: Adlai Stevenson, Leonard Bernstein, Maurice Chevalier, Sammy Davis Jr., Charles Addams, former Deputy Secretary of Defense Roswell Gilpatric, Andy Warhol, Mike Nichols, the Radziwills. When there was dancing, she wanted, as she told the maître d' at the Sign of the Dove restaurant, "the fastest music you've got," and she learned to twist and swing with it. It seemed an innocent enough distraction from her pain.

BUT A CATALOG of her travels—a nearly incessant holiday—suggests an almost manic discontent, as if she would find in motion what she could not in stillness; for a while, the tone and temper of her life seemed rudderless, purposeless. A partial chronology of these years:

In 1965, Jackie took various vacations in, among other places, Aspen, Acapulco, Lake Placid, London, Hyannisport, Newport and Sun Valley.

In 1966, she was off to Gstaad, Rome, Buenos Aires, Madrid, Seville, Honolulu and a dozen other desirable holiday spots.

In 1967, her itineraries included Antigua, Montreal, Acapulco, London, Dublin, Florence and Rome. But her visit to Southeast Asia that autumn was unusually significant, for Jackie was not merely a sightseer.

Since the summer of 1966, Cambodia had entertained no diplomatic relations with Washington. After conferences between Averell Harriman and officials at the State Department, it was agreed that Jackie—who was, in the words of Defense Secretary Robert McNamara, "absolutely overwhelmed by the tragedy of Vietnam"—might improve America's relations with Cambodia and thus, however indirectly, help end the conflict. It must be done, however, without any overt sign of politics or political involvement, nor could she visit or even publicly address the topic of Vietnam.

Accompanied by David Ormsby-Gore, Jackie arrived in Cambodia in November, explored the ancient Angkor ruins and pleaded with Prince Sihanouk to intercede with the Vietnamese for the release of captured American civilians. As it happened, this was a long time in coming, but as Sihanouk himself admitted, her visit alone was "a very great contribution to a moral and sentimental rapprochement between our two peoples." Jackie continued her quiet but firm opposition to the war after her return home. She visited wounded veterans at several government hospitals and stood with student radicals at the Institute of Politics, which she feared was becoming sedate and too identified with the Establishment—"TMBS," as she said: too many blue suits.

WHEN SHE WAS in America, Jackie traveled regularly from Manhattan to Hyannisport to Newport and to her new country estate in Somerset County, New Jersey.

Aware of the power of her identity and presence, she sometimes allowed her name to be used for a good cause. On rare occasions, she would quite deliberately risk the crush of gawkers and photographers by attending an event whose value she endorsed, such as a charity dinner for a hospital. But she asked for promises that her arrival not be announced in advance—and if it was, and if her forthcoming presence was exploited for mere publicity, she immediately withdrew her offer of support.

One such incident occurred when the board of Cedars-Sinai Medical Center in Los Angeles asked her, through their contact Pierre Salinger, to attend a major fund-raising dinner. He reported back to Arthur Wilde, the director of publicity and public relations for the center, that yes, Jackie would be pleased to attend, but since a score of hospitals was making similar requests, she wanted complete silence about her participation until her arrival in California. As the date of the event drew near, however, two members of the hospital's board flew to New York, collared a photographer, and came to the lobby of her apartment. They then sent word that they were waiting: "We want to have our picture taken with you!"

That was the end of that. "Jackie at once withdrew her offer to come to Los Angeles," Arthur Wilde recalled years later, "and I didn't blame her at all—nobody did who had any sense. These men were rightly and soundly criticized. They wanted to turn a good opportunity for the hospital to their own personal advantage, and they ruined everything." There were a number of such incidents. Jackie would simply not be used for personal aggrandizement.

ALTHOUGH SHE SEEMED to do little but grace the company of those who longed to include her, and in most cases to pay her way, few of her travels escaped being detailed in the press. The headlines about Jackie's glittering life became ever more fatuous. Even *The New York Times* considered the slightest item newsworthy:

- ❖ "Mrs. Kennedy Spends Quiet New Year's Eve in Aspen" (Jan. 1, 1965)
- ❖ "Mrs. Kennedy Rides Chair Lift" (Jan. 2, 1965)
- ❖ "Mrs. Kennedy Ill With Flu" (Nov. 5, 1965)
- ❖ "Mrs. Kennedy Buys Horse" (Dec. 8, 1965)

Each of these "stories" was only a short paragraph or two, becoming more and more absurd until the following item of monumental silliness, here reproduced in its entirety, appeared on March 24, 1966, under the headline MRS. KENNEDY SHOPS:

Wearing a checked coat in white, orange and yellow, Mrs. John F. Kennedy dropped into the Chez Ninon custom salon at 487 Park Avenue yesterday for an hour's shopping that came to orders for seven designs.

Like a Hollywood star or anyone briefly lauded or even notorious for a crime, Jackie had to do almost nothing except be noticed from time to time. Hence, she became the most popular cover girl for the movie magazines.

Movie Mirror's cover story was "Jackie's in love with her new surroundings!"

Inside Movie trumpeted that at one of her parties she served "hot and cold hors d'oeuvres."

Modern Screen revealed that television actor Robert Vaughan, who never met her, considered Jackie his intellectual ideal.

Photoplay asked its readers to send in replies: Ought Jackie to devote herself exclusively to her children and the memory of her dead husband? Ought she to begin to date, privately or publicly, and eventually remarry? Ought she to marry right away? They did not, of course, ask if anyone thought it was anybody's business.

Screen Album simply went for soap-opera narration: "Her life seems over. She is like a garden in which everything has withered."

Motion Picture flatly blamed Lee as a "bad influence" on her sister for taking her to discotheques, as if Jackie did not, indeed, decide exactly what she wanted to do each day.

Readers snatched up everything, even the cover story of *Movie Stars,* when starlet Connie Stevens wrote, "I Found God in Your School: Connie Speaks to Caroline." Connie had done nothing of the sort: she was doing so only in the pages of *Movie Star,* which came up with this stunning coincidence: Connie once attended a Convent of the Sacred Heart in the West, and Caroline was enrolled at the Convent of the Sacred Heart in Manhattan. Life could certainly be surprising.

IT WAS ALSO empty of a permanent and devoted attachment.

"It's been quite a lonely life for her," said Rose Kennedy sympathetically about Jackie early in 1968. Despite the rash presumptions of many who regarded Rose simply as the pious, detached grande dame, the matriarch of the Kennedy clan knew about loneliness from her own marital experience. Her statement was profoundly true: for Jackie, life had become emotionally forlorn, despite and even because of her nonstop socializing and the never-ending trek to parties, nightspots, ports and spas.

232 / DONALD SPOTO

Jackie was thirty-eight, a widow of more than four years, and a single mother whose children, then ten and seven, had no father. The American public, she was often reminded when she read a magazine or watched television, imagined that she might forever remain on a pedestal of chaste and noble widowhood—the Dowager Queen of Camelot. She found this rarefied height cold and isolated, however, and she cared not one whit for public approval of her private life. At the same time, she refused to do anything that would embarrass the Kennedys— most of all, her brother-in-law Bobby, whom she loved dearly, to whom she was bound in a shared grief and whose presidential aspirations she wholly endorsed.

But Jackie was, after all, a healthy woman who longed for the satisfactions, security and comfort a loving mate could provide. She knew enough about herself and of life to realize that merely any attractive, adoring man would be insufficient to her needs; this sort of man could readily be delivered to her door. But the emotional shelter she yearned for—the confidence, tenderness and fidelity of someone upon whom she could rely without question and who was not attracted to her because she was the Widow Kennedy—well, that was another amalgam altogether. Jackie needed an older, mature man who had already marked out his own firm place in life, one who would share her love of culture, literature and the arts, one who loved children and would not be jealous of her devotion to Caroline and John, and one who could provide both material benefits and protection from publicity. Men like that were not available in profusion.

While she waited, she was not immune to the blandishments of a few handsome sophisticates. But discretion always characterized her life, especially the most intimate aspects of it, and discretion she required of her gentlemen callers. In any case, none of her intimacies was ever pursued to marriage until the autumn of 1968.

She had first met architect John Carl Warnecke when they had worked together to save Lafayette Square, in Washington; he had known the Kennedys for years and had also designed homes for some family members. Not long after the assassination, Jackie turned to him to create the memorial to John Kennedy at Arlington National Cemetery. Six feet three inches tall and a former college football player,

Warnecke was ten years Jackie's senior, a courtly, articulate and eligible bachelor, several years divorced.

For two years, from the autumn of 1964, they sustained an episodic but, according to Warnecke, passionate romance that reached its zenith during the summer of 1966, when Jackie took her children and followed Warnecke to Hawaii, where he had been commissioned to design the state capitol. The end of the romance, in December 1966, was the collective result of Robert Kennedy's strong disapproval, Warnecke's sense of Jackie's subsequent withdrawal from him, and a need on his part to pursue his career more seriously than their relationship had permitted.

Less likely a suitor was the urbane, cultivated Lord Harlech—Sir David Ormsby-Gore, also ten years Jackie's senior and Britain's ambassador to the United States during the Kennedy administration. He had known Jackie since 1954 and on her important journey to Southeast Asia—as well as on various sojourns in Palm Beach, Mexico, Rome and New York. Harlech was a contender of whom the public approved, for they liked the idea of their fair lady becoming a titled lady.

Whatever the precise category of their affection, the relationship was complicated for them both—until Harlech's wife was killed in an accident in early 1968. Jackie and David continued, until Jackie's second marriage, to dine and attend the theater together. In early October 1968, for example, they went to a performance of Mart Crowley's play, *The Boys in the Band,* a hilarious and poignant work that was the first to express, openly and successfully, the complexities of homosexual life in America. Jackie, neither prude nor Puritan, counted Rudolf Nureyev, William Walton, Truman Capote, Leonard Bernstein, Lemoyne Billings and others among her gay friends; she considered Crowley's play the best she saw that season.

Up to the time of his death in 1985, Harlech made no statement about Jackie other than to firmly deny a romance—an assertion, it must be said, that jibed with the avowal of Jackie's old friend Charles Bartlett, who had accompanied them to Southeast Asia.

Roswell Gilpatric was also in devoted attendance. Twenty-two years older than Jackie, he had been Deputy Secretary of Defense under Kennedy and had later joined a New York law firm. Until the summer of 1968, he, too, accompanied her on a sufficient number of trips—to the Yucatán, for example, where, Gilpatric recalled, "she wasn't content just to see the Mayan ruins by car in the daytime, as the average twentieth-century tourist does. She also insisted on seeing them by moonlight, on horseback, to get the feeling of the way it was. And once she tossed herself into a pool near the ruins with all her clothes on." Gilpatric's wife knew that her husband and Jackie were "very, very close—let's just say it was a particularly warm, close, long-lasting relationship"—a comment that, she must have known, revealed as much as it did not.

Throughout their romance, Jackie had written "Ros" affectionate notes he kept for years until they were stolen and published in 1970. In the first, she wrote of the "spell that will carry over" after they shared a day in the country. In another, she praised Gilpatric's "force and kindness," and in a third she was frankly effusive: "You wrote me a letter that I think about a lot—I am grateful for what you said—I know you understand." She also wrote that she was "very touched— dear Ros—I hope you know all you were and are and will ever be to me." Hardly the stuff of a torrid novel, and certainly not inappropriate language for even a platonic friendship. But the letters were at least provocative enough to confirm Mrs. Roswell in her pursuit of divorce proceedings.

FROM THE TIME Jackie purchased her Manhattan apartment, Aristotle Onassis had been a frequent visitor—but he was, as he said, "the invisible man." As it happened, he owned a suite at the Pierre Hotel, twenty-five blocks south. Perhaps the apparent improbability of friendship, much less romance, between them discouraged the paparazzi from suspecting that there was indeed more than met the eye when they dined at restaurants in Paris or New York, or when he attended dinner parties at her apartment. After all, Maria Callas was known to have Ari's undiluted attention.

But the relationship between the Greek tycoon and the American widow continued, however episodically, and they shared a holiday in January 1968 when Jackie learned about her grandfather Lee's death at the age of ninety. Jackie had not been close to her grandfather in recent years, for he was no admirer of John Kennedy, and at this time Ari was a gentle, comforting presence, just as he had been after Patrick's death.

In New York the following month, Ari told his biographer, Willi Frischauer, about Jackie: she had, he said, captivated him since their cruise in August 1963. "He was lyrical," recalled Frischauer of that February evening. "He seemed transfixed by her glamour and fame," and he compared her to a diamond—"cool, sharp at the edges, fiery and hot beneath the surface!" Ari asked for Frischauer's absolute confidence about the depth of his involvement.

In March, Jackie and Ari were spotted at Mykonos, a Greek restaurant in Manhattan, but since Margot Fonteyn and Rudolf Nureyev were with them, few eyebrows were raised. Very quietly the friendship was becoming amorous. Jackie confided in Roswell Gilpatric, by now no longer a romantic interest but still a good friend: she felt Onassis was a man she could rely on, that he had a protective attitude about her and her children and that with him she felt secure and safe.

Soon, feeling protected and safe mattered more to her than anything, for Jackie's life was again struck by tragedy as the year 1968 proceeded. On April 4, Dr. Martin Luther King Jr. was assassinated in Memphis at the age of thirty-nine. She had followed and supported Dr. King's leadership in the civil rights struggle and had joined him and Robert Kennedy in registering her protest against the Vietnam conflict. His death affected her deeply, and at once she rushed to the King home in Atlanta to comfort his widow and to attend the funeral.

In May, Jackie and Ari boarded the *Christina* in Florida and slipped away for a Caribbean cruise. From there they proceeded to Newport, where she introduced him to her mother and stepfather.

Not long after their return to New York, there was again dreadful news, this time from Los Angeles. Just after midnight on June 5, immediately following his victory in the California Democratic presidential primary, Robert Kennedy was shot twice in the head as he was leaving the Ambassador Hotel. After emergency surgery, he clung uncertainly to life throughout that day. In the early evening, Jackie arrived—alone, aboard a private plane Ari had chartered; it would not, he knew, be appropriate for him to escort her. She was at

Bobby's bedside with Ethel and two of Bobby's sisters when he died just before two o'clock on the morning of June 6. He was forty-two years old.

Jackie was shattered, and for perhaps the first time since Jack's assassination, she turned to her ancient faith for support. "The Church is at its best at the time of death," she told Bobby's press secretary, Frank Mankiewicz.

> The rest of the time, it's often rather silly little men running around in their black suits. But the Catholic Church understands death. I'll tell you who else understands death—the black churches. I remember at the funeral of Martin Luther King, I was looking at those faces, and I realized that they know death. They see it all the time, and they're ready for it in the way in which a good Catholic is.

And then, in a wounded, detached tone, she concluded: "We know death. As a matter of fact, if it weren't for the children, we'd welcome it."

At the funeral in St. Patrick's Cathedral in New York, Jackie's haggard, dazed appearance and detached demeanor caused old friends like Lady Bird Johnson to fear that she might indeed be suffering a complete emotional breakdown. But for the support of a few who were close to her, she may have indeed collapsed. From then on, her decision to become Mrs. Onassis—often proposed by Ari but so far gently turned aside—became firm. "I wanted to go away," she said later. "They were killing Kennedys, and I didn't want them to harm my children. I wanted to go off. I wanted to be somewhere safe." This cannot be called a paranoid reaction.

"Of the thirty-six ways of escape," according to an ancient Chinese proverb, "the best is to run away."

ONCE AGAIN, ARISTOTLE Onassis was at the ready, and soon Jackie's melancholy seemed to abate. When she was in New York during this unofficial courtship that year, the artist Aaron Shikler, who was rendering Jackie's portrait, noticed that "the melancholy widow I had been painting was transformed—she became jollier, gayer, much more re-laxed and girlish."

In early July, Ari arrived in Newport, where he spent more time with the Auchinclosses and further ingratiated himself with Caroline and John. Not only was he always laden with gifts for the children, he also took a real interest in their lives. Whereas he was emotionally uninvolved with his own daughter, Christina, and had only wavering confidence in the abilities of his son, Alexander, Ari compensated for these distances by virtually adopting Jackie's children. At the end of the month, Onassis was invited to Hyannisport, where he met Rose, Ted and Joan Kennedy. When Bobby was alive, Jackie's relationship with Ari had been a close family secret. Now things were moving forward more openly. But Jackie would make no move without in-forming her in-laws, even if she no longer felt that she required their permission.

The public, in the meantime, longed to know more and more about Jackie's romantic life and her plans. This thirst—both reflected and nourished in weekly magazines—confirmed her desire to quit America. She had never asked to be seen as a paragon of virtue or as the widowed queen-in-exile. Her fame, which she neither understood nor encour-aged, was a constant annoyance, while the public saw her as something of a social artifact. More to the point, her legion of admirers kept her like a butterfly in amber and never wanted her to do anything that would change their adoration of a brave, bereaved woman who was dedicated to her children. Perhaps most odious of all in this process of transforming human beings into gods was one massive, collective pre-sumption. It was taken for granted that Jackie was required to court the approval of the world, to have its permission to move, to love, to marry, to change anything more significant than a sofa's fabric.

Then, almost buried and virtually ignored, there appeared a tiny item in the *The New York Times* on August 6, reported from Athens: "Senator Edward M. Kennedy and Mrs. John F. Kennedy arrived in Greece today to spend a vacation as guests of Aristotle S. Onassis, the shipowner." Ted had telephoned Onassis and requested a meeting, and Ari genially invited them both to Skorpios. "As I did not expect a dowry," said Ari, who had a sense of humor, "there was nothing to worry about." Dowry or no, he was, as he told Frischauer, "uneasy" about the meeting. Money was his vocation, but he resented its intrusion into his romantic life.

As it happened, Ted Kennedy made no financial requests or deals with Ari at all: he was there to meet his sister-in-law's prospective husband again and to demonstrate that not all the Kennedys were against the marriage.

Nevertheless, for years rumors persisted about the outlandish monies settled on Jackie that summer, to be paid to her both during the marriage and after Onassis's death—millions of dollars annually, an outrageous clothing and expense budget and all sorts of perquisites. But the truth is quite otherwise, as Onassis's primary attorney and close friend, Stelios Papadimitriou, confirmed in 1998. It was not Jackie who had contrived to have a prenuptial agreement: it was Onassis himself, who had to consider the complex Greek inheritance laws and his son's and daughter's situations; both children were against their father's remarriage. In light of these two conditions, Ari asked Jackie to waive her automatic right under Greek law to inherit 25 percent of his estate. This she did without hesitation.

There was not, as so often claimed, a 170-clause agreement, stipulating financial details and even the fine points of intimate marriage obligations. The fact is that Ari gave Jackie just over $2 million when they married, and that, for the moment, was the single financial arrangement. She demanded no additional money then or in the future, and although she certainly entered the marriage aware that she would be afforded a privileged and secure life, she did not marry in search of extravagant wealth. Among others, Papadimitriou insisted on this fact, which, he admitted, even he was at first surprised to discover.

DURING AUGUST AND September 1968, the secret of an impending marriage was still kept, for Onassis wished, if he could, to deal with Maria Callas gently by gradually withdrawing from her. But Callas did not get the hint. "He doesn't love Jackie," the singer said. "He just likes to be admired by very important women. So he will change me for another, more important woman. But I am certain he does not love her at all."

In his fashion, of course, he did, and he showed it by presenting her with the fabulous forty-carat Lesotho diamond ring as an engagement gift. "I am always searching for the consummate woman," he once said. The opening words of Jane Austen's *Pride and Prejudice* were yet again corroborated: "It is a truth universally acknowledged, that a single man in possession of a good fortune must be in want of a wife."

But Ari prized his fiancée not only because she was perhaps the greatest prize he could show off to the world. He was also a genuinely solicitous man, and Jackie evoked his long-repressed paternal instincts. Ari was also one of the perhaps few available men who could marry Jackie without either being dominated by her image or intimidated by the memory of John Kennedy.

As far as Jackie was concerned, the cynics would say—and they eventually did—that it was F. Scott Fitzgerald who was right: rich girls don't marry poor boys. "She felt a great need for financial security and for physical protection against intrusion," said Arthur Schlesinger, "and this great piratical figure provided for those needs." But in addition, the vast range of those who worked with Onassis—from Papadimitriou to Kiki Faroudi Moutsatsos, Ari's business secretary and personal assistant during the last nine years of his life—remember him as a charming, sympathetic and generous man of great charm, despite his frequently quick temper, his crudeness and bouts of Aegean melancholy. Like Jackie, Ari was intensely private and a perfectionist; like her, too, he appreciated intelligence and wit.

Certainly, material benefits were considerations for Jackie: she wanted to find a protective place and presence to shield her and her children from both danger and publicity. These were, it seems, not entirely well-considered goals: what, for example, about the children's education? Would the three of them permanently leave America? Change their citizenship? Renounce their roots? Doubtless, these were concerns she believed she could eventually resolve. For the moment, it was refuge she sought, and Ari offered her a haven abundant with every benefit.

Jackie would also be able to spend as much time as she wished at or near the sea and at her New Jersey retreat. But this was not a woman who fled only to the ocean or the country for refuge: she also appreciated the great cities of the world. For the kind of refreshment that comes with solitude, it was the beaches that attracted her—Hyannisport,

Newport, Palm Beach, the Yucatán, the Caribbean. In her childhood she had most often drawn herself standing by the seashore, her place for reflection. At the time of her engagement to Kennedy, she had chosen for the editors of *Life* magazine the photos of herself and Jack sailing off Cape Cod. The waters of the world were always her refuge, and she had loved the Greek Isles with a special predilection ever since 1963. And for vigorous exercise, there was her horseback riding in New Jersey.

But if one asks whether she married for love or for the material benefits Onassis offered, the answer could perhaps only be "yes" to both. The presumption that Jackie—or anyone else, for that matter—ought to or even could marry someone "for love alone" is the language of soap opera, an emotional conceit from the land of Camelot fairy tales, and fairy tales only half read.

Henry James's novella *Washington Square,* to name only one classic work, concerns precisely the ambiguity of motives that defines human emotions and decisions. Is Morris Townsend in love with Catherine Sloper for herself, or because she is an heiress? Or is not her social and financial status in fact an aspect of that self? Conversely, is Catherine in love with Morris because she loves him for himself, or because she sees him as a means of escape from her father and a passage to emotional security? Does not his appeal include his function as liberator, just as hers includes her function as heiress?

To put the matter another way, it is perhaps impossible to discuss so-called "pure motives" even in the case of the saints, for single and pure motivation is not the province of humankind. Loving for the sake of love, with no thought of compensation for self, is not given to humans. As Thomas More famously reminded, "Only God is love right through."

In assessing Jackie's decision, it may also be helpful to remember the type of men she most admired as partners and friends—strong men with heroic ambitions, men who aimed and achieved. Always attracted to dynamic heads of state and cultural ministers, she was drawn to great men the way she rose to great events. In this regard, she was yet again like her grand spiritual ancestors, the noble consorts of kings and emperors. Now, in 1968, she was again to solemnize a relationship with a man who had attained the success that had eluded her father. Indeed, more than any man in her life, Ari was the quintessential father fig-ure—lavish, tolerant, attentive, comforting, cosseting, adoring. As she had said five years earlier, she found him "a vital person who had come from nowhere."

Finally, the question so often asked in 1968 was how so beautiful a woman could find Onassis physically appealing. This, it must be said, was for the most part an American concern. Those immersed in a culture that worships youth and physical charm felt that Jackie's dark glasses must have blinded her. For them, no one would be permissible except a Robert Redford or a Paul Newman: the fairy tale must continue.

When Janet Auchincloss announced, through Nancy Tuckerman, the impending marriage in October, the reaction was swift and damn-ing. "She went from a Greek god to a goddam Greek," snarled one New Yorker. Onassis was two inches shorter than his fiancée, said another, "but he is taller when he stands on his money."

"To us, she was royalty, a princess, and I think she should have married a prince—or at least someone who looked like a prince." So ran the typical response, recorded and reinforced many times that au-tumn in newspapers all over the world. An air force pilot took another line, speaking of Jackie, as did so many, as if her marital prospects were like a game-show choice: "I was pulling for the Prime Minister of Canada [Pierre Trudeau]. He would have given her the chance to be a First Lady again." No, don't open door number one, Jackie: that's only a two-week vacation. Select door number two: there's a fabulous new refrigerator there, it'll last forever.

The ceremony was held in the presence of only her children and a few relatives and friends, in the tiny chapel of Skorpios on October 20, 1968. European reaction was fast and furious: *France-Soir* called the event "sad and shameful." *Il Messagero* proclaimed that John Kennedy was dying for a second time. *Bilt-Zeitung* mourned that "America has lost its saint." Asked her reaction, Maria Callas raised her chin, pulled herself up regally and replied, "Jackie did well to give her children a grandfather. Ari is as beautiful as Croesus." Like everyone else who read about the wedding, Callas was astonished at the ring Ari presented his bride: a ruby-and-diamond band that cost $1.25 million.

A few voices were raised above the fracas. The great actress Giu-lietta Masina, wife of Federico Fellini, wisely observed that "myths, when they are human, are fatally subject to wear and tear, disparities and loneliness. Why marvel if a woman at a certain point tears off all the veils that cover her like a monument—a thirty-nine-year-old monument, still beautiful, extremely alive, obligated to a role that does not belong to her? I say that if she wishes to begin all over again, it is right that she do it!"

In no time, and perhaps to no one's surprise, some people decided to pass eternal as well as temporal judgment on the bride: here was a Catholic woman contracting a forbidden marriage to a divorced man. A few churchmen, quick to discuss church rules but apparently unaware of the spirit of Christ himself, concluded that Jackie was a public sinner worthy of excommunication.

To his everlasting credit, Richard Cardinal Cushing of Boston, one of America's most influential prelates, responded quickly. He had tended to the Kennedys' spiritual needs since the 1950s; he had married them and he had buried them; and now he was swift and damning— not of Jackie, but of those who were condemning her.

As it happened, just before she flew to Greece for her wedding, Jackie had quietly slipped up to Boston, to take counsel with the cardinal. Now, when he was asked about the state of her soul, he had no patience. "Months ago," said this wise and compassionate pastor,

I knew full well that Jacqueline Kennedy was going to marry Aristotle Onassis. I know what she has been going through for many, many months. I have been contacted by many of those who are identified in high places with the administration of the late President Kennedy, and I have been contacted by others intimately related and associated with the Kennedy family, to stop all this from taking place—namely, that Jack's widow, God rest him, would marry Aristotle Socrates Onassis.

Well, I would have no part.

Now I turn on the radio and I hear people are knocking her head off, criticizing her and so forth. All I am able to tell you is this: *caritas*—charity!

Why do people send so many letters, condemning her, condemning me? I never would condemn anybody!

And this idea of saying she's excommunicated, she's a public sinner—what a lot of nonsense! Only God knows who is a sinner, who is not.

Why can't she marry whomever she wants to marry? And why should I be condemned for saying it, and she be condemned for doing it?

Perhaps because of the cardinal's refusal to condemn, Rose Kennedy offered Jackie enormous emotional support. Twenty years earlier, she had thought it a tragedy of eternal consequence when her own daughter Kathleen, then a twenty-eight-year-old widow, had been involved in an adulterous affair with a married man she intended to make her husband.

But time and suffering had tempered Rose's inflexibility.

"It seemed to me the first basic fact was that Jackie deserved a full life, a happy future," she said later. "Jack had been gone five years; thus, she had had plenty of time to think things over. She was not a person who would jump rashly into anything as important as this, so she must have had her own very good reasons."

Jackie never forgot Rose's kindness, and in a way, it brought the two women closer than they had ever been. "When I married Ari," Jackie recalled, "she of all people was the one who encouraged me, who said, 'He's a good man' and 'Don't worry, dear.' She's been extraordinarily generous. Here I was, I [had been] married to her son and I have his children, but she was the one who was saying, 'If this is what you think is best, go ahead.' "

In this matter, Jackie was evidently able, like her mother, to reconcile her conscience with the Roman Catholic Church's legal, canonical proscription against marriage to a divorced person. And of both the quality of her conscience and of the state of her soul, neither cleric nor layman may ever pass judgment: they may offer only an opinion on her legal status, not her spiritual state. On this absolute prohibition against assuming the prerogative of divine judgment, Church history and ecclesiastical law are unambiguous—as that good pastor, Cardinal Cushing, appropriately reminded everyone concerned.

———

MOUTSATSOS, WHO SAW Jackie and Ari almost every day while they were together in Greece over the next several years, finally spoke her mind on the gleeful but false reports that the union was simply a loveless charade. "This was a marriage that included many moments of love and affection. I will not say that this love was strong enough to overwhelm catastrophic obstacles later placed in its path by the sad fates that ruled their lives. Yet it was their own unique brand of love that joined this couple and held them together."

But even during the honeymoon that autumn, there were tensions, for to Ari's great dismay, his two children resented Jackie—not for herself, but because they cherished the futile fantasy that their mother, who had remarried, would eventually come back to their father. "I didn't need a stepmother, but my father needed a wife," Alexander, then twenty, said rudely.

As for seventeen-year-old Christina, those who were close to the family agreed with Kiki Moutsatsos: she was virtually ignored in favor of her brother. "She did not have one completely happy moment in her entire life. Alexandros was his son; Christina was his second child." Throughout Jackie's marriage, Ari's children—also, alas, ignored by their mother—labored to avoid their new stepmother. Everything she did to please them was doomed to failure. Alexander took refuge in flying small planes and having affairs with much older women; Christina overate, alternating binge-eating with amphetamines, to which she eventually became addicted.

This animus toward Jackie must have been aggravated by Ari's attention to her two children. While Caroline and John attended school in America, Jackie—who spent more and more time in Manhattan—brought them to Greece for virtually every holiday, short or long. There, Ari further alienated Alexander and Christina by lavishing gifts and affection on the two children.

But Jackie persevered in her attempts to be kind to Alexander and Christina; in time she at least won over the daughter. "She always tries to please him in everything," Christina said of Jackie and her father. "She's always asking what she can do for him, how she can help him. If I had to choose, I'd say that my father is more important to Jackie than vice versa. Jackie is my stepmother, but also my great friend." So much for the unfounded news reports that Jackie and Christina were sworn enemies.

As for Alexander, Jackie achieved something remarkable: she arranged for father and son to spend more time together. The result was a new closeness that revived Ari's hopes that the Onassis empire would one day be expertly managed in the succeeding generation. Alexander—although not, unfortunately, Christina—was once again the center of his father's dynastic and emotional life.

Still, there were difficult shoals to negotiate. Jackie spoke no Greek, and although Ari's English was more than rudimentary, most of his social conversation was conducted in his native tongue. In addition, his mastery of English stopped far short of nuance and subtlety, which were precisely the qualities Jackie so prized even in ordinary discourse. Ari's family and employees routinely spoke Greek, thus Jackie was excluded from many conversations. As far as the arts and culture were concerned, Ari owned some masterworks, but only as investments: he was no more cultivated than Jack. It was perhaps inevitable, then, that Jackie would essentially maintain her home base in New York, where her friends and acquaintances shared her interests.

The complexities of the new marriage must have made even more difficult the fifth anniversary of Jack's death, which was marked just a month after the wedding. Ari was in Athens on business, and his sister Artemis, who loved Jackie, had come to visit her on the *Christina*. On November 22, Artemis noted that Jackie was sad and withdrawn.

"I am having a very bad day," Jackie said. "I know I should be happy now, but all I can think about today is Jack and what happened to him in Texas. Sometimes I think I will never be able to be truly happy again. I try, but I cannot forget the pain. When I feel happy, I am always just waiting for this great pain to return."

And with that poignant admission, Jackie began to weep. All through the quiet evening, her sister-in-law tried to comfort her.

Part Three

❧

Mrs. Onassis
1969-1994

CHAPTER ELEVEN

1969-1975

*E*very moment one lives is different from the other," Jackie said in 1972. "The good, the bad, the hardship, the joy, the tragedy, love and happiness are all interwoven into one single indescribable whole that is called life. You cannot separate the good from the bad—and perhaps there is no need to do so. After all, I have been through a lot and I have suffered a great deal. But I have had lots of happy moments. And so I have come to the conclusion that we must not expect too much from life, and we must not take things for granted."

IN NOVEMBER 1963, Jackie had been thirty-four years old and was the world's most famous and admired woman—enveloped in privilege, living at the center of influence, observed by all observers.

Then, in a matter of seconds on that blazing-hot day in Dallas, she had experienced something so horrific that its psychological and emotional devastation is perhaps impossible to imagine. With the awfulness of the murder, she was at once thrown from a position she effectively shared at the center of the country's life. She had to find her own deepest resources—and she had to do so at once, with no time for reflection, without even the passing of a few hours. But what she did and how she comported herself that funereal weekend constituted the defining moment of her life: she rose to history and to her own destiny magnificently. Rudely bereft of her husband and of a familiar home, she was now responsible to raise, quite alone, her two young children. Most widows are not forced to take their children and vacate their homes immediately after their husbands' burials.

It would be petty and even downright iniquitous to say, as some indeed have said in subsequent years, that Jackie had no choice in what she did that weekend or that she acted out of self-aggrandizement or that she was simply a first-rate amateur actress who found a great role to perform before a worldwide audience. On the contrary, Jackie was a living archetype of courage and grace in the face of disaster: this was real life, not a copy of it in the theater.

As her life shifted, so did the terms of her journey. She had, first, to proceed through and within a world that cherished its preconceived notions of what she was and its preordained demands of what she must do. Obsessed with the props and paints of its fantasy, the world felt it had a right to approve every detail: where Jackie lived, with whom she socialized, what she wore, where she took her children, whom she loved. It was, of course, impossible for her to please, no matter what she did or did not do.

And what did she do? She simply went ahead with her life, neither encouraging her celebrity nor acknowledging that the public's perceptions were important. In this regard, she was nothing like a promoter of fame: as a matter of fact, she took a firm stand *against* fame.

She kept public silence. She refused to submit to television or magazine interviews. She rejected every request to explain herself, to set forth her program of life, to justify, to plead her case. Instead, she was willing to try, to explore, to wander, to be vulnerable, to err, to keep on seeking. By such a sequence, she became one of the first notably independent women. In her insistent self-sufficiency, she formed her own life; she moved along the paths that seemed right to her. And when they were sometimes revealed to be blind paths, she turned aside and somehow found a light through the forest.

AS THEY BEGAN life together in 1969, the range of their differences at once became glaringly apparent to Jackie and Ari—not only in virtually every kind of taste and preference but in the matter of where they wished to spend time. She liked classical ballet, he preferred belly dancers. His homes in Paris, Montevideo and Monte Carlo had no attraction for her as permanent addresses. In the anxious aftermath of Robert Kennedy's murder, she had said she wanted to live outside America. But it soon became clear that this was unreasonable. Her children, she realized, had been uprooted enough. They were Americans, they were Kennedys: she would not uproot them, would not try to transplant them to an alien culture.

Hence, Jackie said in the spring of 1969 that she had no intention of surrendering her home on Fifth Avenue to share Ari's suite at the Pierre Hotel when they visited New York. Just when the gossips were proclaiming that the former Mrs. Kennedy would surely leave America and become the leader of the international jet set—why, here she was, in New York more than ever! In fact, Jackie never moved to Greece, nor did Mr. and Mrs. Onassis ever share more than brief interludes in the house on Skorpios.

One reason was that Ari's business involvements took him all over the world—hence his multiple addresses. It was crucial for him to maintain a hotel address in America, rather than a private one, so that he would not be taxed as an American resident. When the two traveled to New York that winter, therefore, their separate residences did not pass unnoticed by the press. "Jackie is like a little bird that needs its freedom and its security," Ari said, "and she gets them both from me. She can do exactly as she pleases—visit international fashion shows and travel and go out with friends to the theater or anyplace." And then the ominous finale: "And I, of course, will do exactly as I please." During 1969 they were apart 141 days—40 percent of the year. In the future the absences would be even more protracted.

AS IT HAPPENED, this turned out to be a comfortable arrangement. Frequently in New York, Ari visited her apartment and gave her children affection and told them of presents awaiting them, among them a speedboat, a sailboat and ponies. Their reactions to him were not hard to understand: invariably grateful, polite and never resentful of Ari's presence in their mother's life, Caroline and John were at first wary. Caroline never really warmed to Ari—perhaps because she had clearer memories of Jack; John, on the other hand, had a warmer relationship with Ari—perhaps because he had no such memories.

Their Greek stepfather dined with Jackie at home or at a favorite restaurant, and occasionally he spent the night with her. But whereas he preferred late dinners and nights on the town, she preferred supper at home with the children, reading a good book in her favorite chair, and retiring early so she could breakfast with Caroline and John and see them off to school.

Her children's education was of critical importance to her. Caroline transferred to Concord, a private school in Massachusetts in 1971, but John was still attending the Collegiate School in Manhattan; Jackie wanted to remain near them both. Sometimes their classmates or parents of their classmates were hesitant to include the famous Kennedy children in social events, outings and short trips. When that happened, Jackie contacted them, including them in her plans and making it clear that yes, she wanted her children to have normal ties with friends—an assumption not often made about the offspring of celebrities.

When it was clear that Jackie would not be abandoning New York, she became all the more desirable as a consultant and board member for various artistic and dance companies. She lent her name rarely, her presence more often.

But there was more. It was mostly unknown that for six months in 1971, she volunteered once a week as a teacher's aide at the McMahon Memorial, a shelter for homeless and battered children in the heart of Spanish Harlem on East 112th Street. At the time, her work there was unknown even to Nancy Tuckerman, still Jackie's full-time assistant, although she was paid by her official employers, Olympic Airways: "It was something she wanted to do very privately." This was not surprising, for Jackie always had an intimate rapport with children. John Glenn recalled that she took special care to chat with his teenage children when they visited the White House. She did not regard herself, he said, as the great lady to whom everyone should pay court: she took the initiative, she went to them and engaged them in conversation.

Similarly, more than once Jackie visited wounded Vietnam soldiers at veterans' hospitals. The staffs recalled their surprise when she turned up and spent hours chatting with astonished patients, asking what they needed, sometimes even arranging transportation for their families to visit from distant places. She realized, Jackie told friends, that there were people who had endured terrible things—far more awful, she said, than anything she had been through in 1963.

Her opposition to the war, in fact, became stronger and more vocal, as her old friend Secretary of Defense Robert McNamara learned when he visited her at 1040 Fifth Avenue. "She had grown very depressed by, and very critical of, the war," he said, adding that "she became so tense that she could hardly speak. She suddenly exploded. She turned and began, literally, to beat on my chest, demanding that I 'do something to stop the slaughter!' . . . Jackie—this dear friend whom I admired enormously—erupted in fury and tears."

FROM 1969 ON, as Jackie told friends, she could not seem to go through a single year without the death of one she loved. In November 1969 she was at Joe Kennedy's bedside when he died at Hyannisport, at the age of eighty-one. According to the nurse who had attended Joe during the years of his incapacity, Jackie was "the only one who completely accepted Mr. Kennedy's condition" and was therefore able to visit him with real compassionate understanding. Jackie never lied to Joe, never offered empty promises, never minimized his suffering as so many others did—like those who, said nurse Rita Dallas, "pretended not to notice that one entire side of his body was paralyzed" or that he could not communicate by speech.

Then, in November 1970, she was back in Massachusetts for the funeral of her dear friend Cardinal Cushing. The son of a poor blacksmith, Cushing had been widely praised as a friend to people of all faiths and no faith. Those who had suffered racial injustice mourned him perhaps especially. A good pastor, he had worked until the month before he died, when, ravaged by cancer, he finally had to leave his office. Joe Kennedy and Richard Cushing, perhaps more than any other men, were the loving father figures in Jackie's life; no one could replace them.

IN JULY 1969, Jackie marked her fortieth birthday; she did so without any of the wild fanfare desired by Ari and some of his retainers. He presented her with a forty-carat diamond and a fabulous pair of sapphire-and-ruby earrings representing the Apollo 11 moon landing that month, which had originally been Jack Kennedy's dream. The earrings were, however, far too heavy to be worn, and Jackie occasionally showed them to friends encased in their velvet box. For a while it might have seemed that Ari was competing with Richard Burton, who was smothering Elizabeth Taylor with precious gems.

More than appreciating extravagant gifts, Jackie derived enormous pleasure redecorating the Onassis yacht and the house on Skorpios. At first Ari was delighted with her choices: the exterior of their home was repainted a bright Mediterranean pink—the Pink House, Jackie always called it, her ironic sequel to the White House—and the rooms there and aboard the *Christina* were refurnished, their splashier aspects toned down, the frank vulgarity of many items replaced. Her activities were a reprise of her behavior in Georgetown in 1953, when she refurbished, shopped, spent lavishly, bought clothes.

But as the renovation progressed, she met Ari's resistance, for he considered her redecoration, somewhat oddly, as a threat to his primacy—not, as Jack had complained, to his pocketbook. With that, there began to appear, slowly but inexorably, a gulf between husband and wife that was noticeable to everyone. Ari became weary with the work she was having done on the house, and he was often annoyed because her idea of relaxation was settling down with a book. "All Jackie does is read," he complained, and flew off to Paris or Athens, leaving her to her paints and her reading. She joined him presently or eventually, or, like Penelope, she simply awaited the return of her wandering Ulysses. Meanwhile, the summers and school holidays longer than a day or two she reserved for Caroline and John, with whom she traveled to Europe, Greece or Hyannisport.

As always, her time with them during school breaks was inviolate. Typical of her sharing with them was a long weekend in Greece, when Jackie politely shuffled Ari and company off for a shopping tour so that she could be alone with her children. She invited them to bring her their pop music, she listened and tapped in time to it; she read magazines they liked; she involved herself completely in their tastes and fashions. Nothing was so youthfully silly that she could not find a modicum of fun in it, and when she had advice or parental correction, she counseled with the utmost loving gentleness. By all accounts, there was never even the briefest breach between Jackie and her children; the bond between them strengthened over the years.

People readily spotted Jackie at an airport or a restaurant. But they did not know that reading occupied most of her time. "She reads as much as anybody I know," said Truman Capote, "and a book a day isn't unusual for her." Capote was not, for once, exaggerating. Jackie had always been a voracious reader and book collector, but now it was more than a pastime: it was becoming something central to her life, almost a vocation. History, biography, books on art and dance, classic novels, poetry, important first fiction—her reading was wide and eclectic, and as friends knew, she retained extraordinary amounts of information. William Manchester, for one, was astonished during their interviews at her acute recollection of minute details concerning place, time, weather—details precisely confirmed by his subsequent research.

In addition to reading, Jackie insisted on maintaining her riding life. About the time of her marriage to Ari, she had given up the rental in Bernardsville and leased Windwood, an unpretentious seven-room, gray clapboard house in Peapack, a small village in Somerset County, New Jersey. Nestled among old oaks and clear brooks rushing by, Jackie took the children to Windwood, where they painted watercolors, took long walks and enjoyed the absence of any company but themselves. This was Jackie's sacrosanct time with her children.

PERHAPS INEVITABLY, ARI was soon revisiting his former mistress, the fiery and exigent Maria Callas. In mid-May 1970, he spent almost an entire week at her Paris apartment; on the twenty-first the couple posed happily for photographers who had tracked them down at Maxim's. Their smiling faces appeared in newspapers and magazines worldwide. At once, Jackie swept into Paris and arranged for herself and Ari to be photographed at the same restaurant. She was, it seemed, unwilling to be the complaisant wife again. But Ari was a man accustomed to pursuing his own ways. From here on in, he went his way and she hers. "I will do exactly as I please," he had said.

Soon the Callas-Onassis affair was taking on the spirit of a bad French novel—especially when, four days after Jackie's arrival in Paris, la Callas was rushed to the American Hospital at Neuilly. Reporters were told that she was suffering from sinus trouble, but a nurse who recognized the value of a few thousand francs said yes, Callas had taken a handful of sleeping pills.

"He is my best friend," Callas said wanly to a reporter about Ari as she was recovering—adding, as if he were Almighty God, "he is, he was and he always will be." With that sacred assent, she observed that "when two people have been together as we have, there are many things that tie you together. He knows he will always find cheerfulness, mutual friends and honesty when he sees me." To which Jackie's friends may have thought, *Ouch!* But there was more. Of his wedding to Jackie, Callas said with an icy stare: "Frankly, I didn't know about the wedding. And frankly, I don't think *he* knew about the wedding. You'll have to ask—her!"

THERE WERE ADDITIONAL family tensions.

While she was in New York in the spring of 1972, Jackie had a call from her cousins Phelan and Bouvier Beale, sons of her aunt Edith, Black Jack's sister. Aunt Edie had married over a half century earlier and had been subsequently abandoned by her husband. An eccentric but harmless lady who had once longed for a career in show business, she had been left with three children and only her family to rely on for support. They had installed her in a rambling, twenty-eight-room house called Grey Gardens, near the beach in East Hampton. But as the Bouvier fortunes had faded over the years, so had the quality of Aunt Edith's life. Grandly theatrical in her gestures, proudly adhering to extreme forms of politeness and aristocratic manners, she became a neurotic if harmless recluse, living on dreams of past elegance and broken hopes.

In 1952, her thirty-four-year-old daughter, also named Edith, had come to Grey Gardens to help care for her mother and also because, despite her beauty, she was a dreamy, somewhat erratic maiden lady unable to realize her own ambitions as a song-and-dance star. By 1972, Grey Gardens was a dilapidated wreck without adequate running water or operable toilets. Worse, mother and daughter shared the rooms with more than thirty cats—not all of them still alive—and a menagerie of raccoons, badgers, possums and otters that crawled all over, littering the house with urine and feces. The stench roused a passerby to action, and soon the Suffolk County health commissioner arrived, prepared to order the demolition of Grey Gardens. When he learned of the identity of the occupants' famous relative, all journalistic hell broke loose.

At that point, the Beale brothers contacted Jackie, who rushed out to East Hampton to see the horror for herself. There she found the mother and daughter, who had no desire to leave for safer, cleaner quarters. "Mother wants to stay in this house," said Edith the Younger in her impeccably patrician Long Island inflection, which perfectly replicated Jackie's. But Jackie was politely insistent; immediately she and Lee financed such repairs to the house as the two eccentrics would permit. Asked if she liked the improvements being made, Edith Beale the Elder grandly announced, "No, I hate it." By early autumn the place was officially inhabitable, but Jackie had no legal right to take further action. The ruckus also attracted the attention of the documentary filmmakers, brothers David Maysles and Albert Maysles, who took three years to complete *Grey Gardens,* a hypnotically clear-eyed view of the two Edies in their merry and pathetic absurdity.

THIS WAS AN embarrassment to Jackie. But real tragedy came in January 1973, when Alexander Onassis took off in a light aircraft from Athens. Moments later the plane crashed. Over the next day, Alexander lingered, mortally injured, while Jackie and Ari flew from New York with a prominent Boston neurosurgeon. Expert care was ineffectual, and on January 23, Alexander died at the age of twenty-four.

Once again Jackie was at the bedside; once again she rose to the moment, comforting Ari, Christina and Alexander's aunts and cousins. After his son's death, said Kiki Moutsatsos, "there was no longer any reason [for Onassis] to continue to exist." He was so devastated that his close friend and adviser Miltos Yiannacopoulos feared he might suffer a complete breakdown. Ari, who so often gave the impression that he needed no one, was profoundly affected by a loss for which there was no compensation.

In the last three years, he had proudly been able to balance a marriage, an affair and a deepened intimacy with his son that was preparing Alexander to eventually assume the Onassis dominions. By 1973, however, the Callas affair had dwindled into a difficult attachment based mostly on habit, a kind of emotional collusion neither party could disjoin. His life with Jackie, too, was a mostly dispassionate arrangement, whereby each essentially left the other alone. The only fire left in the soul of Aristotle Onassis was the hope that his empire would outlast him, but now the repository of those hopes had been harshly taken from him.

"No woman, no matter how much he loved her, could fill the void Alexander's death created," said Moutsatsos. Ari spent more time with Callas, but he returned from their visits still inconsolable and defeated. However disappointed Jackie felt, there were now other troubles that rendered her anxious and concerned, not only for her marriage but also for Ari's health.

When he was with Jackie, Ari frequently turned against her. There must be some ancient curse, he said. Everything had begun to go wrong in his life when he married her. His business dealings began to fail, he lost his children to death and drugs, his friends abandoned him—all this was her fault, he raved. Having lost hope in the future of his legacy and his name, Ari sank into a black despair. She was Circe, he shouted, luring him to his doom. His obsession with death and these strange, atavistic outbursts frightened Jackie and left her baffled and sad.

"I saw the biggest fights between them you could ever imagine," recalled photographer Peter Beard, who spent four months on Skorpios with Ari and Jackie. "He would blow up all the time—tantrums about everything, yelling and screaming at her." Beard described Jackie's re-action as one of "patience." When he asked why she had married him in the first place, she was frank: for the privacy, Jackie told Beard.

Ari changed his will, greatly reducing the inheritance Jackie and her children were to receive after his death. As it happened, he had successfully lobbied for a change in the Greek law that provided an automatic one-quarter of a man's estate to his widow. Rumors that he had also decided to divorce Jackie are impossible to corroborate: on the contrary, such close associates as Miltos Yiannacopoulos and Kiki Mout-satsos insist that Ari "never discussed the subject."

Wanting to be diverted from the increasing pressures of being with her husband, Jackie called Pierre Salinger and asked him and his wife to join them for a cruise to Acapulco: good, quiet company in a warm climate, she thought, would be helpful to Ari. But during the journey, he became only more withdrawn and depressed.

"I was with [Jackie] and Ari in Acapulco the winter after Alexander Onassis was killed," recalled Jackie's friend Eleanor Lambert. "When it was midnight and the fireworks began, Ari started to sob. Jackie put her arms around him and held him. It was so touching because he was not kind to her. But she stuck by him in this awful time when he was mourning so terribly." He strolled the deck alone late at night, Kiki Moutsatsos recalled, muttering in Greek, drinking ouzo. Back on Skorpios, he often sat at Alexander's tomb, downing hefty glasses of liquor and talking to his dead son.

THE GREEK TRAGEDY continued without interruption. Ari's ex-wife Athina, who had divorced the Marquess of Blandford and had married Onassis's archrival, Stavros Niarchos, sank into madness after her son's death. She wandered about, asking friends and strangers, "Where is my baby? I want to see my baby!" To the great dismay of Ari and his daughter, Christina, the woman moved more and more away from reality, and on October 10, 1974, she was found dead in her Paris apartment. Athina, who throughout her life had access to fabulous wealth but had been emotionally indigent, was only forty-five. There was not much Jackie could say to Ari or Christina to convince them that they were not in some way responsible for this untimely death.

By now, Jackie had learned to find simple consolations for herself: time in America with her children and casual days and short trips with friends like Peter Beard, who was preparing to publish a book of African folk tales. A world traveler, Beard had lived near Isak Dinesen's farm in Africa. For his book, he had supplemented her photos with his own; the text was by Kamante Gatura, Dinesen's cook. Jackie read the manuscript, loved it and offered to write an afterword—which, of course, was wonderful news for Beard and his publisher.

In America, her refuge was often, as usual, her time in the New Jersey countryside. In the autumn of 1974, she gave up her second lease. In a moment of what he later claimed was absurd weakness, Ari bought Jackie a $200,000 estate in Bernardsville; the property included a two-story frame house on ten acres of lush hunt country. Outside, she had it painted yellow with white trim; inside, she furnished it with comfortable, chintz-covered country pieces.

That same season, Jackie and Lee assembled their drawings and memoirs of their 1951 trip to Europe. *One Special Summer* was published in 1974; Beard's book, *Longing for Darkness,* appeared the following year. Jackie had never lost interest in photography, and her friendship with Beard revived it. After visiting the recently established International Center of Photography in New York, Jackie was so impressed that she wrote a reportorial appreciation of it. William Shawn, editor of *The New Yorker,* heard about the museum and of Jackie's interest in it, and he happily accepted her essay for anonymous publication in the January 13, 1975, issue, where it appeared in the "Talk of the Town" section without attribution.

A week after Jackie's article appeared under the title "Being Present," she pitched herself into another activity, this one more visible. The Landmarks Preservation Commission had recently declared New York's Grand Central Station a historic building. But the owners of the great structure, the Penn Central Railroad, claiming economic hardship, wanted to replace it with a fifty-five-story office building and lobbied to have the landmark status declared unconstitutional.

On January 21, a judge agreed. He did not, however, take into account the influence of Jacqueline Kennedy Onassis. As soon as she heard about the planned demolition, she telephoned Kent Barwick, director of the Municipal Art Society; within days they called a press conference, announcing the formation of the Committee to Save Grand Central. For three years, the case dragged through the courts, and the committee raised money and rallied public support. The cause, according to Barwick, proved ultimately successful mostly because of Jackie's presence, time and effort: "She brought an enormous visibility to the campaign," he recalled years later. "By standing up and speaking out for the terminal, she made it a success. And she made it not just a struggle involving New Yorkers, but people all over the country, who sent in five-dollar bills and notes of support."

"A big corporation shouldn't be able to destroy a building that has meant so much to so many for so many generations," said Jackie. "If Grand Central Station goes, all of the landmarks in this country will go as well. If that happens, we'll live in a world of steel and glass. We have so many beautiful buildings of the past, and so this is, in a sense, an issue that represents all issues."

Throughout this time, as the Municipal Art Society's memorial exhibit declared, "Jacqueline Onassis played a prominent and dedicated role, one she continued long after the U.S. Supreme Court upheld the right of municipalities" to declare certain structures worthy of landmark status. She also joined the society's board. It was an appropriate role for Jackie, who appreciated the value of historic sites far more than did most developers—even, some would say, more than most New York politicians. "No matter how inconvenient the time and the place [for meetings of the Municipal Art Society]," recalled her colleague, writer Brendan Gill, "when trouble was brewing, she never failed to appear on the barricades and to put up with the importunate, rat-a-tat questioning of reporters and photographers, to say nothing of the occasional unwelcome embrace of a gross publicity-hungry politician." After Jackie's death, the Municipal Art Society memorialized her efforts by naming an annual award for her.

NOW THINGS HAPPENED quickly. Confined with the flu to his suite at the Pierre Hotel, Ari began to have alarming symptoms of something more serious—transient double vision, a tendency for his eyelids to droop, extreme fatigue and an unusual slurring of speech. After a week in New York Hospital, he learned from doctors that he was suffering from myasthenia gravis, a progressive muscular disease. At first, the symptoms seemed benign and manageable with corticosteroid injections, and Ari flew off to Athens. Upon his arrival, he took to his bed at Glyfada, the seaside suburb of Athens where he maintained a home.

But by February 3, his heart function was compromised by another bout of the flu; the next day, Jackie left New York for Athens, taking along a cardiologist, Dr. Isidore Rosenfeld. Hours after their arrival, Ari collapsed with severe gastric pain: it was determined that he was having a gallbladder attack. On February 6, Jackie, Christina, Ari's sister Artemis and a team of doctors accompanied Ari to Paris, where he refused to go directly into the hospital but instead proceeded to his apartment on Avenue Foch. Three days later, his condition worsened, and he underwent surgery at the American Hospital to remove his gallbladder. What might otherwise have been an uneventful recovery was complicated by the rapidly advancing myasthenia gravis and his weakened heart. On February 12, he was put on a respirator and was given massive infusions of antibiotics.

A week later, Ari seemed to rally, and Jackie returned to New York. Over the next several weeks, she crossed the ocean regularly, but she was no longer warmly received at the hospital by Ari's two other sisters, Merope and Kalliroi, who fought with Christina about the care of Onassis. Maria Callas, frantic for news, was barred and no reports of Ari were relayed to her; Jackie, on the other hand, was merely tolerated.

On March 12, 1975, Ari's doctors told Jackie that he was in no immediate danger of dying and that she could fly to New York for a few days to see her children; Caroline had been working on a television documentary that was to have its premiere. But on the fifteenth, while Jackie was still in New York, Ari suddenly developed severe pneumonia that did not respond to medication. That evening, at the age of sixty-nine, he died. She at once flew back for the funeral and burial and released a brief comment to the press:

> Aristotle Onassis rescued me at a moment when my life was engulfed with shadows. He meant a lot to me. He brought me into a world where one could find both happiness and love. We lived through many beautiful experiences together which cannot be forgotten and for which I will be eternally grateful.

The world was more interested in the disposition of the vast Onassis fortune than in the last rites. Simply summarized, Ari left a fortune of about $1 billion. Jackie, at his request, had signed a quitclaim by which she forfeited any inheritance other than $250,000 annually and a stipend for her children until their twenty-first birthdays. But Christina's lawyers soon urged her to come to more generous terms with her stepmother, for Jackie was now twice widowed and still much loved worldwide: a quarter of a million annually out of a billion or so was a comparative pittance. Eventually Christina willingly assigned $26 million to Jackie, who, after taxes, was left with the tidy sum of about $19 million.

Soon Jackie met with a wealthy and influential New York diamond merchant who frequently counseled friends with vast estates. His name was Maurice Tempelsman. The press took note of this new alliance, saying only that "friends say he has merely been giving her some financial advice."

FOR THE REMAINDER of 1975, Jackie was mostly in America with her children and her friends. She gladly joined David Rockefeller, Brooke Astor and others in forming the Citizens' Committee for New York City, which mustered volunteers to work in areas affected by budget cutbacks. This was no quixotic venture: as with the Municipal Art Society, she attended meetings and traveled to Albany and Washington to lobby on behalf of the city's needs. She also served on the board of the American Ballet Theater and helped to promote commissions for a community textile factory in a poor section of Brooklyn.

According to John Doar, director of the Bedford-Stuyvesant Project, Jackie felt that African culture itself could provide inspiration for African-American business. She helped to develop the project by bringing in entrepreneurs who worked with local talent on cloth designs and organized an exhibit of them at the Metropolitan Museum of Art. For the first and only time, Jackie then invited photographers to 1040 Fifth Avenue, where they had a field day taking pictures of the materials she had sponsored, which had now become table and napkin embellishments in her own home.

In later years, similar efforts on behalf of minority interests and projects drew her out. She traveled to Los Angeles, for example, on behalf of a program to assist youths in the ghetto; she walked through some of the most depressed neighborhoods, visited families and a community center and listened to disaffected teenagers. This was no Lady Bountiful on a walkabout among the miners: Jackie's presence, as she knew, raised money for specific worthy causes. And when she urged friends to consider donations—to the Coalition for the Homeless in Los Angeles, for example, or to lobby on behalf of a worthy cause like the Equal Rights Amendment, which she heartily supported—she backed her ideals with practical action as well as contributions.

ON HER OWN, Jackie jogged in Central Park, took up yoga, read constantly, and dined at home with Caroline and John more often than at restaurants with the so-called Beautiful People. But to a few confidantes she said that being the wealthy Widow Onassis was fine as far as it went, but it did not go far enough. With all her money, she was, according to Halston, who designed some of her clothes, "very conservative in her buying, more so than many other women—she doesn't spend large amounts and she wears simple clothes."

In June and July, Jackie spent several weeks at Hyannisport, reading the Greek poet Cavafy, taking long walks on the shore and visiting with Rose Kennedy. She could no longer remember Jack's voice, she told Rose sadly, and she could not bear to look at pictures of him; Rose, an expert in coping with grief, was a great comfort.

On July 29, Jackie turned forty-six—not typically a significant marker, but for Jackie it was a time of serious reflection. She could not foresee a lifetime of respectable, luxurious retirement, merely waiting for grandmotherhood. What to do? "I have always lived through men," she told a friend. "Now I realize I can't do that anymore." This statement marked a moment of important self-awareness. Jackie had been raised in a family and culture that taught her to derive the meaning of her life from associations with powerful, influential men, those who granted material security as a sign that she was accepted.

That autumn, Caroline was studying in London, and John was about to turn eighteen and head to college. Jackie could not putter, plan dinner parties and arrange flowers for the rest of her life. Meeting with various friends, she wondered aloud about her future. "We had lunch one day," recalled Letitia Baldrige, "and she seemed to me somewhat down and sad, with no clear idea of where she was going. I told her that she had such a fine mind, such a keen intelligence—she should be using it to the fullest." The two old friends discussed working for a foundation, "but we saw that this wasn't right for her. And then a thought occurred to me," continued Baldrige. "I was working on a book for the Viking Press, and I told her about it and asked, 'What about publishing?' As it happened, Tom Guinzburg, president of Viking, was an old acquaintance of Jackie."

Books, of course, were Jackie's great passion. "She had reached that moment so many women find," said Baldrige. "She needed to get involved, to put her mind to work, and publishing seemed perfect. When we discussed it, suddenly she brightened." Jackie met with Guinzburg, who had been a college chum of her stepbrother. On September 18, Guinzburg announced that the following week Jacqueline Onassis would join Viking as a consulting editor. He deflected reporters' questions about her salary, which was $10,000 a year. "I always wanted to be some kind of writer or reporter," Jackie said. "But after college, I—I did other things."

She had not held a paying job since 1953 at the *Washington Times-Herald,* but nothing could be more natural than for Jackie to enter the world of publishing. She had, after all, written poems and stories since childhood; had produced the highly entertaining *One Special Summer;* and had edited *Profiles in Courage.* She had single-handedly produced *The White House: An Historic Guide,* selecting all the items to be presented, editing the text, designing the layout and even choosing the typeface. She was also a brilliant correspondent and had written the afterword for Peter Beard's book and an essay for *The New Yorker.*

Jackie, said Guinzburg, "moves in a wide circle of social, political and international contacts" that would make her invaluable to Viking. This was certainly true, but more to the point was her keen intelligence, her unerring taste, her impressive literary background, her refined sense of language and her extraordinary knowledge of literature, history and art. She needed only an introduction to the practical details of editorial meetings and schedules.

"I expect to be learning the ropes at first," she told a writer from *Newsweek.* She knew she had to "sit in at editorial conferences, discuss general things, maybe be assigned to a special project. Really, I expect to be doing what my employer tells me to do." Asked what title she would have, Jackie suggested "Apprentice." No, said Guinzburg, that would not do. Then what, asked Jackie, is the lowest title in publishing? Associate editor, he replied. "Then that's what I'll be."

ON THE MORNING of September 22, 1975, Jackie's doorman at 1040 Fifth Avenue whistled for a taxi. Wearing a gray shirtdress, she asked the driver to take her to 625 Madison Avenue, where Guinzburg introduced her to the company's other employees and then escorted her to a small office. "She got into publishing because she knew it would be an educational experience—she would learn something every moment—and she became a superb editor," said Nancy Tuckerman.

The staff at Viking could not be blamed for having been suspicious and doubtful at first, but soon they learned that they had a new colleague with formidable gifts.

"Before she came, everybody at Viking was reasonably skeptical," recalled editor Barbara Burn. "After she arrived, we were all pleasantly surprised that she wasn't a stuffed shirt with a funny voice. She was really very serious about what she did." Added Jackie's assistant, Rebecca Singleton: "She's smart, funny and remarkably stimulating." Jackie expected no preferential treatment. She got her own coffee, stood in line to wait to use office machines, made her own phone calls and never gave the slightest indication that she was the most famous woman in the world.

Before long, she acquired her first book for Viking, and perhaps no subject could have been more appropriate as Jackie's editorial debut. She brought to the public a book accompanying a traveling museum exhibit about the changing role of women in the eighteenth century— an ideal publication, she felt, for the upcoming Bicentennial of 1976. Taking its cue from Abigail Adams's plea to her husband John and the newly formed government, the book was called *Remember the Ladies: Women in America, 1750–1815*. Its judicious use of diaries, artifacts, portraits, engravings and artwork enabled readers to understand the demands of early American life and to appreciate the much-disregarded gallantry of women during that period.

But Jackie was neither unrealistic nor prim. When she and a researcher discovered that centuries ago women chewed a certain bark to induce abortions, Jackie insisted that this fact be included: she did not want the book to avoid the controversial, she said—she also wanted it to be earthy. And when they turned up Martha Washington's letter describing Georgetown as "a dirty hole," Jackie laughed, adding that nothing had changed.

As the first book she had acquired, *Remember the Ladies* immediately signaled its editor's primary aesthetic commitments—to history, art and the traditions of the eighteenth century. Published in 1976, the book also gave Jackie an opportunity to go on record in support of the Equal Rights Amendment and to demonstrate that she stood solidly with women's struggles, both in the past and present.

THUS BEGAN THE third act of Jackie's life.

So many celebrities, when their day in the sun has dimmed, retreat into splendid, self-imposed exile—only, in many cases, to emerge with their memoirs or to capitalize on the accident of fame.

Jackie would have none of that.

From September 1975 to her death in the spring of 1994—almost nineteen years, which was close to one-third of her life—Jacqueline Bouvier Kennedy Onassis was a working woman. Not because she needed to earn a living, but because she longed to have a life—not as the widow of two of the most important men in the world, but as a woman doing something on her own, with her own sense of identity. Her career as an editor was the ideal way of being herself, for in a way, her entire history, as well as her talents, had prepared her for serious intellectual work—to appreciate aesthetics, to encourage excellence and to be a creative and active participant in its achievement.

Most of all, the part of her life that had been something of a blind alley—the ceaseless activity, the hopping from this resort to that haven, the ceaseless wandering—forever ended. Wealthy she might have been, but Jackie no longer sought security in her wealth. In a way, her life became simpler, her needs less elaborate. She could have lived on a far grander scale—liveried chauffeurs, grand country estates, a far more opulent Manhattan home and a more dramatic presentation of self. But all these she eschewed.

Within the first few weeks of work that autumn, Jackie stepped into a Manhattan cab at her front door. After a moment or two, the driver glanced in his mirror and recognized her. But he said nothing until they arrived at the Viking offices.

"Lady," he said, turning around to accept the fare, "you work—and you don't *have* to?"

That was right, she replied softly.

"I think that's great!" he said, waving her off to her job.

CHAPTER TWELVE

1976-1979

*I*n 1975, Caroline Kennedy graduated from Concord Academy and decided to study abroad for a year before going on to Radcliffe College at Harvard University. Almost eighteen, she was ready for a bit of the world, and Jackie had no desire to keep her within a cocoon of security, which she knew would forestall an important kind of education.

Paris had been mother and daughter's first choice, but during one holiday Jackie and Caroline met a young man from England named Mark Shand, who had taken art history courses at Sotheby's and was launched on a career as an art dealer. A friendship was struck, and London was hailed as the place for a bright girl like Caroline. After consultation with various of Jackie's British friends, the arrangement was sealed. Caroline would enroll in the same program at Sotheby's.

At first, she lived in the Holland Park section of Westminster, with the family of Hugh Fraser, a Member of Parliament who had daughters Caroline's age; he was recently divorced from his wife, the author Antonia Fraser. But Jackie and Caroline were unaware that Fraser had been targeted by Irish terrorists, who made good their threats that October. A bomb was detonated outside the Fraser home, destroying his car and killing a neighbor only moments before he was to drive Caroline to the underground station, where she took the train each morning for her classes at Sotheby's. The incident ended her stay with the Frasers: Caroline was subsequently installed in the Radziwill home.

At Sotheby's "Works of Art" course, a ten-month program in the visual and decorative arts, Caroline took part in an ambitious educational program that rivaled any university curriculum in gravity and thoroughness. There were daily classroom lectures, visits to London's numerous galleries and museums, trips to English country homes, observation of auctions and inspection of art treasures. When Jackie was asked why she had encouraged Caroline to study in this particular curriculum, she replied in terms that could have been uttered by a dowager in a Henry James novel: "She will have money, and she will be better off for having the taste not to waste it."

But Caroline turned eighteen that November, and all was not study. As it happened, Mark Shand dropped his girlfriend and was soon seen regularly squiring Caroline to Annabel's, a trendy Mayfair nightclub; to movies; and to weekend house parties in the country. Shand was a glamorous escort with estimable social contacts. He was, for example, a friend of Nicky Soames, Winston Churchill's grandson; a chum of young and fabulously wealthy Lord Hesketh, a racing maven; and a confidant of various rich and sometimes idle luminaries whose haunts were the chic spots in and around London.

As it happened, Mark Shand's sister Camilla was married to Andrew Parker Bowles, who had once dated the queen's daughter, Princess Anne. None of these connections hurt Caroline's London social life. Meantime, her brother John's prospects flourished closer to home, where, at fifteen, he was maturing into a handsome boy, a sophomore at the Collegiate School whose major interests were riding and skiing.

THEIR MOTHER'S LIFE was more serene than ever. Pitching herself into serious work, Jackie spent most of her time at home and practically none of it on the Manhattan party circuit. She dined early with John, saw that he completed school assignments, sometimes invited a few friends to supper in the apartment, and read books and manuscripts as if her salvation depended on it. She did her own shopping, jogged in Central Park, practiced yoga, went to weekly sessions with a psychotherapist, took taxis and, on weekends, drove to her country home in New Jersey.

When she accepted invitations to what are often called "events," they tended to be recitals, ballets, readings, art exhibits and openings of photography shows. Often, from the spring of 1976 onward, her financial adviser, Maurice Tempelsman, escorted Jackie. When Stanislas Radziwill died of a heart attack that June, for example, Maurice accompanied her to London for the funeral.

PERHAPS NO MAN in New York society kept a lower profile than Maurice Tempelsman. Financier, diamond merchant, confidant of tycoons and heads of state, he was a man of intelligence, sophistication and sharp wit; although he was certainly wealthy, he had nothing like the fortune of Onassis. Balding and stocky, Maurice seemed another father figure in Jackie's life; in fact, he was only a month younger. He guided her fortune, protected her from public rudeness, befriended Caroline and John, and shared Jackie's cultural interests. Utterly indifferent to the trappings of glamour and fame, he was the ideal companion and counselor for Jackie. He was also married and the father of three grown children.

His own background could not have been more different from Jackie's. Born into a Jewish family in Belgium in August 1929, Maurice and his family had fled to America at the outbreak of World War II. His father was a diamond broker, and Maurice quickly ascended in the family business.

From the time he moved into Jackie's home in the mid-1980s, he was her only companion. Why did they not legalize the union? Part of the reason may have had to do with the tangle of financial complications for them and for their children if they did so.

But there may have been other reasons. Both were in their late forties, both had been chastened by disappointments in and outside marriage, and both prized occasional solitude and a certain autonomy. Jackie, of whose disposition more is known, found her career intensely rewarding, and she appreciated the emotional and psychological strength she drew from her independence. As she had admitted, she realized that she could no longer live through men. Outgrowing— through work and friendships—the insecurities that had still clung to her, Jackie became more fully herself than ever. "They don't need marriage," said Maurice's cousin, Rose Schreiber, in 1991, "because in many respects they are already married. They lack the piece of paper, but there's a spiritual bond."

Jackie and Maurice, close for eighteen years, were a devoted couple for at least twelve: their commitment to each other was inviolable, it was more successful than many legal marriages, and it lasted longer than any of her marriages or relationships. Although they were seen together more and more, the press, marvelous to relate, seemed to take no notice until shortly before her death—and even then the reporting was respectful to the point of deference. Perhaps this was because, in the final analysis, there was absolutely nothing ostentatious or glitzy about them—and because Jackie's life had become quiet, serious and entirely respectable, devoted as she was to her children and her work.

When it was appropriate, Jackie attended school events in which Caroline or John was involved, but, her friends recall, she never did so without her children's permission. At such times, she was another beaming, proud parent, sharing with other beaming, proud parents the typical little tales of childhood pranks and pratfalls. People soon got over their initial awe. Here was a mother among mothers.

Old friends saw a profound change in Jackie. After having been married to a president and then to a man of incalculable wealth, she was able at last to realize—especially as her children were quickly approaching their own maturity—that her life was gaining a depth and gravity she had perhaps never imagined.

IT MAY BE precisely at this point that the so-called enigma of Jacqueline Bouvier Kennedy Onassis is resolved—in her sense of process, her willingness to absorb suffering into her journey, her willingness to grow and change, her refusal to rely on mere fame or social status to provide any depth at all.

Contrary to the opinion of some sophisticates, it was in and through her work and in her quiet but consistent return to the faith of her forebears that, beginning in the late 1970s, Jackie developed what might be called a profoundly Catholic sense of things. This sense has nothing to do with matters parochial and is not, ultimately, primarily something traditionally "religious."

This deserves some brief elaboration.

A "Catholic sense of things" is usually taken to mean attitudes about piety or, even wider of the mark, the mere repetition of certain culturally determined doctrinal formulae. Certainly, expressions of worship and belief constitute important elements in all the world's great religions, Catholicism markedly among them. But precisely because they are the human expressions of transcendent realities, these forms point beyond themselves. Words and gestures, like the words and gestures that communicate and represent human love, do not contain or exhaust the reality: they are carriers toward that reality, which is God Himself, Who stands behind words and forms, and Who may only imperfectly be glimpsed behind human expressions.

A Catholic sense of things is, on the other hand, far more than a static immersion in academic or pious forms. It takes seriously indeed the idea that God has once and for all entered into human matter and experience: Christians call this the mystery of the Incarnation. The corollary of this primal assertion is that God loves what He has made and saves it beyond death. In the Catholic scheme of things, nothing human is outside the order of grace, which carries human destiny forward and provides a way of coping with darkness and confusion. The Catholic sense of things holds, along with the ancient Christian texts, that "all time belongs to Him, and all the seasons." There is no room in authentic Catholic faith for a rejection of the world or contempt for the body.

To be sure, Jackie was no theologian, and her religious education had been virtually nonexistent. But the Catholic sense of things got through to her over the years—in her reading, in her aesthetic life, in her commitment to what is beautiful in the world. Steeped in and surrounded by the spirit of French iconography, art and poetry, the lively loveliness of dance and the richness of Western philosophy, she developed a deeply religious sensibility that went beyond the merely pious. Above and beyond this, there was in Jackie a fundamental trust—a conviction about transcendent mercy and ultimate meaning.

At about this time, she came upon a copy of the writings of the medieval English solitary Julian of Norwich, a woman of great wisdom and mystical insight. Julian's utter confidence in divine Providence was expressed in a famous passage: "All shall be well, and all shall be well, and all manner of thing shall be well." Faith is built on such unshakable trust.

As she began to chat with a few sensitive and sensible clergymen at the Church of St. Thomas More on East Eighty-ninth Street, and sometimes with the Jesuits at St. Ignatius Loyola on Park Avenue, Jackie understood that Catholicism endorsed her fundamental approach toward life, that it meant an embrace rather than a denial or rejection of the human. This sense, she was learning, insists that—in the words of the Bible—the Spirit breathes where He will, and that it is precisely through the opening of oneself through contemplation that things eternal enter in and take root. "If you cut people off from what nourishes them spiritually and historically," Jackie said in a rare public appearance, "something within them dies." She was, at the moment, quietly exploring the roots of Western Christian mysticism.

One need not be a churchman, much less a philosopher or theologian, to absorb this spirit, to be washed with its atmosphere. It begins with a love of all that is good, all that is possible, and does not depend on book learning for its depth. Jackie's Catholic sense refused to accept the final opacity of the universe, refused to believe that one is forever doomed to one's own limitations. Since childhood, her personality had been essentially contemplative. Now, as she neared the age of fifty, that part of her flourished.

THAT ALL THIS paralleled her growing relationship with a man from a devout Jewish background ought not to evoke surprise. The more Jackie knew of her Catholic heritage, the more she came to appreciate its intrinsic Semitic basis. The deepest logic of her relationship with Maurice was, after all, that they both became more themselves—their identities, in other words, were not diminished by any bogus, romantic idea of self-abnegation.

Because she was as respectful of the interior privacy of others as she jealously guarded her own, none of this was much considered during Jackie's lifetime. But her religious vision owed a great deal to Richard Cushing, that craggy, compassionate cardinal of Boston. He was her friend and spiritual guide not only when she had decided to marry Onassis, but earlier—when she married Jack, when her first pregnancy failed, when she lost Arabella, when Patrick died and, of course, after the assassination.

Thanks to Cushing, Jackie's conscience had in critical times been relieved. Through his ministry, she was able to break free from a life that had become cramped and stifled. Because of his wisdom, she was set free to explore—to make, appropriately, a Greek odyssey. As Cushing knew, Jackie was never a traditionally pious Catholic. But her vocation was larger than parochial. In the last years of her life, she became more than a sophisticated and smart lady: she came into her own as a wise, even profound woman.

BUT SHE DID not become some idealized, stained-glass-window saint. Jackie retained an earthy appreciation of the world and of her own carnality. After the death of Onassis but before the commitment to her relationship with Maurice, she seems to have enjoyed a number of intimacies that became more or less frankly sexual. After her death, the journalist Pete Hamill, for one, wrote that they "went around together for a while," and after the death of John Jr., Hamill reminisced in *The New Yorker* about visits to Jackie's apartment and his casual afternoons with the boy at sixteen.

There were one or two other brief romantic attachments during the late 1970s, but nothing—rumors to the contrary—like the platoon of young lovers imagined by a few unscrupulous gossipmongers, who found it impossible to adduce convincing evidence for their tabloid assertions. "I just don't understand," she once said, "why sometimes [the tabloids] work so hard at hurting me. There are so many more important things to do."

For her, these relationships had their own truth and were perhaps, more than anything, an attempt to heal the disappointment and pain in her past. Jackie had been raised in a tradition that expected exclusivity in romantic love, but fidelity had not prevailed in her two marriages. In a way, the brief attachments she formed in her late forties— when she was at liberty for the first time to explore the nature of her own desires—enabled her to learn precisely what she did not want.

Jackie was, to put the matter briefly, a woman with an enormous capacity for learning, for appreciation, for hard work, for sheer elation—she was, in other words, someone with a great soul. She had known all life's excitements, the grandeur, the grief, the loneliness, the frustrating isolation. Now, as she approached fifty, she was having the most transforming experience of all: the clouds of fear, and the concomitant dependence on men and money, were passing beyond her.

EARLY IN 1976, another clergyman saw the depth of her insights. Jackie had read *St. Patrick's Day With Mayor Daley and other things too good to miss*, a collection of essays by Eugene C. Kennedy, at the time a Catholic priest and a professor of psychology at Loyola University in Chicago; he was not related to the Kennedys of Boston. Impressed by the quality of his writing, she telephoned him from her office at Viking and suggested that he do a full biography of Daley—who, of course, she had known from Jack's campaign days. Daley, Chicago's mayor since 1955, was one of the most powerful and controversial leaders in American politics.

"From the start, she was the most extraordinary editor—involved in every aspect of the book's life," recalled Kennedy, who later left the priesthood but not his ministry as a respected psychologist and author of dozens of important works on a variety of subjects. "She also had a wonderful sense of humor—she didn't crack jokes or make funny remarks, but she saw and was able to enjoy the ironic aspect of life, and she had a playful way about her."

The biography, eventually published as *Himself! The Life and Times of Mayor Richard J. Daley,* began when Jackie flew to Chicago to meet with Kennedy and to gain Daley's confidence and cooperation.

Where did Jackie want to go to lunch? Kennedy asked. A nice, quiet French restaurant in a chic part of town?

"No," Jackie replied, "someplace low-down and dirty"—an ordinary hamburger joint would be fine.

Did she require special arrangements or protection to avoid being accosted? A police escort, perhaps?

"Oh, no—I never want anything like that! The best thing we can do is just walk fast!"

As it happened, the mayor was not eager to see Jackie—not because he disliked her, but because he was, perhaps not unreasonably, wary of a full investigation into his career. Jackie did not meet with Daley on her trip, for he claimed that some city problem required his presence. Jackie laughed at this excuse, recognizing the old Irish blarney she knew so well. "It's odd," she said. "After Jack's election, Daley could have asked for anything. But he wanted only one thing: to spend a night in the White House!"

Try as he did to avoid her, Daley did not reckon with Jackie's persistence. Her counterplay was set in action that summer, when she decided to attend the Democratic Convention—for the sole purpose, as Eugene Kennedy recalled, of seeing Daley in a place and a position where he could not refuse to see *her*. Kennedy—who for the occasion put aside his clerical garb and wore collar and tie—escorted her. "It was fascinating and really quite amusing," he recalled. "For one thing, Walter Cronkite and his colleagues couldn't figure out who I was," and so there was a buzz about Jackie's new friend, whom no one could identify. Perhaps no one could have guessed that he was celibate and that their friendship was of course entirely platonic.

Everyone tried to get Jackie's attention that evening, but she ignored the shouting reporters and photographers and instead went out of her way to greet George Wallace, the ailing governor of Alabama, who was then a paraplegic, confined to a wheelchair after being shot. She had loathed his ideology, but his suffering touched her.

Finally, Democratic Party chairman Robert Strauss arranged for Jackie and Daley to meet below the convention floor. "Actually, Daley revered her," said Kennedy, "and she just sprung on him the idea of the book, in a straightforward way. Typically, he replied, 'I'll give it some thought.'" Jimmy Breslin remembered that another man who was present came out of that meeting room and said with astonishment, "That's some sight inside! Jackie Kennedy is sitting with Dick Daley! I thought it was some kind of an emotional visit, but she's trying to get him to do a book. She acts like she really works!"

Which she did—hence the book was eventually published, despite the absence of Daley's active involvement. "She understood the rules, the demands and the discipline of producing a book," Kennedy discovered, "and she loved to talk about being an editor."

"It expands your knowledge," Jackie said about her new career. "Each book takes you down another path. [I hope] some of them move people and some of them do some good. . . . Part of an editor's job [requires that] you keep asking everyone—friends, authors, agents, experts, anyone with access to a particular world—if they know of a person who should be published or a subject that should be treated."

Even more than talking about it, however, Jackie relished doing the job. The symbiosis that links writer and editor is a delicate and often difficult one. But without exception, the more than sixty writers who had the benefit of Jackie's editorial guidance in the publication of nearly one hundred books over nineteen years admired her and were grateful for her considerable contributions. "The fact is that she was fiercely bright and talented," said Eugene Kennedy, who later wrote two novels Jackie edited, *Queen Bee* and *Father's Day*. "She understood that writers, like fine china being prepared for shipment, need to be packaged gently and supported strongly for the long journey from blank paper to publication day. Her style was encouragement—that of a coach prompting as good a performance as possible out of a long-distance runner."

Kennedy recalled, for example, the time when, after spending hours working on the manuscript of a novel he had sent to Jackie, she telephoned him: "No woman would react that way to a man," she said of a female character she considered too passive. "A real woman would kick him all over town." Later, with novelists Elizabeth Crook and Dorothy West, among others, Jackie was invariably on the mark: she especially warned them against repetition or sentimentality, which, she rightly said, "backfires on you."

REAL WOMEN FROM another era were much on her mind during 1976 and 1977. After the book on eighteenth-century American women, it was not surprising that Russians of the same time attracted her attention, too. After studying dozens of books on the subject and collaborating with Diana Vreeland, consultant to the Costume Institute of the Metropolitan Museum of Art, Jackie edited *In the Russian Style*, a lavishly illustrated book on prerevolutionary fashion. Designed to coincide with a Met exhibit, the pictures and text, excerpted from period letters and other documents, celebrated the fairy-tale clothing, jewelry, headdresses and styles worn by Russian royals, aristocrats, bourgeoisie and peasants.

But Jackie was not merely content to read previously published books. In July 1976, she traveled to Moscow and Leningrad with Met director Thomas Hoving, where they met with the Ministry of Culture.

As for the heavy, cumbersome garments they researched, Jackie observed, "You love to see them the way you love to see *Gone With the Wind*. But wouldn't you rather wear your blue jeans than wander around in a hoop skirt?" *In the Russian Style* was published in January 1977. By that time Jackie was busy at work preparing *The Firebird and Other Russian Fairy Tales,* a book as much of interest to adults as to children, illustrated by Boris Zvorykin, a master decorative artist.

As much as she enjoyed her work, there was, of course, inevitable pressure on the job, precisely because she took so seriously her responsibilities to colleagues and authors. To counteract the stress, Jackie continued classes in yoga with a respected trainer and practitioner named Tillie Weitzner. Until her final illness, Jackie was prompt and ready for her sessions when Tillie arrived at 1040 Fifth Avenue. "Not only was she kind and considerate to work with," her instructor recalled, "but she was completely devoted to the practice of yoga and gave herself to it religiously for a quarter of an hour each day."

Disciplined about maintaining her figure, Jackie had, Tillie noticed, a remarkable simplicity about her person at all times. She wore little makeup and scarcely any jewelry; her fingernails were never fashionably long, for she kept them at reasonable length, the better to wield her editorial pencil; and she liked to get down to business on the floor or mat wearing an old yoga suit. Like so many other colleagues, friends and acquaintances, Tillie was, at first, astonished by Jackie's unpretentious private life. Rarely had any of them met anyone whose reality was so at variance with the public misperception that she was a woman of cold glamour and aloof respectability.

Another visitor, as much a friend as an author, was Eugene Kennedy. In June 1977, during one afternoon at her apartment, their discussion about ideas for books was interlaced with numerous references to John F. Kennedy. Because her guest was, at the time, still a priest, she easily confided in him. He had the clear impression, he recalled, of a woman undeceived by life, with a realistic idea of human nature, and above all, an abiding love for her first husband.

There was, Eugene Kennedy recalled years later, "almost a palpable reality in the room that day. She had an enormously profound and deeply seasoned love for a man who had been dead fourteen years," a man whose photograph was prominently displayed in her library. Much earlier, she had confided to Bill Walton that Jack was the love of her life; those who knew her well in later years had precisely the same perception. "One of the things I loved about my husband," Jackie said on the phone to another man, someone she had never met, "was the way he devoured life—like a man sucking the meat out of a lobster claw. The books he read, the food he ate, the boats he sailed . . ."

As always, Jackie's major concern was the future of her children as well as their respect for the past. Her son arrived home from school the afternoon of Eugene Kennedy's visit and casually told them that there had been a question about his father on a history test. "How striking it was," Kennedy remembered thinking, "that this young man had the experience of studying his father as President of the United States!" When John left the room, Jackie spoke about the possibility of her son's entering politics. "She certainly did not want him to take that route precipitously, but rather to have a solid education in another field before—or if . . ." recalled Kennedy.

But Jackie was tremendously candid: her great joy was in keeping John F. Kennedy's memory alive for her children, along with keeping her children away from the brutal glare of publicity. During their formative years she gave them every opportunity to define themselves as separate and apart from the undifferentiated mass of Kennedy cousins.

From the time he was twelve, for example, she saw to it that John was sent off for outdoor adventures that were more than merely vacations. He spent time at an Outward Bound project in Maine and with the National Outdoor Leadership School in Kenya, and at fifteen he and his cousin Timothy Shriver went to Guatemala as part of a team helping earthquake survivors. During the summer before college, he spent two months with the Peace Corps in South Africa. Thanks to Jackie, John was, recalled Harris Wofford, "serious, idealistic, open," with a remarkable "eagerness and lack of pretense." No one in any of these or other projects—and no one at school—could recall him seeking special prerogatives or treatment: he made no secret of his dislike for Secret Service protection, which he was glad to see terminate when he was sixteen.

———

AS IF TO further free her for a new life, it was perhaps ironic that parts of Jackie's family history were drawing to a close during this period. In November 1976, stepfather Uncle Hughdie died at seventy-nine, after years of frail health. Recently, he had lost most of his fortune in failed investments, and Merrywood had been sold. Soon after, Janet was forced to sell Hammersmith Farm to ten businessmen, who paid $875,000 and maintained it as a private Newport museum. With Merrywood also sold, Janet retired to a house in Georgetown.

Jackie provided for her mother's comfort and care by establishing a million-dollar trust fund for her. Although their relationship had been courteous, Jackie and Janet had not been close for years. When a friend once expressed admiration for Jackie—that she had always displayed the same good spirit—Janet replied coolly, "I don't know whether anybody ought to want to stay exactly the same—there must always be room for improvement." This statement fairly synthesized Janet's tone and attitude, particularly after Jackie returned to work: Janet seemed, for some odd reason, unable or unwilling to take into account that in fact her daughter had greatly changed.

Next, Jackie learned that her aunt Edie, ill with pneumonia, had been taken to Southampton Hospital and had been placed in a cramped, airless ward. At once, Jackie ordered a better room for her and arranged for the finest care, for which she gladly assumed the cost. Contentedly daffy to the end—and, when she wanted to be, impossibly peevish— Edie died soon thereafter at eighty-one. Although Jackie and Lee had paid for the rehabilitation of Grey Gardens a few years earlier, the house had mostly returned to its state of disrepair. At the funeral service, Edie's voice rang out with gleeful, girlish abandon from the ancient recordings she had made decades earlier: those same renditions of Romberg, Berlin and Gershwin with which she had entertained children and adults at Jackie's childhood birthday parties now rattled the church windows. Not long after the funeral, Little Edie—by then fifty-nine— moved to Canada and, later, to the warmth of Florida, where she could occasionally be persuaded to tell visitors that yes, it was *she* whom that Jack Kennedy had really wanted to marry.

JUST AS JACKIE had settled happily into the routine of working at Viking, there occurred an irreparable break in her friendship and collaboration with Tom Guinzburg. The problem burst forth in crisis in October 1977, but the seeds had been sown earlier that year.

Nancy Tuckerman was by now employed at another publisher, Doubleday. One day, she and Jackie had lunched with Lisa Drew, an editor at that house. Months before, a British literary agent had submitted to Drew the manuscript of a novel by Jeffrey Archer, set a few years in the future and titled *Shall We Tell the President?*—the premise of which was the attempted assassination of President Edward M. Kennedy. Drew, saying that the novel was utterly tasteless and without merit, had turned it down flat. But by that summer, she had heard that Viking, of all houses, had bought the novel for publication.

"How about this Jeffrey Archer book that Viking bought?" she asked Jackie over lunch with Tuckerman, presuming, quite naturally, that Jackie knew about the acquisition.

"Who's Jeffrey Archer?" asked Jackie. "I don't know anything about it! What's it about?"

"It's a political thriller, and Ted Kennedy's a character, and I thought they might have mentioned it to you."

"I don't know anything about it."

Lisa Drew let the matter rest, but after lunch Jackie went directly to Tom Guinzburg's office and asked to know the details.

"Don't you worry about it," replied her boss. "It's not anything that you're going to have anything to do with."

And that was that—until the novel appeared and John Leonard in *The New York Times* published the first review. Concluding his critique with a negative assessment, Leonard wrote, "There is a word for such a book. The word is trash. Anybody associated with its publication should be ashamed of herself." The implication was clear: by her presence at Viking, Jackie had at least tacitly supported the book. In a separate statement, Leonard minced no words: "She should have objected [to publication of the book]," he told the *Times*. "She could have stopped its publication if she wanted to."

This, of course, was not so. Jackie had not been consulted when Viking had acquired the book. She knew nothing about its contents, apart from what she had learned at her lunch with Lisa Drew. Guinzburg had not been forthcoming with her, and in any case, she had no right of veto against the publication of books by other editors.

When Jackie objected to this misrepresentation, Guinzburg, alas, waffled, going so far as to tell *The New York Times* that she had been "generous and understanding ... at the time we discussed this book and before the contract was signed." This, too, was not true, for Jackie had simply been told of its forthcoming publication and had followed Guinzburg's advice not to read it; he later told the *Times* differently, however, and Leonard's statement added to the implication that Jackie had approved of the project. There was Guinzburg, said Jackie, hurt and bitter, "on the front page of *The New York Times*, saying that I knew all about exactly what happens in this book, and I didn't know about it at all!"

"Last spring, when I was told about the book," she said in a statement to the press, "I tried to separate my lives as a Viking employee and a Kennedy relative. But this fall, when it was suggested that I had had something to do with acquiring the book and that I was not distressed by its publication, I felt I had to resign."

Soon she did just that, hurt by what she considered an old friend's betrayal and depressed by an aspect of publishing she had not yet encountered. Many, then as later, felt that the novel's publication ought indeed to have been forgone by Viking—and that the company ought not, in an excess of insensitive bad taste, to have risked offending a valued colleague whose life had been twice blighted by the assassination of Kennedy brothers.

BY THE END of 1977, then, Jackie was again idle—but not for long. Soon thereafter, she invited Lisa Drew to 1040 Fifth Avenue, and they discussed Doubleday. When Jackie asked about working there, Drew assured her it would be both safe and gratifying—Nancy Tuckerman was there, after all, and the executive officer of Doubleday, John Sargent, had escorted Jackie around town for a while. There were quiet negotiations, and Jackie accepted the position of associate editor at a salary of $15,000 per year. In February 1978, she reported to Doubleday's offices at 245 Park Avenue, a few blocks north of Grand Central Station.

At once, she set out in search of interesting new projects. After seeing actor George Hamilton on a television talk show, she expressed interest in his autobiography. But the proposal submitted by Hamilton's ghostwriter presented him as a figure of historic significance whose story included world culture and the great men of our time. At this, Jackie frowned and delivered one of her incisive *bons mots:* after all, she said, he was George Hamilton—not Alexander the Great. Similarly, she read a press release about a book by Dolly Parton that offered, according to Parton, "a little bit of truth, a little bit of humor, and a little bit of dirty stuff, to make it sell." Jackie's withering reaction: "It sounds like another cultural watershed."

Her own cultural watersheds were reading and purposeful travel. Whereas once she had gone from place to place for distraction, now her journeys were purposeful and mostly linked to work. That May, she made her first journey to Israel, for the dedication of the Jewish Diaspora Museum in Tel Aviv. Accompanied by Karl Katz, who was the moving force behind the museum, Jackie then went on to visit kibbutzim, to meet with students, and to explore biblical sites in the Holy Land. According to Katz, Jackie knew her Scripture well, both Old and New Testaments, and she required no instruction on the connection between place and incident. As a coda to the journey, she planted a tree in Israel's John F. Kennedy Memorial Forest.

In the summer of 1978, after scouring Cape Cod and the offshore Massachusetts islands, Jackie paid $1.15 million for 375 acres on the southeastern tip of Martha's Vineyard, in order to have a seaside summer residence. Three years later, architect Hugh Newell Jacobsen completed the estate at an eventual cost of an additional $3.1 million; there was a main house of just over three thousand square feet and a small guesthouse. For the rest of her life, this was the refuge for her and her family; here she invited several old friends, a few new coworkers, two or three of her authors and one President and First Lady.

In October, her children accompanied Jackie to the dedication of Harvard's John F. Kennedy School of Government. Exactly one year later, they were again an attractive trio at the opening of the John F. Kennedy Library at Columbia Point, Boston. With her usual sharp wit, Jackie characterized the attitude of some present: "I think they really wanted Caroline to come out skipping in a little girl's dress."

To mark their twenty-first and eighteenth birthdays in November 1978, she brought Caroline and John to Manhattan from Radcliffe (where Caroline was a junior) and Phillips Academy (where John was a senior, preparing for graduation the following June). A modish disco party was held for 125 guests at Le Club, on East Fifty-fifth Street.

JACKIE CELEBRATED HER fiftieth birthday in July 1979 more quietly, sailing in Nantucket Sound and going ashore to survey the progress of her home-in-progress at Gay Head. As workmen hammered the cedar shingles and installed bleached oak floors, someone in the family handed her a copy of a little lyric they had found, one she had written on her tenth birthday, lines that expressed her lifelong love of the sea:

> *When I go down by the sandy shore,*
> *I can think of nothing I want more*
> *Than to live by the booming blue sea*
> *As the seagulls flutter round about me.*

Just as she had told Lady Bird Johnson about the happy times in the White House, so Jackie was now able to recall gratefully the times of her life at the seaside on Long Island and to embrace what it had offered.

"We spent the first four summers of our marriage at Hyannisport," she said, admitting that she had once "fought against the idea—I thought it was too close [to the Kennedys], and I wanted to be away from the compound." And then her voice changed: "Sometimes I think that time heals, although you forget certain things. I can't remember Jack's voice exactly anymore, and it's still hard to look at pictures of him." Her gaze swept over the waters of the Sound. "But now I am glad to be back here."

When the poet Stephen Spender asked what she felt her proudest accomplishment was, she was typically refreshing: "I think my biggest achievement is that, after going through a rather difficult time, I consider myself comparatively sane." She was, of course, much more than that. Time and experience had by now erased whatever sense of grandeur might have lurked within her fifteen years earlier. All that remained—and they were everything to her—were work, family, art and a gradually deepening commitment to Maurice Tempelsman. To all who knew her, Jackie was contradicting F. Scott Fitzgerald with a vengeance: her life had not only passed through a second act but was

now fully engaged in a third. With quiet insistence and constant delib-
eration, she was reaching a profound serenity. She was, indeed, no
longer living through a man's identity, but through a constant deepening of her own.

In the meantime, her widowed mother was still on her lifelong
course for the properly wealthy mate. In August 1979, at the age of
seventy-one, Janet seemed to have found one for a third time. Demonstrating the truth of the old French maxim that *plus ça change, plus
c'est la même chose,* Janet Norton Lee Bouvier Auchincloss married a
retired investment banker named Bingham Morris. The couple retired
to Southampton, Long Island, for by this time Hammersmith Farm
had been sold and was being transformed into a tourist attraction.

As 1979 drew to a close, Jackie visited Newport for one last time,
passing through the rooms of her youth and commenting unsentimen-
tally to Caroline about her early life and her social debut there thirty-
two years earlier. As rock music from workmen's radios blared through
the house, the bygone social amenities of floor-length crinoline petti-
coats, long white gloves, formal tea dances and chaperoned parties
seemed remote and improbable, the almost forgotten props of a world
that now existed only in memory.

CHAPTER THIRTEEN

1980-1992

ne of the things I like about publishing is that you don't promote the editor—you promote the book and the author," said Jackie. This was not merely an attitude, it was a way of connecting concretely with her writers and colleagues. As the 1980s began, Jackie produced some of the most interesting books of the decade and, as she brought new talent to public perception, it was perhaps inevitable that her own skills were also widely recognized.

"When I first met Jackie in 1980, she had a small internal office, no window, no frills," recalled Marianne Velmans, who sold British publishing rights for Doubleday in a London office; the following is her estimation, frequently echoed by others during Jackie's sixteen years with the company:

> I found her amazingly easy to deal with, approachable and friendly, relaxed and completely professional. She projected no formality or airs—on the contrary, she was entirely natural in everything she did and said, even when we rode in the elevator and she swiftly and casually put on her dark glasses and head-scarf, the disguise she often wore to preserve her privacy. I found it odd, however, that for many people outside, it was as

if this important third part of her life didn't exist. She was usually spoken of and written about as if she were this character from the past. But she was very much a person of the present.

This is an important observation, for in perhaps the most critical aspect for Jackie—her concern with excellence as the route to happiness for herself and others—the most influential part of her life coincided with the longest division. She had been John Kennedy's wife for ten years and First Lady for less than three. There ensued five years of wandering widowhood and then five years as the wife of Aristotle Onassis. Now all that was followed by nineteen years as an editor— almost a third of her lifetime.

Whereas many others with her fame, privilege and cachet wrote memoirs and promoted themselves, Jackie set to work: "I want to live my life, not record it," she said more than once. "Why sit indoors with a yellow pad writing a memoir when you can be outdoors?" But did she not want to correct the errors, the gossip—to have her own voice heard? Jackie dismissed all that: "The river of sludge will go on and on. It isn't about the real me. I want to savor life, not write about it. I'd rather spend my time feeling the mist of the ocean up at Martha's Vineyard."

NEWS OF MURDEROUS acts blared daily from televisions and news-papers in 1980 and 1981, all inevitably bringing back Jackie's darkest memories. John Lennon was shot to death; soon thereafter, President Reagan and Pope John Paul II were gravely wounded by the gunfire of other madmen. President Sadat of Egypt was assassinated by terror-ists. Closer to home, groups of American conspiracy mavens made headlines almost weekly, insisting that John Kennedy's death was the result of some orchestrated collusion. They managed to have Lee Har-vey Oswald's body exhumed in a futile attempt to prove their theories.

Meanwhile, Jackie benefited not only the world of publishing but also the lives and careers of many authors. "I'm drawn to books that are out of our regular experience," she remarked late in her career, "books of other cultures, ancient histories. I'm interested in the arts in general, especially the creative process. I'm fascinated by hearing artists talk about their crafts. To me, a wonderful book is one that takes me on a journey into something I didn't know before."

She also brought her personal convictions about ethics and moral values to her work, encouraging former Congressman Carl Elliot to write *The Cost of Courage* and Jack Bass to undertake *Taming the Storm,* both important books about civil rights, with particular reference to the South. "These are subjects that people should care about," she said, presenting the books to Doubleday's sales force.

Equally so, her love of ballet led her to publish *Blood Memory,* the memoirs of the formidable Martha Graham, as well as the autobiography of Gelsey Kirkland, a gifted but troubled young ballerina who worked through serious drug addictions and returned to the stage. *Dancing on My Grave* became a bestseller, and in the process Kirkland said that Jackie "helped me recover my life and my career. This was no small gift, and she gave it over and over through the years."

Jackie's sense that her own career was a vocation, not just a job, is directly related to what another of her authors, Olivier Bernier, called the "informed sympathy" of her critical work. She worked on five of his books on French social and political history. According to Bernier, she had "a rare ability to make an author feel that what he was doing mattered. She cared enormously about books—not only about their content, but also the way they looked. The world is full of self-important people, [but] no one could have been more self-effacing than Jackie when she was working with her author . . . [and] she helped improve the book without ever being intrusive."

Ruth Prawer Jhabvala, whose novel *Poet and Dancer* she edited, found that Jackie's "empathy was so total . . . I felt I could lean on her strength, [which] came from her own vulnerability: she was aware how you felt because she felt it herself and knew exactly when and how you needed her support."

The architect and writer William La Riche, a friend during the last eight years of Jackie's life, also experienced her generosity. Although they never produced a book together, Jackie became, he said, his "great literary encourager." In early 1987, over lunch at the Restaurant Raphael, La Riche and Jackie discovered a shared enthusiasm for Greece and Greek poetry. She knew by heart C. P. Cavafy's poem "Ithaka"— and, in tune with its lyrical sentiment, she well understood, as La Riche put it, "that the destination gives the journey, that the journey gives the life."

"As a trusted friend, Jackie was," he added,

> eager to connect on the deepest possible level, and she had a greater capacity for empathy than anyone else I had ever met. The truth is that she was the most spiritually generous friend I have ever known—a woman with an amazing ability to see into one's life more deeply and usefully than one could imagine. I once asked her how, during the most painful moments of her life, she had the strength to go on, and she replied, "It never occurred to me not to."

La Riche found that the quality of her listening was "the counterweave, barely visible, that lent the casual weave of conversation its hidden order. And the intensity of her listening—of her silence—was absolute."

He learned, too, of her sense of adventure.

> We drove from Manhattan to Princeton in her old 1971 BMW. The windows didn't quite work, but she had a powerful engine put in, and she loved to speed. We were on our way to visit Nina Berberova, a Russian writer, then almost ninety, who had fled St. Petersburg after the Revolution and whose work Jacqueline had read and much admired. As we passed through the Lincoln Tunnel, Jackie urged me to cross a double line in order to pass a truck—"Just gun it, William!" she urged me.

JACK VALENTI, WHO had known Jackie since 1963 and was special assistant to President Johnson, wrote his first novel for Jackie: "She had a gift for inspiring insecure authors," he recalled, adding that she was "incapable of either a mean or graceless gesture." At the same time, she was direct in her literary criticism—in the pointed ways in which, as novelist Elizabeth Crook said, she shaped the work.

"She knew where drama was, and where it wasn't," Crook recalled, adding that Jackie frequently wrote "CUT" and "DELETE" on manuscript pages. "Cut baby crying . . . Overkill. Can you delete? . . . Much of Kate and William's relationship is cloying. You must eliminate some of her angst, their coy dialogues, her hemming and hawing, etc. . . . Baby Samuel is so overdescribed it could turn one off babies. . . . This is pretty trite—can you recast? Don't let yourself go overboard with the dog. There is too much about the stump of his tail."

She edited nonfiction with equal perception. Francis Mason, who worked with Jackie on a book about George Balanchine, delivered an unwieldy manuscript of 650,000 words representing the memories of 115 people who worked with the choreographer. "You have a new form of biography here," Jackie said wryly, "but you have to focus on the recollections that fill out Balanchine's portrait. Cut their autobiographical reminiscences and repetitious adoration and concentrate on what each has to say on what Balanchine was really like as a man and an artist. Readers will then know what Balanchine and ballet are all about." When she saw Mason's hesitation, she added, "Blame it on me. I'm the editor."

Her praise was equally detailed. "I am so impressed [with] what you have done, I just can't tell you," she wrote to a young novelist. "You have pared down and tightened a sprawling, overwritten first draft into an immensely moving novel." Composer and conductor André Previn, whose memoir Jackie published (*No Minor Chords: My Days in Hollywood*), said that he could not imagine anyone "not being the better for having worked with her."

But Jackie was never solemn, and she knew when unorthodox styles could be valuable—as, for example, when she published Larry Gonick's *Cartoon History of the Universe,* which she called "very accurate, and a much better account of how civilization developed than many more serious ones I've read." To the astonishment of some colleagues, she then worked with Jann Wenner, the publisher of *Rolling Stone,* to publish a selection of that magazine's best selections from a twenty-five-year period.

In her sixteen years at Doubleday, Jackie published seventy-three books; the total would have been greater but, like every other editor in the business, the editorial board turned down some of the ideas she had championed. Frequently, if she still believed in the prospective book after such a rejection, Jackie had no hesitation in trying to make the project work for another publisher, and on such occasions she virtually became the agent for a struggling writer.

DURING THOSE YEARS, her colleagues at Doubleday admired, respected and came to have enormous affection for her.

"This was not a rich lady who pulled rank—she never did that. There were never any prima donna antics, nor was she having fun with something she didn't take seriously," said Stephen Rubin, the company's president and publisher. The key to a good working relationship with Jackie, he and others learned, was "to treat her like anyone else—then you were fine from Day One. But if you treated her like the legendary Mrs. Kennedy or Mrs. Onassis, you ran into problems."

At work as elsewhere, Jackie never called any attention to her personal history. She rarely mentioned her years as First Lady or her marriage to Onassis. Once, she and Rubin had a conference call with an important woman: "I hope you're going to ask the hard questions," Jackie said nervously, "because I'm terrified!" Similarly, after one editorial meeting, she stopped another editor in the hall to make a comment about a book under consideration. The editor was impressed with the depth of her remark and asked why she had not mentioned this at the meeting. "Oh," Jackie replied softly, "Jack always told me to distrust the first thing that comes into my mind."

Marly Russoff, a vice president at Doubleday, also recalled that Jackie rarely spoke of herself: "She was always interested in other people. With authors, she had curiosity, interest and a deeply nurturing quality. She saw herself not as a person who had a vision, but as someone who experienced, admired, enjoyed."

Her intelligence and lack of pretense also made her impatient with bores. "She could read people at once," said James Fitzgerald, a senior editor at Doubleday, summarizing a widely held impression. "And if they said things they thought she wanted to hear, she was very quickly irked with them."

Occasionally she revealed something of her inner life in the way she described others. The lawyer, literary critic and writer Louis Auchincloss was related to her stepfather's family, and she had confided in him in 1952 about her engagement to John Husted. Auchincloss brought her the fascinating turn-of-the-century diary of Adele Sloane, his wife's grandmother, which Jackie edited and published as *Maverick in Mauve*. At the publication party, Jackie spoke of her fascination for Sloane.

What was so moving to me was the spirit of this woman, the dignity with which she lived her life, and her basic character. You think of the mauve decade and all their extravagances, their private trains, the jewels, the weddings, and then you realize that she would have to live through terrible troubles as well—that her life would seem to be ideal, and then tragedy would strike—losing her child, for example. Her life was not so perfect, after all. She had enormous difficulties, but somehow her spirit and her character would carry her through. You realize, especially when she writes so movingly about the death of her child, how difficult her life could be.

She could have been speaking of Jacqueline Kennedy Onassis.

She did this once again, when Carl Sferrazza Anthony was preparing his book *First Ladies,* and she responded to his statements and queries with handwritten emendations.

"If there was one sphere where Jacqueline had great influence [during the White House years], it was fashion," Anthony had written—to which Jackie added "much to her annoyance."

Anthony also quoted Jackie's statement, "if you bungle raising your children, I don't think that whatever else you do well matters much." She added a rhetorical comment: "And why shouldn't that be an example, too?"

James Fitzgerald recalled his last meeting with Jackie, on a Fifth Avenue corner. "We were waxing proud about our children, standing there like two grinning fools. There we were, opening our wallets, riffling through photos, which of course fell to the pavement and started to blow about. We raced and stooped to gather them, bumped our heads on the way up, laughed uproariously and, without stopping, went on with our glowing comments about our kids. I think that when she spoke of them, she shone with unusual warmth. That's the typical Jackie, the Jackie I'll always remember."

OF THE DUTIES of First Lady, Jackie had once said, "She will have an official role which she must play and accept with grace." And to this, Jackie appended a significant self-disclosure, phrased in the third person: "She had no doubts that she could. Jacqueline Bouvier had been reared in the Puritan ethic of doing one's duty to the fullest and had confidence in her social, administrative and intellectual abilities." That was more true in the last decade of her life than ever it had been, and she knew it. "Maybe now people will realize that there was something under that pillbox hat."

She also knew when her fame could serve the moment—not only regarding landmarks and causes, but also even bad weather. The Irish novelist Edna O'Brien, whose work Jackie admired and whom she invited to 1040 Fifth Avenue on several occasions, was to meet Jackie for a movie one rainy afternoon. But the show was sold out, and Jackie invited O'Brien home for tea. Since there was no cab in sight, Jackie approached a limousine awaiting a passenger's return from shopping. "Excuse me, sir," she said to the astonished driver, "but if you have a few moments to spare, would you mind taking two damp ladies home?" The man did not, of course, deny them or himself the favor.

AT WORK, SHE was not merely an acquisitions editor who turned over the task of line editing to assistants—a growing custom in publishing since the 1980s. "She did her own editing," Rubin added. "She was involved in all aspects of production, cover design, choice of typeface— and so, with her impeccable taste, her books always looked great—and she was available and accessible to us at all times. If we needed to reach her at home or on vacation, we knew how to do so." As publisher, Rubin of course wanted smart editors and cooperative colleagues: "She was certainly among the best. She was smart—and a lot of fun. I remember when she introduced her son to me: 'John, this is the man who gives me money to buy books.' She wanted him to see her as a working mother in a professional situation."

In addition, Jackie was, according to Rubin, "as wily and clever and manipulative as any superb editor can be when she wanted to sign up a book and get the money she wanted for an author. She never consciously set out to buy books that would be bestsellers—only to buy those books that interested her. But the reason she had so many best-sellers was due to the sheer breadth of her interests. She was very good about the business aspect of things, and although she hated publication parties, she was the first to arrive and the last to leave—that was another way of honoring the author and the book."

To be sure, not every project proceeded smoothly: perhaps the most exasperating experience of her formidable career was trying to extract a publishable manuscript from the pop singer Michael Jackson. She agreed to edit the book and made several trips to Jackson's home in California. As it happened, Jackson had no intention of revealing anything about himself other than a few vague remarks about his music and performances. Most of all, recalled J. C. Suarès, the book's art director, Jackie was fascinated by Jackson's obsessive secrecy—particularly about his sexual orientation—"and the star's ambiguity," he added, "only made her more curious."

When the first draft of the manuscript arrived on Jackie's desk in the spring of 1985, she saw at once that it was only a lengthy press release and hence unpublishable. Calmly but firmly, she told Jackson that he must, with the help of his writer Robert Hilburn, speak more openly about his childhood and career. But it was not to be. The book was changed and changed again, twice delayed and eventually published three years later. After some initial success among Jackson devotees, *Moonwalk* sank, unmoored by substance and unmourned by its editor.

"She never shied away from eccentrics," recalled her colleague Fitzgerald. He introduced her to the photographer William Eggleston, whose book *The Democratic Forest* Jackie enthusiastically agreed to edit when Fitzgerald left to work for another publisher. "I went to her office to see how she and Eggleston were getting along," Fitzgerald remembered, "and there he was, standing on top of Jackie's desk, showing her certain Prussian military steps! She wasn't fazed at all. She thought that after all everybody was a little eccentric."

Jackie was also keen on Jonathan Cott's *The Search for Omm Sety,* a book about the experiences of an English lady named Dorothy Eady, who claimed to be the twentieth-century reincarnation of an ancient priest of Isis. "She was mad for ancient history, of course," Fitzgerald added, "and this book was just right for her." And to Cott, Jackie counseled, "Let us understand [in the book] what it meant for Dorothy Eady to come to know the meaning and purpose of her life. Dottiness was her cover-up!"

She was, of course, especially pleased when she had the opportunity to present a book about her beloved France. She commissioned Deborah Turbeville to do *Unseen Versailles,* a book of photographs about the château, bringing in Louis Auchincloss to provide the text. And she was elated when she edited Auchincloss's *False Dawn,* a series of biographical essays about historic women.

Auchincloss, by this time one of the country's most respected writers, the author of dozens of works of fiction and literary criticism, was, of course, familiar with every aspect of the editing process. But even his considerable experience did not prepare him for a long editorial memo Jackie sent—notes on his work that, he later said, revealed why she was "a writer's dream as an editor" and that made him wonder, "Where would you find her today in a world of megapublishers?" A few extracts from her notes to Auchincloss:

"The most uncomfortable thing I have ever had to do is edit your immaculate writing. I hope and expect that you will object vociferously and that I will learn a lot from you in the process....

"[The book] is a little too concentrated in spots, more for an English audience than an American one. Could you get a little more air flowing through it in places where information is more tightly packed? Could we have some lovely stories, some waspish stories?

"Would it distort an occasional essay to give an anecdote here and there, to more fully describe a person, a place? I have always thought that Henriette d'Angleterre must have been one of the most enchanting women who ever walked on this planet. Could we have more about her? ... I would like to know what Anne of Austria looked like. Do you want to describe her horrible marriage to Louis XIII and the conception of Louis XIV? ... It is anecdotes that readers love and remember....

"I want every chapter to be a novel so that I can know more about these people and imagine them in their settings, and of course that is impossible in an essay. I do look forward to our lunch and am prepared to be told that I am an utter dolt."

PRIVATELY, HER LIFE by this time was serene in ways she had never before known. Maurice Tempelsman, now permanently but amicably separated from his wife, Lily, guarded Jackie's privacy and remained her most discreet companion. Unlike Kennedy and Onassis, who were invariably busy with other duties, not to mention people, Maurice made Jackie feel as if she mattered more than anyone in the world. She responded in kind, with complete devotion. In 1984, for example, when he suffered a mild heart attack, he was attended daily at the hospital by Jackie; after his release, she worked on manuscripts at home for two weeks in order to be with him around the clock.

But it was the undiluted fidelity and the daily demonstrations of commitment that proved the reality: neither one of them dominated the other. They supported each other's separate interests, even if they did not always attend the same activities together. Jackie rode with hunt clubs in New Jersey and Virginia and jogged in Central Park, neither of which held any appeal for Maurice. When his business concerns sometimes required him to travel to Belgium or South Africa, Jackie went to China with her friend I. M. Pei, who had designed the Kennedy Library. They visited his family home, where Jackie was fascinated by Chinese wall calligraphy, particularly two panels that counseled "See Fragrance" and "Read Paintings." Returning to New York, Jackie painted two pictures for Pei in Chinese style.

But Jackie and Maurice frequently traveled together—as when Gelsey Kirkland made a comeback in London at the time her book was published. The couple attended the performance with Marianne Velmans and her husband, the editor Paul Sidey. "Going to the ballet with Jackie Onassis," he recalled, "turned our little group into something of a sideshow while the lights were up, and Marianne and I were very conscious of being on a conspicuous outing. During the interval, we talked about ballet, babies and books. Jackie was vivacious, charming and witty, and Tempelsman discreet, courteous and self-effacing."

HOSTING SMALL DINNERS for friends and colleagues, strolling through Central Park, going out to dine, to the opera or ballet or a movie, they seemed like a staid married couple. When Federico Fellini came to New York to promote a new film, he and his wife Giulietta Masina dined at 1040 Fifth Avenue. Jackie, who much loved Fellini's masterworks, discussed them in detail. When he playfully asked if she would like to appear in one of his films, she had a quick reply: a better choice would once have been her eccentric aunt and cousin, the two Edie Beales—ideal characters for a Fellini film, she said.

Meanwhile, Maurice increased the value of Jackie's fortune, ensuring the financial future of her children and grandchildren and establishing them as wealthy in their own right—not simply as Kennedys. Caroline and John came to love and trust Maurice, for they saw how important he was in their mother's life. He was very much a part of the family, as friends realized; indeed, Jackie, Caroline and John spent more time with Maurice than they ever had with Jack or Ari. To make the matter completely agreeable, it happened that Maurice's three children, Leon, Rena and Marcy, were not at all resentful of Jackie; they all remained on good terms with Maurice.

JOHN F. KENNEDY JR. was never called "John-John" by anyone who knew him personally. The nickname derived from the misunderstanding of a Washington reporter, who one day heard the president call twice to his son ("John! John!"). To family and friends, the boy was always called John—and never Jack, which designated only his father. In time, he preferred, as do many juniors, to be known simply as John Kennedy, which in adulthood was the imprint on his business card.

By 1979, when he graduated from Phillips Academy in Andover, Massachusetts, he had reached his full height, an inch over six feet, and he had the sort of face and figure that led *People* magazine—on whose cover he appeared no less than seven times—to designate him the "Sexiest Man Alive." Handsome son of a slain president and an idealized mother, he was the heir apparent onto whom, up until the time of his death, a fantastic national fantasy was attached. Remarkably, in the modern age of celebrity worship and of the so-called Beautiful People, neither the constant glare of the cameras, the endless pursuit of the paparazzi, the requests for autographs nor the ceaseless adulation turned his head. Thanks to Jackie's wise nurturing, John by all accounts became an unaffected, enormously likable man who wore lightly the burden of his name and looks.

"I grew up living a fairly normal life," he said. "I thank my mother for doing that. I always took the bus to school and the subway all over town. Limo cars? Forget it!" As for his ancestry: "It's complicated, and it makes for a rich and complicated life. . . . But it's hard for me to talk about a legacy. It's my family. We look out for one another. The fact that there have been difficulties and hardships or obstacles makes us closer."

The characters and personalities of Caroline and John as they matured attested to Jackie's success as a single mother. "She was determined to maintain her children's privacy in order to make their lives as normal as possible," recalled Arthur Schlesinger Jr. "They were brought up unspoiled, modest, hard-working, well-mannered, friendly to their contemporaries, courteous to their elders." John himself was forthright: "My mother parented for two. She was deliberate in ensuring that my father's interests and concerns were part of our upbringing—and of some of her own, too, which were not his"—by which he meant a certain aesthetic sophistication. Praised for having turned out so well, he invariably deflected the praise: "My mother would be glad to hear you say that. She took a lot of pride in being a good mother. I'm glad people think it worked."

John and Caroline were inspired to appreciate the Kennedy legacy but not to allow it to limit or determine them. Jackie tempered the Kennedy toughness with a humanizing warmth that was evident in an anecdote she told Bobby Kennedy's friend, speechwriter and adviser Richard Goodwin. "When John was a little kid, he fell on a ski slope and he was crying. Bobby came over to him and said, 'Kennedys don't cry.' And John looked up and said, 'This Kennedy cries.'" Similarly, when asked how he had enjoyed a weekend family reunion in Hyannisport, John replied, "Oh, it was a lot of Kennedy stuff—a bit much for me." Interestingly, John Kennedy as an adult neither looked nor sounded like a Kennedy: his looks favored the Bouvier line, his character—one of good-humored, self-deprecating, unself-conscious and unpretentious dignity—he learned from his mother.

Jackie also saw to it that John and Caroline were Americans first, which is why she kept them in American schools, even after she married Onassis, instead of transferring them to some chic Swiss or French or English academy for the children of the jet set. Nor did she, after their time in the White House, turn them over to nannies or surrogate parents: "It isn't fair to children in the limelight," she insisted, "to leave them to the care of others and expect they will turn out all right." When the historian Doris Kearns Goodwin congratulated her on achieving the extraordinarily delicate balance that kept her children not only free of scandal but also a close team, Jackie smiled: "It's the best thing I've ever done."

Among her other achievements was to inculcate in Caroline and John a steely wariness of the public's adoration that never became a general suspicion about people. John's friend Dave Eikenberry spoke for many when he summed up this sort of graceful wisdom: "John assumed the best about people and never became cynical about their motives, and that's amazing, given the sycophants he had to deal with every day. It took enormous fortitude for him to stay well grounded in the face of his bizarre celebrity, but he did it." Jackie's counsel had been simple: "Don't let them steal your soul."

Among other bizarre bits of speculation, the rumor mill ground out the fiction that Jackie did more than guide her children—that she in fact directed them. But before and after her death, John took every opportunity to dispel this notion: "Contrary to any general opinion on the matter, my mother has never had an agenda for me or my sister."

The freedom extended to choice of career—as did the gossip, which insisted that Jackie would not allow John to become an actor but instead forced him to attend law school. "It was never anything but a hobby," he insisted, discussing his participation in school theatrical productions. "I never imagined it as a profession. It was a temporary diversion, and if you look at it psychologically, it was probably a way of temporarily getting away from being myself—it was never something I considered as a career."

Nor did his mother overprotect him. Returning home from school one day, John eluded the Secret Service and raced his bicycle into Central Park, only to encounter a mugger, who made off with the bike. Jackie was unfazed: it was all part of the New York experience, and John would learn something from it. "He must be allowed to experience life," she said, "and unless he is allowed freedom, he'll be a vegetable." Unwilling to extend the publicity attending this incident, she refused to press charges against the hapless, homeless perpetrator when he was arrested.

Jackie worked to ensure that John and Caroline were included in normal school events, that they were treated without fuss by their teachers, peers and other parents. She also saw to it that her apartment was open to her children's friends. In this regard, it became normal procedure for arriving young guests to be greeted by the most famous mother in the world, who smiled and welcomed them: "Hi! I'm John's mother."

In fact, the son could be sensitively protective of his mother. Jackie recalled a time when young John showed her a picture book called *A Child's Life of JFK*. Before handing it to her, he said, "Close your eyes, Mummy," and she heard him tear out a page. "I couldn't help but look at what he didn't want me to see," Jackie said years later. "It was a picture of the car. . . ."

His mother was, of course, enormously proud in 1983, when John was awarded a degree in history from Brown University—which he had chosen over Harvard, the traditional Kennedy alma mater—and then went on to New York University Law School. After taking his law degree, he made news by twice failing the bar exam (which is not, in fact, an unusual occurrence for candidates in the profession). "I'm very disappointed," he told the paparazzi at his heels. "But you know, God willing, I'll go back there in July and I'll pass it then. Or I'll pass it the next time after that, or when I'm ninety-five. I'm clearly not a major-league genius, but I hope the next time you guys are here it will be a happy day." On his third attempt, it was.

After passing the bar and serving four years as a prosecutor in the Manhattan district attorney's office, John abandoned the law and seemed, to some, to founder for a while. Then, two years later, in 1995, he turned to a career Jackie would have equally applauded: he and a business partner launched the political magazine *George*, to which John brought a high degree of realistic idealism. Over the next four years, he also brought an astonishing combination of wit and gravity to this publication. Involved in every aspect of presenting each issue, he understood clearly that politics has in our own time become an element of popular culture. In *George* he published extended and highly intelligent interviews he conducted with people as diverse as Fidel Castro, Gerry Adams, Louis Farrakhan, George Wallace, Gerald Ford and a dozen others.

In 1996, two years after Jackie's death, he arranged a secret ceremony on an island off Georgia, where, far from the press, John, almost thirty-six, married thirty-year-old Carolyn Bessette, a Calvin Klein publicist. Thus ended the tabloids' running tally of his romantic entanglements with a handful of girlfriends. But not, alas, the everlasting national coverage of John F. Kennedy Jr.

That obsession ended only after the tragic events of July 16, 1999. John, his wife, Carolyn, and her sister Lauren Bessette were reported missing. An inexperienced pilot, he had been at the controls of his own single-engine airplane, which encountered disorienting nighttime haze during a short trip from New Jersey to Martha's Vineyard. The three bodies were recovered five days later, in waters not far from the site of Jackie's former summer home. The only cold consolation for the many who loved and admired John F. Kennedy Jr. was that Jackie, five years gone by this time, had been spared this tragedy.

Only after John Kennedy's death did the press and public learn that he had been deeply and personally involved in a wide variety of important charitable works. He had set up foundations for the education of those who work with the mentally handicapped; he had developed programs for the poor and for disadvantaged children; and he had worked hard to include in his professional and personal life a habit of service. The range and reach of his concerns, it became clear, signified a man who was much more than the handsome, rich, socially well-connected scion of a famous family. Cynics to the contrary, Jackie had indeed succeeded. As John had said, "She parented for both . . . I'm glad people think it worked."

CAROLINE KENNEDY AND her boyfriends were also subjected to media scrutiny. For a brief time one summer in Manhattan, she was insistently pursued by a deranged admirer who camped outside her door, insisting he would become her husband; instead, he was remanded for psychiatric evaluation. After graduating from Radcliffe, Caroline worked as a coordinating producer in the film and television department of the Metropolitan Museum of Art, and then she began law studies at Columbia University. She, too, seemed to have not much taste for it, and never practiced for even one day.

At the age of twenty-eight, on July 19, 1986—the groom's forty-first birthday—Caroline married Edwin Schlossberg, a designer of museum interiors and exhibitions, a writer and a scholar with a Ph.D. from Columbia. Later, she collaborated with former classmate Ellen Alderman on *In Our Defense: The Bill of Rights in Action*, in 1991; four years later, their second volume appeared, *The Right to Privacy,* about which Caroline Kennedy certainly had something to say.

That done, Jackie's daughter settled into a quiet private life. She and her husband made Jackie a grandmother in 1988, 1990 and 1993, with the births of Rose, Tatiana and John. "Imagine that!" Jackie told her colleagues at Doubleday. "I'm a grandmother!" And no one doted more on the new generation than this grandmother.

ON JULY 24, 1989, Jackie's mother, Janet, died at the age of eighty-one from the effects of Alzheimer's disease. During her illness, as Jackie's stepsister Nina Auchincloss Straight recalled, "Jackie subsidized her home, organizing and arranging down to the last detail her personal effects, the staff, surroundings and daily routines—all of which enabled Aunt Janet to sail through those later years with a smile."

Four days later, Jackie turned sixty, on July 28. Unlike many in her family, she was a woman who had lost touch with nonessentials; she knew that a great deal of what passed for life in the modern world was, as she said, sheer periphery, just so much space debris. She had been called to a life she could never have anticipated when she was a debutante or an inquiring photographer, and she was aware that she was an important part of twentieth-century history. To deny this would have been an affront to Providence.

But Jackie never believed her fame meant that she herself was important or that it reflected her own earned glory: she simply accepted her part and tried to dispatch it the best she knew. "I'm sixty-two now," she said in 1991, "and I've been in the public eye for more than thirty years. I can't believe that anybody still cares about me or is still interested in what I do." As her close friend Nancy Tuckerman remarked, "She didn't really think of herself as being famous. She thought that people who accomplished things in their own right—they were the ones who should be famous, not her." That she, too, had "accomplished things" and continued to do so never occurred to her.

It fell to those who knew and loved her to appreciate that she was a woman with a great and capacious soul. She had experienced a full quota of the excitements of life and had at last put them aside in favor of pride in work and family, and in a life that was in many ways rich in contemplation. A universe of experience was alive within her—

the viewpoint and vision of an artist, writer, photographer, poet and woman of consummate taste and sensibility.

"She was interested in just about everything," said Bruce Tracy, an editor who had worked with Jackie at Doubleday. "One could never second-guess her opinions, which frequently surprised us. And she was deeply concerned about everyone who worked with her. Once, we were at a critical point in publishing a certain book. My first trip to Europe was coming up—a trip I had scheduled a long time before. I went to Jackie feeling a little awkward about this and thinking, Well, maybe I should cancel. But her response was swift and to the point: 'Of course you have to go, Bruce—life comes first!' "

Tracy added that Jackie "had a real gift for seeing what was important and what not, and when some of us got bogged down in details, she always gently brought us back to the larger issue. Why was she the ideal editor? Because of her immense curiosity, remarkable intelligence and passionate love of language and books."

What Tracy called her concern for colleagues was much in evidence. Scott Moyers, who went directly from graduate school to work at Doubleday as a temporary editorial assistant, was enormously valuable to Jackie in handling everyday details. But against his hopes, he was not hired as a full-time employee, therefore having none of the benefits applicable to such a position. When she learned that Moyers was offered a full-time job with another publisher, Jackie leaped from her desk and hurried to speak with Stephen Rubin. Immediately, Moyers was engaged as a full-time employee, and with a substantial raise.

"She took such joy in her work," Moyers recalled. "I have an image of Jackie, rubbing her hands together in delight about a book and saying, 'Hot spit!' Her pleasure in publishing was infectious, and in the summer, when she was away for several months [according to the terms of her deal with Doubleday], a great light seemed to go out at the office. You had to readjust yourself, but it was difficult—she made such a difference."

Not the least way she made a difference was her sense of humor. First Lady Barbara Bush, accompanied by the usual government protection, visited Doubleday one afternoon to discuss with her own editor her forthcoming book, written in the voice of her dog. Seeing the Secret Service agents, Jackie smiled and joked, "Can't I ever get rid of you guys?"

CHAPTER FOURTEEN

1993-1994

*I*n June 1993, Jackie and Maurice traveled to France, where they visited Arles, traveled by riverboat along the Rhône River, and explored the underground caves that had so fascinated Maurice in his childhood. Jackie hoped to spend some time at Pont-Saint-Esprit, the Bouviers' ancestral village not far from Avignon, but she came down with a summer cold and then felt unusually weary. They returned to Martha's Vineyard and the quiet seclusion of her house.

Among the visitors Jackie and Maurice entertained in August were President Clinton and his family, who joined Caroline and a small representation of the Kennedy clan for a cruise aboard Maurice's yacht. Her political instincts intact, Jackie stopped Maurice as he was on his way to greet the First Family. "Teddy," she said, summoning her brother-in-law, "*you* go down and greet the president—after all, Maurice isn't running for reelection!"

Another guest was Lady Bird Johnson, then eighty-one. She had been widowed for twenty years as Jackie had been for thirty. The two old friends, who had shared so much happiness and heartache over almost four decades, ate lunch under an arbor of vines. They spoke, said Mrs. Johnson later, about authors and books and their children, but not of the past. There was so much in the present to be grateful for, they both agreed. Mrs. Johnson felt that Jackie seemed to have reached a peaceful harbor in her life, safe at last with the work and the people she loved and trusted.

To her annual Labor Day beach picnic, Jackie as usual invited the Kennedys, to whom she showed off her infant grandson, Jack. Neighbor Carly Simon, for whom she edited a quartet of children's books, joined her in singing "Itsy-Bitsy Spider" to the baby. In no time at all, Jackie said, the child would be grown up, and she looked forward to watching him swim in the Sound and riding with her in her kayak, which she paddled energetically all summer long. A few friends regretted they had not gone out in the kayak with her: not to worry, she promised—they would do just that, first thing the following summer. Back in New York, she regularly took her grandchildren for walks in Central Park, for rides on the carousel, and for ice-cream cones. Strollers and joggers frequently spotted her ambling along with John or Jack, with Caroline or Tatiana—and, more often, walking with Maurice, her hand gently holding his arm.

AT DOUBLEDAY, JACKIE was warmly welcomed back after her summer holiday. She also supported an important event at the Brooklyn Academy in early October. Ballet dancer Jacques d'Amboise had coached a thousand children from every ethnic background in New York in performances set to music from each of the past five centuries. The sheer scope and the catholicity of it delighted her. Jackie also visited the tuition-free Children's Storefront School in Harlem, still thriving after thirty years. Its founding director, Ned O'Gorman, recalled that she met the students, joined the school's board and made several substantial contributions. It was a memorable day, although O'Gorman thought she looked frail, despite her animated spirit and warmth with the youngsters.

She could not seem to shake the summer flu she had caught in Europe, but that same day she raced home to prepare for the formal dinner celebrating the centenary of the Municipal Arts Society. A few days later she flew to Boston for the dedication of a new museum attached to the Kennedy Library. Throughout this time, there were almost daily meetings or telephone calls with her authors.

Although Maurice, Caroline and John urged her to slow down a bit, the better to regain her strength and throw off a lassitude that sometimes suddenly descended upon her, Jackie was off to New Jersey and Virginia for weekends in the hunt country. Charles Whitehouse, a riding companion, remembered a conversation they had about being fit, about feeling winded after a ride. She never had that problem, Jackie said, because she jogged regularly around the Central Park Reservoir.

But one Saturday afternoon in November, Jackie tumbled from her horse. Unconscious for a few moments, she was taken to a Virginia hospital, where a physician found a swollen lymph node in her groin. Assessing it as the sign of an infection, he treated her with antibiotics, and she seemed to respond, but not entirely. When Jackie returned to New York, she felt weaker than ever and was compelled to cancel a few editorial meetings.

But her spirits were undimmed as friends found her preparing eagerly for the holidays. To many people that holiday season, in fact, Jackie seemed somehow more beautiful than ever, almost transparent, especially since she dismissed any conversation about illness and, as always, turned her attention to others. Age, her invariable slimness and a little bit of cosmetic surgery had only accented the character in her fine, strong features. To her stepsister, Nina, she described her life in terms of a roller coaster. In a moment of philosophical reflection, she added that "in the end, all you really have are happy memories."

Jackie added to that store of memories, both for herself and her family, by planning a splendid Christmas for her family, complete with a lovely tree in her apartment and a first trip to the ballet for her granddaughter Rose. Jackie and Maurice then began a Caribbean cruise during Christmas week, but suddenly she became ill with severe pains in her back and abdomen. Now there was a second swollen lymph node in her neck. They returned at once to New York, where Jackie submitted to a variety of tests at New York Hospital–Cornell Medical Center.

THE WINTER OF 1993–94 was an unusually bitter one in the Northeast: the cold was unrelenting, and snow seemed to fall almost daily from early January to late March. In Central Park and in the suburbs there were drifts as high as ten feet. Jackie longed to take Rose, Tatiana and Jack into the park to build snowmen. Her grandchildren, she wrote in a note to Caroline, were a great blessing in Jackie's life: through their eyes and their wonder about the world, she herself was seeing it as if for the first time. She concluded by thanking her daughter and son-in-law for sharing their children with her.

But once her test results were reported, trips to the snowy park were out of the question. Calmly, Jackie received the results: a diagnosis of non-Hodgkin's lymphoma, a particularly virulent form of cancer that can rapidly spread throughout the body. The swollen nodes in her groin and neck were the classic first signs of this condition.

Chemotherapy and radiation were her only recourse, but this protocol demanded interruption of her work at Doubleday, which would mean that she would have to inform her colleagues of the situation. As she took people into her confidence, her manner was invariably calm and optimistic: this was a nuisance, an annoyance, but soon everything would be set right. Such was her spirit as she tried to put a good face on a terrifying and debilitating illness. Once again, the courage that had served her so well since girlhood supported her and others during a cold and frightening winter; the "guts and gumption" that had been enjoined on her at Miss Porter's characterized her disposition one more time.

"When she told me she was ill," recalled Stephen Rubin, "she did it in her typically Jackie fashion. She was so generous that she seemed more concerned about my reaction than about herself. I think she was very frustrated by her illness, and for a remarkably long time, even though she was growing more and more frail, she came in to the office and did her work."

Matter-of-factly and with no plea for sympathy, Jackie also told Bruce Tracy and Scott Moyers, for they would have to assume many of the editorial tasks scheduled for that season. For weeks, remembered Moyers, she came to the office right after her chemotherapy treatments, insisting that the medical procedures were not too bad—at least she could read while the drugs were being transfused into her system. She gamely wore bandages on her arms, where the needles had punctured her veins, and scarves and turbans and eventually a wig when her hair fell out.

In February, one blizzard followed another. Rumors about Jackie's declining health swirled around Manhattan and as far as the international press. So many calls came to her home and office that it was necessary to make a statement. Although there was no indication that the treatments were helping, Jackie asked Nancy Tuckerman—who, as so often over the years, spoke for her—to put a good face on things. "The doctors are very, very optimistic," Tuckerman said, when, in truth, no one was.

To everyone's amazement, Jackie soldiered on through February and March, although it was clear that she was becoming more gravely ill each day. She wrote notes to people who were sick or in trouble, and gave her name and support to fund-raisers for ballet companies. For close friends of long standing—Arthur Schlesinger and Eugene Kennedy among them—she managed a laugh: "I don't know why I did all those push-ups!" And with a quiet confidence she deflected anything like morbid concern for her illness: to many people, she said that they must not worry and then, quoting Julian of Norwich, whether they recognized the source or not, she added, "All will be well."

Except for a sinus infection years earlier and the aftermath of child-birth, Jackie had known no illness at all during her sixty-four years. Still, there was no expression of terror or outrage; now, as usual, it was she who comforted others, promising to return, as soon as she might be able, to her regular routine. There seemed to her so much left to do and so much more to become.

No one could ever remember Jackie complaining during her ordeal, even when her illness was at its most punishing. She wondered about it, she asked questions about it and, until any hope of cure was sheer folly, she fought calmly and courageously, enduring the ravages of chemotherapy with astonishing equanimity.

Nor did she, even for one day, forget her authors. "Stay calm!" she wrote in a note to Elizabeth Crook, whose new novel would soon be published. "You have a winner!"

Similarly, Pamela Fiori, editor in chief of *Town & Country,* had made an appointment months earlier to discuss excerpting in the magazine one of Jackie's books—a collection of photographs by the society and fashion photographer Toni Frissell, who, as it happened, had taken pictures of the Bouvier-Kennedy wedding in 1953. Fiori expected the meeting to be canceled because of Jackie's illness, but when she arrived at Doubleday, there was Jackie. With good cheer and enthusiasm, Jackie "plopped on the floor next to me" and opened a children's book and a folder full of photos. Mortally ill though she was, she was "downright bubbly." There is a legion of witnesses to this spirit in her final months.

But Jackie was neither unreasonably optimistic nor, as the popular argot runs, in denial. She had already transferred title of her New Jersey property to her children for the sum of one dollar. Then, on March 22, after several conferences with Maurice, her children and her attorneys, Jackie signed a lengthy and complex will. This thirty-eight-page document set up a trust for her children and grandchildren, in such terms that taxes would not annihilate her handsome estate.

There were also cash bequests outright: $250,000 apiece to Caroline, John and Nancy Tuckerman; $125,000 to her cook and housekeeper, Marta Squbin; $100,000 to her niece, Alexandra Rutherfurd, daughter of her late half sister, Janet; $50,000 to Providencia Paredes, who had been her devoted White House maid; and $25,000 each to Lee Nasso, her accountant; Marie Amaral, her maid at Fifth Avenue; and Efigenio Pinheiro, her butler. No provision was made for her sister Lee ("because I have already done so during my lifetime"), but for each of Lee's two children there was a trust fund of $500,000.

Perhaps most significant of all was another decision Jackie had made some time earlier. She wished to be buried beside John F. Kennedy and their two children, Arabella and Patrick, at Arlington National Cemetery.

ENDURING FOUR COURSES of chemotherapy took a toll as terrible as the disease itself: on April 14, Jackie collapsed at home and was rushed to the hospital for surgical repair of bleeding ulcers, caused by the adjuvant steroid injections. This dangerous condition was treated, but at the same time it was discovered that the cancer had spread deep into her lungs. Throughout the ordeal, Maurice was always constantly present at the hospital and at home, helping her to the doctors, taking her to the bathroom, holding her hand, caressing her cheek. Early in the year, he had set up a temporary office in her apartment so that he would never have to leave her side.

After learning about the rapid advance of her disease, Jackie sat wordlessly with Maurice for a few moments, and then suddenly asked him to call her office. She had scheduled an appointment with one of her authors for that day, and she did not want him to arrive and find her absent. "Oh, this condition is so annoying," she told a friend during an overseas phone call later that afternoon, as if she had nothing more serious than a lingering cold. "I'm losing my hair, but maybe I'll start a new fashion trend in turbans!" Indeed, she wore a colorful headscarf on Easter Sunday, when she went to the New Jersey house for the last time. Singing with her grandchildren in a weak voice but with unstinting gaiety, she sang words of the seasonal tune—"In your Easter bonnet, with all the frills upon it . . ." Caroline and John were with her, as they were daily that spring.

By the end of April, Jackie was alarmingly weakened. She had severe pains in her arms and legs, and there were periods of frightening confusion—all signs that the cancer had reached her spinal cord and brain. During yet another hospital sojourn, a tube was inserted directly into her skull to reduce pressure and to deliver appropriate drugs, but this was a desperate measure. Soon her speech and gait were affected—but not the smile with which she always greeted family and friends. In a brief reply to a note from Louis Auchincloss, she wrote simply, "All will be well. I promise."

When she was alert and had sufficient energy, Jackie begged Maurice to take her to Central Park, if only for a few minutes. "Oh," she whispered one afternoon in early May, her eyes shining, "isn't it something? One of the most glorious springs I can remember—and after such a terrible winter!"

On Sunday, May 15, Jackie, Maurice, Caroline and little Jack crossed Fifth Avenue to Central Park. Soon they were near the spot that brought back such vivid memories for Jackie, an event her parents had for decades after gleefully recited.

When she was just a child, she had wandered away from Nanny Bertha Newey, who had taken her and her infant sister for an outing. While Miss Newey became mildly hysterical, Jackie, alone but undaunted, calmly approached a policeman: "My nurse and sister seem to be lost!"

Now, as roller skaters whizzed by and other nannies pushed carriages with newborns, Jackie and her loved ones sat for a few moments in the warm spring sunshine.

That night, she was restless and in terrible pain. On Monday morning she developed shaking chills and a violent headache. She also became frightened and disoriented. Maurice and a nurse took her to New York Hospital, where she was given antibiotics for pneumonia. She seemed to rally, but by Tuesday night, she suddenly went into a quick decline. Another scan showed that the disease had now invaded her liver and that her kidneys were failing. Physicians had to admit at last that the situation was hopeless. Suddenly lucid, and without fear or hesitation, Jackie asked that all treatment be withdrawn and that she be taken home.

She arrived at her apartment on Wednesday afternoon. Relatives and close friends were summoned that evening and throughout the next day, while Jackie slipped in and out of consciousness, her breathing deep and erratic.

EVERYWHERE AROUND HER were the signs and symbols of her extraordinary life: art and manuscripts, photographs and books, correspondence, keepsakes and souvenirs, seashells and scrapbooks for remembrance—all the things that recalled and represented the contours of each decade.

The albums were a guide to a remarkable history. There were pictures of the society debutante, the shy eighteen-year-old with the broad smile and quick humor, eager to get on with her life. There was the earnest Sorbonne student and the fearless traveler, absorbing so much of the Old World and grafting it onto the New. Here, too, was the Inquiring Camera Girl, asking questions and popping flashbulbs. There were recollections of Senator Kennedy's exquisite bride, and of the radiant young First Lady who had charmed all the world. The mementos of the work she had accomplished behind the scenes for disarmament and civil rights were invisible, known only to a few. But it would be absurd to say that the world was not a better place for her influence.

In the books on her library shelves could be found descriptions of the grieving young widow on that bleak November weekend when her life was at its critical midpoint. There she stood, embracing her children, then, as always, thinking not first of herself but of them, of the nation, and of the world. She had spoken through her presence—had expressed in silence the deepest meaning of courage and loyalty, of commitment and loss. Never mind what the tattlers and meddlers had dredged up over the years: she knew the truth of her commitments and the hidden purpose her devotion had served, both for herself and those she loved. Even the tenebrous tangle of her marriage to Ari was not without meaning: the journey had been rich, the wandering, finally, rewarded by an arrival at a new place.

If Jackie had stood for one thing, in her life and in her distinguished career as an editor, it was that everyone was a part of history, that every life was important and had its secret richness. To her it was of no consequence that she enchanted millions. But it counted enormously, for Jackie, that she shared with as many people as possible all the things and ideas, the lives and gifts and mercies that had first enthralled and enriched her. If real eminence is characterized by this kind of spiritual generosity, then Jackie was one of the great women of the age, worthy to take her place with those in history who had first enchanted her.

She had been known as Miss Bouvier for twenty-four years, as Mrs. Kennedy for fifteen years, as Mrs. Onassis for twenty-five years. But throughout her lifetime, she was Jackie to just about everyone— relatives, friends and strangers alike. In a culture that feeds on personal revelations and pleas for sympathy, she offered very little of the former and demanded none of the latter. She impressed all who knew her with her profound empathy, but she found unacceptable the notion that she or anyone else was a victim of anything at all. On the contrary, for her we are all, in the most hidden and true sense, the recipients only of Life itself, mysterious but finally benevolent. With the bereavements she bore, Jackie believed that a terrible winter would somehow yield to a glorious springtime. That conviction did not desert her at the end. *All will be well . . .*

LATE IN THE afternoon of Thursday, May 19, the family asked a priest to read the ancient blessings of the Church, and to anoint Jackie for her last journey. By midevening, the noise of traffic down below on Fifth Avenue had diminished. In the apartment, there were only the whispers of those she loved who had come to say good-bye. Caroline and John, who had been raised in these rooms, sat silently, holding their mother's hands; Maurice left the room only rarely, to escort a visitor or to comfort someone who was overcome with emotion.

Just after ten o'clock that night, there was one long, deep sigh, and then Jackie was still.

By morning, the editors of the *New York Daily News* had chosen their banner for the day of the funeral: two plain words that perhaps summarized the feelings of countless people, near and far, those who knew her and those who did not. It seemed that everywhere, as the headline stated, people were brought together by a single quiet sentiment:

MISSING HER

Notes

For brevity, details of interviews conducted for this book are supplied only at the first citation; unless otherwise stated, subsequent quotations from the same source derive from the identical interview with that source.

Interviews from the John F. Kennedy Library Oral History Program are abbreviated *JFK:OHP*. Such citations include the source, the interviewer, the date, and the page number of the official transcript.

CHAPTER ONE: 1929

4   "excluded the vulgar parvenus": Cited in Steven Gaines, *Philistines at the Hedgerow*, p. 190.

4   "None seek it": "Maidstone, East Hampton," *Social Spectator* (which rather grandly identified itself as "The Resort Magazine of Society"), July 1958.

4   "almost completely unknown": Ibid. The lady cited was one Mrs. Harry L. Hamlin. On the development of the Hamptons after World War II, see, e.g., *Holiday*, June 1947.

5   On the business interests of James T. Lee, see Christopher Gray, "Quality Developer with a Legacy of Fine Buildings," *The New York Times*, Mar. 12, 1995.

5   For the history of the Lee and Bouvier families, see, e.g., four books by Jacqueline's cousin John H. Davis—*The Bouviers: Portrait of an American Family*, his 1993 revision, *The Bouviers: From Waterloo to the Kennedys and Beyond; Jacqueline Bouvier: An Intimate Memoir;* and *The Kennedys: Dynasty and Disaster, 1848–1983*.

5   "Better a bad decision today": See the obituary for James T. Lee in *The New York Times*, Jan. 4, 1968.

9   "I think . . . [that] it was simply inconceivable": Davis, *Jacqueline Bouvier*, p. 29.

10   "a most devastating figure": Carl Sferraza Anthony, *As We Remember Her*, p. 9.

12   "Long Island Society mostly bases its claims": Mrs. John King Van Rensselaer (in collaboration with Frederic van de Water), *The Social Ladder*, p. 282.

16   For the detailed description of Lasata, see Davis, *The Kennedys*, pp. 167–68.

17   "clings to the conservative fashions": Van Rensselaer, p. 282. See also James Tanner, "East Hampton: The Solid Gold Melting Pot," *Harper's Bazaar*, August 1958.

CHAPTER TWO: 1930–1936

21   "Darling little Jackie Bouvier": *East Hampton Star*, Aug. 3, 1931.

21   "Mother and daughter, riding their mounts": Davis, *Jacqueline Bouvier*, p. 22.

22   "Little two-year-old Jacqueline Bouvier": *East Hampton Star*, Aug. 14, 1931.

23   "Is this Rhinelander 4–6167?" The story has been widely reported—e.g., by Jackie's friend Mary Van Rensselaer Thayer, in "Jacqueline Kennedy," part I, *Ladies' Home Journal*, Feb. 1961.

23   "Hello, Ernest": Ibid.

24   "What's a midwife?": Quoted in Claire G. Osborne, ed., *Jackie—A Legend Defined*, p. 17.

26   "one of the pillars of women's education": An address given by Virginia C. Gilder-
      sleeve, dean of Barnard College, in October 1928, on the occasion of the dedication
      ceremonies of the new building for the Chapin School, at 100 East End Avenue.
      Privately published by the Chapin School and used with kind permission. On the
      school, see its alumnae publications and the annual *Bulletin of Information*.

26   "truest to the *Social Register*": Phyllis La Farge, "A Warm-hearted Guide to Certain
      Girls' Schools," *Harper's*, Apr. 1963. Despite the title, the article is scrupulous in its
      assessment of both social and academic realities.

27   "She could see a misspelled word": The alumnae bulletin of the Chapin School,
      marking the seventy-fifth anniversary in 1976.

29   "Jackie, you never have to worry": Davis, *The Kennedys*, p. 174.

31   "She succeeded admirably": Ibid., p. 180.

32   "I hear you are summoned": Thayer, loc. cit.

32   "the most inquiring mind": Gordon Langley Hall and Ann Pinchot, *Jacqueline Ken-
      nedy*, p. 68; also cited in Carl Sferrazza Anthony, *First Ladies: The Saga of the Pres-
      idents' Wives and Their Power*, vol. 1, p. 475.

32   "She was very funny": Nancy Tuckerman, in the catalog *The Estate of Jacqueline
      Kennedy Onassis*, p. 16.

CHAPTER THREE: 1937–1943

35   "I'll never forget the night": Anthony, *As We Knew Her*, p. 27.

35   "Relations between [the couple]": Berthe Kimmerle's statements were given in the
      divorce hearing on June 9, 1939; they are cited in, e.g., Davis, *Jacqueline Bouvier*,
      p. 47.

37   The events of Christmas 1937 have been frequently reprinted—e.g., in Thayer, loc.
      cit.; in Bill Adler, ed., *The Uncommon Wisdom of Jacqueline Kennedy Onassis*, p. 1;
      and in Osborne, pp. 18–19.

38   "She was, once upon a time": John H. Davis to DS, Jan. 21, 1999.

39   The newspaper account of Janet's lawsuit against her husband was published in,
      e.g., the New York *Daily Mirror* on Jan. 26, 1940.

41   "strangely let down": Quoted in Anthony, *First Ladies*, p. 486.

41   "My love of art was born there": Anthony, *As We Knew Her*, p. 23.

43   "enormous individuality": Janet Lee Auchincloss, in Laura Bergquist, "Jacqueline—
      What You Don't Know About Our First Lady," *Look*, July 14, 1961.

43   "Row after row": Anthony, *As We Knew Her*, p. 24.

45   "It was a peaceful, golden life": Gore Vidal, in Bergquist, loc. cit.

45   John Davis provided the detailed description of Hammersmith Farm.

47   "two happy and rewarding years": In a signed letter on White House stationery,
      dated October 27, 1963, to the Holton-Arms School, on the occasion of the com-
      pletion of its new quarters.

48   "expected and tolerated only solid effort": Nancy Noyes Lusher, in *Holton-Arms, 1901–1981,* privately published by the Holton-Arms School.

50   "the temperament and talent of a writer": Janet Lee Auchincloss, quoted in Anthony, *As We Knew Her,* p. 19.

CHAPTER FOUR: 1944–1949

51   "All my greatest interests": Anthony, *As We Knew Her,* p. 25.

51   "If you were a Farmington girl": Ibid., p. 32; see also *Grey Gardens,* a film by the Maysles brothers. Stephen Birmingham has given a superb reflection on Miss Porter's School in *Jacqueline Bouvier Kennedy Onassis,* pp. 42–47.

52   "No previous education": Birmingham, pp. 45–46.

52   The lines from Emerson are found in *May-Day and Other Pieces* (1867), "Voluntaries, III."

53   "I just know that no one will ever marry me": Widely quoted—e.g., in Ellen Ladowsky, *Jacqueline Kennedy Onassis,* p. 16.

53   "She observed the conventions": Arthur Schlesinger Jr., in the London *Times,* May 21, 1994.

53   "Jackie was an avid reader": Nancy Tuckerman, in the Sotheby's catalog, p. 18.

53   "All my Farmington friends": Adler, pp. 9ff.

54   "It happened gradually": Quoted in Anthony, *As We Knew Her,* pp. 35–36.

55   "I'm still so dazed": Ibid., p. 32.

56   "Who are you *today?*": Quoted in Cass Canfield, *Up and Down and Around: A Publisher Recollects the Time of His Life,* p. 237. By the time Canfield's book was published, it should be noted, his son Michael had married and divorced Lee Bouvier.

58   "America is a country of traditions": Cholly Knickerbocker's syndicated column in, e.g., the *New York Journal-American,* Sept. 2, 1947.

59   "Newport": Quoted in the cover story for *Time,* Jan. 20, 1961.

59   "Young men were constantly trying": Letitia Baldrige, *In the Kennedy Style,* pp. 12–13.

60   "Progress is my watchword": Lucy Greenbaum, "Vassar Picks a Woman and Breaks Tradition," *The New York Times Magazine,* Mar. 31, 1946.

61   "She was very secretive": Harriet de Rossière, cited in Davis, *Jacqueline Bouvier,* p. 117.

61   "roamed wonderfully through the fields": Joan Ellis Ferguson, in the *Vassar Alumnae Quarterly,* autumn 1994.

62   "a tall, thin young congressman": Cited in Anthony, *As We Knew Her,* p. 37.

64   "She was also much more private": Ibid., pp. 26–27.

65   "I suppose it won't be long": Mary Van Rensselaer Thayer, "Jacqueline Kennedy," Part II, *Ladies' Home Journal,* Mar. 1961.

CHAPTER FIVE: 1950-1952

70   "It's so much more fun": Thayer, loc. cit., Part II.

70   "I never worked harder": "The World of Jacqueline Kennedy," on the NBC television network, broadcast Nov. 30, 1962.

71   "I look at a male model": Cited in Osborne, pp. 34–35.

73   "I didn't want her to go": Flora Rheta Schreiber, "What Jackie Kennedy Has Learned from Her Mother," *Good Housekeeping,* Sept. 1962.

75   "She was no longer the little girl": *Time,* Jan. 20, 1961.

75   The meeting between JFK and Jackie Bouvier has been widely documented—e.g., in Joan Meyers, ed., *John Fitzgerald Kennedy . . . As We Remember Him*, p. 51; Thayer, loc. cit., Part II; and the Associated Press, *Triumph and Tragedy: The Story of the Kennedys.*

75   "would have a profound, perhaps disturbing influence": Jackie described herself in these words to Mary Van Rensselaer Thayer, who documented them in the third person: "Jacqueline Kennedy," *Ladies' Home Journal*, Apr. 1961.

76   The quotations from the summer journal are drawn from Jacqueline and Lee Bouvier, *One Special Summer.*

80   "Do you want a serious career": The exchange between Waldrop and Jackie has been variously documented—e.g., in Thayer, "Jacqueline Kennedy" (Part II), *Ladies' Home Journal*, Mar. 1961. See also Anthony, *As We Knew Her,* p. 60.

80   "She was soft-spoken": Chuck Conconi, "Girl Reporter," *The Washingtonian,* July 1994.

82   "rather naïve": Ibid.

82   "That's it!": Louis Auchincloss, in *Quest: New York from the Inside,* May 1997.

82   "Jackie seemed more relieved": Mini Rhea, "The Young Jacqueline Kennedy As I Knew Her," *Ladies' Home Journal,* Jan. 1962.

83   "shameless in their match-making": "The World of Jacqueline Kennedy," NBC-TV, Nov. 30, 1962.

85   "I fixed it": Harold H. Martin, "The Amazing Kennedys," *Saturday Evening Post,* Sept. 7, 1957.

85   "He was always able": Theodore C. Sorensen, *Kennedy,* p. 28.

85   "He spent half of each week": Meyers, p. 64.

85   "I think my destiny is": Often confided by JFK—e.g., to Gunilla von Post, with Carl Johnes, *Love, Jack,* p. 29.

86   "but just as swiftly": Thayer, "Jacqueline Kennedy," *Ladies' Home Journal,* art. cit.

87   "She didn't know whether anybody": Quoted in Anthony, *As We Remember Her,* p. 71.

87   "a man so vain": Evan Thomas, "Grace and Iron," *Newsweek,* May 30, 1994.

88   "I always go to Hyannisport": JFK, quoted beneath photos in the JFK Museum in Hyannisport, Massachusetts.

88 "We don't want any losers": Quoted in Lord Longford, *Kennedy,* pp. 6–7.

89 "Just watching them wore me out": Adler, p. 17.

89 "She was terribly sweet to me": Kennedy, *Times to Remember,* p. 298.

89 "Never once did this suitor": Anthony, *As We Remember Her,* p. 73.

89 "His chariness of marriage": Betty Spalding, quoted in Doris Kearns Goodwin, *The Fitzgeralds and the Kennedys,* p. 771.

91 "Jackie was different": Lemoyne K. Billings, quoted in Goodwin, p. 770.

CHAPTER SIX: 1953–1955

95 "he couldn't be less interested in me": Anthony, *As We Remember Her,* p. 74.

98 "that he'd be drawn away": Goodwin, p. 771.

99 "We hardly ever talk politics": "Life Goes Courting with a U.S. Senator," *Life,* July 20, 1953.

99 "a young woman of almost extravagant beauty": *Vogue,* Sept. 15, 1953.

100 "the two mothers sitting there": Kennedy, pp. 300–01.

100 "I gave everything a good deal of thought": Paul B. Fay Jr., *The Pleasure of His Company,* p. 160.

101 "He was such a wonderful, exciting person": Gunilla von Post to DS, Jan. 25, 1999.

101 "If I had met you one week before": Gunilla von Post, *Love, Jack,* p. 32.

104 "It was just like the coronation": "The Senator Weds," *Life,* Sept. 28, 1953.

104 "a rare and noble spirit": Davis, *The Kennedys,* p. 222.

104 "intruded on the kind of honeymoon": Fay, p. 163.

105 "You ought to write a series of grandfather stories": Richard J. Whalen, *The Founding Father: The Story of Joseph P. Kennedy,* p. 441.

106 "I found it rather hard to adjust": "The World of Jacqueline Kennedy," NBC-TV, Nov. 30, 1962.

106 "I married a whirlwind!": Many times—e.g., for the cameras in 1962, included in the television documentary "Jackie Onassis—An Intimate Portrait," Ellen M. Krass Productions (1993).

106 "It was difficult": JFK to Hugh Sidey, quoted in *Remembering Jackie—A Life in Pictures,* by the editors of *Life,* n.p.

106 "They talked about their children": Ibid.

106 "hated the artificiality": Betty Beale Graeber to DS, Jan. 4, 1999.

106 "Jack kept assuring us": Goodwin, p. 773.

108 "I was alone almost every weekend": Ibid., p. 772.

108 "for two weeks—with you as crew": von Post, p. 41.

108 "I don't know if you are still dangerous": Ibid., p. 48.

111 "She asked me if I could suggest": Jules Davids, letter to Rev. Brian McGrath, Aug. 5. 1957, quoted in *The New York Times,* Oct. 18, 1997.

111   "for your assistance": Ibid.: JFK to Jules Davids, Feb. 27, 1956.

112   On Jackie's influence on the so-called Kennedy Doctrine, see DeVallon Bolles, "About Jacqueline Onassis: Her Secret Role in Foreign Policy," *New York Newsday,* May 25, 1994.

113   "Jackie played a very interesting role": Arthur M. Schlesinger Jr., to DS, Mar. 19, 1999.

113   "He was thin": JFK:OHP: Dr. Janet G. Travell, interviewed by Theodore C. Sorensen, Dec. 26, 1974, p. 4. All subsequent quotations from Dr. Travell are drawn from this interview and are abbreviated JFK:OHP/Travell.

113   "There were two steps": JFK:OHP/Travell, p. 1.

114   "that he was born with": Ibid., p. 3.

116   "Jack's unhappy marriage": von Post, p. 71.

117   "I talked to my father": Ibid., pp. 102–03.

117   Gunilla von Post met John F. Kennedy once more, while they were both visiting New York, in April 1958. They greeted each other in public, and that was the extent of the encounter.

CHAPTER SEVEN: 1956–1960

121   "someone who understands what courage is": Allida M. Black, *Casting Her Own Shadow,* p. 178.

121   "His clothes and hairdo": Herbert S. Parmet, *Jack: The Struggles of John F. Kennedy,* p. 442.

121   The speech in support of Stevenson, read by JFK and drafted by Jackie, is preserved in the John F. Kennedy Library, Boston.

122   "never had a chance to talk with Jack": Kenneth P. O'Donnell and David F. Powers

123   *"Johnny, We Hardly Knew Ye": Memories of John F. Kennedy,* p. 119.

125   "for a long time, she wouldn't listen": Michael R. Beschloss, *The Crisis Years: Kennedy and Khrushchev, 1960–1963,* p. 98n.

125   "Look, it's a trade-off": Anthony, *As We Remember Her,* p. 103.

125   "My mother thinks that the trouble with me": Quoted in Adler, p. 9.

125   "My sweet little house": Hall and Pinchot, p. 141.

126   "There have to be big, comfortable chairs": Meyers, p. 73. JBK said substantially the same words on NBC-TV ("The World of Jacqueline Kennedy"), Nov. 30, 1962.

126   "He never created another life": Charlotte Curtis, "Lee Radziwill in Search of Herself," *McCall's,* Jan. 1975.

127   "The appearance": The description is from Janet Travell, *Office Hours: Day and Night: The Autobiography of Janet Travell, M.D.,* p. 320. Further medical details are in JFK: OHP/Janet Travell.

128   "We were just going, frankly, for a vacation": Beschloss, p. 99.

128   "If I decide to run": *Newsweek,* June 23, 1958.

129 "The Senator was not often to be seen": Maud Shaw, *White House Nanny: My Years with Caroline and John Kennedy, Jr.,* p. 58.

129 "She was as nervous as a kitten": Ibid., p. 60.

129 "Nothing disturbs me as much": Quoted in Adler, p. 74.

131 "always cheerful and obliging": O'Donnell and Powers, p. 142.

131 "staring resolutely straight ahead": Ben Bradlee, *A Good Life: Newspapering and Other Adventures,* p. 206.

131 "underneath a veil of lovely inconsequence": Arthur M. Schlesinger Jr., *A Thousand Days: John F. Kennedy in the White House,* p. 17.

132 "It was assumed that she was not politically involved": John Kenneth Galbraith, *Name-Dropping: From F.D.R. On,* pp. 126ff.

132 "She breathes all the political gasses": Donald Wilson, "Jackie Kennedy," *Life,* Aug. 24, 1959.

132 "You couldn't tell": Osborne, p. 57.

133 "She was not a natural-born campaigner": Kennedy, p. 313.

133 "He was fighting": Nancy Gager Clinch, *The Kennedy Neurosis,* p. 148.

134 "This is the closest I've come": Laura Bergquist, loc. cit.

134 "Jackie is superb in her personal life": Anthony, *First Ladies,* p. 576.

134 "She loosens Jack up": Bergquist, loc. cit.

134 "Acapulco": Wilson, loc. cit.

134 "It's not the right time": Bergquist, loc. cit.

135 "If Jack didn't run": Adler, p. 26.

136 "subliminally": *U.S. News & World Report,* May 30, 1994.

137 "I never know what she's going to do": Nancy Dickerson, *Among Those Present: A Reporter's View of Twenty-five Years in Washington,* p. 64.

138 "Jackie's drawing more people": O'Donnell and Powers, p. 156.

138 On Jackie's visits to small towns in Wisconsin, see "Kennedy's Wife Charms Voters," *The New York Times,* Mar. 11, 1960.

138 "You shake hundreds of hands": Anthony, *First Ladies,* p. 589.

139 "while she was talking": O'Donnell and Powers, p. 157.

139 "She didn't want any part of it": JFK/OHP: Elizabeth Gatov, interviewed by Dennis J. O'Brien, June 25, 1969, pp. 20–21.

139 "Well, write what you want": Burton Hersh, *The Shadow President: Ted Kennedy in Opposition,* p. 9.

139 "I think it's so unfair": *The New York Times Magazine,* May 31, 1970.

140 "It's the only way I can see him": *The New York Times,* Apr. 20, 1960.

140 "I just can't believe it": Anthony, *First Ladies,* pp. 589, 592.

140   "I couldn't spend that much": Nan Robertson, "Mrs. Kennedy Defends Clothes; Is 'Sure' Mrs. Nixon Pays More," *The New York Times,* Sept. 15, 1960.

140   "That's the last thing": Margaret Truman, *First Ladies,* p. 31.

140   "When you are First Lady": Adler, p. 50.

141   "What? Nothing about the press?": *U.S. News & World Report,* May 30, 1994.

142   "it felt like the sides of the car": *The New York Times,* Oct. 20, 1960.

144   "the complexity of man's social involvement": Martin Luther King Jr., *Stride Toward Freedom,* p. 81.

144   "I was and am": Harris Wofford to DS, March 26, 1999.

145   "It is a rare thing": To Arthur Schlesinger Jr., cited in Adler, p. 43.

145   "She seemed dazed": Meyers, p. 101.

146   "I have thought about that": Nan Robertson, "Election 'Unreal' to Mrs. Kennedy," *The New York Times,* Nov. 11, 1960.

146   "I feel as though I have just turned into": *Time* (cover story), Jan. 20, 1961.

147   "Mrs. Kennedy will have so much news": Bess Furman, "Active Role Set by Mrs. Kennedy," *The New York Times,* Nov. 23, 1960.

147   "after eight years of Eisenhower": Helen Thomas, *Dateline: White House,* p. 3.

149   The account of JBK's labor is based on Shaw, pp. 77ff.; Helen Thomas, pp. 3–4; *U.S. News & World Report,* Dec. 5, 1960; and a detailed report in *Time,* Dec. 5, 1960.

149   "I'm never there": O'Donnell and Powers, p. 233.

150   The names given to other newborns were reported in *Life,* Dec. 5, 1960.

150   "You're Mrs. Kennedy": Marianne Means, *The Woman in the White House: The Lives, Times and Influence of Twelve Notable First Ladies,* p. 267.

150   "I didn't know if there was one": Mary Van Rensselaer Thayer, *Jacqueline Kennedy: The White House Years,* p. 8.

150   "Oh, God": Cited in Adler, p. 46.

150   "Well, she's awfully young!": Mamie Eisenhower to J. B. West, *Upstairs at the White House: My Life With the First Ladies,* p. 194.

151   "She brought a daughter to the White House": Means, p. 269.

151   "It was so crowded": Thayer, p. 11.

CHAPTER EIGHT: 1961

153   "She guarded her privacy": Alvin Spivak to DS, March 16, 1999.

153   "Jackie referred to the women": Helen Thomas to DS, March 16, 1999.

154   "chic and sharp": Gwen Gibson to DS, March 16, 1999.

154   "just one of the fox hunters": Dolores Philips and Lewis Lapham, "She's Just One of the Fox Hunters," *Saturday Evening Post,* Feb. 23, 1963.

155   "PROTECT ME": Adler, p. 70.

155   "John was born prematurely": Anthony, *As We Remember Her,* p. 129.

156   "the woman my husband is supposedly sleeping with": Quoted in Truman, p. 41.

156   On the presidential mistresses, see, among others, Parmet (who, unlike many other chroniclers of the president's sex life, is not at all hysterical about it), p. 111.

156   JFK and Marilyn Monroe could never be called lovers unless a single sexual experience qualifies. On the colossal exaggeration of the Kennedy-Monroe relationship, see Donald Spoto, *Marilyn Monroe: The Biography.*

156   "She must have made reference": Diana Trilling, "A Visit to Camelot," *The New Yorker,* June 2, 1997.

158   "Mrs. Kennedy was trying to grope": West, p. 239.

159   "a President's wife could no more afford": Garry Wills, *Reagan's America: Innocents at Home,* p. 186.

160   "I was warned": Anthony, *First Ladies,* vol. 2, p. 28.

160   "only the best": *The New York Times,* Feb. 15, 1962.

161   "no previous perfect White House": Truman, p. 35.

163   "Is there such a thing as Shoppers Anonymous?": Nicholas Fraser, Philip Jacobson, Mark Ottaway, and Lewis Chester, *Aristotle Onassis,* p. 244.

164   "to distinguish between material things": Bernard Taper, *Balanchine: A Biography,* p. 263.

166   "Relaxed and uninhibited": West, p. 195.

166   "Reporters": Means, p. 289.

167   "life is not so short": Emerson, *Letters and Social Aims* (1876).

167   "the Grace of God is in courtesy": Hilaire Belloc, "Courtesy" (1898).

167   "Will you tell whoever it is": West, p. 255.

167   "Really, she had the enthusiasm": Betty Beale Graeber to DS, Jan. 4, 1999.

167   "the intimacy and conviviality": Baldrige, p. 31.

168   "We used to have to come": Trilling, loc. cit.

168   "authentic furniture": "A Tour of the White House with Mrs. John F. Kennedy," CBS-TV, Feb. 14, 1962, with Charles Collingwood.

169   "must have a reason for being there": JBK to Hugh Sidey, cited in *Life,* Sept. 1, 1961.

169   "he tells me, 'That's your province' ": Means, p. 290.

170   "I feel strongly": *Time,* May 30, 1994.

171   "Jackie was great fun": JFK/OHP: Charles Bartlett, interviewed by Fred Holborn, Jan. 6, 1965.

171   "She's poetic": Bergquist, loc. cit.

171   "In their eyes, she was ... strictly": Truman, p. 32.

171   "My wife is a very strong woman": Anthony, *First Ladies,* vol. 2, p. 52.

172   "I'm sure she discussed things": Ibid., p. 56.

173   "I talked to her like a movie star": Oleg Cassini, *In My Own Fashion: An Autobiography,* p. 54.

174   "I know that I am": JBK to Oleg Cassini, Dec. 13, 1960; reproduced in Oleg Cassini, *A Thousand Days of Magic: Dressing Jacqueline Kennedy for the White House,* p. 220.

174   "a great sense of history": Ibid., p. 20.

174   "the French courts of Napoleon": Ibid.

174   "the best-dressed woman in the world": Ibid., p. 192.

174   "Just send me an accounting": Cassini, *In My Own Fashion,* p. 308.

175   "Jackie was new in capital letters": Truman, p. 37.

175   "such marvelous taste": Betty Ford, with Chris Chase, *The Times of My Life,* p. 101.

176   "As it must to all women": *The New York Times,* Dec. 17, 1961.

176   "After dining out": *The New York Times,* Aug. 26, 1962.

177   "Mrs. John F. Kennedy slept late today": Ibid., Aug. 17, 1962.

177   "She helped him . . . to understand France": JFK/OHP: Hervé Alphand, interviewed by Adalbert de Segonzac, Oct. 14, 1964, p. 5.

177   "her charm, beauty": "Kennedys Hit the Road: A Visit with Neighbors," *Life,* May 26, 1961.

178   On the entire Max Jacobson matter, see Boyce Rensenberger, "Amphetamines Used by a Physician to Lift Moods of Famous Patients," *The New York Times,* Dec. 4, 1972.

179   "a problem with the neck": JFK:OHP/Travell, p. 18.

180   "vanished within minutes": *The New York Times,* Dec. 4, 1972.

180   "Jackie was an inveterate reader": Mary Barelli Gallagher (with Frances Spatz Leighton), *My Life With Jacqueline Kennedy,* p. 164.

180   "The radiant young First Lady": *Time,* June 9, 1961.

181   "as if Jack were President of FRANCE": Cassini, *A Thousand Days of Magic,* p. 29.

181   "Well, I'm dazzled": *Time,* June 9, 1961.

181   "I do not think it altogether inappropriate": Ibid.

181   "Your wife knows more French history": O'Donnell and Powers, p. 289.

181   "dazzling and cultivated": Charles de Gaulle (trans. Terence Kilmartin), *Memoirs of Hope: Renewal and Endeavor,* p. 255.

182   "pure and regal": Cassini, *In My Own Fashion,* p. 309.

182   "Jackie wanted the public monuments illuminated": JFK/OHP: John A. Carver Jr., interviewed by William W. Moss, Dec. 9, 1969.

183   "I'd like to shake *her* hand first": Beschloss, p. 207.

183   "Why don't you send me one?": Widely documented—e.g., in O'Donnell and Powers, p. 301.

183   "Oh, Mr. Chairman": Beschloss, p. 207.

183   "I have never been happier": *The New York Times,* June 11, 1961.

184   "I don't know if he is or not": Beschloss, p. 235.

184   "most indiscreet": Ibid., p. 466.

184   "Kennedy—No! . . . Jackie—Sì!": *The New York Times,* Dec. 17, 1961.

184   "She has a great flair for publicity": Kenneth Sydney Davis, *The Politics of Honor: A Biography of Adlai E. Stevenson,* p. 469.

184   "That's Me, Jackie," words and music © 1961 by Gwen Gibson and Sidney Schwartz. Used with the kind permission of Gwen Gibson.

186   "dressed, coifed and made up": *Time,* June 9, 1961.

186   *"C'est la politesse des rois"*: E.g., to Cassini, *A Thousand Days of Magic,* p. 49.

186   "My goal was to dress her like a queen": Ibid., p. 62.

186   "the new U.S. Royal Family": Bergquist, loc. cit.

CHAPTER NINE: 1962–1963

187   "a star": *Newsweek,* Feb. 26, 1962.

187   "as soon as she saw": Ibid.

188   Nina Burleigh, in *A Very Private Woman: The Life and Unsolved Murder of Presidential Mistress Mary Meyer,* pp. 328–30, has documented each date of Meyer's presidential assignations.

188   "What are you going to do, Jack?": JFK/OHP: Charles Bartlett, interviewed by Fred Holborn, Jan. 6, 1965.

189   Arnaldo Cortesi's account of JBK's meeting with Pope John appeared in *The New York Times,* Mar. 12, 1962.

190   "He's such a good man": Adler, p. 96; see also Cassini, *A Thousand Days of Magic,* p. 112.

190   "full of life": John Kenneth Galbraith, *Ambassador's Journal: A Personal Account of the Kennedy Years,* p. 317.

190   "didn't seem to mind": Ibid., p. 322.

190   "her excellent sense of theater": Ibid., p. 323.

191   "the most extraordinary": Marjorie Hunter, "49 Nobel Prize Winners Honored at White House," *The New York Times,* Apr. 30, 1962.

191   "realized that the whole occasion": Trilling, loc. cit.

191   "ever present when it comes to writing art": André Malraux's speech of January 1963 is cited in Pierre Galante, *Malraux,* p. 223.

191   "Thank you for all that you did": John Bartlow Martin, *Adlai Stevenson and the World: The Life of Adlai Stevenson,* p. 757.

192   "If we were only thinking of ourselves": O'Donnell, p. 325; see also Beschloss, p. 469, and Sorensen, p. 693.

193   "I watched him sitting there": O'Donnell, p. 325.

193   "physically exhausted": Baldrige, p. 136.

193   "I'm taking the veil": Adler, p. 58.

194   "He never wanted": Beschloss, p. 631.

194   The gift brought from Rome by JFK to JBK is described in Schlesinger, p. 730.

194   "He was such a beautiful baby": O'Donnell and Powers, p. 377.

194   "He wouldn't take his hands off": Sorensen, p. 367; see also Associated Press, *Triumph and Tragedy,* p. 185.

194   "The loss of Patrick": O'Donnell and Powers, p. 378.

197   "My favorite country": *U.S. News & World Report,* Sept. 7, 1956.

198   "All that really counts": *Time,* Mar. 24, 1975.

198   "an alive and vital person": Bradlee, p. 219.

199   "She didn't enjoy political trips": "Remembering Jackie," *The New Yorker,* May 30, 1994.

200   "It is the charm of her shyness": Joseph A. Loftus, "President's Wife to Campaign in '64," *The New York Times,* Nov. 15, 1963.

200   "I am a very shy person": Maryam Kharazmi, "Jackie is the same as Mrs. Onassis," *Kayhan International* (the English-language newspaper of Teheran, Iran), May 24, 1972. Also cited in *The New York Times,* May 25, 1972.

200   JBK's comments to the President's Commission on the Assassination of John F. Kennedy, headed by Chief Justice Earl Warren, were taken on June 5, 1964. They were reprinted in full in *The New York Times,* Nov. 23, 1964. Mrs. John Connally's diary was printed, along with an interview, in Michael Beschloss, "An Assassination Diary," *Newsweek,* Nov. 23, 1998.

201   Regarding the pathology and autopsy reports on the death of John F. Kennedy, see, e.g., Lawrence K. Altman, "Doctors Affirm Kennedy Autopsy Report," *The New York Times,* May 20, 1992.

201   "We saw pieces of bone": O'Donnell and Powers, pp. 27–28.

203   "She was absolutely stoic": Muriel Dobbin to DS, Dec. 22, 1998.

204   For some of these reflections, I must acknowledge the perceptive and finely expressed thoughts of Margaret Truman, pp. 44–45.

205   "very humble, the same as Lincoln's funeral": JFK/OHP: Larry Arata, interviewed by Pam Turnure (no date), p. 6.

206   "She looked like a ghostly apparition": Pierre Salinger to DS, March 16, 1999.

206   "My children": West, p. 279.

206   "It's just like Versailles": Charles Lawliss, *Jacqueline Onassis, 1929–1994.*

206   "I had never understood the function": Quoted in Nigel Hamilton, *JFK: Reckless Youth,* p. xxiii.

207   "I have peace in my heart": Travell, *Office Hours,* p. 366.

207   "I would to God": Lady Bird Johnson, *Lady Bird Johnson: A White House Diary,* p. 14.

208   "I didn't have anyplace to go": JBKO to Joseph Frantz, in an interview for the Lyndon B. Johnson Library: Jan. 11, 1974, New York. Transcripts of the interview are on file at the LBJ and JFK libraries.

209   "She was orderly": Lady Bird Johnson, p. 11.

209   JBK's letter to President Johnson, preserved in the Lyndon B. Johnson Library in Austin, Texas, was published in Merle Miller, *Lyndon: An Oral Biography,* pp. 335–36.

210   "I wish you a happy arrival": Quoted in *American Heritage,* Sept. 1994.

211   Theodore White's account of his meeting with JBK was first published in *Time,* July 3, 1978, and then in his book *In Search of History: A Personal Adventure.* The original presentation of the Kennedy years as Camelot appeared under his byline as "For Kennedy—an Epilogue," *Life,* Dec. 6, 1963.

213   "There was no Camelot": Dean Rusk (as told to Richard Rusk), *As I Saw It,* p. 323.

CHAPTER TEN: 1964–1968

216   "I know my husband was devoted to me": Billy Baldwin, "Jacqueline Kennedy Onassis: A Memoir," *McCall's,* Dec. 1974.

216   "I never had or wanted a life": Pearl Buck, *The Kennedy Women,* p. 89.

217   "I should have known that it was asking too much": *Look,* Nov. 17, 1964.

217   "I explained that it was really difficult": JBKO to Frantz/LBJ Library interview, as above.

217   "was as grateful to Jackie Kennedy": Salinger, *P.S.,* p. 164.

219   "Why are you all running away?": Nan Robertson, "Mrs. Kennedy Thanks 800,000 Who Expressed Their Sympathies," *The New York Times,* Jan. 15, 1964.

221   My observations on JBK as a kind of royal American movie star are not dissimilar from some earlier reflections on the queen of England; see Donald Spoto, *The Decline and Fall of the House of Windsor.*

222   "People tell me that time will heal": Adler, p. 125.

223   "Jackie wanted an authoritative history": Edwin Guthman to DS, April 16, 1999.

224   "You will be under great pressure": Schlesinger, *Robert Kennedy and His Times,* p. 761n.

225   "It's very upsetting": Baldwin, loc. cit.

226   "Going back to our childhood days": Robert D. McFadden, "Jackie, New Yorker," *The New York Times,* May 22, 1994.

227   "The curtain style stayed the same": Martin Filler, "Jackie, Queen of Arts," *House Beautiful,* Sept. 1994.

227   "Unless you had some knowledge": Amy Fine Collins, "Jacqueline Kennedy Onassis," *Harper's Bazaar,* Aug. 1994.

228 "the fastest music you've got": *Time,* Oct. 1, 1965.

230 "We want to have": Arthur Wilde to DS, Jan. 30, 1999.

231 "It's been quite a lonely life": Buck, p. 93.

233 The Harlech relationship was noted in, e.g., *The New York Times,* June 1, 1967.

233 The Roswell Gilpatric affair was widely known and documented in, e.g., *The New Yorker,* May 30, 1994. Selections from JBK's letters to him were also widely published; see "Social Notes: From Jackie with Love," *Newsweek,* Feb. 23, 1970.

234 "she wasn't content just to see": Susan Sheehan, "The Happy Jackie, the Sad Jackie, the Bad Jackie, the Good Jackie," *The New York Times Magazine,* May 31, 1970.

234 "very, very close": *Newsweek,* Feb. 23, 1970.

234 "the invisible man": Frank Brady, "Jackie and Ari," *The Saturday Evening Post,* Dec. 1977.

235 "He was lyrical": Willi Frischauer, "Jackie & Onassis—What Really Happened," *Good Housekeeping,* Aug. 1975. Frischauer's biography *Onassis* was published before the wedding.

236 "The Church is at its best": Cited in Schlesinger, *Robert Kennedy and His Times,* p. 915.

236 "I wanted to go away": Pete Hamill, "A Private Life Defined by Wit, Compassion," *New York Newsday,* May 22, 1994.

236 "the melancholy widow I had been painting": Byron Dobell, "The Forgotten Portrait," *Town and Country,* July 1995.

237 "As I did not expect a dowry": Fraser, p. 250.

238 "uneasy": Frischauer, loc. cit.

238 "He doesn't love Jackie": Kiki Feroudi Moutsatsos, with Phyllis Karas, *The Onassis Women,* p. 86.

239 "I am always searching for the consummate woman": Brady, loc. cit.

241 "She went from a Greek god": This and the following comments are recorded in Fraser, pp. 255–56.

241 "myths, when they are human": *Time,* Nov. 1, 1968

242 "Months ago": "Cushing Defends Onassis Wedding," *The New York Times,* Oct. 24, 1968.

243 "It seemed to me": Rose Kennedy, pp. 412ff.

243 "When I married Ari": Ibid., p. 413.

244 "This was a marriage": Moutsatsos, p. 97.

244 "I didn't need a stepmother": *Look,* June 30, 1970.

244 "She did not have one completely happy moment": Moutsatsos, p. 128.

244 "She always tries to please him": "Cristina [*sic*] Onassis Talks About Daddy, Jackie and Callas," *Life,* Apr. 14, 1972.

245 "I am having a very bad day": Ibid., p. 225.

CHAPTER ELEVEN: 1969–1975

249   "Every moment one lives": Maryam Kharazmi, "Jackie is the same as Mrs. Onassis," *Kayhan International,* May 24, 1972. The English-language newspaper was published in Teheran, Iran (visited by Jackie and Ari in May 1972 because of his business interests there).

251   "Jackie is like a little bird": *Remembering Jackie* [n.p.].

252   "It was something she wanted to do": *The New York Times,* Dec. 14, 1971.

253   "She had grown very depressed": Robert S. McNamara, with Brian VanDeMark, *In Retrospect,* pp. 257–58.

253   "the only one who completely accepted": *The New York Times,* Apr. 19, 1973.

255   "She reads as much as anybody": Liz Smith, "The New York Life of Jacqueline Onassis," *Ladies' Home Journal,* Feb. 1970.

256   "He is my best friend": Judy Klemesrud, "Maria Callas Speaks Her Mind on Fashions and Friendship," *The New York Times,* Nov. 30, 1970.

257   "Mother wants to stay in this house": *New York Newsday,* May 23, 1972.

257   "No, I hate it": Ibid., July 30, 1972.

257   "there was no longer any reason": Moutsatsos, p. 271.

258   "No woman, no matter how much": Ibid.

258   "I saw the biggest fights": Peter Beard, quoted in Steven M. L. Aronson, "The Missing Years," *Town & Country,* July 1994.

256   "never discussed the subject": Moutsatsos, p. 276.

258   "I was with [Jackie] and Ari": "Remembering Jackie," *Town & Country,* July 1994.

260   "She brought an enormous visibility": Robert D. McFadden, "Jackie, New Yorker: Friends Recall a Fighter for Her City," *The New York Times,* May 22, 1994.

269   "A big corporation shouldn't be able": "Celebrities Ride the Rails to Save Grand Central," *The New York Times,* Apr. 17, 1978.

260   "Jacqueline Onassis played a prominent... role": From the Municipal Art Society's exhibit "The Triumph of Grand Central: The Battle to Save Grand Central Terminal," on display at the terminal.

261   "No matter how inconvenient": "Jacqueline Kennedy Onassis: Remembering the Indelible Style of an American Icon," *Architectural Digest,* Sept. 1996.

262   "friends say": The friends spoke in autumn of 1975; the statement appeared in Winzola McLendon, "The New Jackie," *Ladies' Home Journal,* Jan. 1976.

263   "very conservative in her buying": Ibid.

264   "I have always lived through men": "Jackie on Her Own," *Newsweek,* Sept. 29, 1975.

264   "We had lunch one day": Letitia Baldrige to DS, March 8, 1999.

264   "She had reached that moment": "Jackie on Her Own," loc. cit.

264 "I always wanted to be some kind of writer": Joyce Maynard, "Jacqueline Onassis Makes a New Debut," *The New York Times,* Jan. 14, 1977.

265 "moves in a wide circle": "Notes on People: Jacqueline Onassis Is Editor at Viking," *The New York Times,* Sept. 17, 1975.

265 "I expect to be learning the ropes": Elizabeth Peer, Lisa Whitman, and Phyllis Malamud, "Jackie on Her Own," *Newsweek,* Sept. 29, 1975.

265 "Apprentice," etc.: Jimmy Breslin, "It Was a Life Well Spent," *Newsday,* May 20, 1994.

265 "She got into publishing": "Jackie, New Yorker," *The New York Times,* May 22, 1994.

265 "Before she came": Lawliss, p. 103.

266 "She's smart, funny": McLendon, loc. cit.

267 "Lady, you work": "Jacqueline Kennedy Onassis Talks About Working," *Ms.* magazine, Mar. 1979.

CHAPTER TWELVE: 1976-1979

269 "She will have money": Murray Kempton, "The Second Act Triumph of a Tragic Queen," *New York Newsday,* May 22, 1994.

271 "They don't need marriage": Jessie Mangaliman, "Her Constant Companion," *New York Newsday,* May 21, 1994.

273 "If you cut people off": "Landmark Status Debated in Albany," *The New York Times,* Feb. 9, 1984.

274 "went around together for a while": Pete Hamill, "A Private Life Defined by Wit, Compassion," *New York Newsday,* May 22, 1994.

274 "I just don't understand": Ibid.

275 "From the start, she was...extraordinary": Eugene C. Kennedy to DS, Jan. 21, 1999; see also his tribute: "As an Editor, She Was a Total Professional," *New York Newsday,* May 23, 1994.

275 Regarding the JFK-Daley connection, Letitia Baldrige also remarked that the president always felt "tremendous political gratitude [to] Mayor Richard J. Daley of Chicago." *Of Diamonds and Diplomats,* p. 212.

276 "That's some sight inside!": Breslin, loc. cit.

276 "It expands your knowledge": In *Ms.,* loc. cit.

278 "You love to see them": Maynard, loc. cit.

278 "Not only was she kind": Tillie Weitzner to DS, Jan. 24, 1999.

278 "serious, idealistic, open": Harris Wofford, "A Tribute," *Newsweek,* special memorial edition, summer 1999.

280 "I don't know whether anybody": JFK/OHP: Janet Lee Bouvier Auchincloss, recorded interview by Joan Braden, Sept. 5, 1964, p. 23.

281 "There is a word for such a book": *The New York Times,* Oct. 10, 1977.

282 "Last spring": Deirdre Carmody, "Mrs. Onassis Resigns Editing Post," *The New York Times,* Oct. 15, 1977.

283 "I think they really wanted": Breslin, loc. cit.

284 Jackie's poem was published in *People* magazine, July 13, 1981.

284 "We spent the first four summers": Kennedy, p. 431.

284 "I think my biggest achievement": Quoted often—e.g., in Adler, p. 138.

CHAPTER THIRTEEN: 1980-1992

286 "One of the things I like": John F. Baker, "Editors at Work: Star Behind the Stars," *Publishers Weekly,* Apr. 19, 1993.

286 "When I first met Jackie": Marianne Velmans to DS, Mar. 21, 1999.

287 "I want to live my life": E.g., to Pierre Salinger, *P.S.,* p. 209.

287 "Why sit indoors": To David Wise, cited in *Newsweek,* May 30, 1994.

288 "These are subjects": Baker, loc. cit.

288 "helped me recover my life": Anthony, *As We Remember Her,* p. 326.

288 "informed sympathy": *A Tribute to Jacqueline Kennedy Onassis,* p. 6.

288 "empathy was so total": Ibid., p. 11.

288 "great literary encourager": William La Riche to DS, Mar. 19, 1999. Among La Riche's comments here, some are excerpts, cited with his kind permission, from *Brief Pilgrimage of Witness,* an unpublished memoir of his friendship with Jackie.

289 "She had a gift for inspiring": *A Tribute,* pp. 30–31.

289 "She knew where drama was": Elizabeth Crook, "Remembering Jackie Onassis, My Editor," *Publishers Weekly,* June 27, 1994.

290 "You have a new form of biography here": Francis Mason, in *Ballet Review,* spring 1995.

290 "not being the better": *A Tribute,* p. 22.

290 "very accurate": Baker, loc. cit.

291 "This was not a rich lady": Stephen Rubin to DS, Jan. 28, 1999.

291 "She was always interested": Grace Glueck, "The World Through Her Eyes," *The New York Times,* May 22, 1994.

291 "She could read": James Fitzgerald to DS, Ap. 15, 1999.

292 "If there was one sphere": Carl Sferrazza Anthony, "The Substance Behind the Style," *Town & Country,* July 1994.

293 "Excuse me, sir": Edna O'Brien to DS, Mar. 20, 1999.

294 "and the star's ambiguity": J. C. Suarès and J. Spencer Beck, *Uncommon Grace: Reminiscences and Photographs of Jacqueline Bouvier Kennedy Onassis,* p. 8.

295 "a writer's dream as an editor": Auchincloss, loc. cit. The excerpts from Jackie's notes to his book *False Dawn* are taken from the same periodical.

296   "Going to the ballet with Jackie Onassis": Paul Sidey to DS, Mar. 4, 1999.

297   "Sexiest Man Alive": Cover story, *People,* Sept. 12, 1988.

297   "I grew up living a...normal life": "Politics, Publishing and Personality: The Words of JFK, Jr.," *Newsday,* July 19, 1999.

298   "It's complicated": *Larry King Live,* Sept. 28, 1995.

298   "She was determined": Arthur M. Schlesinger Jr., "Brought Up to Be a Good Man," *Time,* July 26, 1999.

298   "My mother parented for two": To Katie Couric, NBC-TV *Today* show, May 14, 1999.

298   "When John was a little kid": On *Meet the Press,* July 25, 1999.

298   "Oh, it was a lot of Kennedy stuff": *U.S. News & World Report,* July 26, 1999.

298   "It isn't fair to children": Ibid.

299   "It's the best thing": *Meet the Press,* July 18, 1999.

299   "John assumed the best": Eric Pooley, "The Art of Being JFK, Jr.," *Time,* July 26, 1999.

299   "Don't let them steal your soul": Evan Thomas, "Living with the Myth," *Time,* July 26, 1999.

299   "Contrary to any general opinion": *Vogue,* June 1993.

299   "It was never anything": To Don Imus, *Imus in the Morning* radio show, May 22, 1997.

299   "He must be allowed to experience life": *The New York Times,* July 19, 1999.

300   "Close your eyes": *U.S. News & World Report,* July 26, 1999.

300   "I'm very disappointed": *New York Observer,* July 19, 1999.

302   "Jackie subsidized her home": Suarès and Beck, p. 15.

302   "I'm sixty-two now": To Jayne Wrightsman, cited in Adler, p. 151.

302   "She didn't really think of herself": Anthony, *As We Remember Her,* p. 331.

303   "She was interested in just about everything": Bruce Tracy to DS, Feb. 1, 1999.

303   "She took such joy": Scott Moyers to DS, Jan. 28, 1999.

CHAPTER FOURTEEN: 1993-1994

306   "in the end, all you really have": Suarès and Beck, p. 17.

308   "Stay calm!": Crook, loc. cit.

308   "plopped on the floor next to me": Pamela Fiori, "Jacqueline Bouvier Kennedy Onassis, 1929–1994: In Loving Memory," *Town & Country,* July 1994.

310   "All will be well": Auchincloss, loc. cit.

313   MISSING HER: *New York Daily News* headline, May 23, 1994.

Bibliography

Abbott, James A., and Elaine M. Rice. *Designing Camelot: The Kennedy White House Restoration*. New York: Van Nostrand Reinhold, 1998.

Adler, Bill, ed. *The Uncommon Wisdom of Jacqueline Kennedy Onassis*. New York: Citadel, 1994.

Andersen, Christopher. *Jackie After Jack*. New York: Morrow, 1998.

Anthony, Carl Sferrazza. *As We Remember Her*. New York: HarperCollins, 1997.

———. *First Ladies: The Saga of the Presidents' Wives and Their Power, 1961–1990*. 2 vols. New York: Morrow, 1991.

Ariès, Philippe (trans. Patricia M. Ranum). *Western Attitudes Toward Death: From the Middle Ages to the Present*. Baltimore: Johns Hopkins, 1974.

Associated Press. *Triumph and Tragedy: The Story of the Kennedys*. New York: Associated Press, 1968.

Baldrige, Letitia. *Of Diamonds and Diplomats*. Boston: Houghton Mifflin, 1968.

———. *In the Kennedy Style*. New York: Madison Press/Doubleday, 1998.

Beale, Betty. *Power at Play: A Memoir of Parties, Politicians and the Presidents in My Bedroom*. Washington, D.C.: Regnery Gateway, 1993.

Beschloss, Michael R. *The Crisis Years: Kennedy and Khrushchev, 1960–1963*. New York: Edward Burlingame Books, 1991.

———, ed. *Taking Charge: The Johnson White House Tapes, 1963–1964*. New York: Simon & Schuster, 1997.

Birmingham, Stephen. *Jacqueline Bouvier Kennedy Onassis*. New York: Grosset & Dunlap, 1978.

———. *The Right People: A Portrait of the American Social Establishment*. Boston: Little, Brown, 1968.

Black, Allida M. *Casting Her Own Shadow: Eleanor Roosevelt and the Shaping of Post-War Liberalism*. New York: Columbia University Press, 1996.

Boller, Paul F. *Presidential Wives*. New York: Oxford University Press, 1988.

Bouvier, Jacqueline and Lee. *One Special Summer*. New York: Delacorte/Eleanor Friede, 1974.

Bradlee, Benjamin C. *Conversations with Kennedy*. New York: Norton, 1975.

———. *A Good Life: Newspapering and Other Adventures*. New York: Simon & Schuster, 1995.

Buck, Pearl. *The Kennedy Women*. New York: Cowles/John Day, 1970.

Burleigh, Nina. *A Very Private Woman: The Life and Unsolved Murder of Presidential Mistress Mary Meyer*. New York: Bantam, 1998.

Canfield, Cass. *Up and Down and Around: A Publisher Recollects the Time of His Life*. New York: Harper's Magazine Press, 1971.

Caroli, Betty Boyd. *First Ladies*. New York: Oxford University Press, 1987.

Carter, Rosalynn. *First Lady from Plains*. Boston: Houghton Mifflin, 1984.

Cassini, Oleg. *In My Own Fashion*. New York: Simon & Schuster, 1987.

———. *A Thousand Days of Magic: Dressing Jacqueline Kennedy for the White House*. New York: Rizzoli, 1995.

Clifford, Clark, with Richard Holbrooke. *Counsel to the President: A Memoir*. New York: Random House, 1991.

Clinch, Nancy Gager. *The Kennedy Neurosis*. New York: Grosset & Dunlap, 1973.

Colacello, Bob. *Holy Terror: Andy Warhol Close-Up*. New York: HarperCollins, 1990.

Cook, Don. *Charles de Gaulle: A Biography*. New York: Putnam's, 1983.

Cutler, John Henry. *Cardinal Cushing of Boston*. New York: Hawthorn, 1970.

Damore, Leo. *The Cape Cod Years of John Fitzgerald Kennedy*. Englewood Cliffs, N.J.: Prentice-Hall, 1967.

David, Lester. *Jacqueline Kennedy Onassis: A Portrait of Her Private Years*. New York: Birch Lane/Carol, 1994.

David, Lester and Irene David. *Bobby Kennedy: The Making of a Folk Hero*. New York: Dodd, Mead, 1986.

Davis, John H. *The Bouviers: Portrait of an American Family*. New York: Farrar, Straus & Giroux, 1969. See also his 1993 revision, from the same publisher, *The Bouviers: From Waterloo to the Kennedys and Beyond*.

———. *Jacqueline Bouvier: An Intimate Memoir*. New York: John Wiley, 1996.

———. *The Kennedys: Dynasty and Disaster, 1848–1983*. New York: McGraw-Hill, 1984.

Davis, Kenneth Sydney. *The Politics of Honor: A Biography of Adlai E. Stevenson*. New York: Putnam, 1967.

de Gaulle, Charles (trans. Terence Kilmartin). *Memoirs of Hope: Renewal and Endeavor*. New York: Simon & Schuster, 1971.

De Pauw, Linda Grant, and Conover Hunt. *Remember the Ladies: Women in America, 1750–1815*. New York: A Studio Book/Viking Press, 1976 (edited by, among others, Jacqueline Onassis).

Dickerson, Nancy. *Among Those Present: A Reporter's View of Twenty-five Years in Washington*. New York: Random House, 1976.

The Estate of Jacqueline Kennedy Onassis (the catalog for the auction). New York: Sotheby's, 1996.

Fay, Paul B., Jr. *The Pleasure of His Company*. New York: Harper & Row, 1966.

Ford, Betty, with Chris Chase. *The Times of My Life*. New York: Harper & Row and the Reader's Digest Association, 1978.

Fraser, Nicholas, and Philip Jacobson, Mark Ottaway, and Lewis Chester. *Aristotle Onassis*. New York: Lippincott, 1977.

Gabler, Neal. *Life the Movie: How Entertainment Conquered Reality*. New York: Knopf, 1998.

Gaines, Steven. *Philistines at the Hedgerow: Passion and Property in the Hamptons*. Boston: Little, Brown, 1998.

Galante, Pierre. *Malraux*. New York: Cowles, 1971.

Galbraith, John Kenneth. *Ambassador's Journal: A Personal Account of the Kennedy Years*. London: Hamish Hamilton, 1969.

————. *Name-Dropping: From F.D.R. On*. Boston: Houghton Mifflin, 1999.

Gallagher, Mary Barelli (with Frances Spatz Leighton). *My Life with Jacqueline Kennedy*. New York: David McKay, 1969.

Goodwin, Doris Kearns. *The Fitzgeralds and the Kennedys*. New York: Simon & Schuster, 1987.

Graf, Henry F. *The Presidents: A Reference History*. New York: Charles Scribner's Sons, 1996.

Graham, Katharine. *Personal History*. New York: Knopf, 1997.

Gutin, Myra G. *The President's Partner: The First Lady in the Twentieth Century*. New York: Greenwood Press, 1989.

Hall, Gordon Langley, and Ann Pinchot. *Jacqueline Kennedy*. New York: Frederick Fell, 1964.

Hamilton, Nigel. *JFK: Reckless Youth*. New York: Random House, 1992.

Hersh, Burton. *The Shadow President: Ted Kennedy in Opposition*. South Royalton, Vt.: Steerforth Press, 1997.

In Memoriam: Jacqueline Bouvier Kennedy Onassis, 1929–1994. New York: Doubleday, 1995.

Jensen, Amy La Follette. *The White House and Its Thirty-Three Families*. New York: McGraw-Hill, 1962.

Johnson, Lady Bird. *Lady Bird Johnson: A White House Diary*. New York: Holt, Rinehart and Winston, 1970.

Kennedy, Rose Fitzgerald. *Times to Remember*. New York: Doubleday, 1995.

King, Martin Luther, Jr. *Stride Toward Freedom*. New York: Harper & Row, 1958.

King, Norman. *The Woman in the White House: The Remarkable Story of Hillary Rodham Clinton*. New York: Birch Lane, 1996.

Klein, Edward. *Just Jackie*. New York: Ballantine, 1998.

Ladowsky, Ellen. *Jacqueline Kennedy Onassis*. New York: Park Lane Press, 1997.

Last Will and Testament of Jacqueline Kennedy Onassis, The. New York: Bill Adler/Carroll & Graf, 1997.

Lawliss, Charles. *Jacqueline Onassis, 1929–1994*. New York: JG Press, 1994.

Leamer, Laurence. *The Kennedy Women*. New York: Villard, 1994.

Longford, Lord. *Kennedy*. London: Weldenfeld and Nicolson, 1976.

Lowe, Jacques. *Jacqueline Kennedy Onassis: The Making of a First Lady*. Los Angeles: General Publishing Group, 1996.

McBrien, Richard P. *Catholicism*. San Francisco: HarperSanFrancisco, 1994.

McNamara, Robert S., with Brian VanDeMark. *In Retrospect*. New York: Times Books/Random House, 1995.

Madsen, Axel. *Malraux*. New York: Morrow, 1976.

Martin, John Bartlow. *Adlai Stevenson and the World: The Life of Adlai Stevenson*. Garden City, N.Y.: Doubleday, 1977.

Means, Marianne. *The Woman in the White House: The Lives, Times and Influence of Twelve Notable First Ladies*. New York: Random House, 1963.

Meyers, Joan, ed. *John Fitzgerald Kennedy ... As We Remember Him*. New York: Athenaeum, 1965.

Miller, Merle. *Lyndon: An Oral Biography*. New York: Putnam's, 1980.

Moutsatsos, Kiki Feroudi, with Phyllis Karas. *The Onassis Women*. New York: Putnam's, 1998.

O'Donnell, Kenneth P., and David F. Powers. *"Johnny, We Hardly Knew Ye": Memories of John F. Kennedy*. Boston: Little, Brown, 1972.

Osborne, Claire G., ed. *Jackie—A Legend Defined*. New York: Avon Books, 1997.

Parmet, Herbert S. *Jack: The Struggles of John F. Kennedy*. New York: Dial, 1980.

Rattray, Jeannette Edwards, under the direction of the Golden Jubilee Committee chaired by Julian S. Myrick. *Fifty Years of the Maidstone Club: 1891–1941*. East Hampton, N.Y.: At the Maidstone, 1941.

Remembering Jackie—A Life in Pictures. New York: Warner Books, 1994.

Reston, James. *Sketches in the Sand*. New York: Knopf, 1967.

Robinson, Harlow. *The Last Impresario: The Life, Times, and Legacy of Sol Hurok*. New York: Viking, 1994.

Rusk, Dean (as told to Richard Rusk). *As I Saw It*. New York: Penguin, 1990.

Salinger, Pierre. *With Kennedy*. Garden City, N.Y.: Doubleday, 1966.

———. *P.S.: A Memoir*. New York: St. Martin's Press, 1995.

Schlesinger, Arthur M., Jr. *A Thousand Days: John F. Kennedy in the White House*. Boston: Houghton Mifflin, 1965.

———. *Robert Kennedy and His Times*. Boston: Houghton Mifflin, 1978.

Shaw, Maud. *White House Nanny: My Years with Caroline and John Kennedy, Jr*. New York: New American Library, 1966.

Sorensen, Theodore C. *Kennedy*. New York: Harper & Row, 1965.

Spoto, Donald. *The Decline and Fall of the House of Windsor*. New York: Simon & Schuster, 1995.

——. *Marilyn Monroe: The Biography*. New York: HarperCollins, 1993.

Suarès, J. C., and J. Spencer Beck. *Uncommon Grace: Reminiscences and Photographs of Jacqueline Bouvier Kennedy Onassis*. Charlottesville, Va.: Thomasson-Grant, 1994.

Sulzberger, C. L. *Seven Continents and Forty Years: A Concentration of Memoirs*. New York: Quadrangle/New York Times, 1977.

Taper, Bernard. *Balanchine: A Biography*. New York: Times Books, 1984.

Tapert, Annette, and Diana Edkins. *The Power of Style: The Women Who Defined the Art of Living Well*. New York: Crown, 1994.

Thayer, Mary Van Rensselaer. *Jacqueline Kennedy: The White House Years*. Boston: Little, Brown, 1971.

Thomas, Helen. *Dateline: White House*. New York: Macmillan, 1975.

——. *Front Row at the White House*. New York: Lisa Drew/Scribner, 1999.

Travell, Janet. *Office Hours: Day and Night: The Autobiography of Janet Travell, M.D.* New York: World Publishing, 1968.

Tribute to Jacqueline Kennedy Onassis, A. New York: Doubleday, 1995.

Truman, Margaret. *First Ladies*. New York: Random House, 1995.

Van Rensselaer, Mrs. John King (in collaboration with Frederic van de Water). *The Social Ladder*. New York: Henry Holt, 1924.

von Post, Gunilla, with Carl Johnes. *Love, Jack*. New York: Crown, 1997.

West, J. B., with Mary Lynn Kotz. *Upstairs at the White House: My Life With the First Ladies*. New York: Coward, McCann & Geoghegan, 1973.

Whalen, Richard J. *The Founding Father: The Story of Joseph P. Kennedy*. New York: New American Library, 1964.

White, Theodore H. "The Camelot Documents, 1963–1964," in The Papers of Theodore H. White, 1915–1986, unpublished documents at the John Fitzgerald Kennedy Library.

White, Theodore H. *In Search of History: A Personal Adventure*. New York: Warner Books, 1978.

Wills, Garry. *The Kennedy Imprisonment: A Meditation on Power*. Boston: Little, Brown, 1982.

——. *Reagan's America: Innocents at Home*. Garden City, N.Y.: Doubleday, 1987.

Index